THE RESEARCHER'S
GUIDE TO
AMERICAN GENEALOGY

THE RESEARCHER'S GUIDE TO AMERICAN GENEALOGY

By
Val D. Greenwood

With an Introduction by
Milton Rubincam

GENEALOGICAL PUBLISHING CO., INC.
BALTIMORE
1978

© 1973
Genealogical Publishing Co., Inc.
Baltimore, Maryland
All Rights Reserved
Fifth Printing 1978
Library of Congress Catalogue Card Number 73-6902
International Standard Book Number 0-8063-0560-6
Made in the United States of America

PREFACE

In my opinion most prefaces are too long, and are, therefore, seldom read. With this in mind let me state as briefly as possible my purpose and plan in writing The Researcher's Guide to American Genealogy.

As an instructor of genealogy on the college level I became increasingly frustrated each time I taught a course in American genealogical research, for there existed no comprehensive textbook on American records. Valuable time was wasted explaining background information and fundamentals to students who ought to have been forearmed with a good text. Reading assignments often lacked substance and had to be scattered among three or four books to cover even the most superficial data on the various records.

Six years ago I decided that something needed to be done. The good information on American records which existed needed to be combined under one cover and then it needed to be enlarged upon to make it more meaningful to the student. Since I knew of no one else working on such a project, I decided to do it myself. I had previously talked to other genealogists about a cooperative venture, but we never got any writing done—just talking—and there was no promise that we ever would. Under these circumstances my course was set. Perhaps if I had not been so naive about the size of the task before me I might never have undertaken it.

Thousands of hours of research and planning are represented in this volume and, though I am sure it is not perfect, I feel that it fulfills my original objective—to provide a meaningful and comprehensive guide to the records used in American genealogical research. There is no other book like this in existence.

Part I of the book deals with basic principles of genealogical research as they apply to American ancestral problems and Part II (the unique feature of this volume) deals exclusively with those records in which the student will do most of his research. Here the records are examined in some detail and their use and value to the genealogist are discussed and exemplified.

A number of persons have given assistance and encouragement to this project, and I am deeply indebted to each of them for the suggestions given, the information provided and the encouragement offered. I am grateful to the genealogists, public officials and record custodians who took time to answer my queries and look up information for me. I am grateful to those authors who have so graciously given permission to quote them and to use their materials. I am grateful to the genealogists, professional and amateur, who have known of my work and have given suggestions and offered encouragement to hasten the project to completion. And I am especially grateful to my wife, Peggy, who uncomplainingly sacrificed my company for so many evenings during the years I have been writing. She also read the manuscript and made suggestions to add to its clarity.

I offer no magic formula for genealogical success—I have none. There are no fail-proof solutions to genealogical problems. The key to success lies in hard work, use of available tools and adherence to correct research principles.

This book is dedicated to my own American ancestors and also to those students who will use the book to further the science of genealogy.

V. D. G.

TABLE OF CONTENTS

PART I
BACKGROUND TO RESEARCH

PART II
RECORDS AND THEIR USE

LIST OF ILLUSTRATIONS AND CHARTS

ILLUSTRATIONS AND ChnRTS (continued)

INTRODUCTION

During the past four decades a great many works have been published concerning the sources and techniques of genealogical research. Beginning in 1930 with Donald Lines Jacobus's great classic, <u>Genealogy as Pastime and Profession</u> (completely revised by the author and brought out in a second edition by the Genealogical Publishing Company, 1968), the best works in the field include Gilbert Harry Doane's <u>Searching For Your Ancestors</u> (1937, and later reprints), Archibald F. Bennett's <u>A Guide for Genealogical Research</u> (1951), <u>Finding Your Forefathers In America</u> (1957), and <u>Advanced Genealogical Research</u> (1959), E. Kay Kirkham's <u>Research in American Genealogy</u> (1956), Derek Harland's <u>A Basic Course in Genealogy</u> (1958), Ethel W. Williams's <u>Know Your Ancestors</u> (1960), The American Society of Genealogists' <u>Genealogical Research: Methods and Sources</u> (Vol. I, 1960, Vol. II, 1971), and George Olin Zabriskie's <u>Climbing Our Family Tree Systematically</u> (1969). In addition, many articles on procedures and sources have appeared in <u>The American Genealogist</u>, the <u>National Genealogical Society Quarterly</u>, and other periodicals. And in 1958 Noel C. Stevenson published an anthology of articles in <u>The Genealogical Reader</u>.

At the time of their publication the books named above filled a long-felt need, and, indeed, are still indispensable in various aspects of genealogical work. Most of them describe the basic records used by the researcher, discuss the areas (states and counties) where the records are preserved, and suggest methods for evaluating evidence. Mr. Zabriskie's work emphasizes the need to <u>plan</u> a genealogical campaign and the systematic collection and analysis of data which will result in correct conclusions, or at least conclusions based on the preponderance of evidence.

Now, Val D. Greenwood has produced a book that is different from its predecessors. It, too, has long been needed in the complicated business of tracing families. He discusses in detail many subjects only lightly touched upon or not covered by other authors. He has no sections on regions, except in the case of Canada (Chapter Twenty-four), and a necessary "Special Note on Virginia" in Chapter Eighteen. All parts of the country are mentioned, but chiefly in connection with his discussion of classes of records.

Mr. Greenwood delves deeply into the historical background of our records systems, providing us especially with an understanding of the legal aspects of genealogical research. Many family historians do not under-

stand such terms as "administration cum testamento annexo," "administration de bonis non," "degree of relationship," "per stirpes," "estate tail,"
the "rectangular survey system," the "antenuptial contract," or the measurements of land (acre, chain, furlong, perch, pole, etc.). All of these
are defined in the book. Chapter Eighteen, "Court Records," should be
studied with care, for here we have a full explanation of the American court
system and of the types of records the American genealogist encounters.

The author stresses the need to base one's work on primary sources—
not on printed books. He is a member of The Church of Jesus Christ of
Latter-day Saints, which has accomplished so much for the preservation of
records in this country and abroad, but he does not hesitate to point out the
ways and means whereby Mormons could improve their research techniques.
He is realistic in his approach to genealogy. If people are afraid of finding
"family skeletons," he recommends that they "stay out of closets." If their
ancestors do not measure up to their own social standards, he suggests that
people "stay away" from genealogy. He writes easily and with a sense of
humor—a necessary ingredient in our work!

Genealogy is recognized as one of the auxiliary branches of history,
but whether it can be considered an exact science has been debated for many
years. In an article published in 1933 in The American Genealogist Donald
Lines Jacobus wrote: "Sciences which relate wholly or in part to human
nature are considered the least exact. History and biography may be exact
as to dates, but in so far as they deal with human motives, the 'why' of historical and personal events, they can never hope to be absolutely correct.
Genealogy, as one of the sciences in which human nature is a factor, is
considered to be one of the less exact sciences. As practiced by many of
its devotees, it is certainly one of the least exact. Yet it is entitled to rank
higher, provided only that proper scientific methods be pursued." After
reviewing the reasons why scientific methods of research are unpopular
with many genealogical students and writers, he concludes: "It must be
confessed, in view of such chaotic conditions, that genealogy in this country to-day is very far from being an exact science, although the many
workers in this field who now employ scientific methods are doing much to
make it one."

Mr. Greenwood's book demonstrates that genealogy is an exact science
—if its practitioners carry out the methods insisted upon by Mr. Jacobus.
He points out that the genealogist must work like the research chemist or
anyone else who does research. He must first determine what others may
have already done with the same problem. He must carefully and systematically seek out everything he can find on the problem. He must analyze
his findings and make sound judgment of their validity. He must study the
material and sift the information very carefully. He must determine his
objectives, based upon his analysis, and plan his research. Then he must
gather data from primary sources and record them systematically so that

he will have a complete record of all he has done. And finally, like the chemist, he must analyze his data to ascertain whether he has attained his objectives "and synthesize them into meaningful form." These steps are basic to the research process; if the researcher follows them Genealogy is indeed an exact science.

Mr. Greenwood's book is a significant contribution to the field of Genealography, which may be defined as "the study of the history of genealogy and of genealogical research procedures."

Milton Rubincam,
F.A.S.G., F.N.G.S., F.G.S.P., C.G.

PART I

BACKGROUND TO RESEARCH

CHAPTER ONE

UNDERSTANDING GENEALOGICAL RESEARCH

There is a familiar song which alleges that happiness is "different things to different people."[1] Sadly the same seems to be true of genealogy —not because it actually is different things, but because it is widely misunderstood. With this in mind, let us offer two basic definitions before we proceed further:

> GENEALOGY: That branch of history which involves the determination of family relationships. This is not done by copying but rather by research.

> RESEARCH: An investigation aimed at the discovery and the interpretation of facts and also the revision of accepted theories in light of new facts.

You should never approach a pedigree problem as a student in a history class would pursue knowledge of secular history. If the history student has an assignment to study the American Revolutionary War he will probably read an assigned text (or a chapter therein), perhaps check an encyclopedia, and, if he is especially diligent, read about the subject in other history books. But he takes someone else's word for everything—that is, if he believes what he reads.

If you have a genealogical problem you may well begin in the same place as did our history student—you can read printed genealogies and family histories, and well you should, but the prevalent notion that when you are copying someone else's records you are doing research is a gross misconception. This is also true when it comes to copying published and compiled works—they are only someone else's records.

Before you progress very far in genealogical research you ought to be on the same plane as the author of the textbook used by our history student —and perhaps even beyond that point. You will be engulfed in searching out and studying original documents and accounts, doing work to dig out the

---

[1] Quoted with permission of Belwin-Mills Publishing Corp., Rockville Centre, New York, 11571. All rights reserved.

facts, to interpret those facts, and to compile them into a meaningful and usable format.

Though a branch of history, genealogy is a subject which you cannot approach in the same way you would approach most other branches. In genealogy you cannot make a brief general summary of a historical period —but must consider the details of each ancestral problem individually and thoroughly.

One other significant difference between the study of history and the study of genealogy is that genealogy is a technical rather than an academic subject. It is a "how-to" subject in which you must learn and apply certain principles and facts relating to many academic disciplines. You must actually learn how to do the research. The study of history, on the other hand, is mostly informational.

I. THE NATURE OF RESEARCH

As a genealogist you must work much like the research chemist or anyone else who does research. The steps are as follows:

1. Just as the chemist, before you begin work on your actual problem, you must first make a study to see what others may have done already with the same problem. This is secondary research. In genealogy we call it the "preliminary survey."

The chemist will carefully and systematically seek out everything on the problem that he can find. How foolish it would be for him to spend ten years (or even one year or one month) on a special project only to find, upon presenting his findings to his colleagues, that someone else had already accomplished the same work. It is no less foolish for you to do the same thing in genealogical research.

2. As the scientist completes this secondary research, he must analyze what he has found and make some judgment of its validity. He must study the material and sift the information very carefully. If he accepts it he will begin his own research where it leaves off; but if he questions part of it or if he rejects it totally, his point of beginning will be quite different. But in any case his activities will be influenced by what has already been done. The same is true of the genealogist.

3. The chemist's next step will be to determine his objectives, based upon his analysis, and to plan his primary research. He should know by now what his problems are and should be able to decide how he will seek their solutions. The genealogist must do the same.

4. After this both the chemist and the genealogist will gather data from primary sources and record them systematically so that they will have a complete record of all they have done. Their approach will be logical and in complete agreement with their plans. The only difference is that the chemist's primary sources are his own research and experimentation

while the genealogist's primary sources are documents.

5. Then as they complete their gathering of relevant data, they will evaluate those data—analyze them to ascertain whether they have reached the objectives set earlier and synthesize them into meaningful form. If the desired objectives have been reached then they will begin the entire cycle again with a new problem. If not they will also complete the cycle again but will probably skip the secondary research step (unless sufficient additional information has been brought to light to make it profitable) and continue the quest with a fresh analysis of the problem in light of the recent failure.

6. A sixth step, not a part of the actual research process yet very important to it, is to make the results of your research findings available to others (perhaps by publication).

These steps comprise the cycle of research. They are basic to the research process. The explanation we have given of them here is greatly over-simplified as the steps themselves are not clear-cut. We have divided them only for clarification and discussion so that you might better understand what is involved in actual research. But the basic process is the same whether you are a research chemist or a research genealogist.

Also, by dividing the research process into its components we are able to observe some other interesting phenomena. Note that of the six steps listed three of them (the second, third and fifth) involve analytical activity of some type. So we see that in most research one of the chief attributes of the researcher is the ability to evaluate and analyze properly. Almost anyone can search records if he is told what to search, but to make an accurate evaluation of what is found is usually much more difficult, as is the ability to set reasonable objectives and to plan for their fruition—this requires both aptitude and training.

Another thing we can readily observe from this research cycle is that many would-be genealogists do not use all of the steps required for complete research. Too many spend their entire efforts on secondary research, thinking they are doing all that can be and needs to be done by copying the records of others and searching old family histories. This is the approach to research used by a lady who recently approached the reference desk at a large genealogical library, a printed family history open in each hand. She carefully laid the two books on the counter and then, apparently quite perturbed, queried the reference assistant as to which one was correct. One book said that the father of a certain ancestor was one man while the other claimed it was someone else. The assistant examined the two sources and explained that he did not know the answer to the problem. He said it would be necessary for her to check some original source materials for her answer. Her reply: "I don't have time to do that!" And so she did not do it.

Others feel that secondary sources are generally so unreliable they cannot be bothered with them at all, so they spend all of their research

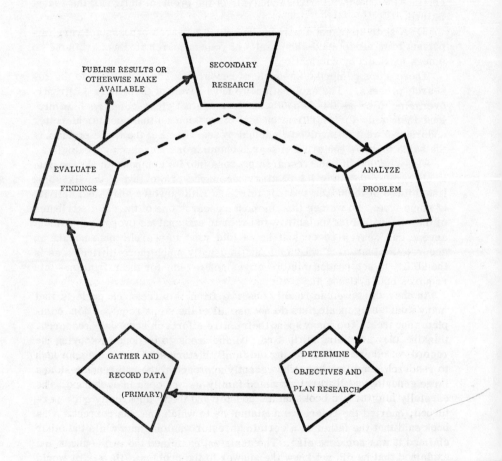

THE RESEARCH PROCESS

hours working in original records not caring whether anything has been done before. To illustrate partially the extent and seriousness of this approach here are some impressive figures: In the first four months of 1968 there were 96,904 family group records submitted to The Genealogical Society of The Church of Jesus Christ of Latter-day Saints by patrons. Of these 24,296, or 25 per cent, were duplicates of records already on file with the Society—the research already completed. [2]

One of our most satisfying experiences in teaching genealogical research came one day when a student sat in class, scratched his head intuitively, and then philosophized: "Research in genealogy isn't really any different than research in any other field." This is a truth that many of us are too long in learning, and he figured it out all by himself.

II. GENEALOGY AND SCIENCE

In our discussion thus far we have not really come right out and claimed that genealogy is a science, yet we have certainly hinted at this idea and hope you have gotten the message. It might be well, however, to pursue this idea a little further.

First let's define the word science and look at its etymology. It comes from the Latin term scientia which means "having knowledge," and Webster gives the following definitions:

1. Originally, the state of fact of knowing; knowledge.

2. Systematized knowledge derived from observation, study, and experimentation carried on in order to determine the nature or principles of what is being studied.

3. A branch of knowledge or study, especially one concerned with establishing and systematizing facts, principles, and methods, as by experiments and hypotheses... [3]

These definitions all clearly apply to genealogy when it is properly practiced. However, as practiced by many it falls short in some respects. We can truthfully say that genealogy should be a science—it deserves to be a science—but the methods of some tend to lower it to the level of a mere pastime built upon false premises.

---

[2] The Church of Jesus Christ of Latter-day Saints, "Services to Help Avoid Duplication," The Priesthood Bulletin IV (November, 1968), p. 12.

[3] From Webster's New World Dictionary of the American Language, Second College Edition. Copyright 1970 by the World Publishing Company, Cleveland, Ohio. By permission. All rights reserved.

Genealogy will reach its proper place of respectability among the sciences only as we, its devotees, adopt sound scientific principles in our research. We must learn to consider all facts and all evidence before we reach our conclusions. No scientist would do less. When tempted to do less than your best you should remember two things:

1. Those who come after you will eternally judge you by what you have actually produced and not by your ability.

2. An error on an ancestral line extended many generations can be mammoth, even colossal, in its effect. One wrong ancestor on a line extended five short generations will have those who follow working on 32 wrong lines, and on 64 wrong lines in six generations, and so on, doubling each generation.

Thus to the definition of genealogy we gave earlier, let us add the word scientific and say that GENEALOGY IS THAT BRANCH OF HISTORY WHICH INVOLVES A SCIENTIFIC STUDY FOR THE DETERMINATION OF FAMILY RELATIONSHIPS.

III. COMPLETING THE GENEALOGICAL PICTURE

Perhaps the one thing that would improve the quality of genealogical research being done more than any other single factor would be a concern for complete families rather than just direct lines. Genealogy involves much more than just a pedigree with its names, dates and places. Though such a pedigree is a basic essential, it can be very deceptive if it is all you have.

For example, if a man was born in 1845 and his father was born in 1780, such a connection may appear dubious until you know (because you have gathered data on the complete family) that the father was 20 years older than the mother (born 1800), that she was his second wife, and that the son in question was the last child in a large family, the eldest being born in 1820. Knowing all this you can put the problem into proper perspective and it does not seem unusual at all, but only by seeing the complete picture is this possible.

On the other side of the coin we often have pedigrees alleging to be true, that look quite logical and possible, that prove otherwise when we get information on the entire family. (One of the children may have been born when his alleged mother was 65 years old or perhaps when she was 10.) Yet if we had dealt with only the direct line and not with complete families these incorrect connections might have been accepted—as they so often are.

All good genealogists now agree on the importance of compiling complete families with complete data on the members thereof. The late Donald Lines Jacobus, writing on this matter, said:

For many reasons it is advantageous in doing genealogical research to consider the family group, not to look upon each ancestor as an isolated individual, or as a mere link in a chain of descent. One of the most important reasons is that it enables us to check the chronology. Very often the relations of dates determine or negate the possibility of an alleged line of descent, or provide clues which might otherwise elude detection. It is a good idea to write out the full family history, or chart of relationships, while working, inclusive of "guessed" dates where positive dates are not known. It is an aid to the memory as well as to the imagination, if the eye can see the members of the family grouped together. [4]

The Latter-day Saints (Mormons) have especially stressed the importance of the family as a unified group because of their religious tenets, but even many among them have much to learn about the importance of the complete family to accurate research. There is too great a tendency among ancestor hunters to see how far back they can go rather than how accurate and complete they can be. Somehow it seems to matter little whether a pedigree is accurate or not just so long as it goes back a long way. Maybe this is what the Apostle Paul was talking about in his epistles to Titus and Timothy when he instructed that they should not "give heed to fables and endless genealogies..." (I Tim 1:4 and Titus 3:9).

There are myriad sheets and forms available from suppliers of genealogical materials on which you can compile family groups. Some are designed as work sheets and others as complete and final record forms to be used only after research on a family is completed. These sheets can make your job much easier. [5]

Another thing that will add to the quality of your genealogical research, as well as to your success, is the concern you have for everyone of the surname of interest that you find living in the localities where your ancestors lived, rather than having concern only for those whom you can already identify. This measure is closely allied to the compiling of complete fam-

---

[4.] Donald Lines Jacobus, "Genealogy and Chronology," _Genealogical Research: Methods and Sources_, ed. by Milton Rubincam (Washington, D.C.: American Society of Genealogists, 1960), p. 29. By permission.

[5.] Some members of the LDS Church have been falsely misled into believing that complete family groups are no longer important to research now that the church's Name Tabulation Program has been introduced. They would do well to remember that research and good research methods have not been altered in any way. The only thing that has changed is the criteria for submitting names to the Genealogical Society for ordinance work.

ilies. As you search a geographical area where your ancestors are known to have lived, every record relating to every person with the same surname (in all of its spelling variations) should be read and carefully recorded in your research notes. You may not identify these persons with your ancestors immediately, but most of them will probably fit into place as you analyze your findings and put the complete families together. If the surname you seek is a common one, however, there are likely to be some exceptions. There may even be persons whom you will prove are definitely <u>not</u> related to your ancestors, but this is also useful.

As an example of this principle let's describe a hypothetical (though certainly not unusual) situation: You are searching for the records of your ancestor Charles Pebble in Mugwump County in an effort to identify his father. You find nothing. However, if you had extended your search in the Mugwump County records for everyone named Pebble (in all its variations) you would have found the will of one John Peppell, probated in 1805, wherein he named "my brother Charles" as executor and also bequeathed to his son James an old saddle which he had "bought from my father, Thomas Peppell."

This may or may not be your Charles who is referred to by John Peppell as his brother. This information would have to be analyzed as it relates to other evidence, but the possibilities are obvious.

If families are related, the records of the area where they lived will usually tie them together, but you must exhaust the records for that surname. And you must not be too upset if you find the name spelled a variety of ways (Pebble, Peppell, Pebbel, Pepple, Pebell, Peble, Peple, Pebel, etc.). If your ancestor could not write (which is quite a common situation) his name was spelled the way it sounded to whoever happened to be spelling it at the time. More is said about spelling in Chapter Two.

IV. GENEALOGY AND HISTORICAL BACKGROUND

Genealogy and history (religious, economic, social and political) cannot be separated. Men cannot be dissociated from the times and places in which they lived and still be understood. It is impossible to recognize the full extent of research possibilities if you are not aware of the background from which your ancestors came.

For example, without a knowledge of the religious background of an area you could neither appreciate the customs of its people nor understand the type of records produced.

History actually dictated the types of records kept, together with the format and content of those records. It also dictated those which were not kept and those which were lost or destroyed. History dictated social stratification, patterns of migration and settlements, and even occupations. Hostile Indians, wars, land policies, political figures and legislation, persecutions, disease, epidemics, droughts—all of these factors and many more have had a profound effect on genealogy and genealogical records in America.

If you can understand the forces which shaped men's lives then you can better understand those men. If your ancestor was of age to fight in the Civil War you would miss a good bet if you did not investigate the records of that war. If you find that he did not serve then perhaps his religious affiliation should be examined more closely. He may have been a conscientious objector on religious grounds (as were the Quakers and others)—this too would be significant.

V. NOTHING BUT THE FACTS

If you are afraid of skeletons then stay out of closets. And if you are ashamed to have ancestors who do not meet your own social standards then stay away from your genealogy. There are illegitimate children in the best of families—none of us is free from this. An outlaw or the proverbial horse thief may show up on any pedigree. You will also find the opposite—nobility and social status. But remember well the words of Sir Thomas Overbury which he wrote in 1614:

> The man who has not anything to boast of but his illustrious ancestors is like a potato—the only good belonging to him is underground. (CHARACTERS)

It is also very true that often some of the most shameful carryings-on took place in the most illustrious families. Chaucer puts it very nicely in the "Wife of Bath's Tale:"

> It is clear enough that true nobility
> Is not bequeathed along with property,
> For many a lord's son does a deed of shame
> And yet, God knows, enjoys his noble name.
> But though descended from a noble house
> And elders who were wise and virtuous,
> If he will not follow his elders, who are dead,
> But leads, himself, a shameful life instead,
> He is not noble be he duke or earl.
> It is the churlish deed that makes the churl. [6]

Regardless of what you find, your first responsibility is to the truth. A true report, regardless of the nature of the facts, is the responsibility of

---

[6]. Theodore Morrison (trans. and ed.), "The Wife of Bath's Tale," The Portable Chaucer (New York: The Viking Press, 1940), pp. 250-251. By permission.

the genealogist as it is the responsibility of any historian or scientist. Those who attempt to alter or color the truth are a liability to the science of genealogy—they are the millstone which tends to drag us all down. They are not genealogists and do not deserve the title.

Never be ashamed of the truth or of your ancestors. After all, who knows how they might feel about you!

VI. WHAT IS EXPECTED?

Is it necessary to be a professional genealogist in order to be successful in locating your ancestors? Should this work be left to the professionals? The answer to both of these questions is the same—a resounding (yet qualified) NO!

With proper instruction and discipline many persons can and do become proficient genealogists and have the deeply satisfying experience of seeking —and finding—their ancestors. But whether you seek your ancestors out of pure curiosity, out of a desire to join a patriotic or hereditary society, out of the intrigue of the study, for religious motives, or for any other reason, the requirement is the same—you must know what you are doing.

It can also be appropriately stated at this point that no matter how good your tools may be and no matter how complete your collection, such tools are of little worth if you are not skilled in their use.

If you had a severe attack of appendicitis in some remote place and could not get to a hospital, you would be grateful for the surgeon who came along with a tin can, a pocketknife and a needle with thread (all of which he would surely boil) to take care of you in your predicament. In fact you would probably much prefer this to being in the most modern hospital in the world, with the best available equipment, and the hospital janitor to perform the operation. When it comes right down to bare facts, we see that tools are not the most important thing—knowledge is. However, after you have the knowledge there is much to recommend being properly tooled. Certainly you would much prefer to have both the skilled surgeon and the modern hospital. Can't this same principle apply to genealogical research?

We would not think of turning a man loose to do research (of even the most basic type) in a chemistry laboratory filled with equipment and chemicals without some instruction. We would tell him about both the equipment and the chemicals. It is true, is it not, that the more he knows about these things, the better his chances for success will be? Lack of knowledge may not only result in failure but may also produce some disasterous results. Yet how often does a person with a similar lack of genealogical experience and know-how undertake "research" in the historical and documentary laboratory?

Is it any wonder that some get discouraged and that the results are often unsatisfying and even disasterous? Is it any wonder that so many compiled genealogical records lack credibility and so many printed family histories and genealogies are pure tripe?

If you have an aptitude for history and the social sciences, are good at remembering details, and enjoy intellectual problem-solving, then you have the basic aptitudes required by the genealogist. You should be able to learn quite easily the things you will need to know in order to use the available tools properly—you merely need a guide. Instruction and guidance, together with the empirical knowledge of actual practice can prepare you to be a good genealogist, even though not a professional. You do not have to be an expert in all phases of genealogical research to be a good genealogist; you need only to be an expert on genealogical research in the specific geographical locality where your problem is—you can become an expert one step at a time.

VII. THE PROFESSIONAL GENEALOGIST

If you desire to pursue genealogy as a vocation the requirements are no different. You must have good instruction and plenty of practical experience while you are learning, but beyond this you must be able to devote yourself whole-heartedly to the pursuit of information. You must be more than a scientist; you must be a detective as well. More than ever you must be able to remember and to catagorize details. You must be especially painstaking in the recording of information and sources, and you must be able to do these things rapidly. These qualities, of course, are improved and intensified through greater use, but you should be aware of their necessity before you pursue genealogy as a profession. As the satisfaction is great, so are the demands.

What can the professional genealogist do? Can he find work? If so, where? These questions are legitimate and are often asked by those interested in the field. There are several possibilities:

A. FREE-LANCE RESEARCH

Anyone, living almost anywhere, can do research on a free-lance basis for those wishing to engage his services. It is usually to the free-lancer's advantage, however, to live near and have access to libraries or other genealogical research facilities, but if you are free to travel this is not necessary. Large cities, especially Washington, D.C., have their advantages, but again, living in or near such places is not essential. Most free-lance researchers build up their clientele by their reputations for good work. If he does a good job the person he does it for will tell others. So, once he gets started, a good genealogist has no problems. Many have several months' work ahead of them all the time.

The LDS Genealogical Society in Salt Lake City, Utah, has a program for accrediting free-lance genealogists. Persons who pass tests showing their proficiency in doing genealogical research in specific geographical areas of the world are accredited to research in those areas, and their names are placed on a list of "recommended" researchers which the Society distributes upon request. Most of these persons live in or near Salt Lake City where they can take advantage of the facilities and records in the Society's library. Generally these persons do not travel extensively but write letters to local officials and/or researchers and record searchers when the Society does not have microfilms of the records they need.

Anyone who feels he can pass the tests (in a given geographical area) and has had extensive practical experience (a minimum of 1,000 hours) doing research in the records of the locality of his interest is welcome to take the tests. [7] For the U.S., different tests are given for New England, the middle-Atlantic states (Delaware, New Jersey, New York and Pennsylvania), the South, and the middle-West. He may take the test in as many areas as he likes so long as he meets the requirements.

A national Board for Certification of Genealogists was formed in Washington, D.C., in 1964 which is also good and which adds stature to the researcher's credentials. It certifies, for a period of five years (renewable at the end of that time for another five-year period) persons found to be qualified as professional Genealogists, American Lineage Specialists, and Genealogical Record Searchers. The Board has devised a Code of Ethics for professional workers in this field which has been accepted by leading genealogical organizations. For further information about certification you should write to Richard E. Spurr, Executive Secretary, Board for Certification of Genealogists, 1307 New Hampshire Ave., N.W., Washington, D.C. 20036.

B. FREE-LANCE RECORD SEARCHING

A record searcher is a person who does nothing more than the mechanics of the research—finds records, searches them and records his findings. His function is extremely important because many persons need to have records searched to which they do not have personal access. Above all he must be able to follow instructions and do just what he is asked to do. He might make suggestions, but should never make a search that is not authorized and expect to get paid for it. The record searcher does not usually make as much money as the genealogist; but good record searchers, espe-

---

An exception to the 1,000 hour time requirement is offered to those who have satisfactorily completed the equivalent of this through genealogical research courses at Brigham Young University in Provo, Utah, and Ricks College in Rexburg, Idaho.

cially those who are free to travel, are in great demand, and, if they are good, they can command a good price. Like researchers these persons are also usually located near large genealogical collections or libraries. There is a great need for record searchers who will go into courthouses, churches, cemeteries and other places where they might find working conditions cramped, uncomfortable and dusty. As mentioned earlier, certification is available for Genealogical Record Searchers.

C. LIBRARY AND ARCHIVES WORK

More and more libraries, historical societies, patriotic and hereditary organizations, and archives are demanding persons who are knowledgeable in genealogy—persons who can take care of their collections and answer correspondence of a genealogical nature. If you are interested in this phase of genealogy you should consider the study of library science in connection with your study of genealogy. Library training is essential for those who would pursue this course.

D. EDITORIAL WORK OR WRITING

Hundreds of genealogical and historical periodicals are currently being published in the United States. These publications demand not only qualified editorial personnel but are an endless market for good, well-written material. Many persons in other areas of genealogy also do free-lance writing for such publications, but to do any kind of writing you need an above-average command of English. Generally those who write genealogical articles do so because they like to write, for there is very little monetary reward.

E. TEACHING

The market for genealogy teachers is scant, but it is growing. If you desire to teach genealogy we recommend that, in addition to genealogical training and experience, you should pursue an advanced degree in some related field of the social sciences—perhaps history or library science—but above all you should qualify yourself as a genealogist and as a teacher.

Brigham Young University in Provo, Utah, offered a program leading to a bachelor's degree in genealogical research for five years, and both BYU and Ricks College, Rexburg, Idaho, have offered two-year associate degrees in genealogy. Though neither school still offers the degrees, they have the broadest and most diversified genealogical curricula available. Some other institutions in the U.S. offering courses in genealogy are American University, Washington, D.C.; Samford University, Birmingham, Alabama; Western Illinois University, Macomb; and The Church College of Hawaii, Laie. There are others overseas.

F. COMPUTER TECHNOLOGY

With the movement of electronics into the fields of demography and genealogy there is a growing need for persons who have background in computer science and mathematics as well as in genealogy. If you are interested in this area you should plan your schooling accordingly. Future possibilities in this field seem good.

VII. CONCLUSION

Regardless of the impetus which inspires you to pursue the study of American genealogy, one point is clear: Success and competence are dependent on both adequate instructional guidance and practical experience. Remember that a book, no matter how good, can go only so far. A good cook book does not make a good cook, though it surely helps. Edwin Slosson summarized the matter appropriately:

> One cannot, of course, become a scientist by merely reading science, however diligently and long. For a scientist is one who makes science, not one who learns science. A novelist is one who writes novels, not one who reads them. A contortionist is one who makes contortions, not one who watches them. Every real scientist is expected to take part in the advancement of science, to go over the top... But of course the number of those who are in reserve or in training must always outnumber those at the front. [8]

The way is clear and the goal is attainable. You can be a good genealogist if you are willing to pay the price--not just here and now but all along the way. If you are, be you amateur or professional, the rewards and the satisfaction can be great.

Good luck!

---

8. Edwin E. Slosson, "Science from the Side-Lines," Chats on Science (New York: Appleton-Century-Crofts, 1924), p. 140. By permission.

CHAPTER TWO

FAMILIAR RECORD PRACTICES: PROBLEMS AND TERMINOLOGY

In order for you to be a good genealogist you must be familiar with the basics of genealogy. Every area of study—whether physics, chemistry, sociology, medicine, law, art, photography or genealogy—has its own basic vocabulary or jargon and its own rules. You must know these to succeed in the field.

We have a friend who comes from Sweden, so when we come upon a term in our Swedish research that we do not understand, we call and ask him about it. Often the term is not familiar to him even though he was born and raised in that country. This is not a problem of his not understanding Swedish but rather of not having the vocabulary needed by the genealogist. We can toss out certain English language terms to the man on the street here in America, too, with the same result. Thus the purpose of this chapter is to help bridge the gap across some of the more common problem-terms and also to look carefully at other practices and problems inherent in American genealogical research. Other specific terms and problems are discussed in every chapter of this book.

I. HANDWRITING

Perhaps you wonder why handwriting is discussed in an American research text. Most American records are recent enough that the handwriting is not too different from your own—or is it? Actually there are enough serious problems, especially in the colonial period, that a brief discussion should prove useful. Handwriting is always a problem. Even in our own time some of us write so that others of us cannot read it except with great difficulty. (Sometimes we can't even read our own handwriting after it gets cold.) But if your ancestors were in America in the 1600's, and even the 1700's, you will find enough carry-over of Middle English in the records that a study of the simpler Middle English alphabets would prove beneficial. [1]

---

[1] Excellent helps in studying Middle English can be found in David E. Gardner and Frank Smith, Genealogical Research in England and Wales, Vol. III (Salt Lake City: Bookcraft, 1964).

SOME MIDDLE ENGLISH WRITING
WITH ITS MANY UNFAMILIAR CHARACTERS

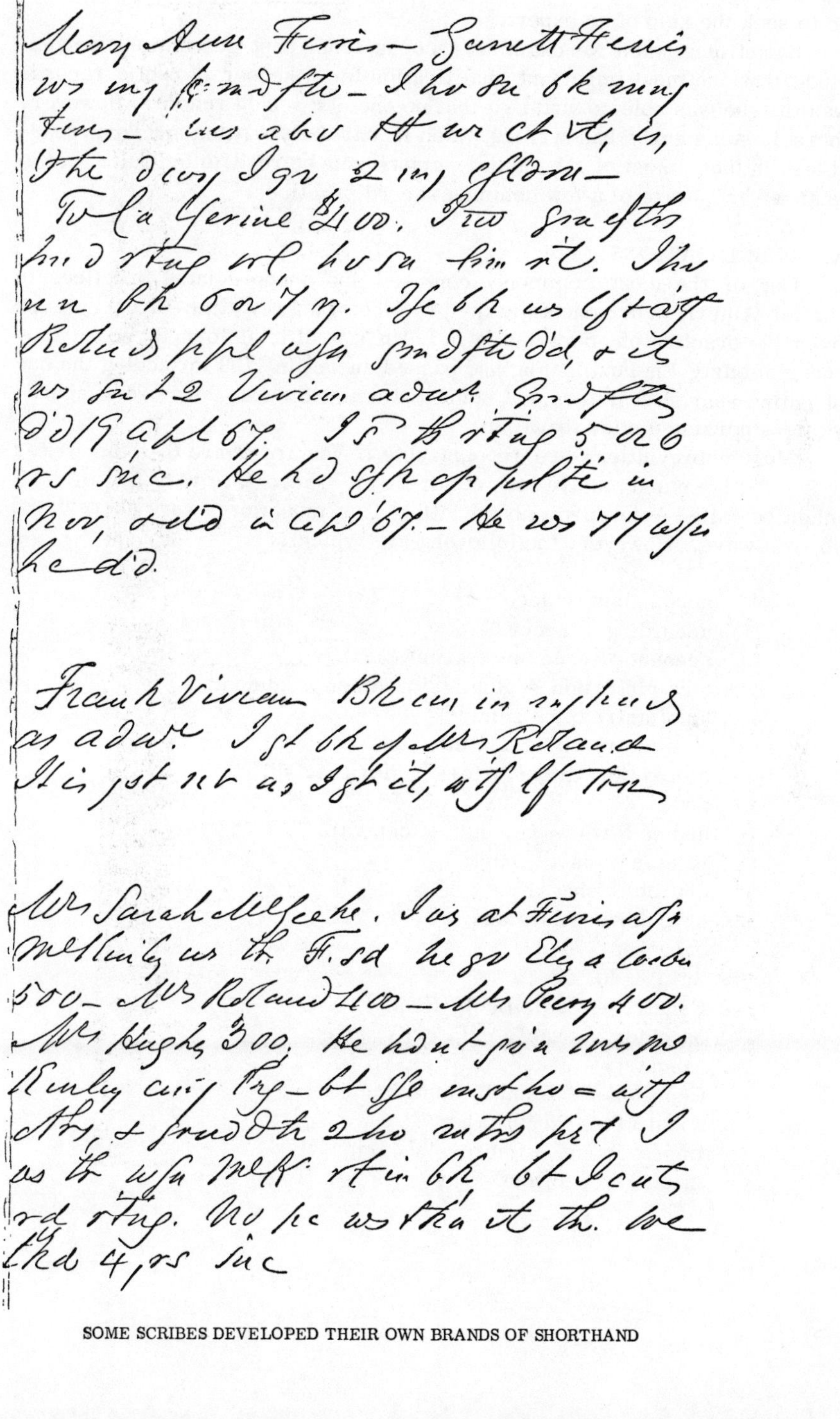

SOME SCRIBES DEVELOPED THEIR OWN BRANDS OF SHORTHAND

Many records in early America were not written in English at all but in other European languages; however, this is another problem and we will not deal with it here. Your best action when you meet that situation would be to seek the help of an expert.

Sometimes when we examine records from past generations we conclude that the most important qualification for a keeper of public records was that he was able to write so that no one else could read it. However, there is some early handwriting which is carefully written and very readable. In fact, most of the earlier scripts can be read (often quite easily) when we are aware of a few common record practices.

A. ABBREVIATIONS

One of the most commonly confused and unappreciated practices in earlier American documents is the practice of abbreviating—a carry-over from the practice of abbreviating in Latin (the official formal record language of early England). England passed an act in 1733 forbidding the use of Latin in parish registers, but some Latin and the extensive use of abbreviations persisted after that time.

Most abbreviations are recognizable if you are aware that the writer was using them and you are looking for them. There were very few of what might be called "standard" abbreviations, and most words were abbreviated several ways. However, the following are typical:

accomptant - accompt^t
according - accord^g
account or accompt - acco^t, acc^t
administration - admin^{ion}, admon., admon:
administrator - admin^r
administratrix - admin^x
aforesaid - afors^d, fors^d, afors:, afsd.
and - &
and so forth - &c, etc. (etcetera)
captain - capt^n, capt:
church - chh
daughter - dau, dau^r
deceased - dec^d
ditto - do, d^o
Esquire - Esq:, Esqr, Esq.
executor - exec^r, ex^r, ex^{or}, exor:
executrix - exec^x, ex^x, ex^{ix}
Gentleman - Gentl^n, Gent:, Gent.
honorable - hon^{ble}, hon:
improvement - improvem^t, improv^t
inventory - invent^y, inv:

Junior - Junr, J^r, Jun:
Messieurs - Messrs, Messrs
namely - viz, viz: vizt (videlicet)
paid - p^d
pair - p^r
per - p^r
personal - person^l, p'son^l
probate - prob^t
probate register - p. regist^r
received - rec^d, recv^d
receipt - rec^t
record - rec^d
register - reg^r, regist^r
said - s^d
Senior - Senr, S^r, Sen:
testament - testam^t, testa:
the - ye, y^e (This usage is a carry-over from the ancient An-
glo-Saxon letter, <u>Thorn</u>, which was similar to
the <u>Y</u> and had the <u>TH</u> sound. Other words beginning with the same sound were also thus
written: y^{en}, y^{ere}, y^{is}, y^t, etc.)

A good example of what you might find is shown in the account of Elizabeth Hodsdon's administration of her deceased husband's estate in 1763, York
County, Massachusetts (now Maine):

The acco^t of Eliz^a Hodsdon of her admin^{ion} of the Estate of her
late Husband John Hooper the third late of Berwick in ye County
of York dec^d Intestate. The S^d accompt^t chargeth her self with
the person^l Estate of S^d Dec^d as p^r Invent^y £21·13· - ...

Let's point out a few important things from the above example:
Most of the abbreviations are formed by merely shortening the word,
sometimes even as we might abbreviate it today, but then putting the last
letter (sometimes even two or three letters) of that word above the line.
This is called <u>superior letter</u> abbreviation. Another form is that of <u>termin-
ation</u>—that is, merely cutting the word to be abbreviated short and putting
a period or a colon (:) after it, or by drawing a line (———) through it like
this: T̶h̶o̶ (for Thomas). In very early periods often only the first letter of
the word was used.
Another common form of abbreviation was the contraction. A word like
<u>parish</u> might be contracted to <u>p'ish</u>, or <u>present</u> might be contracted to <u>p'sent</u>.
In these examples an apostrophe (') is used, but at other times contractions
were also made by putting a curved line (⌣) above the contracted word like

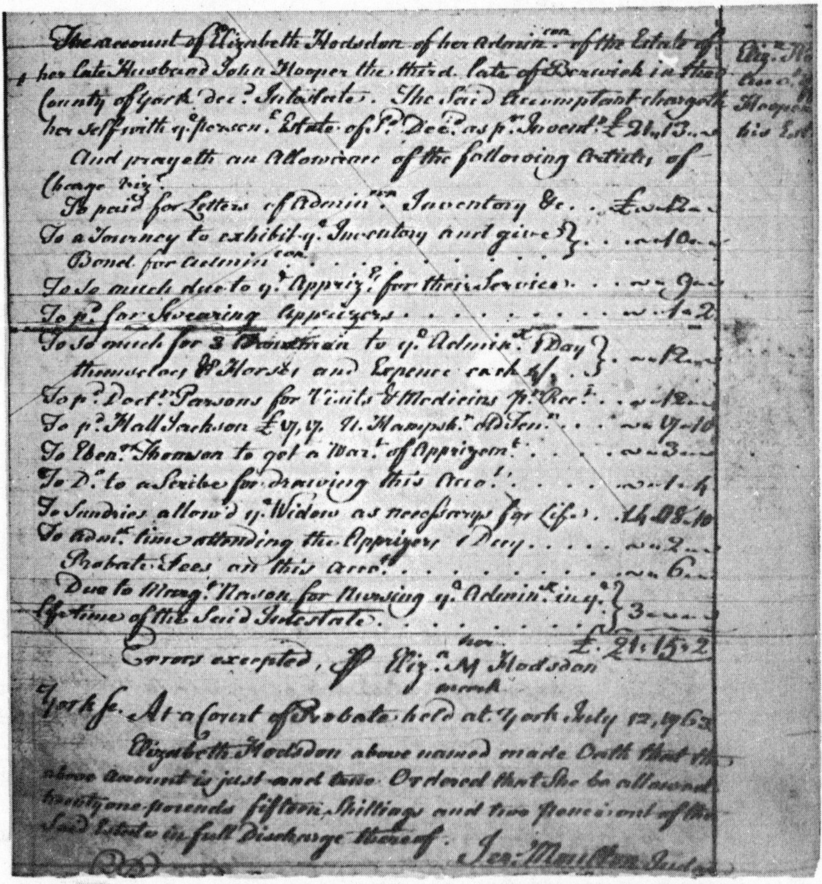

A DOCUMENT WITH EXTENSIVE ABBREVIATIONS

this: p$\overset{\frown}{\text{s}}$ent. You will also find occasions where a word with a double consonant was written with only one consonant and a line drawn over it to show that it should be doubled. For example, common might be written as co$\overline{\text{m}}$on. This was especially used in connection with the letters m and n, and the line was sometimes curved (co$\overset{\frown}{\text{m}}$on).

In actual practice any word might be abbreviated in several different ways depending on the scribe. In many instances the abbreviation for two different words might even be the same, but most can be recognized within the context of the writing.

B. NAME ABBREVIATIONS

Given names are often abbreviated as is Elizabeth (Eliz[a]) in the example. Ordinarily names were abbreviated in the same way as other words; however, there are a few exceptions to this rule also. Here are just a few popular name abbreviations:

Aaron - Aar[n]
Abraham - Abra[m]
Andrew - Andr[w], And[w]
Arthur - Art[r], Arth[r]
Barbara - Barb[a]
Benjamin - Benj[a], Benj[n], Benj:
Charles - Cha[s], Char[s]
Christopher - X[r], Xopher, Xofer
Daniel - Dan[l]
David - Dav[d]
Ebenezer - Eben[r]
Franklin - Frankl[n], Frank[n], Frank:
Frederick - Fred[ck], Fredr[k]
George - Geo:, G[o]
Gilbert - Gilb[t], Gil[rt]
Hannah - Ha$\overline{\text{n}}$ah
James - Ja[s], Jas:
Jeremiah - Jer[a], Jerem[a], Jer:
Jonathan - Jonath[n], Jon[n], Jon:
John - Jno:, Jno
Joseph - Jos, Jos:
Leonard - Leon[d]
Margaret - Marg[t]
Nathan - Nath[n]
Nathaniel - Nath[l], Nathan[l]
Patrick - Patr[k]
Richard - Rich[d], Rich:

Robert - Robt, Rob:
Samuel - Saml, Sam:
Stephen - Steph^n
Thomas - Thos, Tho: , ~~Tho~~
Vincent - Vinc^t, Vinc^{nt}
Virginia - Virg^a, Virg:
Wilford - Wilf^d, Wilf:
William - Willm, W^m, Will:
Zachariah - Zach^a, Zachar^a, Zach:

Many other names were also frequently abbreviated (and many of those shown were abbreviated in different ways), but most can be recognized quite easily. Nearly every given name of any length and often even surnames will be found abbreviated at one time or another. If you have trouble identifying an abbreviated name you may find it written out some other place in the same record, though this is not always the case.

C. IRRELEVANT CAPITALS

There was a tendency to capitalize words for no apparent reason, and capitalized words might be found anywhere within a sentence. There seems to have been more of a tendency to capitalize nouns, but it was not consistent. Some writers simply capitalized certain letters whenever they began a word with them, and there is some variation from scribe to scribe.

D. PUNCTUATION

There is no punctuation in the Hodsdon example except the periods at the ends of the sentences. There are two main types of exceptions to this kind of punctuation in early records: (1) In some writing you will find an occasional comma, and (2) In other writing you will find no punctuation at all.

One practice followed by some scribes was to use dots (·) to indicate pauses. A dot on the line indicated a brief pause, a dot above the level of the writing indicated a full stop, and a dot between the words indicated a phrase separation. These dots, when used, took the place of all other punctuation.

E. LOOK-ALIKE LETTERS

Another problem, only partially observable in the sample documents shown in this chapter, is that many letters look almost exactly like other letters. The capital letters I and J are very difficult to distinguish between as are also U and V. (In the original Roman alphabet there was only one letter for each.) L and S and even T and F are also easily confused. However, much depends on the scribe, and there are frequently other capital letters which are confusing. You must study the handwriting very carefully in order to make a distinction whenever there is a problem. Initials in names are the chief villains so far as this problem is concerned and are especially troublesome in census returns (and these are in the nineteenth century) and other lists of names.

Small, or lower case, letters also cause many misunderstandings. Curlicues on the letter d above the line and on y and g below the line can be troublesome as they often run into other letters, even on other lines of writing. But they are not much trouble when you recognize them for what they are. Another troublesome character is the long s (ʃ). To the inexperienced observer this may appear as either an f or a p or even as a double f or double p depending on how it was used. It was seldom used at the beginnings or endings of words but was almost always used as the first letter of the double s and frequently in other instances. This usage persisted into the middle 1800's.

In early writing (this is strictly from Middle English) the small e was made to resemble the modern-day o, and it can cause errors if undetected. Another difficult problem is the similarity between the n and the u and all other letters with up and down strokes (minims) in a series. We still have problems with these in our modern chirography. Some scribes in the 1600's put a crooked line (ʃ) above one of the letters when there was more than one letter with these up and down strokes in sequence. Thus punish might appear as punish.

There are also other important practices and problems that we need to consider.

F. WORD DIVISIONS

When a word was divided at the end of a line it was not divided with a hyphen (-) as in modern usage, but rather with either an equals sign (=) or a colon (:) and often at the beginning of the line where the last part of the divided word was being continued rather than at the end of the preceding line (and sometimes in both places). As we mentioned earlier, colons were also used quite frequently in forming suspension abbreviations. These two usages should not be confused even though they may be confusing.

G. NUMBER PROBLEMS

Numbers can also cause difficulties. Many of the numbers that people wrote two or three hundred years ago are different from the same numbers as we write them. Numbers and dates written in the Arabic form should be studied carefully to make sure they are being properly interpreted. Sometimes numbers may not look like numbers at all and you may erroneously try to make something else out of them. The <u>8</u>, for example, was often made to lie almost flat on its side, and most scribes would write a series of numbers (as a year) without lifting the pen from the paper. Also, Roman numerals are found with great frequency in older records and familiarity with them is essential.

H. LATIN TERMS

You may encounter some Latin terms or their abbreviations with which you may not be familiar. These are not generally extensive in American records but, as a carry-over from British and European practice, they are common enough that you ought to be aware of some of those most frequently used outside of legal and court records. Consider the following:

Anno Domini (A.D.) - in the year of our Lord
circa (c., ca., circ.) - about
et alii (et al.) - and others
etcetera (etc., & c) - and so forth
item - also, likewise
liber or libro - book or volume
nepos - grandson
obiit (ob) - he died, she died
requiescat in pace (R.I.P.) - may he (or she) rest in peace
sic - so, thus (intentionally so written to show exact reproduc-
                tion of original)
testes - witnesses
ultimo (ult.) - last
uxor (us, vx) - wife
videlicet (viz, vizt) - namely

If you come across other Latin terms (and you assuredly will), there are many reference books and dictionaries you can use. The likelihood of your encountering records written entirely in Latin in American research is quite remote; however, the possibility is not excluded and, should you find such records, you should never try to make a translation on your own (unless you have a good background in the language), even when the words appear familiar. In Latin the way a word ends determines the meaning, and the ending of one word can change the meaning of an entire sentence. Thus in such cases you should seek the help of someone who knows the language.

I. NOT THE ORIGINALS

If you use any records which are not originals—either manuscript or published—remember that they too are subject to the same errors of which we have been speaking. Many of the persons who make extracts and/or abstracts of original records are not completely qualified to do so, and many who are qualified make honest mistakes. In either case the effect is the same. Persons who make copies of indexes (or indices if you prefer) can also have the same problems. A name can be misread and thus be incorrectly indexed, or a document can be missed completely. These things can happen even in making the original index, so every index and every secondary source must be approached with due caution.

J. A GENERAL RULE

In any record the most important thing to do when you have difficulty in reading it is to study the handwriting very carefully and learn how to read that particular hand. (It's worth the time if the record has information you need.) You should study it solicitously, read and "translate" a small portion of it word-by-word and note how the various letters are formed. The more difficult problems you will have to study letter-by-letter, comparing similar characters in the same handwriting until you recognize the word in question. This is especially important when you are reading names, as in a census, since some names are easily confused with others at first glance. Some relief lies in the fact that documents of the same kind contain set phrases and words which seldom vary from one instrument to another. You should be familiar with these words and phrases before you attempt to read them in any early script.

When you are working with vital records certificates it is sometimes difficult to apply these rules completely because the certificate of concern is usually the only example you have of the handwriting in question. In such situations you must do your best with what you have but you must be very, very careful.

For more help with handwriting problems refer to E. Kay Kirkham, How to Read the Handwriting and Records of Early America, 2nd ed. (Salt Lake City: Deseret Book Co., 1964). This book provides a good guide to the solutions of many of the handwriting problems you will encounter in American records.

K. SPELLING

The lack of standardized spelling and the use of phonetic spelling can be very sticky problems for the genealogist. If you go back just 100 years you will find that there was not a large percentage of the population that could read, fewer still who could write (many of these being able to write only their names), and fewer still who could spell. Most persons who did write did not concern themselves particularly with standard spellings, but rather

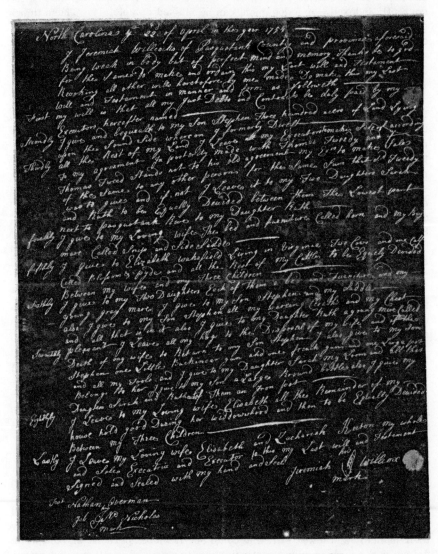

FIGURE 4——THE WILL OF JEREMIAH WILLCOX

spelled the words they wrote just as they sounded—phonetically—with local accents and all. You should also realize that the early settlers of America were emigrants from many foreign lands. There were many accents and when records were made the scribe wrote what he heard, accent and all. (Note that the examples of various records given in this book have retained original spellings and that the errors are not ours.)

What is the significance of these facts? It means that oftimes you will be called upon to decipher scripts in which you will puzzle over simple words just because they are misspelled and in an unfamiliar hand. However, the main problem is in the spellings of names (especially surnames) and places.

In the will which he made in 1754 in Pasquotank County, North Carolina, Jeremiah Willcox's surname is spelled two different ways—Willcox and Willcocks (see Figure 4). In other documents it is spelled still other ways—Wilcox, Wilcocks, Wellcox, Wellcocks, Welcocks, etc.—but Jeremiah could not write himself (he made a mark for his signature) so he probably had no idea as to what the correct spelling really was or if it was ever being spelled correctly. The name and its spelling were entirely at the mercy of the person who chanced to make the record.

This points up the fallacy of a common practice which we see in many modern families—that of assuming that if the name is not spelled in a certain way it cannot belong to the same family. Persons with such ideas pass over important genealogical records because the name happens to be spelled with an a rather than an e, with an ie rather than a y, or with one n rather than with two. We must be especially careful of this when the two related spellings of a name are found in the same geographic area. The connection is not always guaranteed, as it is not guaranteed even when the spelling is exactly the same, but it is worth investigating the possibility.

Also, because of this spelling problem, we must be extremely careful in our use of indexes. We must consider every possible spelling of the name sought. It is very easy to overlook some of the less logical (to us) possibilities and thus many valuable records. Local dialects and foreign accents often make a significant difference. The pronunciation of a name may be quite different in Massachusetts than it is in Georgia, and so might its spelling.

In law this is called the Rule of "Idem Sonans." This means that in order to establish legal proof of relationship from documentary evidence it is not necessary for the name to be spelled absolutely accurately if, as spelled, it conveys to the ear, when pronounced in the accepted ways, a sound practically identical to the correctly spelled name as properly pronounced.

A few years ago we worked for some time on a problem where the same surname was found spelled 24 different ways in the very same locality, some of them even beginning with a different letter of the alphabet. The original name (supposedly) was Ingold, but the following variations were found: Ingle, Ingell, Ingles, Ingells, Ingel, Ingels, Ingeld, Inkle, Inkles, Inkell,

Ingolde, Engold, Engolde, Engle, Engell, Engles, Engells, Engel, Engels, Engeld, Angold, Angle and Ankold. These several variations were all found in the same family at the same time. Would you have considered all of them or would you have stopped with those that began with the letter I?

Other less likely possibilities for this name are Jugold and Jugle. Such errors could easily occur in an index because of the similarities between the capital I's and J's and the small n's and u's.

Another family changed the spelling of its name from Beatty to Baitey when moving from one location to another. In still another instance the surname Kerr was found interchanged with Carr. Whether these spelling changes were intentional is unknown, but that is how it worked out in the records and the intention makes little difference. In one family three brothers deliberately spelled their surname in different ways—Matlock, Matlack and Matlick. In his history of the Zabriskie family, [2] George O. Zabriskie reports having dealt with 123 variations of that name, though certainly not all in the same locality or at the same time period.

L. MARKS AND SIGNATURES

Very often the records which we use are not the original records but rather copies made in official registers by recorders and clerks, and the signatures on these registered copies are only copied signatures so they are of little consequence when it comes to identifying an ancestor. But even then there can be some value and often it is greater when the person concerned (the ancestor) could not write. That value lies in the mark with which he signed his name because the clerk usually copied the exact mark (as best he could) into the register. If it was an X the value is minimal because so many persons used X's, but if another type of mark was used, it may be useful for identification. This is especially true if your ancestor had a common name, and often those with the most common names used the most distinctive marks in their striving for individuality and identity.

If you can definitely identify your ancestor in a deed (or some other type of record) where he used a distinctive mark in connection with that name, you can be quite sure you have your ancestor. Almost anything except an X can be helpful, and we do not even completely rule out that possibility.

If original documents are available, signatures can be used in the same way but only if the party concerned signed his own name or made a distinctive mark. However, both practices can be tricky and you must be extremely careful.

---

2. George Olin Zabriskie (comp.), The Zabriskie Family (Salt Lake City: Publishers Press, 1963).

M. POORLY PRESERVED RECORDS

Very often during your research you will find that records you need have not survived the onslaught of nature and the ravages of time. In addition to acts of nature, some record custodians have been careless and some users of the records have been inconsiderate. There is not a great deal you can do if the records you need are destroyed or are badly damaged, but you can be more concerned about the records you use so that the same fate will not befall them. Irresponsibility in the use of records is one of the chief reasons why so many records are either damaged or non-existent.

If you are in a position to handle the old, original documents please treat them gently and do not touch them. Regardless of how clean your hands are, skin oil is on your fingers and, in time, the paper will darken in every place it is touched. Turn pages with the eraser end of your pencil or with a rubber finger. Keep your pens and pencils off the records. There is no reason for your leaving any marks on them. Proper document care is very much the responsibility of the record user.

II. EVOLUTION OF THE LANGUAGE

Whenever we deal with writing or language from a different period of time there are semantics problems. The history of linguistic development is a story of constant change. Meanings and usages are not static. They have changed in the past, they are changing today, and they will continue to change as long as men use language to communicate with one another.

Early American colonization is somewhat concurrent with the publishing of the King James Bible in 1611, so let's take a simple example from the Bible to illustrate our point. In Mark 10:13 Jesus said: "Suffer the little children to come unto me..." The same verse in a more recent translation says: "Let the children come to me..."[3] This is the type of problem we are dealing with and it truly can cause us suffering (in the modern definition of the word). Only when you realize that a word might have a different meaning than the one you personally ascribe to it do you really grasp the full impact of how easily you might be misled.

Let's talk a little more about this problem and some of the more common usage variations as they affect American genealogical research.

A. RELATIONSHIPS

Relationships and terms connected with them can be sources of trouble for the uninitiated.

---

3. From The New English Bible, New Testament. © The Delegates of the Oxford University Press and the Syndics of the Cambridge University Press, 1961. Reprinted by permission.

Junior and Senior are terms which we usually think of as indicating a father-son relationship, but in records this was not necessarily true. They were used merely to distinguish between two persons with the same name, usually of different generations, living in the same locality. Very often they were uncle and nephew rather than father and son. In some parts of the United States, particularly the South, it was as common, or even more so, for a man to name his sons for his brothers as for himself. And you should also watch for the changing of designations. A man once known as junior may be called senior after the death of the earlier senior, and then someone of a younger generation may be called junior.

You must be very careful of this usage. We once checked a Daughters of the American Revolution lineage based on a junior-senior, son-father assumption—the junior was allegedly the son of the senior who had served from Virginia in the Continental Line. Research proved that this was actually a situation where they were uncle and nephew—not father and son.

In-law relationships and step relationships can also cause us some problems if we are not careful. In earlier times people often stated that an in-law connection existed when there was actually a step relationship instead. Any relationships created by legal means, including step relationships, were identified simply as "in-law." The following excerpt from a release executed by the heirs of William Bryer, 1738/9, in York County, Massachusetts (now Maine), provides a good example of this.

Know all men by these Presents that we William Bryer Shipwright Richard Bryer Weaver Andrew Haley husbandman and Mary his Wife Caleb Hutchins Caulker and Sarah his Wife Joseph Hutchins Weaver and Elizabeth his Wife William Willson Weaver and Eadah his Wife John Haley Husbandman & Hephzib[a] his Wife all of Kittery in the County of York in the Province of the Massachusetts Bay in New England and William Tapley Taylor of New Hampshire & R   [sic] his Wife Do forever acquit exonerate and discharge our Father in Law Benjamin Hammond of Kittery & Province afors[d] and our Mother Sarah Hammond lately call'd Sarah Bryer from the Demands of us or our or either of our Heirs in and unto any part of the Cattle or Household Goods or moveable Estate of our hon[d] Father William Bryer late of Kittery afores[d] dec[d]...this 31st Day of January Anna Domini 1738/9...[emphasis added].

Another common type of example of this situation is found in the will of Francis Champernoun, dated November 16, 1686, in the same place. We quote in part:

I give and bequeath & confirm unto my Son in Law Humphrey Elliot & Elizabeth his now wife and their heirs forever the other

part of my s^d Island, which I have allredy given by Deed under
my hand and Seal to the s^d Humphery & Elizabeth his wife— Item
I give and bequeath unto my Son in Law Robert Cutt my daughter
in Law Bridget Leriven my daughter in Law Mary Cutt and my
daughter in Law Sarah Cutt and their heires forever all that part
of three hundred acres of land belonging unto me lying between
broken Neck and the land formerly belonging unto Hugh Punnison...

It is easy to see the confusion that this usage can cause if we are not
aware of the possibility. However, this type of problem cannot be predicted.
Usually the records mean exactly what they say in this regard—they say
"in-law" and mean just that. But you must be on your guard for possible
exceptions.

The terms cousin, brother and sister are also of significance because
of varied usage. However, they do not assume so great an importance in
American research as the terms previously mentioned. Concerning these
three, Jacobus said:

The term "cousin" is perhaps the one which is most puzzling
to the untrained searcher. It was applied loosely to almost any
type of relationship outside the immediate family circle. It was
most frequently used to denote a nephew or niece, but it could be
applied to a first cousin or more distant cousin, or to the marital
spouse of any of these relatives, and sometimes to other indirect
connections who were not even related by blood. The first guess
should be that a nephew or niece was meant; if this does not work
out, then try to prove that cousin in our sense of the word was
meant; if this also proves impossible, it may require long and
profound study to determine just what the connection was. This
applies, generally speaking, to the use of the term in the colonies
prior to 1750. No definite and exact date can be fixed, for the
terms nephew and niece gradually supplanted cousin to denote that
form of relationship....

... Husband and wife were identified as one person. Hence,
when a man writes in his will of "my brother Jones" and "my sister Jones,: he may be referring to his own sister and her husband, to his wife's sister and her husband, or to his wife's brother and that brother's spouse.

It is not always possible to decide, in the will of a puritan
around 1650, whether the "Brother Peck" and "Brother Perkins"
whom he appointed overseers of his estate were relatives by marriage or merely brothers in the church. The expression "my
Brother Peck" makes it sound a little more like relationship,
but is not conclusive. The same uncertainty attaches to the use of

the term "Sister" in these early wills. [4]

You will occasionally see the use of the term german (or germane) in connection with some types of relationships, especially brothers, sisters and cousins. Brothers (or sisters) german are children of the same parents (as opposed to half-brothers or sisters), and cousins german are the children of brothers and sisters, i.e. first cousins.

The terms niece and nephew, as mentioned above, can cause confusion in early records. They did not always have the same connotations that we attach to them. Niece derives from the Latin term Neptis and nephew from the Latin term Nepos, which, when translated, actually mean granddaughter and grandson, respectively. In early American records this usage is rarely found but certainly not unknown. In most cases these relationships, when stated, mean the same thing as they do today. During the evolution of meaning you may find it used for either, but by 1690 we have found no use of niece and nephew in this context while finding frequent mention of grandson and granddaughter. However, if you find the word nepos, you can almost count on it meaning grandson.

The term my now wife is very often misunderstood as it appears in various records. It is often misinterpreted to mean that the person making the statement or to whom it applies (as in the will of Francis Champernoun where he mentioned "my Son in Law Humphrey Elliot & Elizabeth his now wife") has been previously married, but this is not necessarily true and the person making the statement had something quite different in mind. Usually the term was used in wills when the testator (the person making the will) wanted to place a limitation on that will which the court would recognize even when he wasn't around to explain. The thing for you to remember is that this was not an explanatory phrase but rather a phrase used to limit the inheritence rights of any future wife in case the "now wife" should die before the will was probated and he should remarry. The person making such a statement in a will may have been previously married, but the statement was not made to protect property against the claims of a previous spouse but always from possible future spouses.

B. TITLES

There were some other terms in quite common usage in earlier periods with which you should become familiar. British America, during the

---

4. Donald Lines Jacobus, "Interpreting Genealogical Records," in Genealogical Research: Methods and Sources, ed. by Milton Rubincam (Washington, D.C.: American Society of Genealogists, 1960), pp. 22, 23. By permission.

colonial period was naturally caught up in many British traditions and usages. Hence the terms of British social rank were also used here though
they commonly lacked the strict meanings and social implications which
had been attached to them in the mother country. In many records (some
of them quite recent) we find persons referred to as Esquire (Esqr) or
Gentleman (Gentl^n).

In Britain a person who had an "Esquire" tacked on the end of his name
was able to bear arms and was next in social precedence to a knight. If he
had "Gentleman" at the end of his name this signified gentle birth also, but
one more step down the social ladder.

The use of these terms became quite loose in England and especially
so in America. Of course even in America the earlier the period, the more
strict the usage. They were mainly used as a designation of the most in-
fluential (or most prosperous) persons in a community. They were used by
the social elite—lawyers, physicians, notable political figures, clergy,
large landowners, magistrates and justices of the peace—but the meaning
was not precise. You will occasionally find these terms in America even as
late as the middle 1800's applied to some public officials such as justices
of the peace and magistrates and church leaders. The most valuable thing
about the use of these titles in America is that they often provide an additional means of identification for the persons so designated as you search
the various records.

The title, Colonel, was also frequently used by many of the old southern planters, and though the title meant nothing so far as military rank was
concerned, it is useful for identification purposes.

Also among the early colonists, the usage of the terms Mr. and Mrs.
followed the English precedent and was used only by the upper classes of
society, those with the "Esquire" and "Gentleman" after their names. In
this connection Mrs. was not a term identifying a married woman but rather
a title of courtesy for a woman of "gentle" birth, married or single. In
this sense it was ordinarily used before both names (given and surname) of
the unmarried woman. However, it wasn't too long before our current usage of the terms became the common usage.

You will also often find the terms goodman and goodwife (frequently
shortened to goody) used in many of the older records you search. They
simply mean the head of a household and the mistress of a household, respectively.

III. NAMING PRACTICES

We have already dealt with problems of surnames so it might be well
now to discuss given names and some familiar practices relating to them
and their use. In both New England and the South, Bible names had great
popularity. However, New Englanders used both common and uncommon

Bible names while their southern cousins stuck with the more conventional. New Englanders are also well known for the frequent bestowal of names of qualities of the soul, or spiritual gifts, upon their children; this perhaps being partially due to their dislike of the old established English names. Faith, hope and charity were more than just words to live by—they were very common female given names. Other popular names for girls included Prudence, Sympathy, Mirth, Kindness, Mercy, Constance, Submit, Silence and Deliverance. Popular male names included Remember, Comfort (also sometimes feminine), Ransome, Consider, etc.

Given names of the past also had more of a tendency to be carried on in a family from generation to generation than they do today, though we still have some tendencies in this direction. Even very unusual names were carried on—a practice which often provides circumstantial evidence for certain genealogical connections. You must be careful, however, and not accept a connection on this basis without some definite proof that such a connection was indeed a fact.

A child very often was given the name of one of his (or her) grandparents. (This custom was more common in some other countries than in America, but it was also quite common here among certain ethnic groups.) Or, he may have been given his mother's maiden surname. A boy might have been given the names of his father's and mother's brothers, and a girl might have been given the names of her parents' sisters. This means that if a man and his brothers all had large families and they came from a large family themselves you will find many contemporary cousins all bearing the same given names—and often very hard to identify which is which as you read of them in the records.

It is quite common for the researcher to find more than one child in the same family unit with the same given name. Usually when this happened it was because one child of that name died and the name was given to one of the later children. Occasionally we find more than one living child in the same family with the same given name, but this is very rare and happened mostly in German or Dutch families or when there was a great age difference between the two children. In the latter case they were frequently the children of two different marriages.

Very often several children were given the same middle name (after middle names became popular), often their mother's or even their grandmothers' maiden surname. This practice, however, does not date back quite so far as some of the others. [5]

---

5. For further discussion on names (especially in New England), see Chapter Five of Donald Lines Jacobus, Genealogy as Pastime and Profession, 2nd ed. rev. (Baltimore: Genealogical Publishing Co., 1968).

IV. SOME SYMBOLS

It also seems wise for us to list a number of symbols widely used by those who compile genealogies. You will encounter these often as you use various secondary sources. Some of the main ones follow:

*	-	born
(*)	-	born illegitimate
X	-	baptized or christened
⌒	-	baptized or christened
∿	-	baptized or christened
O	-	betrothed
∞	-	married
O/O	-	divorced
O-O	-	common-law marriage
†	-	died
⊬	-	died
▢	-	buried
▭	-	buried
††	-	no further issue
(†)	-	no further issue

V. THE CALENDAR

Calendar difficulties may come as a surprise to you unless you have either studied astronomy or have a good background in history. However, the calendar and its transition from the Julian to the Gregorian system and other changes which were involved therewith have considerable impact on many early American genealogical problems.

The main problem of interest and concern here has to do with the changing of the calendars—when the switch was made from the Julian to the Gregorian. In Britain and her colonies (which included most colonies in America) this took place in 1752. [6] Remember that date; it is important. During the period while the Julian Calendar was used, the Christian Church and the countries within which that church prospered used what we call an ecclesiastical calendar (dating back to the Nicean Council of 325 A.D.) which

---

[6]. The Dutch in New Netherland never used the Julian Calendar. They had accepted the Gregorian Calendar prior to their American colonization. These people even continued to use New Style dates in their private records after England had control of their colony. The Quakers did not accept the ecclesiastical calendar but began their year on January 1 even though they otherwise accepted the dates of the Julian Calendar. (Note that the examples in Chapter Nineteen show an exception to this general rule.)

had New Year's Day falling on the 25th of March. This was the day of the Feast of the Annunciation (commonly called Lady Day) which commemorates the visit of the Angel Gabriel to the Virgin Mary to inform her that she would be the mother of the Messiah. [7] You will note that this date is exactly nine months before Christmas, when we celebrate that birth.

Let's take an example to show the effects of this situation. You have several documents (such as wills) recorded in chronological order. The dates on these might run something like this:

> November 14, 1718
> December 26, 1718
> January 3, 1718
> January 22, 1718
> February 16, 1718
> March 5, 1718
> March 23, 1718
> March 28, 1719
> April 12, 1719

This is very simple, isn't it? The main difficulty here is that we are accustomed to beginning our years on January 1, so when we see a date like one of these, say February 16, 1718, we automatically put it in the wrong year—and we are automatically one year off.

One year off isn't bad, you say? That is true unless it can lead you to make incorrect conclusions. If the record in question happens to be a church register and the christenings, etc., of your ancestor's children are recorded therein, then you may have a problem. Let's say you find two christenings on the following dates for children of persons you suppose are your ancestor's children:

> April 1, 1720
> March 22, 1720

If you didn't know that the year 1721 began three days after the second of these two christenings, what would be your conclusion?

Or, what about the case of the man who draws his will in October of 1692 and dies and that will is admitted to probate in February 1692? What would you think?

Because of this problem we use what we call double-dating. This means that whenever a date falls between January 1 and March 24, inclusive, before 1752, it should be recorded to reflect both the ecclesiastical and the

---

7. Luke 1:26-28.

historical calendars. You do this by writing the dates in our previous list as follows:

> November 14, 1718
> December 26, 1718
> January 3, 1718/9
> January 22, 1718/9
> February 16, 1718/9
> March 5, 1718/9
> March 23, 1718/9
> March 28, 1719
> April 12, 1719

And our two christening dates given earlier should be written:

> April 1, 1720
> March 22, 1720/1

And the dates on the will would actually be October 1692 and February 1692/3.

This double-dating indicates that the year was actually (in the case of the christening) 1720, but that if the year had begun on January 1 as it now does, then it would have been 1721. Very simple, isn't it?

There was some pressure for the change to January 1 before it actually took place officially in 1752, and it is not uncommon at all to find double-dating used in many of the early records, especially after 1700. Some other Christian countries were using the new system as early as 1582.

You may also find double-dating used incorrectly in these records on occasion, but do not let this alarm you. You can usually make the corrections. For example, you may find a date incorrectly written as "April 12, 1718/9." This is much the same problem that we have today when we keep writing the old year for a month or so after the new year has begun. It would be corrected to 1719. You might also see some double-dating after 1752. This is merely a case where the writer either had a habit of writing dates that way and could not change or was just opposed to changes.

Also, since the year began in March, you will find March referred to as the first month, April as the second month, and so on. So when you see the months written as 7^{ber} and 8^{ber} (before 1752) they actually mean September and October and not July and August. In Latin September and October mean seventh month and eighth month, respectively. The same principle also applies to November and December so far as the names are concerned—they mean ninth month and tenth month. But regardless of name the other months were also numbered differently. You may find it helpful to remember this—it makes quite a difference.

CHAPTER THREE

ANALYZING THE PEDIGREE AND THE PLACE

I. PEDIGREE ANALYSIS

It goes without saying that you can never arrive at your destination if you do not know where you are going. The person who does not know where he is going is like the proverbial ship that leaves port with no particular destination in mind and drifts aimlessly on the open seas. Unless you have goals you can never accomplish anything; and in genealogy an objective analysis of your pedigree is the thing which will help you visualize possible genealogical goals and channel your efforts correctly for their attainment. This does not actually make research any easier—the work is still there—but it can make it much more fruitful.

Before you can make a satisfactory analysis, however, you must first determine exactly where the research stands as of right now—you must find out what has already been done. This need not take forever as many suppose; it is quite a simple process if properly pursued. This secondary research, or preliminary survey[1] as we call it, includes the use of home and family sources (both those in your own possession and those in the possession of relatives). It also includes two sources peculiar to the LDS Church which are valuable to both Mormon and non-Mormon. These are the Temple Records Index Bureau and the Church Records Archives (commonly referred to as the TIB and the CRA).

The TIB is a card index file which contains genealogical data cards on nearly 40,000,000 persons from many generations and many countries. The CRA is a collection of group record forms of entire families (more than 5,000,000 of them) arranged alphabetically by the name of the father in each family. There is a cross-reference system between these two collections so if there is information in both places it can be detected. You can easily use these two sources, if you desire, by submitting a special form to the Society. Copies of the form may be obtained by writing to The Genealogi-

---

1. For a thorough discussion of the preliminary survey see Norman E. Wright and David H. Pratt, Genealogical Research Essentials (Salt Lake City: Bookcraft, 1967), Chapter 8.

cal Society, 50 East North Temple Street, Salt Lake City, Utah 84150.

The Genealogical Society has prepared "Research Papers" which give additional information on these sources. The titles which are pertinent are:

Series F, no. 1   LDS Records and Research Aids
Series F, no. 2   A Brief Guide to the Temple Records Index Bureau

They are available for 50¢ each from the above address.

Various compiled sources are also essential to your survey, and Chapter Eight discusses these in some detail. Printed genealogies are only a record of the research that someone else has done, and any research you do in them, as important as it may be, is only secondary research.

As you progress through your survey you should make a careful record of all the information you find. You should also keep in mind that the survey is not your ultimate objective and any data found are subject to error. These data are no more reliable than the persons and the research methods which produced them, and this cannot be determined except by careful study. Your first objective, however, is to gather the data—then you can analyze them.

Some type of pedigree chart (see Figure 2) should be prepared from the information found so that you can get a true picture of what you actually have in relation to the information still required. Family group forms (see Figure 1) should also be completed as far as the information found will allow. If a family group form is used you can readily get a true perspective of the information you have and that which you still need in order to make the record complete for the various families.

Once you have your pedigree and family group forms complete as far as you can determine from your survey, you are in a position to analyze the data they contain and decide exactly what your objectives in research will be.

As you analyze your pedigree you must remember that you cannot do everything at once. It would be folly for you to try to work on every ancestral line simultaneously. Pick a line that needs work—even two or three lines if they are in the same geographical area during the same time period —and you are ready to begin on a problem with a realistic perspective.

II. THE BASIC APPROACH

The first rule to remember is that you must work with the information which you already have. Just as you do not build a house separately from its foundation, genealogical evidence also requires a foundation. This means that you must begin your research on the ancestors about whom you already know something. To do effective research you must have a name,

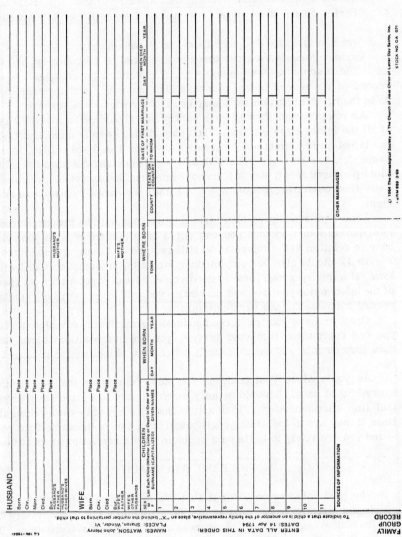

FIGURE 1—A TYPICAL FAMILY GROUP RECORD FORM

8. MATHIUS KELLY of Va.	9. BETSY BLACK	10. MIDDLETON JAMENSON	11. POLLY HARRIS	12. SIMION GILBERT	13. BETSY HUTSON	14. CHARLES BAKER	15. POLLY GIRE or McGUIRE
Brn Chr Die Bur	Brn Chr Die Bur	Brn Chr Die Bur	Brn Chr Die Bur	Brn Chr Die Bur	Brn Chr Die Bur	Brn Chr Die Bur	Brn Chr Die Bur
Mar'd		Mar'd		Mar'd		Mar'd	

4. JAHUE KELLY	5. RHODA JAMENSON	6. QUILLER GILBERT	7. POLLY BAKER
Brn 1782 Of Virginia Chr Die c. 1820 Bur	Brn c. 1791 Of Virginia Chr Die Feb 1881 Kentucky Bur	Brn 1791 Chr Die Bur	Brn Chr Die Bur
Mar'd		Mar'd	

2. WILLIAM SAMUEL KELLY	3. NANCY JANE GILBERT
Brn 1815 Of Virginia Chr Die 20 Mar 1865 Kentucky Bur	Brn 2 Dec 1825 Of Kentucky Chr Die 9 Nov 1908 Kentucky Bur
Mar'd	

1.   JOHN SAMUEL KELLY

Brn   24 Aug 1851   Booneville, Owsley, Kentucky
Chr
Die   8 Feb 1909   St. David, Cochise, Arizona
Bur

Mar'd   16 Mar 1894   to MARY ELLEN SMYTH

FIGURE 2—PEDIGREE OF JOHN SAMUEL KELLY

a <u>date</u> (at least a period of time), and a reasonably specific <u>place</u> or <u>locality</u>. You are wasting your time if these factors are unknown. Too many so-called genealogists find a "desirable" person with the right surname then try to trace the line of descent down until they make a connection. If such methods work then the person who uses them is either a very successful gambler (because of his ability to beat the laws of probability) or else the connections he has accepted are erroneous.

As your first step of analysis ask yourself: "Just what do I know about the person on whom I am doing research?" Analyze very carefully his name, the places with which he was associated, the dates connected with those places, and his relationships to other persons. Usually your research will begin in the earliest place that you find this person, but this is not always true as you may wish to do research in some later places of residence in order to complete the information on the family group record you are preparing.

Ask yourself whether the dates associated with your ancestor are historically significant. Might this person have lived at the right time to have served in one of this country's many wars? Might he or his widow have received a pension for that service? **Did** he die when his children were young? Might you find guardianship records for them? Did he die several years before his wife died? Might she have remarried? Or vice versa? Was he several years older than his wife? Might she have been a second wife? These possibilities and any other possibilities which you observe as you study your pedigree should be carefully noted. You will want to check them out later; as yet they are only possibilities. Many things of significance have occurred which are lost to family tradition.

As an example, let's consider the pedigree of John Samuel Kelly. First, from what you see on the pedigree form illustrated in Figure 2, where should research begin? On Simion Gilbert? On Rhoda Jamenson? Or just where? Quite obviously neither of these persons should be your primary objective to begin with. You do not know enough about them. Though you know a little about Rhoda you still do not have a definite enough locality in which research can be conducted.

There seems to be quite complete information on John Samuel Kelly himself so he would not be your objective unless you lacked information on his complete family.

There are actually only two logical possibilities—William Samuel Kelly and his wife, Nancy Jane Gilbert—and they can be combined into a dual objective. Why? Because you need further information on both of them and it can likely be found in the same locality. More is said later about searching for all persons of both surnames during your research.

Our <u>first question</u>: What do we know about William Samuel and Nancy Jane? Let's list a few things and have you check them out:

1. He is ten years older than she.
2. He died 43 years before she did.
3. He was about five years old when his father died.
4. He died 16 years before his mother did.
5. His mother was about 24 years old when he was born, his father about 33.
6. He came from Virginia and she came from Kentucky. (The use of the word "of" here merely indicates that we are not sure of birth places, and that these are the earliest known places of residence.)
7. They had a son born in 1851 and were apparently married before that year.
8. They resided in Booneville, Owsley County, Kentucky, in 1851. (Note that this is the earliest specific known place of residence we have and is thus quite significant.)
9. Both of them died in Kentucky.
10. We know the names (apparently) of both sets of parents.

Now we ask our second question: Do any of these facts suggest possibilities to be investigated? Yes! So let's list a few of them:

1. Since he was ten years older than she, he may have had a previous marriage.
2. Since she outlived him by 43 years, she may have remarried after his death.
3. Since his mother outlived his father by so many years, she may have remarried also.
4. Their marriage (William Samuel and Nancy Jane's) probably took place in Kentucky since she was from that state and their son John Samuel was born there. (Under these circumstances it is much more likely that he came to Kentucky to marry her than that she went to Virginia to marry him.)
5. If he came to Kentucky before his marriage and if it was his first marriage, he probably came with his mother and her family, possibly a step-father. (Note also that his mother did come to Kentucky. She died there.)
6. They possibly resided in Booneville and Owsley County for more than just the one year (1851) and our research should begin there.
7. His date of death suggests that he may have died in the Civil War. Though he was 50 years old this is still a possibility. (Being from Kentucky, a border state, there is no suggestion as to whether this might be a Union or Confederate Army connection. You would need to learn more about local history.)
8. There is also a possibility of other children both before and after John Samuel since Nancy Jane was 26 years old when John Samuel was born. (There would be none later than 1865 when William Samuel died.)

As research is begun each of these possibilities should be investigated in the appropriate records.

This is the way that every pedigree should be analyzed, not necessarily on paper, though that may prove helpful to the beginner. This is the type of analysis that clearly enables us to put the individual, the locality, the records, and history in their true perspective with one another.

III. GET THEM ALL

During the research for your ancestor it will be to your advantage if you read and extract all information relating to all persons of the surname(s) of interest in the locality of interest. If you do not do it, someday you will be sorry and you will wind up going back through the same records all over again, and it will likely be sooner than you think. You may not be able to identify all of these persons as you find them, but when you begin to synthesize your findings and put them into families most of the pieces will fall into place and the information you have found on those "unknown" persons will often provide clues to help you extend your pedigree. Some persons argue that if the surname is a common one it takes too much time to follow this procedure. Actually the more common the name the more essential this procedure becomes so that proper identification can be ascertained.

An example of the value of this course of action is shown in the Charles Pebble example in Chapter One. The "easy way" of picking out only "the important records" falls short in actual practice.

Also, before research can commence, you must know what records are available in the locality of your problem and what you might hope to find in those records that would be useful in solving your problems. This is an area of American research that is especially fascinating, and somewhat complicated, because you can never be sure what you are going to find in so many of the available records. You can usually get a pretty fair idea, but you will often be surprised by the actual content of many records. Names or titles of records often mean very little as the same types of records in different localities are labeled with different titles. Because of this no record should be sold short or overlooked until it has been put to the test. You can't afford to decide a case without hearing all of the evidence.

It is also essential that you know something about the location of records and the jurisdictions in which they were originally kept.

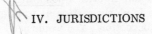 IV. JURISDICTIONS

By jurisdiction we mean the legal or traditional authority to carry out certain activities. A legal jurisdiction is established by law and might have to do with a case in civil court, or it may deal with vital records, or land records, wills, or censuses, etc. A <u>traditional</u> jurisdiction might include christenings (or baptisms), marriages, burials and other activities carried on by a church. Also, activities carried out by private businesses, institutions, fraternal organizations, etc., in behalf of their membership would be in traditional jurisdictions.

To you as a genealogist it is important to know who had jurisdiction of certain activities if you wish to locate and use any records which those activities may have produced.

You will find that the most logical approach to almost every American genealogical problem is the jurisdictional approach—that is, each locality and each jurisdiction of interest must be studied carefully as to its record-keeping procedures before research begins therein. Once you know what records were kept, who kept them, and who is their present custodian you are ready to proceed. And let us emphasize here the necessity of your searching all existing records produced by all jurisdictions or spheres of authority within which your ancestors lived—the home, the church, the county, the state, etc.

Closely related to jurisdictional knowledge is that most essential knowledge of records and their contents. When you search a record you should at least have a general idea of the kind of information usually found in that type of source. To help provide that knowledge is one purpose of this book.

A good example of what we are talking about is found in probate jurisdictions. In most states these records are kept in the county, but if you were tracing ancestors in Vermont it would be worthwhile to know that the records are kept in special probate districts which do not always correspond to the counties. In Rhode Island probate records are kept in the towns, and in Delaware all probate records for the state are kept in one central depository. See why it's important to understand jurisdictions as well as record content?

Also, you should be careful of jurisdictional changes. Records kept in one place at one time may have been kept somewhere else during another period. In New Hampshire, for example, probate and land records have traditionally been kept by the counties, but between 1671 and 1771 both types of records were kept by the province or colony. (This was prior to statehood.) You must know that in order to find them.

V. LOCALITY ANALYSIS

Closely related to the jurisdictional analysis already discussed is an examination of other data relating directly to the locality of your research. You must know much more about that locality than who kept the records and when they kept them. You must consider the history and the geography in minutiae.

If you knew that your great grandfather lived in Zanesville, Ohio, what

would you do to learn more about him?—a very simple question with a not-
so-simple answer. Do you have it figured out?

A. SOME BASIC TOOLS

The first thing you need to do, and this applies whether you are looking
for Zanesville, Ohio; Picabo, Idaho; Punxsutawney, Pennsylvania; or Booneville, Kentucky, is to find out exactly where that place is located.   A gazetteer, a postal directory, an encyclopedia, or a good map may provide
this information.

The dictionary defines a gazetteer as "a geographical dictionary,"[2]
but the term is actually used more broadly to include almost any work which
lists geographical names in alphabetical order. There are several of these
and also several postal directories that might be useful to you, but some
are better than others because they include more places.

To begin with we need to determine in which county of Ohio Zanesville
is located. Since, in America, most (but certainly not all) records are
kept on a county basis, this is an essential piece of datum. You can do
very little toward completing the research picture unless you know that
Zanesville is in Muskingum County. At least one of four good sources of
this information is available in most libraries:

1. United States, <u>United States Directory of Post Offices</u>, Washington, D.C.: Post Office Department (annual). The first section in
this source lists towns alphabetically by state and tells in which county
each one is located. This is not a complete source, however, as it is
limited to only those towns with post offices.

2. <u>Bullinger's Postal and Shippers Guide for the United States and
Canada</u>. Westwood, N.J.: Bullinger's Guides, Inc. (1897—). This
source provides the same information as the post office directory (item
1) except that all towns are listed in strict alphabetical order rather
than by state. It is much more extensive also because it is not limited
only to those towns with post offices. It is good for finding places that
are very small. And, as the title indicates, Canada is also included.

3. <u>Columbia - Lippincott Gazetteer of the World</u>. Morningside
Heights, N.Y.: Columbia University Press and J. B. Lippincott Co.
(1905 and 1952). This is a good source because of the information it
gives about the places listed, but it is not complete in its coverage.
All entries are arranged in strict alphabetical order.

------

2. By permission. From <u>Webster's Seventh New Collegiate Diction-
ary</u> © 1969 by G. & C. Merriam Co., Publishers of the Merriam-Webster
Dictionaries.

4. Webster's Geographical Dictionary. Springfield, Massachusetts: G. and C. Merriam Company (1957). This volume, though it
may not be comprehensive enough to meet your need on every occasion,
does contain some 40,000 entries (worldwide) and can be a useful tool.

Of these sources, though recent editions are generally available, the
older editions have the most value. The names of some places change;
other places become ghost towns for one reason or another. Because of
these facts our slogan might be: "The older the better." We have never
seen the early edition of Columbia - Lippincott, but we are sure there are
a few of them around. We found one catalogued in the Sugar House Branch
of the Salt Lake City Public Library in 1964, but it was not on the library
shelves. When we asked the librarian about it she merely assured us that
it was "too old to be any good anyway." She obviously was not a genealogist.
        Other gazetteers, especially of the individual states, can also be located
and are usually of even greater value in solving locality problems. J. H.
French's Gazetteer of the State of New York (1860) is a good example.
        Maps are also a "must" item for the genealogist. A good map can fill
the same requirement that a gazetteer does; it too will tell you the name of
the county in which a particular town is situated. Unless a map is quite detailed, though, it may not show small towns. Our motto about the older
ones being more useful than their more recent counterparts also holds
true with maps and for basically the same reason—changes. If you can
find an old map of a locality made about the time your ancestors lived there
the boundary and jurisdiction changes will be reflected as the old map is
compared with a more recent one. More is said later about the importance
of understanding these changes.
        Maps also help us understand the geographical and physical features
which often have an important effect upon the genealogical problem. They
may suggest some pattern of settlement and migration and completely rule
out others. A range of mountains is a barrier to migration while a river
may aid migratory travel. It is much easier to travel on water than through
dense forests and undergrowth; however, a river might also be an obstruc-
tion to travel. Crossing it could be difficult if one were not properly
equipped.
        A map also shows the relationship of a town or county to other towns
and counties in the same area. This may suggest other searches to you,
especially if the place your ancestors lived happened to lie near a boundary
line. Too often we tend to restrict our searches by boundaries when we
cannot see relative locations on a map, but the persons who lived there were
never thus restricted. They went where they pleased and records relating
to them are often found in several different places.
        For any locality, detailed local maps are the most valuable. This is an
obvious conclusion since it naturally follows that the smaller the area cov-

ered the better will be the coverage. As has already been mentioned old maps are the best if they can be found; however, if they cannot be located modern maps will suffice. Road maps are surprisingly good and usually serve quite well. They are generally available through service stations, chambers of commerce, magazine and book distributors, and state publicity and/or highway departments.

Most larger libraries and some smaller ones have the Rand McNally Commercial Atlas and Marketing Guide (New York: Rand McNally and Co., annual). This atlas contains excellent maps of the individual states. The maps are very detailed showing nearly all of the towns, water courses, county boundaries and, in places where it is pertinent, township boundaries. These atlases are placed in libraries by subscription and each year the publisher replaces the old atlas with a new one in order to keep the marketing data current. Some small genealogical libraries not subscribing to this service have been able to obtain copies of older atlases through the influence of their U.S. Congressional Representatives.

The maps in this atlas are good for other countries also, but those for the United States are the strong feature of the book, at least from a genealogical point of view. The quality of the U.S. maps, in an atlas of this type, is unsurpassed. Our only criticism of them is that they are too new.

If, after you have checked maps and gazetteers, you are still unable to locate a certain place there are other approaches that should be used. Historical societies and local libraries can often provide information on defunct place names as can books on local history. The reason that a place name cannot be found might be that the town is now a ghost town, the name has been changed, or the place is too small to be found in the regular sources. Regardless of the reason, research cannot be initiated until that problem is solved and the county has been identified.

If your ancestor lived in a large city and you can locate his address in some way (perhaps with an old city directory), a map of that city may help you limit your search. For example, if you can determine that your ancestor lived in Ward 14 of Philadelphia and you want to find him in the 1860 census with his family, you will find it much easier to search the census for just one ward than to search the entire city. You can accomplish in perhaps 30 minutes to an hour what might otherwise take several days.

B. GENEALOGY OF PLACES

Because America is a relatively new country there are some special kinds of research problems caused by constant boundary changes. Due to this you may often have use for maps which show boundary lines only, especially state maps which show county boundaries. These not only help us locate counties in their relationships to each other generally but to specifically locate them in relation to their parent counties and child counties.

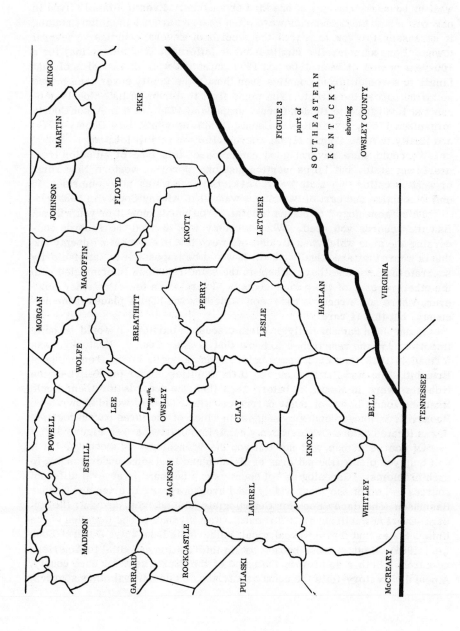

FIGURE 3
part of
SOUTHEASTERN
KENTUCKY
showing
OWSLEY COUNTY

Some of the better maps of this type are found in the 200 Series, 8 1/2" x 11", individual state maps, produced by the American Map Co. in New York City. There are also other good sources.

Almost every early American genealogical problem is affected somewhat by boundary changes of one kind or another. Even if a family lived in only one place the boundaries were often changed around them thus making it necessary for you to search the records of several counties or several towns. For example, if a family lived at Jefferson, North Carolina, for a 100-year period between 1700 and 1800 you might well find records of that family in seven different counties even though the family never even moved so far as across the street. You would first find them in Bath County (organized 1696), next in Bladen County (organized 1734), next in Anson County (organized 1750), next in Rowan County (1753), next in Wilkes County (1777) and finally in Ashe County (1799) where Jefferson is still located.

We could show several good examples of this type of situation from nearly any state, but let us mention just one more: In western New York, or what is called "up-state" New York, the area which now comprises 45 entire counties and part of two others was all in Albany County in 1683.

This "genealogy" of places is vital. You must know it or you will not find the records you need. When a county was divided the records concerning the area which was divided off were left in the original county and that is where they are usually found. It would be impossible to satisfactorily separate them because they are kept in the same registers intermingled with the other records of the parent county. There are a few situations, however, where some records have been copied and the copies placed in the new county, but this is rare.

In our John Samuel Kelly problem discussed earlier, it would be quite important for the researcher to know that Owsley County, Kentucky, was formed in 1843 (just eight years before John Samuel's birth) from parts of Breathitt, Clay and Estill counties. If the families (either the Kellys or the Gilberts) were in Kentucky before 1843 then the records for them would likely be found in one of these parent counties. A map would show where Booneville is located and may suggest in which of the three parent counties it was located before Owsley County came into existence (see Figure 3).

Of course a map will not tell you the "genealogy" of a county, but it will help you picture the patterns of division and lend some understanding to such problems. "Genealogies" of counties can be found in several different sources. Two of the most widely used are George B. Everton and Gunnar Rasmuson. The Handy Book for Genealogists, 6th ed. rev. and enl. (Logan, Utah: Everton Publishers, 1970) and E. Kay Kirkham, The Counties of the United States and Their Genealogical Value (Salt Lake City: Deseret Book Co., 1964). Both of these books contain information essential to American research. Both also provide the name of the county seat for each county. A postal directory tells the county seat, too, as do several other sources.

This information is significant because records are usually housed at the county courthouse in the county seat.

Pedigree analysis is not complete without locality analysis, and our purpose in this discussion has been to illustrate the necessity of having a knowledge of the locality where your genealogical problem exists and to introduce a few basic tools which will provide some answers.

If you will make a good preliminary survey, analyze your pedigree carefully, and then learn all you can about the locality, you will have laid a good foundation on which to do productive and accurate research. Good hard work should now produce some satisfying results.

VI. TRADITION, COMMON SENSE AND HELPFUL CLUES

Do you know the religious affiliation of your ancestor? What was his position in the community? Was he prominent or obscure? Did he have money? These are also factors which would affect your approach to the research problem. If any or all of them can be determined it is that much more to your advantage. Maybe your ancestor was a Quaker or belonged to one of the other religious groups which refused to bear arms in time of war. This would certainly be significant. Maybe he was loyal to Britain during the Revolutionary War. You ought to know.

Family tradition also tells us much about family origins; however, such traditions, on the whole, are notoriously unreliable and no tradition should ever be accepted at face value. Dr. Ethel Williams says, "They have value but should be evaluated."[3] Surely we could add: They should be chewed and tasted but never swallowed. More often than not they do contain threads (sometimes even cables) of truth that, when unraveled, provide useful clues and leads upon which to base research.

However, if family tradition says that you descend from the Mayflower Fullers, do not start in 1620 and try to trace the pedigree down to yourself. That could prove to be a very sad experience. Remember the rule we gave earlier: Work first with the information that you already know—FROM THE KNOWN TO THE UNKNOWN. The house must be built from the foundation up and not from the roof down.

Common sense is practical judgment and ordinary good sense. Much of this is needed by the genealogist as he pursues his ancestors. It is best typified by looking at each problem logically and thoroughly and then proceeding one step at a time to do those things suggested by your analysis.

[3.] Ethel W. Williams, Know Your Ancestors (Rutland, Vt.: Charles E. Tuttle Co., 1960), p. 23. By permission.

CHAPTER FOUR

AN INTRODUCTION TO RESEARCH TOOLS: THE LIBRARY

Just as carpenters have saws, hammers and tri-squares and chemists have beakers, test tubes and graduated cylinders, genealogists also have basic tools. One of the most important of these is the library (if we may be allowed to so classify a library).

I. THE PURPOSE OF LIBRARY RESEARCH

Most genealogical research is not done in libraries, and those who devote themselves solely to the printed word do not understand what genealogy is all about—they do not know the true disposition of research.

However, there are libraries such as the National Archives, The Genealogical Society of The Church of Jesus Christ of Latter-day Saints, and others, including archives and history departments (called also by other titles) and libraries of various states that do have vast collections of primary records, both originals and microfilms. (Such libraries are often more appropriately called archives.) If the record collections of the locality of your genealogical concern are available in a library or archives to which you have access you are most fortunate and should feel no qualms about doing that type of library research. Often you will be able to do research there much easier than you could in the actual record depository. However, if you cannot find the answers you need in these library and archival collections a personal visit to the locality may be necessary.

Histories, periodical literature, etc., must be checked before you begin actual research in primary sources and also as you proceed. Often much information and many important clues can be gleaned in a few well-spent hours in a public library. Consequently this chapter is devoted to libraries and their use.

There are several libraries in the U.S. with large, important collections of printed genealogical materials as well as archival materials. These include:

AMERICAN ANTIQUARIAN SOCIETY, 185 Salisbury Street, Worcester, Massachusetts 01609.

CONNECTICUT HISTORICAL SOCIETY, 1 Elizabeth Street, Hartford, Connecticut 06105.

CONNECTICUT STATE LIBRARY, 231 Capitol Avenue, Hartford, Connecticut 06115.

DAUGHTERS OF THE AMERICAN REVOLUTION LIBRARY—See National Society,...

DENVER PUBLIC LIBRARY, Genealogy Division, 1357 Broadway, Denver, Colorado 80203.

DETROIT PUBLIC LIBRARY, Burton Historical Collection, 5201 Woodward Avenue, Detroit, Michigan 48202.

GENEALOGICAL SOCIETY OF NEW JERSEY, Manuscript Collections, Rutgers University Library, New Brunswick, New Jersey 08901.

GENEALOGICAL SOCIETY OF PENNSYLVANIA, 1300 Locust Street, Philadelphia, Pennsylvania 19107.

THE GENEALOGICAL SOCIETY OF THE CHURCH OF JESUS CHRIST OF LATTER-DAY SAINTS, 50 East North Temple Street, Salt Lake City, Utah 84150.

GREAT FALLS PUBLIC LIBRARY, Third Street and Second Avenue North, Great Falls, Montana 59401.

GROSVENOR LIBRARY, 383 Franklin Street, Buffalo, New York 14202.

HISTORICAL SOCIETY OF PENNSYLVANIA, 1300 Locust Street, Philadelphia, Pennsylvania 19107.

HOLLAND SOCIETY OF NEW YORK, 122 East 58th Street, New York, New York 10022.

INDIANA STATE LIBRARY, 140 North Senate Street, Indianapolis, Indiana 46204.

LIBRARY ASSOCIATION OF PORTLAND, 801 South West Tenth Avenue, Portland, Oregon 97205.

LIBRARY OF CONGRESS, Washington, D.C. 20540.

LONG ISLAND HISTORICAL SOCIETY, 128 Pierrepont Street, Brooklyn, New York 11201.

LOS ANGELES PUBLIC LIBRARY, 630 West 5th Street, Los Angeles, California 90017.

MARYLAND HISTORICAL SOCIETY, 201 West Monument Street, Baltimore, Maryland 21201.

MASSACHUSETTS HISTORICAL SOCIETY, 1154 Boylston Street, Boston, Massachusetts 02130.

NATIONAL GENEALOGICAL SOCIETY LIBRARY, 1921 Sunderland Place, N.W., Washington, D.C. 20036.

NATIONAL SOCIETY, DAUGHTERS OF THE AMERICAN REVOLUTION LIBRARY, 1776 D Street, N.W., Washington, D.C. 20006.

NEW ENGLAND HISTORIC GENEALOGICAL SOCIETY, 101 Newbury Street, Boston, Massachusetts 02116.

NEW HAMPSHIRE HISTORICAL SOCIETY, 30 Park Street (P.O. Box 478), Concord, New Hampshire 03301.

NEW JERSEY HISTORICAL SOCIETY, 230 Broadway, Newark, New Jersey 07104.

NEW YORK GENEALOGICAL AND BIOGRAPHICAL SOCIETY, 122-6 East 58th Street, New York 10022.

NEW YORK PUBLIC LIBRARY, American History and Genealogy Division, Fifth Avenue and 42nd Street, Rooms 315A and 315G, New York, New York 10018.

NEW YORK STATE LIBRARY, Manuscripts and History Section, State Education Building, Albany, New York 12224.

NEWBERRY LIBRARY, 60 West Walton Street, Chicago, Illinois 60610.

ST. LOUIS PUBLIC LIBRARY, 1301 Olive Street, St. Louis, Missouri 63103.

SEATTLE PUBLIC LIBRARY, Fourth Avenue and Madison Street, Seattle, Washington 98104.

SOUTH CAROLINA HISTORICAL SOCIETY, Fireproof Building, Meeting and Chalmers Streets, Charleston, South Carolina 29401.

U.S. LIBRARY OF CONGRESS—See Library of Congress.

VIRGINIA HISTORICAL SOCIETY, 428 North Boulevard, Richmond, Virginia 23219.

WESTERN RESERVE HISTORICAL SOCIETY, 10825 East Boulevard, Cleveland, Ohio 44106.

WISCONSIN STATE HISTORICAL SOCIETY, 816 State Street, Madison, Wisconsin 53703.

The above is not a complete list. There are many other libraries with significant genealogical collections, some of which you might already be aware. Of special note are the libraries of some universities and colleges.

II. THE CATALOG

When you use any library you must understand, first of all, how to use the library's catalog (usually on cards)—the index to the library's holdings. Just as an index to a book, this catalog is in an alphabetical arrangement. It is much more than just a shelf-list; it is a complete index which should enable you to find the location of any book, manuscript or serial within that library by looking in at least three different places in the catalog—under author, title or subject and, in the case of many genealogical sources, locality. A shelf-list does not have this advantage; it is merely a list of holdings by only one category—title, locality, or perhaps by author, but rarely if ever by subject—unless subject and title happen to be the same.

The catalog is usually on 3" x 5" index cards so that it can be up-dated as new books are added to the library collection.

III. CLASSIFICATION

The only reason it is possible for a library to catalog its holdings is that each book is classified and assigned a number. That number is written on the book (usually on the spine) and the books are shelved consecutively.

In the United States there are two popular classification systems in general use—the Library of Congress Classification System (L. C.) and the Dewey Decimal Classification System (named for Melvil Dewey, its originator). Some libraries, such as the LDS Genealogical Society in Salt Lake City, use a modification of one of these systems and there are, no doubt, some libraries that use other systems. However, if you use the card catalog it doesn't matter much which system is used so long as the catalog is complete.

Many libraries have "open stacks" where you are free to go into the areas where the books are shelved and serve yourself, but in those libraries where the stacks or shelves are closed to public access you must fill out a book order slip with the correct information and present it at the designated counter, desk or window and an attendant will bring you the book you want. You will use it and then return it to the desk. In some libraries many books can be checked out (or circulated, as they call it), but most libraries keep genealogy books for library use only.

A. LIBRARY OF CONGRESS

The Library of Congress Classification System, though not so widely used as the decimal system, is becoming more popular. It is sometimes considered the better of the two because it has more latitude for expansion as new areas of learning are developed, and it is especially helpful in classifying large collections in certain subject areas. It is considered a "must" in many large libraries and even many smaller libraries that formerly used the Dewey system are switching.

L. C., as Dewey, classifies according to subject. The system utilizes the letters of the alphabet but knowledge of this classification system will not substitute for your using the library catalog. Browsing is a very risky practice since significant materials will be classified throughout the system.

We will refrain from listing here the various areas of classification. Such a list would add nothing to your ability to use the library properly.

B. DEWEY CLASSIFICATION

The Dewey Decimal Classification System is based on ten major subject divisions, each further broken down into subdivisions through the use of Arabic numbers and decimals. Every classification is based on a three-digit number; and, if the subject is a more minute subdivision of the main subject, additional digits are added after a decimal.

At the LDS Genealogical Society in Salt Lake City the use of the Dewey system has been modified so that research source materials are also assigned the class number for history (strictly by locality) instead of being codified under the usual subject heading. This modification has the advantage that it facilitates browsing.

Knowledge of the classification numbers in either the L. C. or the Dewey systems should never excuse you from using the library catalog. Those numbers are used primarily to facilitate the shelving of the books and to aid library patrons in locating them after they have checked the catalog. Often important works would be completely overlooked if you checked only the stacks where you thought the material you wanted ought to be shelved. Also, there may be such a divergence of material classified in one area that you would probably overlook important materials unless the specific catalog reference were used. Even though the books on one subject are not scattered throughout the library quite so much with the decimal system as they are inclined to be with L. C., there is still no excuse for not using the library catalog.

C. CUTTER CLASSIFICATION

Even when two books are written on exactly the same subject they do not have exactly the same classification numbers. This is because library materials are not classified by subject only but also by author. This is accomplished by assigning a second number—a Cutter number—to each book. The system was named for its originator, Charles Cutter. In the call number as it is written on the book the Cutter number is usually placed directly below the subject class number. In the Dewey system it consists of the first one or two letters (depending on the name) of the author's surname, followed by a number which is assigned to that particular author (determined by formula). [1]

When an author has written more than one book and it is classified under Dewey, the letter-number combination already described will be followed by another letter (sometimes more than one) which is the first letter(s) of the first word of the book title (not including articles). For example, if the book title were "The Search for Your Ancestors" by John Doe then the Cut-

---

[1] Note that the LDS Genealogical Society has also modified its use of Cutter numbers so that the number refers to record catagory rather than author. This works very well since they have modified the Dewey number to indicate locality rather than subject. For further details refer to Norman E. Wright and David H. Pratt, Genealogical Research Essentials (Salt Lake City: Bookcraft, 1967), Chapter 5.

ter number might be something like "D64s." The "D" stands for Doe, the "64" for the number assigned to this author, and the "s" for "Search," the first letter in the title of the book which is not an article. The adjective or article "the," is not considered. Some libraries follow this procedure just as a matter of course even when the author may have written only one book. This system allows for the shelving of books alphabetically by author within each subdivision of the subject and then alphabetically by title.

The L. C. system also frequently uses Cutter numbers to indicate things other than author, and often a book may have two Cutter numbers (seldom more)—one for the author and one for something else (usually placed before the author number). For example, a Cutter number may indicate a locality thus facilitating the arrangement of books in a certain class by their geographic area (if pertinent). Most often when there are double Cutter numbers the first is for the purpose of further subdividing the subject in some way.

It is not necessary here to discuss all of the intricacies of the system nor the many exceptions to the various rules. It is perhaps only necessary to stress again the importance of using the library catalog. Your propensity to browse must be curbed sharply in any library where the L. C. classification system is used.

IV. CONCLUSION

This chapter should contain sufficient information to enable you to use the library catalog to its fullest advantage in locating the materials you seek within almost any library. However, we should stress one more thing: If you have difficulty do not hesitate to ask the librarian for help. He (or she) is there to help those who need it, so you need not be afraid of showing your ignorance. Also, if you are interested in U. S. Government Documents such as maps, gazetteers, etc., and the library you are using happens to be a depository for Government Documents, remember that they present additional problems in locating. The librarian in charge can save you a lot of time and effort with these if you will give him a chance.

Let's look now at some of the materials found in most libraries that can help make your research easier.

CHAPTER FIVE

AN INTRODUCTION TO RESEARCH TOOLS: REFERENCE MATERIALS

The real purpose behind the use of reference sources is to help locate various records and/or to facilitate use of those records. There are many problems that the beginning genealogist struggles to solve which could be solved in a few minutes by using some common and readily available reference source. One of the main differences then between a good researcher and a poor one is his knowledge of, and his ability to use correctly, critical reference works. For our purposes these reference works can be divided into three catagories:

> I.   Guides to locality data.
> II. Guides to secondary sources.
> III. Guides to primary sources. [1]

I. GUIDES TO LOCALITY DATA

In Chapter Three we discussed the value of maps, gazetteers and postal directories as reference tools, but there are also other useful sources that can help us find out about places. There are five types of sources which give data on American localities. They are:

> A. Atlases and maps.
> B. Gazetteers.
> C. Postal directories.
> D. Specialized locality sources.
> E. Local histories.

The following bibliography lists some of the works available in the first four catagories. Some of these sources have already been mentioned in Chapter Three but are repeated here. We make no claims about this being

---

[1]. A primary source is one which had its origin with someone directly involved with the event being reported, near the time of that event. A secondary source is everything else. In law another name for primary evidence is "best evidence." The best evidence available must be considered before judgment is made. See footnote #1, page 78.

Thomas F. <u>A Gazetteer of the State of Pennsylvania.</u> Phila-
hia (1832).

Elias. <u>A Gazetteer of the State of Massachusetts.</u> (2 vols.).
on (1874).

ohn C. and J.M. Niles. <u>Gazetteer of the States of Connecticut</u>
Rhode Island. Hartford (1819).

d, Adiel. <u>A Gazetteer of the State of Georgia...</u> (1827, 1939).
ens: University of Georgia Press (1968 reprint).

's Geographical Dictionary. Springfield, Mass.: G and C.
riam Co. (1957).

DIRECTORIES

r's Postal and Shippers Guide for the United States and Canada.
stwood, N.J.: Bullinger's Guides, Inc. (1897—).

tates. <u>United States Directory of Post Offices.</u>   Washington,
.: Post Office Department (annual).

LIZED LOCALITY SOURCES

rne, Ava H. <u>Maine Place Names and the Peopling of Its Towns.</u>
gor: Furbush-Roberts Printing Co. (1955).

, David Leroy. <u>The Formation of North Carolina Counties,</u>
3-1943. Raleigh: State Department of Archives and History
50).

hade, Abraham Howry. <u>Pennsylvania Place Names</u>. (1925).
ltimore: Genealogical Publishing Co. (1970 reprint).

, George B. and Gunnar Rasmuson. <u>The Handy Book for Gen-</u>
ogists. (6th ed. rev. and enl.). Logan, Utah: Everton Publish-
s (1970).

Thomas P. <u>A Guide to Kentucky Place Names...</u> Kentucky Ge-
gical Survey. (Ser. X, Special Publ. 5). Lexington: College
Arts and Sciences, University of Kentucky (1961).

t, Henry. <u>Boundaries of the United States and of the Several</u>
tes and Territories. (3rd ed.). Washington, D.C. (1906).

l, Ray O., Jr. <u>A List of Places Included in Nineteenth Cen-</u>
y Virginia Directories. (Virginia State Library Publ. 11).
chmond: Virginia State Library (1960).

Joseph Nathan. <u>The American Counties.</u> New York: The Scare-
ow Press (1960).

m, E. Kay. <u>The Counties of the United States and Their Genea-</u>
gical value (3rd ed.). Salt Lake City: Deseret Book Co. (1965).

are some of the sources which you will find essential to your re-

a complete bibliography of reference
that there are many other sources of
relate to specific geographical areas.

A. ATLASES AND MAPS

Adams, James Truslow (ed.). Atl
  Charles Scribner's Sons (1943)
Bartholemew, John (ed.). The 1
  (Mid-Century ed.). London:
  (1955-59).
Everton, George B., Jr. Geneal
  America. Logan, Utah: The E
Fox, Dixon Ryan (ed.). Harper's
  York: Harper and Brothers (19
Kagan, Hilde Heun (ed.). The Am
  United States History. New Yor
  Co. (1966).
Rand-McNally Commercial Atlas ar
  Rand McNally and Co. (annual).
Rand-McNally's Pioneer Atlas of the
  McNally and Co. (1956).
One of the best collections of America
cated in the Library of Congress in W
includes a vast, though incomplete, in
for U.S. counties during the 1800's.
in the various counties at the time the
brary of Congress has published an ex
which is available from the Superintend
ment Printing Office, Washington, D.C

B. GAZETTEERS

The Columbia - Lippincott Gazetteer o
  Seltzer. Morningside Heights, Ne
  Press by arrangement with J.B. Lij
French, John H. Gazetteer of the State
  Washington, New York: Ira J. Fried

---

2. Richard W. Stephenson (comp.), Land
list of 19th Century U.S. County Maps in the
ington, D.C.: The Library of Congress, 1967

search as you undertake learning the things you need to know about the localities of your problems. We will not list local histories in bibliographic form here because of their great multiplicity. However, you need to be aware of their existence (on town, county, and regional levels) because they contain invaluable information about places which is seldom found in other sources. Chapter Eight discusses them in more detail.

II. GUIDES TO SECONDARY SOURCES

Also useful as reference tools are those sources which help us locate secondary source materials pertinent to our genealogical problems. More is said about the value and use of these in later chapters but they can be divided into four major catagories:

> A. Directories
> > 1. of newspapers.
> > 2. of libraries and societies.
> > 3. telephone and city directories.
> b. Bibliographies.
> C. Indexes
> > 1. to periodicals.
> > 2. to published genealogies and pedigrees.
> > 3. to multiple source types.
> D. Texts and specialized reference sources.

Let's look now at a few reference tools in each of these catagories.

A. DIRECTORIES

1. Of Newspapers.
    Ayer Directory of Newspapers and Periodicals. Philadelphia: N. W. Ayer and Son, Inc. (annual).
    National Directory of Weekly Newspapers. New York: American Newspaper Representatives (annual).

2. Of libraries and societies.
    American Library Directory. New York: R. R. Bowker Co. (biennial).
    Directory—Historical Societies and Agencies in the United States and Canada. Nashville, Tenn.: American Association of State and Local History (biennial).
    International Library Directory. ed. by A. P. Wales. London: The A. P. Wales Organization (biennial).

3. Telephone and city directories.
   These give addresses of living persons, including possible relatives, so that they can be readily contacted. Any large telephone
   office or large library will have a good collection of them. Chambers of commerce can also help you locate directories, or even
   names and addresses.

B. BIBLIOGRAPHIES

The American Genealogist, Being a Catalog of Family Histories
   Published in America from 1771 to Date (5th ed.). Albany,
   N.Y.: Joel Munsell's Sons (1900). Reprinted Detroit: Gale
   Research Co. (1967); Baltimore: Genealogical Publishing Co.
   (1967).

Brigham, Clarence Saunders. History and Bibliography of American Newspapers, 1690-1820. 2 vols. (incl. add. and correct.)
   Hamden, Conn.: Shoe String Press (1962).

Brown, Stuart E., Jr. (comp.). Virginia Genealogies—A Trial
   List of Printed Books and Pamphlets. Berryville, Va.: Virginia Book Co. (1967).

Cappon, Lester Jesse. American Genealogical Periodicals: A
   Bibliography with a Chronological Finding-List (2nd print.
   with add.). New York: New York Public Library (1964).

Catalogue of American Genealogies in the Library of the Long Island Historical Society. ed. by Emma Toedteberg (1935). Baltimore: Genealogical Publishing Co. (1969 reprint).

Daughters of the American Revolution. Catalog of the Genealogi-
   cal and Historical Works in the Library of the National Society,
   Daughters of the American Revolution. Washington, D.C.:
   D.A.R. (1940).

Filby, P. William. American & British Genealogy & Heraldry.
   Chicago: American Library Association (1970).

Genealogy and Local History: An Archival and Bibliographic Guide
   2nd ed. rev.). Evanston, Ill.: The Associates (1959).

Gregory, Winifred (ed.). American Newspapers, 1821-1936; A
   Union List of Files Available in the United States and Canada.
   New York: H.W. Wilson Co. (1937).

Hamer, Philip May (ed.). Guide to Archives and Manuscripts in
   the United States. New Haven, Conn.: Yale University Press
   (1961).

Kaminkow, Marion J. (ed.). Genealogies in the Library of Congress: A Bibliography. Baltimore: Magna Carta Book Co.
   (1972).

Lancour, Harold (comp.). A Bibliography of Ship Passenger

Lists, 1538-1825 (3rd ed.) rev. and enl. by Richard J. Wolfe. New York: New York Public Library (1963).

Meynen, Emil (comp. and ed.). Bibliography on German Settlements in Colonial North America. Detroit: Gale Research Co. (1966 reprint).

Newberry Library, Chicago. The Genealogical Index (4 vols.). Boston: G.K. Hall (1960).

Peterson, Clarence Stewart (comp.). Consolidated Bibliography of County Histories in Fifty States in 1961. Baltimore: Genealogical Publishing Co. (1963 reprint).

Slocum, Robert B. Biographical Dictionaries and Related Works. Detroit: Gale Research Co. (1967).

√ Virkus, Frederick A. The Handbook of American Genealogy (4 vols.). Chicago: Institute of Genealogy (1932-43).

√ United States, Library of Congress. American and English Genealogies in the Library of Congress (2nd ed., 1919). Baltimore: Genealogical Publishing Co. (1967 reprint).

_____. American and English Genealogies in the Library of Congress (microcards). comp. by Dr. and Mrs. C. K. Jones. Middletown, Conn.: Godfrey Memorial Library (1954).

_____. The National Union Catalog of Manuscript Collections, 1959-61; Based on Reports from American Repositories of Manuscripts. Ann Arbor, Mich.: J.W. Edwards, Publisher (1962).

_____. The National Union Catalog of Manuscript Collections, 1962; Based on Reports from American Repositories of Manuscripts. Hamden, Conn.: Shoe String Press (1964).

_____. The National Union Catalog of Manuscript Collections, 1959-62; Index. Hamden, Conn.: Shoe String Press (1964).

_____. The National Union Catalog of Manuscript Collections, 1963— (with indexes). Washington, D.C.: Library of Congress (various dates).

Whitmore, William Henry. Bibliography of Genealogy. Albany, New York: Joel Munsell's Sons (no date).

C. INDEXES

1. To periodicals.

Genealogical Periodical Annual Index. ed. by Ellen Stanley Rogers and George Ely Russell. Bladensburg and Bowie, Md.: Genealogical Recorders (annually, 1962—)

Jacobus, Donald Lines. Index to Genealogical Periodicals (3 vols.).

Baltimore: Genealogical Publishing Co. (1963-65 reprint).

New England Historical and Genealogical Register; Consolidated Index, Vols. 1-50 (4 vols.). Boston: New England Historic Genealogical Society (1906-1911). Baltimore: Genealogical Publishing Co. (1972 reprint).

_____. Index (abridged) to Volumes 51 Through 112 (1897-1958). comp. by Margaret W. Parsons. Privately published (1959).

Topical Index to the National Genealogical Society Quarterly, Volumes 1-50, 1912-1962. comp. by Carleton E. Fisher. Washington, D.C.: National Genealogical Society (1964).

Swem, Earl G. Virginia Historical Index (2 vols. in 4). Gloucester, Mass.: Peter Smith (1965 reprint).

2   To published genealogies and pedigrees.

Crowther, George Rodney, III. Surname Index of Sixty-Five Volumes of Colonial and Revolutionary Pedigrees. Washington, D.C.: National Genealogical Society (1964).

McAuslan, William A. (comp.). Mayflower Index (2 vols.). rev. by Lewis E. Neff. Boston: General Society of Mayflower Descendants (1960).

3. To multiple source types.

Biography Index; A Cumulative Index to Biographical Material in Books and Magazines, 1946—. New York: H.W. Wilson Co. (1964).

Index to American Genealogies and to Genealogical Material Contained in All Works As Town Histories, County Histories, Local Histories, Historical Society Publications, Biographies, Historical Periodicals, and Kindred Works (5th ed., 1900, and Suppl. of 1908). comp. and originally publ. by Joel Munsell's Sons. Baltimore: Genealogical Publishing Co. (1967 reprint).

Passano, Eleanor Phillips. An Index of the Source Records of Maryland—Genealogical, Geographical, Historical. (1940). Baltimore: Genealogical Publishing Co. (1967 reprint).

Rider, Fremont (ed.). American Genealogical Index (48 vols.). Middletown, Conn.: Godfrey Memorial Library (1942-52).

_____. American Genealogical-Biographical Index. Middletown, Conn.: Godfrey Memorial Library (1952—).

Stewart, Robert Armistead. Index to Printed Virginia Genealogies; Including Key and Bibliography. (1930). Baltimore: Genealogical Publishing Co. (1965 reprint).

D. TEXTS AND SPECIALIZED REFERENCE SOURCES

Draughon, Wallace R. and William P. Johnson. North Carolina Genealogical Reference—A Research Guide (new ed.). Durham, N.C.: The authors (1966).

Rubincam, Milton (ed.). Genealogical Research: Methods and Sources. Washington, D.C.: The American Society of Genealogists (1960).

Stryker-Rodda, Kenn. (ed.). Genealogical Research, Vol. 2. Washington, D.C.: The American Society of Genealogists (1971).

Williams, Ethel W. Know Your Ancestors. Rutland, Vt.: Charles E. Tuttle Co. (1960).

World Conference on Records and Genealogical Seminar. Seminar papers. Salt Lake City: The Genealogical Society of The Church of Jesus Christ of Latter-day Saints (1969).

III. GUIDES TO PRIMARY SOURCES

In the area of primary source materials there are also some good guides to assist you in finding the records you need. These fall into four main catagories, and some of them duplicate those listed as guides to secondary sources in the previous section because they are guides to both. The four catagories include:

A. Government publications.
   1. National.
   2. State.
B. Texts and specialized reference sources.
C. Special publications.
D. Indexes.

Let's look at them:

A. GOVERNMENT PUBLICATIONS

1. National.

Colket, Meredith B., Jr., and Frank E. Bridgers. Guide to Genealogical Records in the National Archives. Washington, D.C.: The National Archives (1964).

√Davidson, Katherine H. and Charlotte M. Ashby (comp.). Preliminary Inventory of the Records of the Bureau of the Census. Washington, D.C.: The National Archives (1964)

United States, Department of Health, Education and Welfare.

"Where to Write for Birth and Death Records in the United States and Outlying Areas." Public Health Service Publication #630A-1. Washington, D.C.: Public Health Service (revised as necessary).

_____. "Where to Write for Births and Deaths of U.S. Citizens Who Were Born or Died Outside of the United States and Birth Certifications for Alien Children Adopted by U.S. Citizens." Public Health Service Publication #630A-2. Washington, D.C.: Public Health Service (revised as necessary).

_____. "Where to Write for Divorce Records in the United States and Outlying Areas." Public Health Service Publication #630C. Washington, D.C.: Public Health Service (revised as necessary).

_____. "Where to Write for Marriage Records in the United States and Outlying Areas." Public Health Service Publication #630B. Washington, D.C.: Public Health Service (revised as necessary).

United States, Works Projects Administration. Inventories of County Archives, Church Archives, Vital Statistics Records, etc. Published by the various states: Historical Records Survey (1930's and 1940's).

2. State.

Georgia. "Genealogical Research in Georgia." Atlanta: Georgia Department of Archives and History (1966).

New Jersey. Genealogical Research: A Guide to Source Materials in the Archives and History Bureau of the New Jersey State Library and Other State Agencies. Trenton, N.J.: New Jersey State Library (1966).

South Carolina. "Ancestor Hunting in South Carolina." Columbia: South Carolina Department of Archives and History (1969).

B. TEXTS AND SPECIALIZED REFERENCE SOURCES

Rubincam, Milton (ed.). Genealogical Research: Methods and Sources. Washington, D.C.: The American Society of Genealogists (1960).

Stevenson, Noel C. Search and Research: The Researcher's Handbook (new ed.). Salt Lake City: Deseret Book Co. (1964).

Stryker-Rodda, Kenn (ed.). Genealogical Research, Vol. 2. Washington, D.C.: The American Society of Genealogists (1971).

Williams, Ethel W. Know Your Ancestors. Rutland, Vt.: Charles E. Tuttle Co. (1960).

Wright, Norman Edgar and David H. Pratt. Genealogical Research
Essentials. Salt Lake City: Bookcraft (1967).

C. SPECIAL PUBLICATIONS

Research papers of The Genealogical Society of The Church of Jesus Christ of Latter-day Saints, Research Department (including "Major Record Sources of the United States").

United States, Library of Congress. The National Union Catalog
of Manuscript Collections. 1959-61; Based on Reports from
American Repositories of Manuscripts. Ann Arbor, Mich.:
J. W. Edwards, Publisher (1962).

_____. The National Union Catalog of Manuscript Col-
lections, 1962; Based on Reports from American Repositories
of Manuscripts. Hamden, Conn.: Shoe String Press (1964).

_____. The National Union Catalog of Manuscript Col-
lections, 1959-62; Index. Hamden, Conn.: Shoe String Press
(1964).

_____. The National Union Catalog of Manuscript Col-
lections, 1963—(with indexes). Washington, D. C.: Library
of Congress (various dates).

World Conference on Records and Genealogical Seminar. Seminar
papers. Salt Lake City: The Genealogical Society of The
Church of Jesus Christ of Latter-day Saints (1969).

D. INDEXES

Bowman, Alan P. Index to the 1850 Census of the State of California. Baltimore: Genealogical Publishing Co. (1972).

Houston, Martha Lou (comp.). Indexes to the County Wills of
South Carolina. (1939). Baltimore: Genealogical Publishing
Co. (1964 reprint).

Index of Revolutionary War Pension Applications (rev.). comp.
by Frank Johnson Metcalf, Max Ellsworth Hoyt, Agatha Bouson
Hoyt, Sadye Giller, William H. Dumont and Louise Dumont.
Washington, D. C.: National Genealogical Society (1966).

Johnson, William Perry. Index to North Carolina Wills, 1663-1900
(3 vols.). Raleigh, N. C.: The author (1963-68).

McLane, Mrs. Bobby Jones and Inez H. Cline. An Index to the
Fifth United States Census of Arkansas. Fort Worth, Texas:
Arrow Printing Co. (1963).

Magruder, James Mosby. Index of Maryland Colonial Wills, 1634-
1777, in the Hall of Records, Annapolis, Maryland (3 vols.,
1933). Baltimore: Genealogical Publishing Co. (1 vol., 1967
reprint).

New Jersey Index to Wills (3 vols.). (1901). Baltimore: Genealogical Publishing Co. (1969 reprint).

IV. CONCLUSION

This list of reference tools could go on and on because, strictly speaking, any source to which you refer for information can properly be called a
reference tool. And since genealogy is so closely related to so many different subjects, these are myriad. You will use reference sources dealing
with handwriting (calligraphy, chirography and orthography), with history,
and geography, with biography, with bibliography itself, with law, with origins
of words and names (etymology), with dates and calendar problems (chronology), with heraldry and, of course, with genealogical methodology. Some
bibliographies dealing with these various subjects and with others are found
in Norman E. Wright and David H. Pratt, Genealogical Research Essentials
(Salt Lake City: Bookcraft, 1967), and Ethel W. Williams, Know Your Ancestors (Rutland, Vt.: Charles E. Tuttle Co., 1960), as well as many other
sources. At these authors' own admission, however, their bibliographies
are also quite incomplete.

The most accurate and complete genealogical bibliography that exists
is P. William Filby, American & British Genealogy & Heraldry (Chicago:
American Library Association, 1970). It is an essential source for every
genealogist.

Another major catagory of reference sources—those which actually
provide secondary genealogical data—is discussed in Chapter Eight. This
catagory includes various kinds of biographical works—dictionaries,
directories, registers, etc.—which, though reference sources in the usual
sense, do not fit the definition of genealogical reference tools which we gave
in the first paragraph of this chapter. They do not assist us in locating
records nor do they facilitate our use of records. However, they do provide some useful data—some better than others depending on the sources
in which their information originated.

If you can familiarize yourself with the reference sources listed in this
chapter and become aware of the existence of other similar works and know
their value and use you will have acquired one of the major requisites of
the competent genealogist.

CHAPTER SIX

ORGANIZING AND EVALUATING RESEARCH FINDINGS

I. PURPOSE OF RECORD KEEPING

The basic purpose of genealogical research is to gather the details about possible ancestors from the various sources which came into existence during their lives, compile those details into meaningful form and evaluate them to determine genealogical connections. You cannot do this properly without keeping a record of your activities.

In Chapter One we discussed the importance of organizing your research findings into complete families on some type of family group record form. In this chapter we will attempt to show how this can be done effectively—how the information found can be taken through every step, from original source to final family group form, without something being lost along the way—and still allow you to retrace your steps at any time.

Too many of us learn neither the purposes nor the processes of keeping good research notes until too late. And some, much to the consternation of those who wish to check their work or to take over the work where they have left off, never learn. Others are well convinced of the value of good notes but are never quite willing to make the effort required to keep them. They feel that other people should keep good notes but that they are personally justified with something less—that their situation is somehow different.

There is probably no other area where your ability as a genealogist will be judged more critically than in the notes and records you keep during your research and the documentation of your completed records. Regardless of how thorough you are in research and how good you are at correct analyses, if your notes are poorly kept and your records poorly documented the work you do will never be appreciated by any competent genealogist who views it or reviews it. He will probably repeat the same searches because he is not sure what you have done. Then, if he finds your work was good, he will condemn you the more for not keeping a good record. It will cost time and money to duplicate your work if you do only half the job.

When a student writes a library research paper he carefully notes each source checked and what he finds therein. As the paper appears in its final form it is well documented; the information from the various sources is carefully footnoted showing the sources of all information. Genealogical research should require no less than this. Data in the records you compile are acceptable only if their origin is known. Undocumented "facts" have no weight of authority.

In the most practical terms the purpose of good research notes is two-fold:

1. To keep you, the researcher, constantly and completely in touch with the problem in all its aspects. You must know exactly what has been done, why it was done, when it was done and the results of it. You should also be able to tell readily what still needs to be done and why— all this after any length of time.

2. To aid those who follow you so that they can check quickly for completeness and accuracy and/or continue research where you left off. No one should ever have to re-do your work because he is not sure that you did it correctly.

Not only must you keep and organize your research notes, together with the records and documents which you may accumulate, but those notes must indicate the purpose of every search you make. If you do not know why you are searching a particular source perhaps you should re-evaluate. No search should be made without a purpose. Your goals should be outlined carefully and each step should be directed toward reaching those goals.

The purpose of each search should be recorded somewhere in your notes so that anyone looking at those notes will know why you did what you did. Your purposes must be clearly indicated.

Just as it is true with the preliminary survey, so it is true with good research notes and thorough documentation: Everything possible must be done to prevent needless duplication of effort. There is too much to be done and the expense is too great for us to spend time needlessly repeating ourselves and each other.

II. METHOD

There are many different systems of keeping research notes in current use, which is all very well because what pleases us may be distasteful to you. We each have our own ideas about what is best. Any system is good which gets the job done with a proper balance between completeness and simplicity. An imbalance in either direction is serious. It is as bad to spend too much time and effort on over-elaborate notes as it is to be too brief. No system is good if the note keeping takes more time than the research.

Some persons become so involved with keeping notes and setting up filing systems that they forget their real purpose—the proper determination of family relationships. Every effort should be made to make your notes as complete as necessary, but no more complete than your purpose demands. If shortcuts will work use them, but be careful that your shortcuts are not actually booby traps.

Here are two simple housekeeping rules that will help prevent your notes from taking too much time and insure the quality of those notes for years to come:

1. Keep all of your notes on the same size paper. This can be either standard 8 1/2" x 11" paper or legal size, 8 1/2" x 14". Steer clear of paper scraps, backs of old envelopes and odd size papers of all kinds. Actual size is not important if everything is the same size and can be conveniently filed. There are two things you can't control—the size of papers on which other people write letters and the size of photocopied documents—so it is important that you control what you can.

Also, use a good quality paper so that it will not crumble or become brittle after a few years. Newsprint paper is unsatisfactory. A good bond paper will usually serve best, and paper of not too light a weight will be easier to maintain in good condition.

2. Do not recopy your notes. Make your first copy good enough to be your final copy. Some persons diligently type all of their longhand notes so they will look just right when completed. These do look nice but they are hardly worth the time they take. If you are careful your original notes will be completely adequate.

You do not have time to recopy your notes; it is only busy work. And every time something is copied there is a chance of error. Surely we make enough errors already.

When you take notes you should use a good pencil. (Many libraries and record depositories request that pens not be used.) Your pencil should be sharp (Take more than one with you.) and the lead should not be so hard that the writing is too light to read. Neither should it be so soft that the writing smears. (A #3 lead is usually best.) When possible use ink; it will make a better record. Lined paper may also help you make a better record if you have difficulty writing in a straight line.

III. RESEARCH CALENDARS AND NOTES

Though style and form may vary from one person to another, each set of research notes will have certain things in common with every other set. One thing that each system requires is a list of the sources searched. For our discussion we shall call this a RESEARCH CALENDAR, though different persons call it by different names (such as "calendar of search," "source book," "research organizer," "research index," etc.).

This "calendar" is more than a list of sources, but the amount and ar-

RESEARCH CALENDAR

Sidney Orbeck — 1384 Westside Ave, Haysbury, Ga.

Surname(s) of interest: Black, Green / Jackson

Locality of interest: Henrico Co., Va.

Library Call No.	Description of source	Purpose of search	Comments	Date of search	Ms. page
7560 (GS) (film)	Colonial records pt 1 - Bks 1-2 (1677-1693) pt 2 - Bks 3-5 (1677-1739) pt 3 - Indx, Bks 1-5	Blacks and Green were in Henrico Co. before 1700 to about 1795. Looking for any mention.	Found mention of William & Samuel Black, Hayum Green.	13 Sep 1967	1
7559 (GS) (film)	Court records (Brookville, etc.) pt 1 - 1677-1697 (indxd) pt 2 - 1697-1714 (") pt 3 - 1714-1737 (") pt 4 - 1749-1750 (") pt 5 - 1750-1767 (") pt 6 - 1767-1797 (")	Same	Found a few — (see notes)	13 Sep 1967	1-9
Va.Hc (GS)	Marriage bonds, 1780-1861 (typescript)	Same	found nothing	19 Sep 1967	Nil
Va.Hc3 (GS) (microav)	Brady, Eblot (comp.) Virginia Colonial abstracts to 1821 Henrico County, Southside (Richmond, 1956)	Same	found entry relating to Samuel Black (see notes)	19 Sep 1967	9
—	Record of Green family in poss. of Mrs. Nellie C. Reynolds, 321 Weston Drive Clifton, N.O., 58014	For possible Green connection.	Some good information but doesn't fit in yet. (corresp.)	2 Oct 1967	See letn corresp. Extr. 5
(more)					

FIGURE 1—A RESEARCH CALENDAR

rangement of other information varies from person to person. It must, however, be a list of properly identified sources. Too many researchers make lists of library call numbers or of book titles only. Proper note keeping requires more than this.

The list of sources you make on your calendar may include library classification numbers if you wish, but they are the least significant items you will record there since they are often different from one library to another. If you list them it will be for your own convenience only. If you record all other essential data about the source it can be located, if available, in any library. If you include classification numbers you might somehow indicate the library from which each number comes. Perhaps initials of the library would suffice, such as "GS" for the LDS Genealogical Society, "LC" for the Library of Congress, "DAR" for the National Daughters of the American Revolution library, "NBL" for the Newberry Library in Chicago, "NYP" for the New York Public Library and "PC" for the Podunk City Library. Develop your own designations based on the libraries to which you have access. Unless you have access to extensive microfilm collections of original records, such as those at a state archives or at the LDS Genealogical Society, most of your sources will not have classification numbers anyway. They will be the original records from their original depositories.

Source descriptions on your calendar are best written in footnote form if the source is a book or a periodical. Such a description should include:

1. Author, compiler or editor.
2. Title and edition.
3. Place of publication.
4. Publisher.
5. Date of publication.
6. Page number(s) where applicable.

If your source is an original record you will modify this but must always list sufficient information to identify the source completely, leaving no question as to what or where it is. If you use personal interviews, unpublished manuscripts or family records in private hands, then names and addresses are essential. (See Figure 1.)

Perfect footnote form (if there really is any) is not the most important thing, but your form should be consistent from entry to entry and sufficiently detailed that anyone, even those who know nothing about genealogy, can use your references and readily find the sources listed. Any good book on English fundamentals or on the use of libraries will give you guidance in procedures and form in footnotes.

Another item which many persons include on a research calendar is a brief notation of the significant findings within each source. This is optional but it does have some merit.

Often the sources on the calendar will not be searched in the order listed since there is really no one correct order of search. The order in which sources are used is dependent entirely upon the problem at hand and your analysis thereof. This is one reason why the date each source is used should be noted on your research calendar; it will help you recall your order of search at a future date and may suggest the need for repeating a particular search.

Every source searched should be listed on your research calendar without regard to whether anything was found. For this record the important thing is that a source was searched. If negative sources (those in which nothing is found) were not listed, after the passage of time you would probably find yourself searching them again, and again finding nothing. Or those who follow you may search those sources again. Our purpose here is to prevent duplication of research effort.

In addition to being a list of sources searched and the dates of those searches there is another purpose which a research calendar must serve. It must provide a direct reference to the notes of your research and serve as a table of contents.

As you search a particular record, say an 1860 census, and make notes of its contents on pages five through eight of your manuscript notes, on your research calendar adjacent to the entry for that census you will indicate pages "5-8." Next to those sources which prove negative a notation to that effect should also be made. "Negative," or "nothing," or "nil," or anything else which conveys the idea, may be used. (See again Figure 1.)

The question always arises as to whether the research calendar should be limited in some way. Should you make a separate calendar for each objective, for a group of related objectives, for each locality, or should you make just one all-inclusive calendar for everything? You will likely be happier with a system which provides for some kind of limitation. We use a system (and this is quite common) wherein a separate research calendar is kept for each pertinent locality (usually for each county but this varies with the situation). As we do our research in the records of that locality the pages of our manuscript notes, including documents and photocopies—numbered consecutively—are filed in sequence behind the proper calendar. These research calendars thus serve as tables of contents for the notes of all research in the separate localities. When research in a given locality is completed we have, filed together, our research calendar (as a table of contents) and all notes from the research done there. The research calendar and manuscript notes are kept together in either a manila file folder or looseleaf binder. Never use a spiral or solid-bound notebook for keeping notes. They lack versatility—they cannot be added to conveniently and they cannot be spread out during analysis. They are too limiting.

As you keep notes make sure that your name, address and the date are written on every page. This helps prevent possible loss. A typical heading might read something like this:

DATE: 22 June 1972
RESEARCHER: Sidney Orbeck, 138 N. Westside Ave.,
                          Haysbury, Ga.
LOCALITY OF SEARCH: Henrico County, Va.
SURNAME(S) OF INTEREST: Black, Creer, Jackson

One research calendar (it can be more than one page) is all you need if your research is limited to one locality. But as your research expands into other localities your filing system must also expand. To avoid confusion as your files grow you will find it helpful to use some type of systematic arrangement. Some researchers use a system wherein they arrange localities alphabetically, but we prefer to alphabetize surnames. This could create one problem, but it is not serious.

The problem is this: If you arrange surnames alphabetically and you have three surnames (as Black, Creer and Jackson) on one calendar, and obviously the calendar can be filed in only one place, what about the two surnames under which it cannot be filed? One answer is to make three identical research calendars for the locality—one for each of the surnames. However, this leads to a lot of extra work and there is an alternative— cross-referencing.

File your main calendar under the surname Black, then begin a calendar for the surname Creer (and another for Jackson) in Henrico County with the usual heading, and then, instead of re-listing the sources already recorded on the first calendar, write in large letters across the front of the new calendar: "SEE BLACK, HENRICO COUNTY, VA."

Next, file these cross-referenced calendars in their correct alphabetical sequence and the problem is solved.

Another filing problem arises when research on one surname is performed in several localities. Some researchers prefer to arrange localities alphabetically under the surname, and this works well, but we prefer to arrange the localities under each surname in the sequential order in which the surnames are identified with those localities, from the most recent to the most remote (so that you are generally adding on new notes at the end rather than in the middle). For example, if you do research on the Black family beginning in Maricopa County, Arizona, and trace the family from there to Gunnison County, Colorado, then to Osage County, Missouri; Pulaski County, Kentucky; Henrico County, Virginia; and James City County, Virginia, your research notes under that surname would be arranged in just that order with a separate calendar and a separate set of notes for each of those places. This system follows the family as it is followed on the pedigree chart. In the file, at the beginning of each surname, you should keep a copy of the appropriate portion of the pedigree.

In your manuscript notes you should always give adequate reference to the specific source and its location. This will be more detailed in most cases than the reference on the research calendar because you must indicate volume and page numbers for your entries. For example, on the calendar you indicate only that the source was the 1860 census of the locality, while in your manuscript notes you give the exact references for specific entries in which your surnames were found in that census.

The notes you take should also indicate the purpose for which each search is made. Some persons make this notation in their manuscript files while others have a special column for it on their research calendar as illustrated in Figure 1. Your notation may be something quite specific like: "For the death of Charles Black." Or it may be quite general like: "For all families of above surnames in the county." The latter example may be typical for most census searches, and similar references are often appropriate for other records too. However, be cautious about becoming too general; you must tell why a specific source is being searched. In the case of the census search you might state: "Family in area, 1836 to abt. 1875." Do not be afraid to give as much detail as necessary.

It is also essential that your notes include pertinent statements describing the source materials. If the record was not legible, if the microfilm was unreadable because of focus or light, or if there is another problem of any kind which would affect your research, some type of notation should be made. Missing pages (or parts thereof), smeared ink, non-intelligible shorthands, etc. are all significant problems. If you say nothing those who follow must assume the record was perfect.

All research may not be in a specific locality. Often, because of incomplete information and lack of success in the various "finding tools," you may find yourself making an "area search" in an effort to locate your ancestor. For example, you may make a search of the deed indexes in every county in southwest Virginia for a surname or for a specific individual when more definite clues of origin have not been forthcoming. You may find that a search of the 1830 census of every county in Alabama is necessary for the same reason. Such searches are not to be made impulsively because they can be very time-consuming, but there are times when they cannot be avoided if further progress is to be made. Usually these searches can be centralized around what appears to be the most probable location and then expanded as necessary until the required information or clue is found.

Your research calendar, in such a case, must be able to meet your demands. Usually all you need to do is to write, under the "Locality" heading, something like: "Deeds, southwest Virginia counties." The surname heading is filled in as usual, then as the deed indexes of each county are checked, the proper listings can be made on both the calendar and the manuscript notes. The same procedure would be followed with the Alabama census search or any other area search.

If you are making a preliminary survey or searching in various compiled genealogical sources such as family histories, periodicals or biographical works, it is completely appropriate to write "preliminary survey" or "compiled sources" in the "Locality" blank on your calendar.

These calendars and their related notes fit into your filing system quite readily. An area search can easily be filed chronologically in relation to the various localities and the survey-type search can usually be filed at the beginning of the file of the appropriate surname, before the locality notes. This can all be worked out to your liking.

IV. EVALUATING YOUR NOTES

As soon as you exhaust all records pertinent to your problems in a given locality you are ready to evaluate your findings in depth. Since you have been collecting every bit of information on every person of the surname of your interest, and not just on those who are your primary objectives, you will often accumulate a great bulk of material and some quite extensive notes. You will have already made some superficial analyses, but to get all pertinent data from those notes will require very careful study. For the novice this can be especially difficult, and even those of more experience must use great care.

One way to find out just what you have is to take the information in your notes, item by item, and record it on family-group forms. (These should be inexpensive worksheet forms.) Most data must be recorded on more than one worksheet since they pertain to the person both as a child and as a parent, or they may refer to several persons. Always make sure that each item of information is recorded in every possible place. This is important if you are going to make a proper evaluation. There are other ways to tabulate data, but this method is especially useful for the beginner.

Some researchers use family group records as a note-keeping device, taking notes directly from the research sources onto the family-group forms. We are strongly opposed to such a system for two reasons:

1. Complete information on record content is not as easily recorded. The group sheet does not reflect exactly what the record said —only your interpretation of it.

2. The nature of such a system tends to produce an excessive bulk of work sheets, many of which are completely without meaning or value in the final analysis.

As you work, keep your work sheets in alphabetical sequence (by name of husband) so that you can refer back to any sheet instantly. When two husbands had the same name (and this will happen often when you are dealing with all persons of a single surname in a given locality), arrange them chronologically, eldest first so far as this can be determined.

Some researchers make a separate work sheet from the information found in every document or record entry. We oppose this because, just as with taking notes directly onto the work sheets, it is too bulky and many of the sheets have absolutely no value. Every time you can make a positive identification, record the information on the same family group record with all other information on that same family. However, be cautious about two things:

1. Before putting data on a sheet with other data, be absolutely certain that they refer to the same family. Just because you think the family is the same is not enough. If there is any doubt at all make two work sheets. They can be combined later when you have the required proof, if they turn out to be the same.

2. Footnote the information from each source carefully so that there will be no doubt as to which information came from which source. This makes it easy to re-check your work should you so desire. It also makes it easier to solve discrepancies in record information. If you know the sources of two conflicting data you can usually decide which is more likely to be correct, especially when considered in light of other evidence. One means of identifying the source from which a particular bit of datum comes is to record the information from each of the various sources with different colors of ink and/or pencil on your work sheet and then make your footnote or source reference note in the same color. This system is quite satisfactory. [1]

After our research findings have been thus tabulated we can easily see what has been accomplished on our primary objectives and what still remains to be done. In all of this our chief concern should be for the families of our lineal ancestors with collateral families having significance primarily because they are essential to complete research.

As far as possible, complete and finished records should be compiled from the data tabulated, and then, depending on which sheets still indicate a need for work, research continues. The process is continual just as we explained in Chapter One: You must analyze the problem, decide on a proper course of action, search the appropriate records and record the re-

---

[1] For excellent treatment of evaluation of evidence see Norman E. Wright and David H. Pratt, Genealogical Research Essentials (Salt Lake City: Bookcraft, 1967), Chapter 4, or Derek Harland, Genealogical Research Standards (formerly A Basic Course in Genealogy, Vol. 2) (Salt Lake City: Bookcraft, 1963), Chapter 3.

sults, tabulate your findings, evaluate again and then start over.

We have discussed analysis already but let us mention again that without proper analysis there is no sense of direction and it is easy to get lost in mechanics. There must be a good reason for everything you do.

V. ONE MORE STEP

To help you keep your sense of direction and make meaningful evaluations, one more thing is necessary—periodic research reports. If you were doing professional research you would make reports to your patrons as a matter of course. You would explain very carefully the nature of your searches, the results therefrom and the reasons you have done what you have. Too often, however, when you work on your own genealogy you do not give yourself the same courtesy.

Every qualified professional can vouch for the value of the reports he writes to his patrons. (He always keeps a carbon copy.) After not working on a problem for several months, or even several years, he can know, by merely reading the report, exactly where the research stands and what steps are necessary in continuing. Hence the professional strives to make his reports meaningful to both himself and his patrons. When you work on your own pedigree, do you not deserve the same advantage?

As research progresses, you will find it worthwhile to sit down periodically and outline in some detail what you have done and what the results have been since the last such report. A report should be made while both the problem and the research are still clear in your mind. Six things belong in this report:

1. A brief explanation of the problem.
2. A notation of the records you have searched.
3. A statement of your reasons for searching those records.
4. Your findings therein.
5. Your interpretation and evaluation of these findings as they relate to the problem (in whatever detail is required).
6. An outline of the problem as it now stands and suggestions on what needs to be done next.

It is not essential (or even advisable) that the points in this list be numbered and kept separate, but merely that they each be covered.

If you have proved a difficult connection the evidence which verified that connection should be laid out with great care, step by step, so that it can be easily reviewed. When a line or a connection long-accepted by the family is disproved, it is doubly important to make a written report of the details and the evidence. Sources and their contents must be listed with particularity—not just in a general way. Others in the family will question your conclusions, as well they should, and if a careful report has not been prepared, in time you will forget the details of your proof. You will find that it is difficult for some persons to accept new information even when supported by impeccable evidence, so you had better be well prepared. Though all the sources from which your proof was derived are in your notes, this is not the same as having the details of your proof and analysis summarized systematically in a report. These reports become an important part of your permanent research file, and no requirement of record keeping is more important.

It is also useful to accompany your report with visual aids such as small maps, hand-drawn if necessary. Your ancestors can "come alive" by pictures of tombstones, houses, churches, etc.

VI. REMINDER NOTES

As research progresses from day to day, or from one research trip to the next, it is easy to forget the details of your problem and the specifics of what you are doing. When you leave the library or the courthouse you can think of many possibilities that need to be investigated. But when you return a week (or a month) later, most of these ideas have been forgotten and are only recalled as you spend time reviewing the problem. Because of this difficulty with the human memory it is a good idea to drop a note into your research file as you conclude your day's work. This note can say anything you want it to say or need it to say, but its design is to put you back on the track as quickly as possible. It may be a list of sources that need checking or just a note of "things to do next," with reasons. As research is resumed all you need to do is read your reminder and proceed from where you left off.

These reminder notes should never become a permanent part of your research file as they would cause confusion in later years when your files are used by your successor. They should be retained only until they have served their purpose and should then be discarded.

VII. ABSTRACTS AND FORMS

Though Chapter Seventeen discusses extracts and abstracts in some detail, we think it appropriate to introduce you to the subject here during our discussion of research notes. You will find that it is sometimes unwise to copy source materials verbatim. This is especially true when you are working with court records, including both land records and probate records, since there is much verbiage which does not contain genealogical evidence and is only time-consuming if you attempt to copy it. It is therefore a requirement of efficient research to be able to read records of this type and pick out the important details. However, you must always be careful to copy <u>all</u> that is important. When there is a question as to value, include the information in question. It is always better to make your abstracts (as we call them) too detailed than too brief. Even by eliminating unnecessary modifiers and parenthetical phrases you can dispose of much excess without harm to meaning.

Abbreviations may be used, but be wary lest you are unable to interpret them when they are cold. If you use good judgment they can be used to great advantage. Names, however, should always be copied <u>exactly</u> as they appear in the records. This allows for more accurate analysis.

Some persons have special forms which they use for abstracting various types of records. If you like to use them they are good. They can serve as a useful guide to the beginner, but they are not mandatory and most experienced researchers prefer to limit their use. However, forms for extracting census information are a necessity because they save so much time. (This would be true of any source with a tabular format.) The use of abstracting forms must be left to individual preference.

VIII. CARD FILES

In addition to the foregoing, some researchers keep a card index of the ancestors they identify in their research. You may want to consider making such a file, especially if you plan to publish a family history, but it does involve a lot of extra work. If you use it you must list sources on the cards or the file will be worthless. We also recommend that you limit it pretty much to your lineal ancestors or the project will become much too unwieldy.

IX. CONCLUSION

Perhaps there is much more that could be said about keeping research notes, but we think enough has been said to help you set up a system that will work for you. The only thing we will add here is that you should never destroy any of your notes. If it is a question of space, store those files not in current use in boxes under your bed; but somehow preserve them.

Notes should also be made of the research you accomplish through correspondence, but this aspect of record keeping is discussed in the next chapter along with other facets of research through the mail.

The following list outlines the essentials of a workable record-keeping system as they have been discussed in this chapter:

1. Research notes must be simple enough so that anyone can understand them.

2. They must also be complete enough to reflect adequately the research done.

3. They must not be so time-consuming that they detract from your research.

4. They must be neat and orderly on uniform-size, good-quality paper.

5. They should be done well enough the first time that it is unnecessary to recopy them.

6. Keep a research calendar, in footnote form, of all sources searched. This is a list of the sources you search.

7. The research calendar will list sources in which nothing is found as well as those that contain useful information.

8. Notes should include the date of every search made.

9. References to sources searched must be sufficiently adequate that anyone who is so inclined can use them to locate those sources.

10. Research notes must indicate the purpose of every search made.

11. Limit your research calendars in some way. Do not use one calendar for everything. A division by locality (or jurisdiction) is recommended.

12. The research calendar will make direct reference to the notes you take, serving as a table of contents to those notes.

13. Notes should ordinarily be kept in either file folders or in looseleaf binders in preference to spiral or solid-bound notebooks.

14. Your name and address should be on every page of your notes.

15. File notes systematically. A good system is to file them alphabetically by surname and, under each surname, chronologically by locality.

16. Cross-reference research calendars to each other when you have more than one surname in a locality rather than making identical calendars for each one.

17. Keep a copy of the appropriate portion of your pedigree in every research file.

18. Notes must indicate the condition of the records being searched and the conditions of the search itself.

19. Notes, including research calendars, must be suited for the handling and filing of all materials and documents rearched in a survey, in an "area search," or in your regular routine.

20. Notes will be tabulated in some form suitable to you and evaluated periodically to determine if your objectives are being reached.

21. Notes should be as easy to analyze and evaluate as possible.

22. One of the most important parts of the note file is a detailed periodic report of the searches you have made and the results of those searches.

23. Use reminder slips during your research, but do not make them a permanent part of your research files.

24. Never throw away any of your research notes.

CHAPTER SEVEN

SUCCESSFUL CORRESPONDENCE

Correspondence is essential to genealogical research. Complete research cannot be accomplished without it unless you have unlimited funds for travel. Certainly there is no doubt that personal research in the appropriate archives is the best way to obtain information but, since this is often financially impossible, you must write letters.

Writing good letters is not easy and many people expend a great deal of time and effort in genealogical correspondence with very little to show for it. Before we discuss the actual problems of correspondence, however, let's talk about a system for filing correspondence and the materials accumulated as a result thereof.

I. THE CORRESPONDENCE CALENDAR

Just as it is necessary to organize, file and index the information acquired through your personal research, the same requirement exists for data arising from your correspondence. This can be best accomplished by keeping some type of correspondence calendar (or index). This is just as essential to a well-planned, functional record-keeping system as is a research calendar.

There are different forms that a correspondence calendar can take. It is really a matter of personal taste. Wright and Pratt recommend a very simple type of correspondence index which works quite well. [1] It has three simple columns—one for the date of your outgoing letter, a second for your addressee's name and the purpose of the letter, and a third for the date you receive a reply. Another type of correspondence calendar is illustrated in Figure 1. You will note that this form is much like the research calendar discussed in Chapter Six in that it serves as a table of contents and direct reference guide. With the type of system which this calendar represents, a file of letters and documents is usually maintained separately from the manuscript file you keep in conjunction with your personal research, but

---

1. Norman E. Wright and David H. Pratt, Genealogical Research Essentials (Salt Lake City: Bookcraft, 1967), p. 140.

CORRESPONDENCE CALENDAR

Sidney Orbeck – 158 N. Westside Ave., Hyesberg, Ga.   Surname: *Gregg*

Date sent / Money	Follow-up	Date of answer / Refund	Correspondent and address	Subject	Results	Extract number
13 Apr 1969 / $1.50	29 May 1969	5 June 1969 / —	County Clerk, Yolo County, Calif.	Probate of Charles Gregg (d. aft 1908)	Found will (1908)! Received copy – good!	1
10 June 1969 / $2.00	—	21 June 1969 / —	Bur. of Vital statistics, Sacramento, Calif.	Death certif. of Charles Gregg	Received copy – b. Huntram, died 4 July, 1908 Nebr.	2
16 July 1969 / $1.50	—	1 Aug 1969	Huntram Gazette, Huntram, Nebr.	Newspaper ad for possible relative	Ad in news column 29 July – got copy	3
		3 Aug 1969	Wendell Shade, Huntram, Nebr.	Shade is relative (3C1r) – info on Charles Gregg's brothers and sisters	He sent ad – gave	4
4 Aug 1969	—	19 Aug 1969	"	Thank you note for info. Asked abt. Wm. Gregg and about Wilder	Has no more info – says contact Harry Gregg, Seward, Nebraska.	5
3 Sep 1969	—	27 Sep 1969	Harry Gregg, Seward, Nebr.	Info on Gregg and Wilder in Nebr. (false)	Sent info on bros and sisters of Wm. Gregg – told parents of Jne. E. Wilder. knew	6
3 Sep 1969 / $2.50	—	1 Oct 1969 / $2.50	Register of Deeds, York County, Nebr.	Gregg & Wilder deeds (index check) – 1840-1970	Found 3 deeds for Wm. Gregg, 1 for J.C. Wilder – two others for later owners	7
5 Oct 1969 / $8.00	—	26 Oct 1969	"	Copies of 12 deeds on Gregg & Wilder	Got deeds – good info. Wm Gregg from Berkeley Co. W.Va.	8
13 Nov 1969 / $2.00	26 Dec 1969	6 Jan 1970	County Court, Berkeley Co., W.Va.	Gregg wills (index check) 1772-1850	Found 5 wills	9
7 Jan 1970 / $0.60			"	Copies of wills (5)		10
9 Jan 1970 / $3.00			Nat'l Archives, Wash, D.C.	3 Gregg Revolutionary pension files – Va & Pa		11

FIGURE 1—A CORRESPONDENCE CALENDAR

this is not mandatory if you can work it out otherwise to your satisfaction. The only requirement would be that your basic filing divisions be the same for both.

Let's look now at each of the columns on this sample calendar and discuss its value and content:

The first three columns—one for the date the original letter is sent, one for the date(s) of any follow-up correspondence that may prove necessary and one for the date on which the answer is received—provide a quick picture of the status of all correspondence. If there are several queries out at the same time, it can be easily seen which ones have been answered and which require follow-up action. Columns one and three also provide a place to keep track of money sent and refunded in connection with any individual situation.

Note that in column four the complete address of the correspondent is not given. It is unnecessary to include the complete address here since it is on the carbon copy of the letter in your files. (More is said about carbon copies later.) However, if you want to list a complete address, you may do so.

The "Subject" and "Results" columns are for a few brief and appropriate words to help you remember something about your letters and their answers without going completely through the file. These notations should enable you to determine whether you have already written a letter about a particular matter, perhaps several years past, and already received a negative reply.

The "Extract Number" column is for reference convenience. This column makes the calendar a table of contents for your correspondence. There are various ways that correspondence might be numbered, but the system used in the example is quite simple. It merely requires that the carbon copy of your original letter (and any follow-up letters), the letter of reply from your correspondent, and all documents and copies enclosed with the reply all be given the same extract number. The number is conveniently placed in the upper right-hand corner, and each item bearing that number is filed according to date so that you can follow the developments of a correspondence request with relative ease. Manila file folders and loose-leaf binders are best for filing.

A. FILING DOCUMENTS

In filing those documents received by correspondence there are several possibilities. We feel, however, that there is a need to correlate somehow all documents with the letters to which they relate. The reason this question arises is because documents are of so many varied sizes and shapes that it is difficult to keep them neatly in the same file with your letters. One way to file them is to fold them individually and place them in envelopes which are glued to appropriately-numbered and titled sheets of file-size paper. They can then be filed in their proper places among the letters.

Another way is to make a separate file for documents received through correspondence. Documents are given the same numbers as the letters to which they are related and are filed accordingly. This provides a direct-reference system between the two files. One apparent disadvantage of this system is that it creates an additional file. This is not serious but may detract from the simplicity of your filing system.

A third system, widely used, is a combination file. With this system you interfile all the fruits of your research, whether from your personal searches or from correspondence. To use this system you must maintain your manuscript file separate from both your research calendar and correspondence calendar. You must also develop a numbering system that would relate to both. This is not difficult as long as your filing divisions are the same. This can be accomplished by making a separate correspondence calendar for each locality or jurisdiction just as we suggested for your research calendars. (See Chapter Six.)

You must always cross-reference between the two calendars. This requires that you list searches made through correspondence on your research calendar as well as on your correspondence calendar, with a notation to the effect that the results are under a certain extract number in a specific correspondence file.

Just as you can use the same research calendar for more than one surname if in the same locality, you can do the same with your correspondence calendar, but you must cross-reference them. There is no problem in writing about more than one surname in the same letter.

B. TABULATING RESULTS

You must tabulate and evaluate the results of your correspondence just as carefully as you do the findings of your personal research. The best time to do this is immediately upon receipt of the reply. You need to get any important family data recorded on your work sheets and analyzed as soon as possible. Such immediate analysis is important because the next step in your research may be influenced by it. Research, especially by correspondence, often is a one-step-at-a-time process with the next step being dependent on the results of the previous one. You will use the same work sheets to tabulate the results of your correspondence as to tabulate the results of your personal searches.

If you follow with circumspection the basic principles outlined here your correspondence file will be more than just a stack of letters but a versatile and accessible record of your research by mail.

II. REVIEW OF RESEARCH NOTE REQUIREMENTS

At this point it may be useful to point out, in review, the requirements of good research and correspondence notes. Wright and Pratt list five essentials of a good record-keeping system: [2]

1. Initiate a <u>work pedigree chart</u> showing a selected line or two of interest, and include all known genealogical facts....
2. Initiate <u>work family group sheets</u> on those families of special concern, and show all genealogical... facts pertaining to them....
3. Initiate a <u>calendar of correspondence</u> and index letters sent or received which apply to the lines of interest....
4. Initiate <u>calendars of search</u> for each jurisdiction of interest, and list on them bibliographic information for sources searched or to be searched....
5. Maintain a <u>manuscript note file</u> of searches and findings.... [Emphasis added.]

To the five requirements listed by Messrs. Wright and Pratt we would add a sixth—your <u>periodic research reports</u>. These too are essential to good notekeeping.

This chapter and the preceeding one outline in some detail how these requirements can be met satisfactorily. Any rule can be altered to fit your personal preference or circumstance if none of the six essentials listed is neglected. However, so far as American research is concerned, the steps as outlined have proved very workable.

III. LET'S WRITE A LETTER

A. THE "LETTER" FORMULA

There is much to be said about letter writing in general, but there are a few rules which apply more specifically to genealogical correspondence. Let's talk first about six such rules. The initial letters of the key words in these rules spell the word <u>LETTER</u> and provide a simple formula for better genealogical correspondence.

1. <u>LIMIT</u> your requests. Do not ask for too much. There is no more sure way to destroy the good will of someone whose assistance you need than to make an unreasonable request of him. If you know

---

[2]. <u>Ibid.</u>, pp. 139-144.

something about the records held by a certain public official, you are in a better position to judge what a "reasonable request" would be, thus the importance of studying and understanding records. If you need additional information, you can always write another letter (or several) once you have secured the good will of your correspondent. You should never write a relative and ask for "everything you have." The late Archibald F. Bennett told the story of his sister who had never been interested in the genealogical research he was doing until late in life. Not realizing the extent of the records he had compiled, she unthinkingly wrote to him: "Dear Archie, please send me all you have." This was not a reasonable request.

2. <u>Make your requests EASY TO ANSWER</u>. There are several suggestions you can follow to help make your requests easy to answer:

(a). If you want answers, ask specific questions. Do not be vague or beat around the bush.

(b). Do not lose your questions in the body of a long letter. Very often the best procedure is to write your questions on a separate sheet of paper in questionnaire form, leaving space for answers.

(c). Be careful of sending forms such as pedigree charts and family group record forms. Sometimes these forms can be used to advantage in your correspondence, but they are confusing to the average person. If the person to whom you are writing knows little or nothing about genealogy you will likely get a more satisfactory response if you copy any family data you wish to send him in tabular form on a plain sheet of paper. You might then say something like this: "The above information is all I have on this family. Can you make any additions or corrections?" We are not saying that you should never use these forms in your correspondence; we are merely saying that you should use them wisely and with caution. And never send them to public officials.

3. <u>Make TWO COPIES of each letter you write</u>. You do not have a complete record of your research unless you have a carbon copy in your files of every letter you write. There are several reasons why this is necessary; let's consider some of them:

(a). If a follow-up letter becomes necessary it will be much easier to write if you know the specific requests and wording of the original.

(b). As research progresses and you desire information on a specific matter you can tell from your letters if previous attempts have been made to locate the same information. Often we make ourselves offensive by asking for the same non-existent information over and over again because we did not keep a carbon copy of a letter. In the same light we may have located additional data in the interim which would make it possible now to locate the required information, but it is impossible to know unless a copy of the original request is preserved.

(c). A third and very obvious motive is the necessity for such copies in a complete research file.

4. <u>Express THANKS to those who help you.</u> Most of those who assist you through the mail have no legal obligation to do so. Their help is a favor for which you should show your gratitude. On the other hand, however, it is not necessary to apologize for the requests you make.

5. <u>Fair EXCHANGE will work to your advantage.</u> Never expect to get something for nothing; in our time it is often difficult to get something for something. To a public official of whom you have asked a favor, a small sum (with an offer to pay any reasonable additional charges which may be incurred) is a must. Usually if you send an amount somewhere between $1 and $2.50, depending on what you ask, this is sufficient. If you feel that $2.50 is not enough you are probably asking for too much and need to limit your request. If you request copies of specific documents more money may be required, depending on the cost of those documents. This same principle applies when you write seeking favors of newspapers, libraries, historical societies, church officials or other private organizations, except when there are established fees for such services.

When you write to a private individual or a relative, your "fair exchange" is not necessarily monetary unless that person happens to have services for hire as a genealogist or record searcher. You should always offer to pay the cost of making copies of important materials, but more important is your offer to share information and to make the final results of your research available to those interested.

Many public officials, as well as private organizations, may return the money you send, but they appreciate your willingness to pay and will feel more inclined to help if they do not think you are trying to get something for nothing.

6. <u>Provide for RETURN POSTAGE.</u> Ethel W. Williams tells the story of the lady who wrote Abraham Lincoln asking for a bit of advice and his signature for a keepsake. He replied: "When asking strangers for a favor, it is customary to send postage. There's your advice and here's my signature. A. Lincoln."[3] We think this is excellent advice.

It is not necessary to offend close relatives with this practice (though that will seldom happen), but all others will appreciate your thoughtfulness and will often feel a greater obligation to answer your queries.

When you write to a federal agency or to a state agency it is not necessary for you to provide for postage, but letters addressed to of-

---

3. Ethel W. Williams, <u>Know Your Ancestors</u> (Rutland, Vt.: Charles E. Tuttle Co., 1960), p. 271. By permission.

ficials of counties or towns or to newspapers, historical societies, church officials, etc. within the U.S. should include a stamped envelope addressed back to you. The only exception to this would be when you allow money for postage in your remittance or when you are paying a set fee for a service.

B.   THE "4S FORMULA"

In addition to the above rules, which relate especially to genealogical letters, there are other rules which will add to your effectiveness whether your letters are of a genealogical nature or not. Among the most important of these is a formula for clarity promulgated by the U.S. Government. It is called "The 4S Formula."[4] The four S's stand for <u>shortness</u>, <u>simplicity</u>, <u>strength</u> and <u>sincerity</u>. The formula goes like this:

1. Shortness.
    (a). Don't unnecessarily repeat inquiry.
    (b). Avoid needless words, information.
    (c). Shorten prepositional phrases.
    (d). Watch "verbal" nouns, adjectives.
    (e). Limit qualifying statements.

We recall an old maxim which says, "Good things, if short, are twice as good." Most things written can be improved much more by deletions than by additions. A stone is polished by breaking off and wearing down the rough edges, not by filling in around them. Busy public officials, especially, do not have time to read lengthy letters; so if you can say something in one or two words, don't use three or four. A good rule of thumb is that when you are asking favors your letters should never be more than one page long, with adequate (even generous) margins on all four edges of the page. A friend of ours says he never writes a letter that he cannot get on half a sheet of 8 1/2" x 11" paper. He has the right idea.

2. Simplicity.
    (a). Know your subject.
    (b). Use short words, sentences, paragraphs.
    (c). Be compact.
    (d). Tie thoughts together.

Your letters should be written in a friendly, conversational style. Write as you would talk. Try to write from the other person's point of

---

4. G.S.A., Wash. D.C. 58-7468.

view, keeping his interests dominant. Also remember that nothing adds to simplicity more than knowing something about the subject on which you are writing.

3. Strength.
   (a). Use specific words
   (b). Use active verbs.
   (c). Give answer, then explain.
   (d). Don't hedge.

Don't beat around the bush. You should avoid cliches, stilted language and word crutches.

4. Sincerity.
   (a). Be human.
   (b). Admit mistakes.
   (c). Limit intensives and emphatics.
   (d). Don't be servile or arrogant.

Try to be yourself and to "put yourself on paper." As was stated under "simplicity," you should try to write as you speak (that is, your very best speech).

C. OBJECTIVITY

If you can take all four of the "S" principles and draw from them one important idea perhaps it would be the need for objectivity—the ability, in this situation, to look at your own letters and see them for what they really are. If you could do this a good many problems would be solved.

You have undoubtedly experienced writing something that you thought was pretty good at the time, but upon re-reading it later you received quite a different impression. The difference in your reaction on those two occasions is the result of objectivity. It is much easier to be objective about something after it has grown cold and you have removed yourself from it than when the writing is fresh. We were much more excited about the rough draft for this book right after completion than we were later when we went back to re-work and polish it.

It is not practical to let your letters sit for six months before you send them, but if you can be aware of your usual lack of objectivity when something is first written, you can achieve a bit of the objectivity you need. Perhaps a better idea, if your ego can stand it, is to have someone else read and criticize your letters. See if he can understand clearly what you are trying to say and if you are saying it inoffensively. He will be in a better position to judge this. Also, have him check spelling, grammar and punctuation; you may have overlooked something.

Plan your letters. Make rough drafts of them, have them checked and corrected, and then write them (with carbon copies) in their final form. After you have done this reread them carefully before signing. Be prepared to do over any letter which you would not like to receive personally.

If you cannot endure criticism at least let your letters sit overnight before you finalize them. That much time will seldom hurt one, and you can gain a little objectivity even overnight if you try.

IV. HOW DOES THE LETTER LOOK?

This is not a text on business communications, but a brief summary of some items which make a letter look inviting to its recipient is in order:

A. Leave adequate margins on all four edges. Nothing gives a letter a worse appearance than crowding it to the edge of the paper. No matter how neatly you write or type or how well you spell, the letter will look sloppy. If you have to crowd your margins to keep the "one-page" rule, then break the rule.

B. Use short paragraphs and double-space between them. This additional white space on the page breaks up the letter and makes it more attractive and easier to read.

C. Keep your left hand margin straight. Do not wander all over the page.

D. Use proper letter form. Any good English text will give you information on the acceptable forms. Your letters must be business-like or people will think you don't know what you are doing.

E. Type your letters if possible. If you cannot, write neatly, legibly and evenly.

V. TO WHOM DO I WRITE?

One of the genealogist's biggest problems is knowing who has custody of the records and information he needs. This is especially perplexing to the beginner. First of all you should make every possible effort to obtain information from relatives. If you are attempting to locate unknown relatives, a newspaper advertisement in the locality where your ancestors lived might be helpful in locating them. The Ayer Directory (see Chapter Five) lists addresses of newspapers and thus provides a partial answer to this problem.

For information which relatives do not have (and most genealogical information falls into this catagory) you must determine who has jurisdiction over the required records. Record custodians can usually be determined by using proper reference tools. When these fail you can always write to a probable record custodian and ask him about the actual location of the records you need. Later chapters of this book provide information on the location and custody of several kinds of genealogical research sources.

VI. CONCLUSION AND CHECK LIST

In 1964 we picked up a check list designed to help letter writers pinpoint trouble-spots in their letters. This list was distributed in a class taught at the LDS Genealogical Society and its actual origin is unknown. We have taken the liberty to modify that list slightly to fit our needs and are passing it along to you. Questions are worded so that a "no" answer may indicate a problem area. Go through it and see how you fare.

YES   NO

1. Are most of your letters less than one page long? ____ ____

2. Is your average sentence less than 22 words long? ____ ____

3. Are your paragraphs short—always less than ten lines? ____ ____

4. Do you avoid beginning a letter with: "I am doing genealogical research..."? ____ ____

5. Do you know some good ways to begin letters in a natural and conversational manner? ____ ____

6. Can you think of four different words that will take the place of "however?" ____ ____

7. Do you know what is wrong with phrases like: "held a meeting," "are in receipt of," "gave consideration to," etc.? ____ ____

8. Do you use personal pronouns freely, particularly "you?" ____ ____

9. Do you use active verbs ("I read your letter" rather than "Your letter has been read")? ____ ____

10. When you have a choice, do you use little words (pay, help, error) rather than big ones (remuneration, assistance, inadvertency)? ____ ____

11. Whenever possible, do you refer to people by name and title (Dr. Brown, Mr. Adams) rather than catagorically (our researcher, the patron, etc.)? ____ ____

12. Compare your letters with your speech. Do you write the way you talk (your most careful talk, of course)? ____ ____

13. Do you answer questions before you explain your answers? ____ ____

14. Do you resist the use of phrases like: "Attention will be called to the fact," "It is to be noted," "It will be apparent?" ____ ____

15. Do you organize your ideas and data before you write your letters?   ___ ___

16. Have you tried setting off lists of various types into easily-read tables?   ___ ___

17. Do you number and/or indent important points, explanations, etc., and attach explanations to the data they explain?   ___ ___

18. Do you highlight important facts by underlining or by separate paragraphs?   ___ ___

19. Do you re-read your letters before you send them to see if you actually said what you intended to say?[5]

Experience is a good teaching tool, especially when combined with proper instruction and guidelines. If you will carefully follow the guidelines given in this chapter you should obtain good results from your research experience. And though we have no panacea that will guarantee success every time you write a letter, we do guarantee that if you follow good procedures your chances for success will be vastly improved.

---

5. "The Letter Writer's Checklist," instructional hand out, The Genealogical Society of The Church of Jesus Christ of Latter-day Saints (Salt Lake City: unpublished, 1964). Modified and used by permission.

PART II

RECORDS AND THEIR USE

CHAPTER EIGHT

COMPILED SOURCES AND NEWSPAPERS

I. THE NATURE OF COMPILED SOURCES

When we talk of compiled sources we are talking about a great variety of materials. The thing which distinguishes them is that they bring together (compile), in one place, information from more than one root. We have classified them into seven catagories:

    A. Family histories and genealogies.
    B. Local histories.
    C. Compiled lists (dictionaries, directories, registers, etc.).
    D. Biographical works.
    E. Genealogical and historical periodicals.
    F. Compendium genealogies.
    G. Special manuscript collections.

Compiled sources are of relatively recent origin. They have grown almost simultaneously with genealogical interest, for only as people do research are they able to compile the results thereof.

Compiled sources are always secondary (not the original records). In fact some persons use the term "printed secondary sources" to describe them. The term "secondary" is not necessarily a mark of inferiority or unreliability; it merely indicates a greater potential for error since the information is compiled or copied from other sources, often both primary and secondary. Errors are certainly not mandatory in secondary sources, but they are easily made.

Some compiled sources represent extensive research and bring together valuable data of many different origins. If such sources are well documented their value is inestimable—provided the material put forth is based on sound research and evaluation.

You will note that the discussion in this chapter excludes all publications of single-source materials such as censuses, church records, military records, etc. The exclusion is intentional because of the vast area covered by such publications. However, you will find discussion of several of these types of publications in the chapters relating to the records themselves.

We have also omitted indexes, bibliographies and reference tools of all kinds as we have already discussed them in Chapter Five.

Let's look at each of the catagories of compiled sources listed above:

A. FAMILY HISTORIES AND GENEALOGIES

One of the largest and fastest-growing catagories of compiled sources is family histories and genealogies. These are the chief objects of our earlier reference to sources that bring together, in one place, valuable data from many different sources. Because of this "bringing together" they are very useful, but you cannot rely on their accuracy until it has been proven. Too many compilers of such works do not follow proper scientific procedures and many of the connections therein are nothing more than guesses— many of them quite uneducated guesses—and wishful thinking. The late Donald Lines Jacobus discussed four reasons why the compilers of these records have not adhered more prudently to proper research methods:

There are several reasons why scientific methods have been unpopular with many genealogical students and writers. First in responsibility is that all-too-human trait of <u>laziness</u>. It is much easier to make a "likely guess" than to collect data with infinite labor and attention to detail. Second, comes the factor of sheer <u>ignorance</u>. Many compilers of family histories quite evidently have no knowledge of the existence of documentary archives, and assume that the only way the early generations of their family can be put together is by accepting what little is to be found in print and guessing at connections.

A third and very important factor is that of <u>expense</u>. Many amateur genealogists and compilers cannot afford the cost of thorough research in documentary sources. With this factor, the present writer has an understanding sympathy. Yet it is an old maxim that "whatever is worth doing at all is worth doing well," and one may be entitled to ask whether it never occurs to the perpetrators of the worst genealogical atrocities to give consideration to this maxim. And it may be observed that, despite the lack of funds to compile a worthwhile genealogy, the compilers nearly always seem able to raise the funds to publish their productions.

For the professional genealogist, as for the amateur, there are valid excuses for failure to take advantage of the opportunities for original research. The professional, dependent upon his work for a livelihood, is restricted by the limitations of cost set by his client, and these limitations frequently do not permit as thorough a search as should be made. Errors made by professionals very often are due to the fact that, to keep within authorized limits of expense, they were forced to rely to a greater extent than they desired on printed sources of information. No one is responsible for this situation, for a large number of those who employ the services of genealogists are not people of large wealth.

A final reason for the unpopularity of scientific methods in genealogy is the romantic temperament of some of those who pursue genealogy as an avocation or hobby. To people of that type, scientific methods are a bore. It irritates them to be told that a line of descent, innocently accepted from an unmeritorious printed source, is incorrect. They like that ancestral line, and intend to keep it. Denial or question of its accuracy seems to them purely destructive and negative. With people of this temperament, genealogy is not a serious study; it is a mere diversion, and they derive more pleasure from the exercise of their imaginative talent than they could from grubbing for facts. They believe what they want to believe, regardless of facts and scornful of evidence. Let us concede, without argument, that "genealogists" of this type are entitled to their opinions; just as those who believe that the earth is flat are entitled to that opinion. It is entirely natural that these temperamental enthusiasts should oppose scientific methods, and that with the uninformed their opinions may have weight. [Emphasis added.] [1]

It is difficult to evaluate genealogies and family histories, but you can make a fairly good evaluation by answering the following questions as they relate to a specific source:

1. Are the materials which the source presents well documented? Some sources merely state "facts" with no indication of their sources.

2. What kinds of sources are represented in the documentation? Are they primary sources or are they other secondary materials? It could make quite a difference.

3. Are the research and analyses of difficult problems and connections explained in detail so that the bases for their acceptance can be completely understood and even re-examined?

There are some good things written that are poorly documented, but they are the exception and not the rule. And the sad thing about such works is that those using them have no idea of either the completeness of the re-

---

[1] Donald Lines Jacobus, "Is Genealogy an Exact Science?" The American Genealogist, Vol. X, No. 4 (October, 1933), pp. 68-69. By permission.

search or the nature of the analysis. Though the percentage of good family histories and genealogies is low, those of inferior quality can still be useful in providing clues for research. Any information which you have to work with is better than no information at all and can be a great time saver in research. But you must remember that just because something is "in the book" it is not necessarily true. Far too many genealogical authors fall into the catagories described by Mr. Jacobus for you to indiscriminately believe everything you read.

A useful guide to the available published family histories has recently been compiled. It is Marion J. Kaminkow (ed.), Genealogies in the Library of Congress: A Bibliography (Baltimore: Magna Carta Book Co., 1972).

We hope that better-informed, better-trained genealogists will produce a product of higher quality in the future. Perhaps you will be among them.

B. LOCAL HISTORIES

You will find town, county and regional histories among those in this catagory. Many have been written, mostly in the 1800's and early 1900's, and many are still being written. In the eastern states and in some of the middle-western states the writing of such histories has been very popular, and there has been great variation in the quality and reliability of the resulting works. In several states there are published histories of every county (as in New York and Iowa) and in some of the states the number of town histories which have been written is unbelievable.

Regional histories are those which cover more than one county within the scope of the same work. A good example is John Thomas Scharf, History of Western Maryland (1882), 2 vols. (Baltimore: Regional Publishing Co., 1968 reprint).

A feature of many local histories is a biographical section (sometimes in a separate volume) with short historical sketches of prominent citizens and early settlers in the locality. Some of these are quite authentic because the families provided the information, and others contain many errors for the same reason. Those books which specialized in biographical sketches accompanied with pictures of the persons named therein are often referred to by book dealers and genealogists as "mug books" because anyone could get his "mug" in one if he paid the fee, and no one could if he didn't.

Though your ancestors may not have been eulogized in such books as these, you can often find information about them in sketches of their in-laws. For example, there is no biographical sketch of William Jasper Kerr in the published history of Jefferson County, Iowa, but there is a sketch of one of his sons-in-law, John Workman. This sketch says that John's wife, Amanda J. Kerr, was born in White County, Tennessee, October 14, 1825. This is very useful information when you consider that we knew only that William Jasper Kerr came from Tennessee, but did not know the specific county.

These histories, exclusive of any biographical materials, whether they be for town, county or region, provide useful information on the settlement patterns of the locality and on the origins of the settlers. They tell of religion, economics, education and social conditions which might effect research procedure and direction. They tell of geography and terrain, water courses and their effects upon settlement and population. Events molded the lives of the people and were controlled by those people. And even the records that were kept were dictated by the lips of history. No genealogist knows all he should about research in any given area until he knows something of its history; such knowledge is essential to research.

A helpful guide to county histories is Clarence Stewart Peterson (comp.), Consolidated Bibliography of County Histories in Fifty States in 1961 (Baltimore: Genealogical Publishing Co., 1963 reprint). Access to these books can usually be had through local libraries.

C. COMPILED LISTS (dictionaries, directories, registers, etc.)

Many different, though related, types of materials are included under this heading. Any lists—pioneers, early settlers, soldiers, patriots, immigrants, petitioners, etc., etc.—compiled from several (usually original) sources, with some data or information on the persons listed would be included here. Some are quite comprehensive in their general coverage, others are comprehensive in their coverage of specifics, and others are not comprehensive in any way. The purposes for which they were compiled may have been quite different. A few of the important works of this type will give you an idea of the nature of these very useful tools:

> Bancroft, Hubert H. California Pioneer Register and Index, 1542
> -1848. Including Inhabitants of California, 1769-1800, and
> List of Pioneers. Extracted from The History of California,
> 1884-1890. Baltimore: Regional Publishing Co. (1964).
> Coulter, Ellis M. and A.B. Saye. A List of Early Settlers of
> Georgia. Athens: University of Georgia Press (1949).
> Farmer, John. A Genealogical Register of the First Settlers of
> New England (with additions and corrections by Samuel G.
> Drake). (1829). Baltimore: Genealogical Publishing Co. (1964
> reprint).
> Heitman, Francis B. Historical Register and Dictionary of the
> United States Army, from Its Organization, September 29,
> 1789, to March 2, 1903. 2 vols. (1903). Urbana: University
> of Illinois Press (1965 reprint).
> Hinman, Royal R. A Catalogue of the Names of the First Puritan
> Settlers of the Colony of Connecticut. (1846). Baltimore:
> Genealogical Publishing Co. (1968 reprint).

Holmes, Frank R. (comp.). <u>Directory of the Ancestral Heads of</u>
<u>New England Families, 1620-1700</u>. (1923). Baltimore: Gen-
ealogical Publishing Co. (1964 reprint).

Kaminkow, Jack and Marion Kaminkow. <u>A List of Emigrants from</u>
<u>England to America, 1718-1759</u>. Baltimore: Magna Carta
Book Co. (1964).

Noyes, Sybil, Charles T. Libby and Walter G. Davis. <u>Genea-</u>
<u>logical Dictionary of Maine and New Hampshire</u>. 5 parts (1928
-39). Baltimore: Genealogical Publishing Co. (1972 reprint,
5 parts in 1).

Pope, Charles Henry. <u>The Pioneers of Massachusetts, A Des-</u>
<u>criptive List, Drawn from Records of the Colonies, Towns and</u>
<u>Churches, and Other Contemporaneous Documents</u>. (1900).
Baltimore: Genealogical Publishing Co. (1965 reprint).

_____. <u>The Pioneers of Maine and New Hampshire,</u>
<u>1623-1660; A Descriptive List Drawn from the Records of the</u>
<u>Colonies, Towns, Churches, Courts and Other Contemporary</u>
<u>Sources</u>. (1908). Baltimore: Genealogical Publishing Co.
(1965 reprint).

Savage, James. <u>A Genealogical Dictionary of the First Settlers</u>
<u>of New England, Showing Three Generations of Those Who</u>
<u>Came Before 1692 on the Basis of Farmer's Register</u>. 4 vols.
(1860-62). Baltimore: Genealogical Publishing Co. (1965 reprint).

Skordas, Gust. <u>The Early Settlers of Maryland: An Index to</u>
<u>Names of Immigrants, Compiled from Records of Land Pat-</u>
<u>ents, 1633-1680, in the Hall of Records, Annapolis, Mary-</u>
<u>land</u>. Baltimore: Genealogical Publishing Co. (1968).

These sources are usually quite reliable (though not always complete)
because they are based on data found in original records, but, due to their
secondary nature, they do have errors in them just as family histories and
genealogies do. Generally, however, accuracy is somewhat greater because of the nature of the sources and the experience of the persons who
compile such sources. There is usually little information in them that will
prove a genealogical connection, but they are helpful in finding families.

D. BIOGRAPHICAL WORKS

Almost every library contains several useful biographical works. You
ought to investigate the ones in your local library for information on your
American ancestral lines. Of course most of these deal with persons who
have achieved some degree of prominence in one field or another. Even
those which deal with specific geographic areas have information on only

the prominent citizens. Because of this, the average genealogist will often pass them by. He will say: "My ancestors were just common folk," and this is a point well taken if the assumption is true. However, there is a "multiplier factor" in this type of source which makes it much more useful than it might ordinarily be. Though your direct ancestors may not be included, sometimes descendants of these ancestors on lines other than your own have achieved prominence and are included. Since the ancestry of these persons is the same as yours, the value is practically the same. This is illustrated in the case of Robert Lowe: [2]

Robert was known to be the son of William Lowe who had been killed by some outlaws when he first came into Kentucky. It was not known where William Lowe was born or where he came from. Neither Robert nor any of his descendants achieved any prominence that would put their names in any biographical work, but Robert Andrew Lowe, a son of Robert's brother James, did achieve sufficient prominence that he was listed in Who's Who in America. In the short biographical sketch of him it told that his father, James, was born in Laurens County, South Carolina—a breakthrough on the problem.

The possibility that your ancestors had prominent descendants on lines other than your own lines of descent should not be overlooked. And biographical works often provide the needed clues, just as in the Lowe example. Don't overlook in-laws either. You can get the same kind of good data out of these sources as we got from that Iowa county history in the Kerr problem discussed earlier in the chapter.

A good bibliography of some important American biographical sources is Robert C. Slocum, Biographical Dictionaries and Related Works (Detroit: Gale Research Co., 1967). A few of the early American sources listed in this publication include:

Allen, William. The American Biographical Dictionary: Containing An Account of the Lives, Characters and Writing of the Most Eminent Persons Deceased in America From Its First Settlement (3rd ed.). Boston: J. P. Jewett (1857). Originally published in 1809 as An American Biographical and Historical Dictionary.

American Biography, a New Cyclopedia. New York: The American Historical Society, Inc. (1916—).

Appleton's Cyclopaedia of American Biography (7 vols.). New York: D. Appleton (various editions, 1887-1900). New, enlarged ed. was published from 1915-1931 as The Cyclopaedia of American Biography by Press Association Compilers.

---

2. The names used in this example are not the actual names.

The Cyclopaedia of American Biographies (7 vols.). ed. by John
    H. Brown. Boston: Cyclopaedia Publishing Co. (1903). Also
    published in 1904 in 10 vols. under title: The Twentieth Century
    Biographical Dictionary of Notable Americans.

Drake, Samuel F. Dictionary of American Biography, Including
    Men of the Time; Containing Nearly Ten Thousand Notices of
    Persons... Boston: Houghton and Osgood (1879).

Hall, Henry. America's Successful Men of Affairs. An Encyclo-
    pedia of Contemporaneous Biography (2 vols.). New York:
    New York Tribune (1895-96).

Herringshaw, Thomas W. (ed. and comp.). Herringshaw's Na-
    tional Library of American Biography (5 vols.). Chicago:
    American Publishers' Association (1904-14).

Men and Women of America; A Biographical Dictionary of Contem-
    poraries. ed. by John W. Leonard. New York: L.R. Hamer-
    sly (1908).

The National Cyclopaedia of American Biography. New York:
    James T. White Co. (1893-19—).

Officers of the Army and Navy (Regular and Volunteer) Who Served
    in the Civil War. Philadelphia: L.R. Hamersly (1894).

Sketches of Representative Men, North and South. ed. by Augustus
    C. Rogers. New York: Atlantic Publishing Co. (1872).

United States Congress. Biographical Dictionary of the American
    Congress, 1774-1961... (rev. ed.). Washington, D.C.: U.S.
    Government Printing Office (1961).

Who Was Who in America. Historical Volume, 1607-1896. Chi-
    cago: A.N. Marquis Co. (1963).

Who's Who in America. A Biographical Dictionary of Notable
    Living Men and Women. Chicago: A.N. Marquis Co. (1899-
    1900—). Indexes are available.

The salient differences between this type of source and the compiled
lists discussed earlier are that most of these are usually current or semi-
current biography at the time they are published and their purpose is always
biographical rather than either historical or genealogical. Some well-known
sources of more recent American biography are:

The American Catholic Who's Who.
American Men of Science.
Celebrity Register.
Current Biography.
Dictionary of American Biography.
Dictionary of American Scholars.
Leaders in Education.

Who's Who in American Art.
Who's Who in American Jewry.
Who's Who in American Junior Colleges.
Who's Who in Colored America.
Who's Who in Commerce and Industry.
Who's Who in Labor.
Who's Who in Our American Government.
Who's Who in the Central States.
Who's Who in the East.
Who's Who in the Northwest.
Who's Who in the South.
Who's Who in the West.
Who's Who of American Women.

And there are many, many more—some of them for specific states, regions, counties and even cities.

Most of the data in these sources are provided by the subjects and are usually quite reliable.

E. GENEALOGICAL AND HISTORICAL PERIODICALS

This too is an area which is much larger and more comprehensive in scope than is usually suspected by the beginning genealogist. It runs the gamit all the way from the scholarly journal to the mimeographed, one-man, low-budget publication of a specific family. There are literally hundreds of publications—monthlies, bi-monthlies, quarterlies, semi-annuals and annuals—each making its own contribution to the science of genealogy. Governmental units, libraries, historical societies, genealogical societies, patriotic and hereditary societies, families and private individuals all play an important role. Some are excellent, some are good and some are pretty bad.

Many of these periodicals are published on a very restricted basis and copies are almost impossible for the average person to obtain—in fact something which may be of interest to you might well be published without your ever knowing of it unless someone makes a specific effort to inform you or you come across it accidentally. Very few libraries, if any, have all such publications, though several subscribe to all of the most reputable publications. Many have extensive holdings. The New York Public Library receives some 600 genealogical periodicals annually and the LDS Genealogical Society in Salt Lake City subscribes to most of the same ones. Every genealogical library subscribes to at least a few periodicals—usually some of the most important ones.

Following is a list of some of the available genealogical periodicals published in the United States:

> The American Genealogist, 1232 - 39 Street, Des Moines, Iowa 50311.

Car-Del Scribe, Box 746, Burlington, Vermont 05401.

Central Illinois Genealogical Quarterly, 2358 E. Johns Avenue, Decatur, Illinois 62521.

The Colonial Genealogist, The Hartwell Co., 945 2nd Street, Hermosa Beach, California 90254.

Deep South Genealogical Quarterly, Mobile Genealogical Society, P.O. Box 6224, Mobile, Alabama 36606.

The Detroit Society for Genealogical Research Magazine, Detroit Public Library, Detroit, Michigan 48202.

The Genealogical Helper, 526 N. Main Street, Logan, Utah 84321.

The Genealogical Magazine of New Jersey, P.O. Box 1291, New Brunswick, New Jersey 08903.

> The Genealogy Club of America Magazine, Ancestry House, Mendon, Utah 84325.

The G S Observer, The Genealogical Society of The Church of Jesus Christ of Latter-day Saints, Inc., 50 East North Temple Street, Salt Lake City, Utah 84150. (Restricted circulation.)

Georgia Genealogical Magazine, Folks Huxford, ed., Homerville, Georgia 31634.

The Hoosier Genealogist, 140 N. Senate Avenue, Indianapolis, Indiana 46204.

Idaho Genealogical Society Quarterly, 610 N. Julia Davis Drive, Boise, Idaho 83706.

The Kansas City Genealogist, 110 W. 36th Street, Kansas City, Missouri 64111.

Kentucky Ancestors, P.O. Box 14, Frankfort, Kentucky 40601.

Maryland and Delaware Genealogist, Box 352, St. Michaels, Maryland 21663.

National Genealogical Society Quarterly, 1921 Sunderland Place, N.W., Washington, D.C. 20036.

New England Historical and Genealogical Register, 101 Newbury Street, Boston, Massachusetts 02116.

The New York Genealogical and Biographical Record, 122 E. 58th Street, New York, New York 10022.

North Carolina Genealogy, P.O. Box 1770, Raleigh, North Carolina 27602.

Ohio Records and Pioneer Families, 36 N. Highland Avenue, Akron, Ohio 44303.

Oregon Genealogical Society Bulletin, P.O. Box 1214, Eugene, Oregon 97401.

The Register of the Kentucky Historical Society, Old State House, Frankfort, Kentucky 40601.

Southern Genealogist's Exchange Quarterly, 2525 Oak Street, Jacksonville, Florida 32204.

Stirpes (Texas State Genealogical Society Quarterly), 2525 University Drive S., Fort Worth, Texas 76109.

The Virginia Genealogist, Box 4883, Washington, D.C. 20008.

A few of the most widely-circulated of these periodicals are listed in the Ayer Directory of Newspapers and Periodicals, and it is often useful to refer thereto, under the place in which the periodical is published, to determine when the periodical started. However, the Standard Periodical Directory (Lexington, N.Y.: Oxbridge Publishing Co.) and Ulrich's International Periodicals Directory (New York City: R.R. Bowker) have easier-to-use, more complete lists of genealogical periodicals and give the same information.

Contained between the covers of these many periodicals is a wealth of genealogical and historical information. All types of information are included—genealogies, family histories, family sketches, biographical sketches, indexes to otherwise unindexed records, locality histories, information from valuable private record collections, copies of lost records, genealogical queries with useful data, procedural instructions on the use of various record types, guides to record use and research standards, etc., etc.—and most of this information lies hidden and undetected because of limited circulation and lack of indexes (and lack of knowledge of existing indexes).

There are some useful periodical indexes. (Some of the general ones are listed in Chapter Five under "Guides to Secondary Sources.") Among them are Jacobus's Index to Genealogical Periodicals, the Genealogical Periodical Annual (GPA) Index, Swem's Virginia Historical Index and Munsell's Index to American Genealogies. Some periodicals have special indexes of their own which are excellent. These include the Pennsylvania Magazine of History and Biography, the National Genealogical Society Quarterly and the New England Historical and Genealogical Register. There are many others. Indexes to state publications are also frequently found in state libraries and historical societies. For example, the Maryland Historical Magazine is card-indexed at the Maryland Historical Society.

Certainly periodicals should be used when their use is feasible, but even a good thing can be overdone. It would be unwise to spend hours searching haphazardly through periodical literature for information on your ancestors if you didn't know what you were looking for or where to look for it. Also, notwithstanding the great genealogical value of periodicals, it should always be remembered that they are secondary and the possibility of error must be considered.

While we are discussing periodical literature it might be well to note that sometimes there are valuable genealogical and local history data in gen-

eral circulation magazines that are not primarily or ordinarily of a genealogical or historical format. We have in our files an informative article on
probate records from a leading "Sunday supplement" and another on the
history of the Moravian Church in America from a well-known women's
magazine.

F. COMPENDIUM GENEALOGIES

A compendium is a work which treats a broad subject in brief form.
These are usually comprehensive treatises with only abstracts of information. One compiler of a compendium genealogy said it was his objective "to
compress the lineages contained in thousands of individual family genealogies
into a single volume."[3] Genealogical compendia are usually quite inaccurate because the data presented therein are generally from sources other
than original records—usually from family histories or even family members. They are useful but should be used with great care. Some of the
most widely known compendia in American genealogy are:

> d' Angerville, Count Howard H. Living Descendants of Blood Roy-
> al (4 vols.). London, 1959-71 (distributed by Genealogical
> Publishing Co., Baltimore, Md.).

> Hardy, Stella Pickett. Colonial Families of the Southern States of
> America (2nd ed.). Baltimore: Southern Book Co. (now Gen-
> ealogical Publishing Co.) (1958 reprint).

> Mackenzie, George Norbury (ed.). Colonial Families of the Unit-
> ed States of America (7 vols.). (1907-20). Baltimore: Gen-
> ealogical Publishing Co. (1966 reprint).

> Munsell, Joel, et. al. American Ancestry: Giving the Name and
> Descent, in the Male Line, of Americans Whose Ancestry
> Settled in the United States Previous to the Declaration of In-
> dependence, A.D. 1776 (12 vols.). Comp. and originally pub-
> lished by Joel Munsell's Sons (1887-99). Baltimore: Geneal-
> ogical Publishing Co. (1968 reprint).

> Pittman, Hannah D. Americans of Gentle Birth and Their Ances-
> tors: A Genealogical Encyclopedia (2 vols.). (1903-7). Bal-
> timore: Genealogical Publishing Co. (1970 reprint).

> Virkus, Frederick A. (ed.). The Compendium of American Gen-
> ealogy. The Standard Genealogical Encyclopedia of the First
> Families of America (7 vols.). (1925-42). Baltimore: Gen-
> ealogical Publishing Co. (1968 reprint).

[3.] Frederick A. Virkus (ed.), Compendium of American Genealogy,
Vol. 1 (Baltimore: Genealogical Publishing Co., 1968 reprint), p. 5.

G. SPECIAL MANUSCRIPT COLLECTIONS

Some persons go to great time and expense gathering data and materials for publication (or just for the joy of gathering) which are never published for one reason or another. Many of these collections have found their way into libraries, historical societies and archives, but many more still lie hidden away in private collections and family records. The obvious disadvantage of this type of record, even those in libraries and archives, is that it is hard to locate even when you know it exists. Some of them have been microfilmed and this helps, but it does not completely solve the problem. The best guides to such materials are the continuing series being prepared by the Library of Congress with assistance from the Council on Library Resources. [4]

Many family and personal records fall into this manuscript catagory, but mainly they include compilations and collections of original documents of various kinds. If you are using the National Union Catalogs to seek genealogical data, look in the various indexes to these volumes under the heading "genealogy" and not directly under the surname.

II. NEWSPAPERS

Another very useful, though far-from-trustworthy, printed (but not actually compiled) genealogical source is the local newspaper of the geographical area where your ancestor lived. Obituaries, marriage and engagement stories and announcements, birth announcements, probate court proceedings (legal notices), notes of thanks (statements by families of deceased persons expressing appreciation for sympathies extended), news items, etc., can all be sources of important family data. We have known of several situations where the only information that could be found relative to a person's birthplace was in his obituary. Generally, weekly newspapers are your better source because they usually contain more detailed information than do the larger dailies, though there are exceptions.

When you use newspapers, especially older ones, remember that journalism has not always had the "objective reporting of facts" as an avowed goal. Following are some examples of marriage notices and obituaries from early newspapers:

[4.] United States, Library of Congress, National Union Catalog of Manuscript Collections (1959-61; 1962; 1959-62 Index; 1963-64; 1965, Index 1963-65; 1966, Index 1963-66; 1967, Index 1967; ——), First volume publ. Ann Arbor, Mich.: J. W. Edwards (1962); vols. 2-3 publ. Hamden, Conn.: Shoe String Press (1964). Remaining vols. publ. Washington, D. C.: Library of Congress (1965-69——).

A. MARRIAGES

Raleigh Register and North Carolina Gazette—Tuesday, June 10, 1834:

— Marriages —

In this City, on Thursday evening last, by the Rev. Mr. Dowd, Mr. Thomas J. Johnson to Miss Ann Maria Walton.

In this county, on the 29th ultimo, Mr. John M'Cullars to Miss Aley Ann Warren, eldest daughter of Nathaniel Warren, Esq.

In Orange county, on the 8th ultimo, Col Jehu Ward to Miss Martha M'Callian, daughter of John M'Callian, Esq.

In Person county, on the 14th ultimo Mr. Irby Sanders to Miss Sarah Briggs. Also on the 15th Mr. John H. Jones to Miss Rebecca Winstead.

In Franklin county, on the 14th ultimo, Mr. Thomas Debnam to Miss Priscilla Macon, daughter of Nathaniel Macon, Esq.

At Oxford, on the 27th ultimo, Capt. Samuel B. Meacham to Miss Martha Curran.

In Chowan county, by Rev. John Avery Mr. Robert T. Paine to Miss Lavinia Benbury.

B. OBITUARIES

Virginia Argus (Richmond)--Wednesday, August 6, 1806:

— Deaths —

DIED—On Friday evening Mrs. AMBLEM of this city of the most elevated standing in the city, and beloved by all who knew her.

On Sunday morning, Mrs. FRANCES GAUTIER an old and respectable inhabitant of this city.

On the 28th of July last in Goochland county, at their dwelling house, Mr. WILLIAM POWERS and his wife JUDITH, within a few hours of each other; he lay sick 19 days with a dysentery which he bore with christian fortitude; she was taken with a shock of the dead Palsy which carried her off in about twenty six hours; in her health before she was taken ill, she often declared there would not be two days difference in their deaths. They lived 57 years together in a well spent life of conjugal affection, and by their care and industry had raised a plentiful fortune, together with a numerous family; and like Theodocius and Constance, were both buried in one grave, and as they were lovely and pleasant in their lives, in their deaths they were not divided.

You will note from the examples on the previous page that very often the details in early newspapers are sketchy, even for persons of "the most elevated standing." Sometimes, however, these newspaper accounts provide useful data for identifying ancestors and especially in distinguishing them from other persons of the same name. One of the greatest identity problems in research is that of contemporary men with the same names. Any information which helps distinguish one from the other is invaluable.

There is often some difficulty in locating old newspapers which might be of value to your research. If you find this to be true, the best helps are Clarence Saunders Brigham, History and Bibliography of American Newspapers, 1690-1820 (2 vols.), incl. add. and corrections (Hamden, Conn.: Shoe String Press, 1962) and Winifred Gregory (ed.), American Newspapers 1821-1936—A Union List of Files Available in the United States and Canada (New York: H. W. Wilson Co., 1937). These cover extant newspapers published between 1690 and 1936 in the United States and tell the location (specific library, historical society, newspaper office, etc.) of the extant numbers. They tell how often each paper was published (weekly, daily, etc.) and the time period covered by publication. Many libraries have copies of these volumes.

If the newspaper you seek is still in publication the Ayer Directory [5] is a useful guide to its location. The date the paper began publication and whether it has weekly or daily circulation is indicated. If you are unaware of any specific newspaper in the locality from which your ancestor came and you do not have access to Brigham or Gregory you should certainly consult Ayer for possibilities. If there are no newspapers being published (or none were published during the proper time period) in the town where your ancestor lived, get the names of nearby towns from a map (there are maps in Ayer) and check to see if any of those towns had newspapers that might interest you.

A good use for current newspapers, and again weeklies seem to yield the most success, is in locating unknown relatives. You may still have relatives living in places where your ancestors lived many years ago. Though your direct ancestors moved away, some of their brothers and sisters may have remained and today there may be a sizable branch of the family still living in the area. An advertisement in a local paper, with sufficient identifying information, can often produce surprising results. Frequently a kind letter and a small remittance to the editor of the local weekly will put your query in his news columns rather than with the ads. This can be even more effective.

---

[5] The Ayer Directory of Newspapers and Periodicals (Philadelphia: N. W. Ayer and Sons, annual).

III. LIMITATIONS OF COMPILED SOURCES

We have already discussed limitations as they relate to the various cat-agories of compiled sources, but it seems appropriate now to summarize briefly some of the major problems of these secondary materials so that you can establish them more clearly in your mind. It is important that you understand these problem areas, but at the same time you ought not to be-come so obsessed with negatives that you overlook the good points.

Consider the following:

A. ACCESSIBILITY AND AVAILABILITY

Because of limited publication and lack of indexes we cannot always take full advantage of many compiled sources. Of many items which could be useful, we are often never cognizant—others, of which we are aware, we cannot find.

B. RELIABILITY

When it comes to credibility gaps most compiled sources are hard to compete with. The gap is wide and the main reason for it is the fact that scientific research methods were seldom used by many of the authors. All printed sources should be approached with due caution for in them we frequently find that the families are inaccurate and the pedigree connections lack verification. Hence they are often not even good circumstantial evi-dence. Clerical errors are also possible whenever anything is copied, and in research the effect of these can be serious.

C. COMPLETENESS

The most incomplete compiled sources are no doubt family histories and compendium genealogies. Other sources are generally limited in na-ture and are not expected to be complete in quite the same way. We often find that family histories have been compiled without thorough research and by persons not qualified. They are frequently full of information gaps which might have been filled if the research had been better. There are not only incomplete families but also incomplete information on many family mem-bers.

D. DOCUMENTATION

If stated "facts" lack documentation they mean nothing. Too many printed sources indicate that something or other is true but give no indica-tion of the source of the information. Footnotes and/or complete source references are essential in credible secondary sources, and if these do not exist there is no way of determining authenticity. Also, even when complete and detailed source references are given, if they are from other secondary sources they cannot be accepted as facts unless substantiated by data from original sources. Merely finding something stated in two or three different family histories does not make it true. These books often just go on and on quoting each other, accepting something as fact merely because "it's in the book. " Well, to borrow an old bromide, "It ain't necessarily so. "

We have seen books which had some (usually not extensive) documentation and, upon careful checking of the sources listed, have found no resemblance between those sources and their alleged product. This is nothing more than sloppiness and can usually be traced directly to poor methods of record keeping, but it all adds up to poor research. Most writers do not do this; they usually just omit all documentation.

E. OUR DILEMMA

No doubt there are other problems which you will encounter in the use of compiled sources, but the above are the main ones. Mr. William Bradford Brown summed up the whole situation admirably when he wrote in the Pilgrim News Letter:

> When I enter a genealogical room and see the many workers industriously copying from the printed records, I have a feeling almost of dismay, realizing that each one is perhaps adding to the already hopeless tangle of twisted pedigrees. [6]

This is the dilemma into which compiled sources are leading us, and the thing which makes it so serious is the fact that so many uninformed pseudo-genealogists never progress beyond the compiled sources in that "genealogical room" of which Mr. Brown speaks. Their research begins and ends in a library. Jacobus explains the problem further when he says that most family histories are written...

> ... in blissful ignorance of record sources, only scratching the surface of the research, full of erroneous deductions and inconsistencies, bearing evidence of rank amateurishness.... Too often... [the authors] are satisfied to follow what is found in

---

[6.] As quoted by Donald L. Jacobus in Genealogy as Pastime and Profession 2nd ed. rev. (Baltimore: Genealogical Publishing Co. , 1968), p. 61. By permission.

print on the early generations, in total ignorance of its trustwor-
thiness, and to reconcile all difficulties they encounter by assump-
tions and guesses. In view of this situation, it is remarkable that
so many good family histories have been written, and that the
average one is even as good as it is. [7]

Our sentiments exactly!

[7.] Ibid., pp. 64-65.

CHAPTER NINE

VITAL RECORDS

Vital records, as considered here, are primarily civil (or non-church) records of births, marriages and deaths and can be an important source of genealogical data. They do not have a place in every American pedigree problem because they are a relatively recent source in most areas of the country, but where they do apply their use is essential and research is not complete without them.

I. BEGINNING AND BACKGROUND

A. THE COLONIAL PERIOD

The American system of keeping vital records is, in many ways, unique when compared with the systems used by other countries, even though the roots of at least part of the system began on foreign soil. The main roots of American vital records, however, lie in America herself.

Since the early settlers in most of the colonies which later became the United States of America were predominantly British, they followed British customs. Beginning in 1538, shortly after the separation of the English church from the church in Rome, it was required that ministers keep a record of christenings (baptisms), marriages and burials in the registers of their individual parish churches. This was nearly 70 years before the first permanent British colony was established on American soil, and the practice was continued in the early colonies, being implemented and facilitated by statute.

The first known law in the colonies to this effect was passed by the Grand Assembly of Virginia in 1632. This law required the minister or warden from each parish to appear in court once a year on the first of June and present a record of christenings, marriages and burials for the preceding year. [1] These were the traditional events recorded by the church, but, in effect, they provided a record of births, marriages and deaths.

---

[1] United States. National Office of Vital Statistics, Vital Statistics of the United States 1950 (Washington, D.C.: U.S. Public Health Service, 1954), Vol. I, p. 3.

A statute passed by the General Court of the Massachusetts Bay Colony in 1639 required town clerks in that colony to make a record of the actual births and deaths rather than christenings and burials. This act was also different in that it placed the burden for keeping such records upon governmental rather than church officials. Connecticut, Old Colony (New Plymouth) and other colonies soon followed this same pattern.

B. THE SYSTEM GROWS—SLOWLY

As time went by, legal machinery was effected to help collect and preserve the records. The early laws were repeatedly strengthened to better meet this obligation. Again the Massachusetts Bay Colony provides a good example of this strengthening procedure. In 1644 that colony added a penalty to its registration laws for those who failed to report vital events and in 1692 went so far as to establish registration fees. This act of 1692, the most comprehensive vital registration law of the period, empowered town clerks to collect three pence for each birth or death registered and to assess fines upon those failing to report. The act also allowed for the issuance of certificates by the clerks. [2]

None of these early laws was ever very effective. Even much later than the colonial period already discussed, problems plagued those responsible for keeping the records. For one thing, coverage was incomplete. Many towns and cities had legislation but there was not one state which had complete registration coverage before the mid-nineteenth century.

The most significant problem affecting the existing laws was the lack of concern for property rights (the only reason given for the existence of such laws) by a population swelled with immigrants who settled only temporarily, waiting for a chance to move west. The population was so unsettled that the enforcing of these laws was next to impossible.

C. THE TURNING POINT

A better reason than the protection of property rights was needed to induce compliance. And a better reason was finally provided by a group of medical men and statisticians who saw the importance of knowing about births and deaths—especially deaths by cause—in order to fight disease and control epidemics. This held true in both Britain and America. Speaking of the situation in Britain, Sir Arthur Newsholme wrote:

> Panic was a large factor in securing repentance and good works when cholera threatened; as it, likewise, was in an ear-

---

[2.] Ibid., Vol. I, p. 3.

lier century when plague became epidemic; and in both instances the desire for complete and accurate information as to the extent of the invasion led England to the call for accurate vital statistics. It may truly be said that the early adoption of accurate registers of births and deaths was hastened by fears of cholera, and by the intelligent realisation that one must know the localisation as well as the number of the enemy to be fought. [3]

The English-speaking peoples were considerably slower to develop vital registration than were many other peoples of the world, and the entire world was relatively slow. By 1833 only one-tenth of the world's population lived in the areas covered by regular vital registration. This included Austria, Bavaria, Belgium, Denmark, Finland, France, Norway, Prussia, Saxony, Sweden (Some of these countries had vital registration systems operated by their churches.) and five U.S. cities (six per cent of the U.S. population)—Baltimore, Boston, New Orleans, New York and Philadelphia. [4]

Though these five cities were the forerunners in the development of American vital registration, and though some of them had health departments and kept statistics of death by cause, complete records are not available for them from this early period because the laws were ineffective. In Baltimore, for example, it was not until 1875 that death certificates were required by statute.

England and Wales had no vital registration until July 1837 (Act of 1836) when a central registry office was established with responsibility for recording all births, marriages and deaths. This act probably came about in response to the cholera epidemic which took 42,000 lives in Great Britain and Ireland during 1831 and 1832. The Act of 1836 is regarded by many as the turning point in the development of vital registration in both England and the United States. Vital records began to improve consistently from that time. Part of the impetus behind these improved records was the security of property rights, but the chief motivation was the gathering of facts that would facilitate war against disease and poor sanitary conditions.

In the U.S., vital records have never been kept on a national level as they are in Britain, but rather their keeping is largely a state responsibility. At the time our nation's founders framed the Constitution they created a republic in which all rights or duties not expressly given to the federal government were automatically left to the individual states. And practically no one saw need for vital registration in 1787. Hence each state has de-

---

[3.] Sir Arthur Newsholme, Evolution of Preventive Medicine (Baltimore: Williams and Wilkins, 1927), p. 113. By permission.

[4.] United States. National Office of Vital Statistics, Vol. I, p. 4.

veloped its own system of vital registration, but not without the prodding and direction of federal agencies and other interested organizations.

The one man with perhaps the greatest influence on the early development of American vital records was Lemuel Shattuck of Massachusetts. Shattuck was inspired by England's Act of 1836 and made it the model for the statute adopted by Massachusetts in 1842 and strengthened in 1844. This legislation (1844) was the first in America to require central-state filing of records and to provide for standard forms. The American Statistical Association, which Shattuck founded, was the pressure group which worked to secure this legislation. [5] New Jersey was not far behind, making registration of births, marriages and deaths mandatory on a state-wide basis in 1848.

D. VITAL REGISTRATION AND THE CENSUS

Shattuck's accomplishments in Massachusetts vital registration were by no means the end of his influence upon vital records. Because of his work in designing the 1845 census of Boston, he was called to Washington in 1849 to help draw up plans for the 1850 federal census. This census bore the marks of his genius and foresight and also of his interest in vital records. That census inaugurated the most important innovations in the history of the federal census.

It is not our purpose here to discuss the census in detail—that is done in Chapters Ten and Eleven—but some of Shattuck's census innovations do relate to vital records since that census included an attempt to collect vital data by enumeration. He apparently was not convinced that such a system would work, but felt that if it produced any information at all it would be of more value than what was being done otherwise at the time—the old idea that anything is better than nothing.

To the population schedules of the census was added an additional column:

Married within the year?

There was also added a mortality schedule to gather data on persons dying within the census year. In 1860 a column was added to the population schedules to tell the month of birth for those born within the census year. The first birth and death statistics published by the federal government were collected by the decennial censuses up through the census of 1900. [6]

Shattuck's fears for the effectiveness of the system were confirmed, but, for lack of something better, the program was continued. The method

---

5. Ibid., Vol. I, p. 5.
6. Ibid., Vol. I, p. 5.

was quite unsatisfactory. For one thing these enumerations covered only the 12 months immediately preceding the date of the census—only one year out of ten. A second problem was getting people to report events properly, especially deaths. Apparently memories were very short. The 1850, 1860 and 1870 counts of deaths, it is estimated, fell short of the actual number by 40 per cent. [7] With the census of 1880 the census law was amended to withdraw mortality schedules from the enumerators in those cities and states with official registration of deaths and to secure the needed information from the actual death records. [8]

The census as a tool for collecting vital records was not abandoned until the 1910 census when registration within the several states had developed sufficiently to provide better national statistics than enumeration could provide. [9] However, nothing is known of the location of any 1900 mortality schedules except that they were probably destroyed prior to World War I, and those for 1890 were destroyed by fire on March 22, 1896. [10]

In defense of these vital records by enumeration (if indeed they need defense) it must be said that the only other choice was to have practically no vital records at all. [11]

E. ORGANIZATION AND STANDARDIZATION

Registration was working well in a handful of large U.S. cities as early as the mid-1800's, but in the rest of the country the records were very poor. It was this condition which prompted the American Medical Association, in 1855, to adopt a resolution calling for all members to petition their state legislatures to establish vital statistics offices. In 1879 an act of Congress created the National Board of Health which began almost immediately to publish health statistics for cities that could provide them. That their main emphasis was directed toward uniformity of registration is not difficult to appreciate when you realize that from the 24 cities which participated in the program at its outset, 14 separate forms were used. The differences among these forms were so vast that any comparison of data was next to impossible. [12]

The effect of this new national board was almost unbelievable. By

---

[7] Ibid., Vol. I, p. 7.

[8] Katherine H. Davidson and Charlotte M. Ashby (comp.), Preliminary Inventory of the Records of the Bureau of the Census (Washington, D.C.: The National Archives, 1964), p. 110.

[9] United States. National Office of Vital Statistics, Vol. I, p. 7.

[10] Information provided by National Archives in letter of February 1970.

[11] Mortality schedules are discussed in more detail in Chapter Ten.

[12] United States. National Office of Vital Statistics, Vol. I, p. 7.

March of 1880, in only its second year, weekly information was being received from about 90 different cities. Also in 1880 the board called a meeting of all state and local registration officials (which proved to be the beginning of an annual convention) and, among other things, this conclave discussed collection procedures, standard forms and uniform legislation from state to state. [13]

As mentioned earlier, the 1880 census on mortality was operated quite differently from those of 1850, 1860 and 1870. The legislative adjustment which effected this change also put the National Board of Health's Committee on Vital Statistics in charge of the mortality schedules of that census.

Prior to the taking of the mortality census of 1900 the Census Office carried on extensive correspondence with each of the states and with those cities with a population over 5,000. It collected extensive data on registration procedures and then published its findings for the benefit of all registration personnel. It recommended a death certificate form and suggested that all areas adopt it before January 1, 1900. Eighteen states and the District of Columbia adopted the form either wholly or with slight modifications, and 71 major cities in the remaining states followed suit. On this basis it is believed that the 1900 mortality census is 90 per cent complete [14] (if only it were available).

Various interested organizations continued to have tremendous effect on local registration of births and deaths even though they had no direct control. By 1910 registration was considered complete enough that it was no longer necessary to attempt to collect vital information as part of the census. These organizations and their progeny under the Census Office (later the Bureau of the Census; still later the Federal Security Administration; and today the Department of Health, Education and Welfare) have continued their efforts and since 1933 every state in the Union has had a model (uniform) law, or a modification thereof, and is in a national registration area which assures sameness from one state to another, both in procedures and forms used. The last states to actually adopt statewide birth and death registration (Georgia and New Mexico) did so in 1919, but they were close on the heels of half-a-dozen other states.

Useful death records generally developed slightly earlier than birth records, which is normal when you consider the motivation behind the registration movement—the war against disease. And, of the three kinds of vital records being considered here, marriage records have been the slowest to develop. Though in most localities we often find marriage records earlier than either birth or death records, their rate of development has not kept pace. Marriages still have not reached the point of state-wide

---

13. Ibid., Vol I, p. 7.
14. Ibid., Vol I, p. 7.

FIGURE 1
IMPORTANT DATES IN THE HISTORY OF BIRTH
AND DEATH REGISTRATION: UNITED STATES

AREA	RECORDS ON FILE FOR ENTIRE AREA		ADMITTED TO REGISTRATION AREA		AREA	RECORDS ON FILE FOR ENTIRE AREA		ADMITTED TO REGISTRATION AREA	
	DEATHS	BIRTHS	DEATHS	BIRTHS		DEATHS	BIRTHS	DEATHS	BIRTHS
Alabama	1908	1908	1925	1927	Nevada	1911	1911	1929	1929
Arizona	1909	1909	1926	1926	New Hampshire	1850	1850	1890	1915
Arkansas	1914	1914	1927	1927	New Jersey	1848	1848	1880	1921
California	1905	1905	1906	1919	New Mexico	1919	1919	1929	1929
Colorado	1907	1907	1906	1928	New York	1880	1880	1890	1915
Connecticut	1897	1897	1890	1915	North Carolina	1913	1913	1910	1917
Delaware	1881	1881	1890	1921	North Dakota	1908	1908	1924	1924
District of Columbia	1855	1871	1880	1915	Ohio	1909	1909	1909	1917
Florida	1899	1899	1919	1924	Oklahoma	1908	1908	1928	1928
Georgia	1919	1919	1922	1928	Oregon	1903	1903	1918	1919
Idaho	1911	1611	1922	1926	Pennsylvania	1906	1906	1906	1915
Illinois	1916	1916	1918	1922	Rhode Island	1852	1852	1890	1915
Indiana	1900	1907	1900	1917	South Carolina	1915	1915	1916	1919
Iowa	1880	1880	1923	1924	South Dakota	1905	1905	1906	1932
Kansas	1911	1911	1914	1917	Tennessee	1914	1914	1917	1927
Kentucky	1911	1911	1911	1917	Texas	1903	1903	1933	1933
Louisiana	1914	1914	1918	1927	Utah	1905	1905	1910	1917
Maine	1892	1892	1900	1915	Vermont	1857	1857	1890	1915
Maryland	1898	1898	1906	1916	Virginia	1912	1912	1913	1917
Massachusetts	1841	1841	1880	1915	Washington	1907	1907	1908	1917
Michigan	1867	1867	1900	1915	West Virginia	1917	1917	1925	1925
Minnesota	1900	1900	1910	1915	Wisconsin	1907	1907	1908	1917
Mississippi	1912	1912	1919	1921	Wyoming	1909	1909	1922	1922
Missouri	1910	1910	1911	1927	Alaska	1913	1913	1950	1950
Montana	1907	1907	1910	1922	Hawaii	1896	1896	1917	1929
Nebraska	1905	1905	1920	1920	Puerto Rico	1931	1931	1932	1943
					Virgin Islands	1919	1919	1924	1924

[Courtesy of Department of Health, Education and Welfare, U.S. Public Health Service, National Center for Vital Statistics. From Vital Statistics of the United States 1950 (1954), Vol. I, p. 13.]

registration in all states nor has a standard form been accepted by all states. However, all states do keep good marriage records at some level of jurisdiction.

II. THE USE OF VITAL RECORDS

The utility of American vital records is questioned by many in light of the foregoing historical data. These records, in most states, are considered too modern to serve a genealogical purpose. In some respects this is true, but there is sufficient value in them that they should not be passed over lightly. Death records, especially, contain information of exceptional genealogical value even though most of the records are of relatively recent vintage.

The death certificate form calls not only for information on the death but also on the birth (date and place) and on the parentage of the deceased. As an example, if an elderly person, say 82 years old, died in 1915, his death certificate might well provide invaluable information about the family (time and place) for an event which transpired in 1833. Of course some certificates lack some of this information because of a lack of knowledge on the part of the informant. Also, for the same reason (and others) the information on a death certificate might be in error—this is not uncommon. We have a death certificate for one of our ancestors which gives a fictitious name for her father because the informant, a son-in-law, apparently did not want to disclose that the decedent's birth was out of wedlock. Those who willfully give erroneous information create some serious problems for the genealogist.

The information on the death certificate can help you verify information from family sources too. We recently worked on a problem where the female ancestor had never been positively identified even though her name, approximate age and place of birth were all apparently known. The problem was during the census period, but a search of the appropriate census schedules failed to show this person even though there were several families of the correct surname in the area. A death certificate for this woman's son was secured and it showed the maiden surname of his mother (the person for whom we had been searching) as something entirely different from what present family records had stated. Further investigation showed that the death certificate was correct; the person was properly identified and the pedigree was extended.

Dates and places can also be verified through vital records. Whenever there are vital records available in connection with the persons on your pedigree beyond the immediate generation, they should be secured and analyzed for any value they might have in preparing an accurate genealogical record. These records must not be overlooked even when you think you already have the information you need on the person. Dates and places

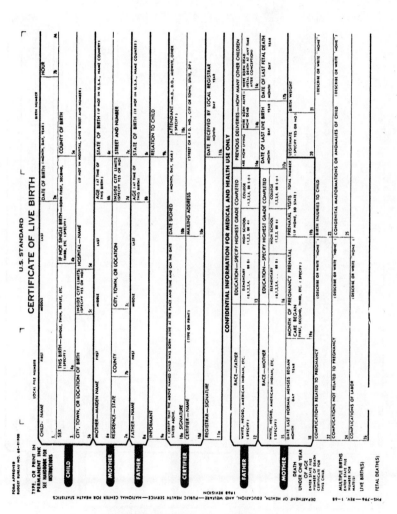

STANDARD CERTIFICATE OF BIRTH
(Certificates with this format are in use in many states.)

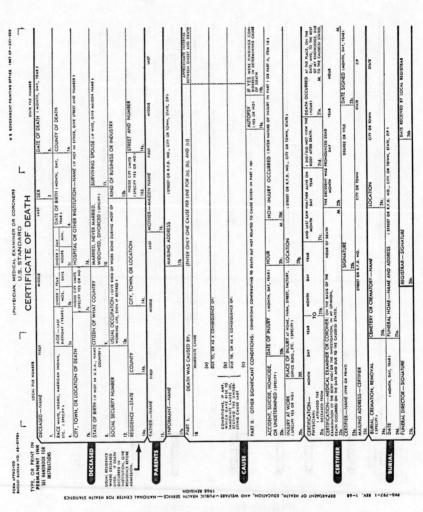

STANDARD CERTIFICATE OF DEATH

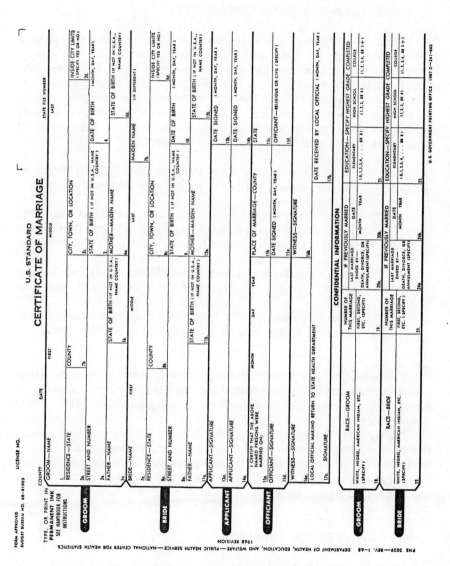

STANDARD CERTIFICATE OF MARRIAGE

passed down in the family are often the victims of copying errors and poor memories.

III. SECURING THE RECORDS

A. SINCE STATE-WIDE REGISTRATION

It is a relatively easy matter to locate and secure copies of those vital records kept since the instigation of state-wide registration in the several states. Much has been written about this and many books have been published with lists of essential data. We could make such a list here too, but data in lists of this kind tends to become outdated rather quickly (especially the prices) so we shall forebear. Rather, we refer you to four booklets (already mentioned in Chapter Five) published by the U.S. Department of Health, Education and Welfare, Public Health Service:

> "Where to Write for Birth and Death Records, United States and Outlying Areas." (Public Health Service Publication No. 630A-1)—15 cents.
> "Where to Write for Births and Deaths of U.S. Citizens Who Were Born or Died Outside of the United States and Birth Certificates for Alien Children Adopted by U.S. Citizens." (Public Health Service Publication No. 630A-2)—15 cents.
> "Where to Write for Marriage Records, United States and Outlying Areas." (Public Health Service Publication No. 630B)—10 cents.
> "Where to Write for Divorce Records, United States and Outlying Areas." (Public Health Service Publication No. 630C)—10 cents.

These booklets are periodically revised in an effort to keep the information current, and they are obtainable from the Superintendent of Documents, U.S. Government Printing Office, Washington, D.C. 20402, at the stated prices.

The format of these booklets includes information on registration areas (usually the states, but also some large cities), the cost of certified copies of certificates, the addresses of the record custodians and some brief remarks relating mainly to the completeness and time period of the records. Everyone doing American research would do well to secure these valuable tools and use them.

B. BEFORE STATE-WIDE REGISTRATION

Locating extant vital records in any state or registration area prior to

MONTANA: "Guide to Public Vital Statistics Records in Montana." (Mar. 1941).

"Inventory of the Vital Statistics Records of Churches and Religious Organizations in Montana. Preliminary Edition." (July 1942).

NEBRASKA: "Guide to Public Vital Statistics Records in Nebraska." (Sep. 1941).

NEVADA: "Guide to Public Vital Statistics Records in Nevada." (Dec. 1941).

NEW HAMPSHIRE: "Guide to Church Vital Statistics Records in New Hampshire. Preliminary Edition." (May 1942).

"Guide to Public Vital Statistics Records in New Hampshire."

NEW JERSEY: "Guide to Vital Statistics Records in New Jersey."
Vol. I, Public Archives. (1942).
Vol. II, Church Archives. (1942).

"Guide to Naturalization Records in New Jersey." (Dec. 1941).

NEW MEXICO: "Guide to Public Vital Statistics Records in New Mexico." (Mar. 1942).

NEW YORK: "Guide to Public Vital Statistics Records in New York State (Inclusive of New York City)."
Vol. I, Birth Records. (Jan. 1942).
Vol. II, Marriage Records. (Aug. 1942).
Vol. III, Death Records. (1942).

"Guide to Vital Statistics Records in Churches in New York State (Exclusive of New York City)."
Vol. I. (May 1942).
Vol. II. (June 1942).

"Guide to Vital Statistics Records in the City of New York: Churches."
Borough of Bronx. (Apr. 1942).
Borough of Brooklyn. (1942).
Borough of Manhattan. (1942).
Borough of Queens. (May 1942).
Borough of Richmond. (1942).

NORTH CAROLINA: "Guide to Vital Statistics Records in North Carolina."
Vol. I, Public Vital Statistics. (June 1942).

NORTH DAKOTA: "Guide to Public Vital Statistics Records of North Dakota." (Aug. 1941).

"Guide to Church Vital Statistics Records in North Dakota." (Mar. 1942).

OKLAHOMA: "Guide to Public Vital Statistics Records in Oklahoma. " (June 1941).

OREGON: "Guide to Public Vital Statistics Records in Oregon. " (Apr. 1942).

RHODE ISLAND: "Summary of Legislation Concerning Vital Statistics in Rhode Island. " (July 1937).

"Guide to Public Vital Statistics Records: Births Marriages, Deaths in the State of Rhode Island and Providence Plantations. " (June 1941).

SOUTH DAKOTA: "Guide to Public Vital Statistics Records in South Dakota. " (Jan. 1942).

TENNESSEE: "Guide to Public Vital Statistics Records in Tennessee. " (June 1941).

"Guide to Church Vital Statistics Records in Tennessee. " (Aug. 1942).

TEXAS: "Guide to Public Vital Statistics Records in Texas. " (June 1941).

UTAH: "Census of Weber County (Exclusive of Green River Precinct), Provisional State of Deseret, 1850. " (Oct. 1937).

"Guide to Public Vital Statistics Records in Utah. " (Nov. 1941).

VIRGINIA: "Index to Marriage Notices in the Southern Churchman, 1835-1941. "

Vol. A-K. (May 1942).

Vol. L-Z. (May 1942).

"Guide to the Manuscript Collections of the Virginia Baptist Historical Society. Supplement No. 1, Index to the Obituary Notices in the Religious Herald, Richmond, Virginia, 1828-1938. "

Vol. I, A-L. (Aug. 1941).

Vol. II, M-Z. (Sep. 1941).

WASHINGTON: "Guide to Public Vital Statistics Records in Washington. " (June 1941).

"Guide to Church Vital Statistics Records in Washington. Preliminary Edition. " (Feb. 1942).

WEST VIRGINIA: "Inventory of Public Vital Statistics Records in West Virginia: Births, Deaths, and Marriages. " (Mar. 1941).

"Guide to Church Vital Statistics Records in West Virginia." (Feb. 1942).

WISCONSIN: "Guide to Public Vital Statistics Records in Wisconsin. " (Sep. 1941).

"Guide to Church Vital Statistics Records in Wisconsin." (Sep. 1941).

"Outline of Vital Statistics Laws in Wisconsin."
(Sep. 1941).

WYOMING: "Guide to Public Vital Statistics Records in Wyoming." (June 1941).

"Guide to Vital Statistics Records in Wyoming:
Church Archives. Preliminary Edition."
(Mar. 1942).

As we do not know where all of these guides are available, we suggest
that a letter to the county clerk or other appropriate jurisdictional authority
in the locality of your interest will usually provide a quick answer as to
whether any vital records are available for any time period prior to state-
wide registration. The booklet on "Where to Write for Birth and Death
Records..." offers some very brief information on this subject.

It might also be appropriate to mention that though these inventories
were up-to-date in 1942, etc., many changes in the interim have outdated
much of what they say.

C. OTHER HELPS

We already mentioned this in our discussion of history, but an interesting thing to note is that registration of births and deaths in large cities
usually antedated state-wide registration by several years. In New Orleans,
for example, there are birth records from 1790 and death records from
1803 while there was not state-wide registration in Louisiana until July 1914.
Four large cities which had vital registration before the states in which they
are located are still self-contained registration districts. They are:

Baltimore, Maryland—from 1875.

Boston, Massachusetts—from 1639.

New Orleans, Louisiana—births from 1790, deaths from 1803.

New York, New York:

Bronx Borough—from 1899. (Records from 1866 to 1897
are in Manhattan Borough.)

Brooklyn Borough—deaths in Kings County from 1847,
others in City Health Department from 1866.

Manhattan Borough—from 1866. (Deaths from 1847 at
Municipal Archives, New York Public Library.)

Queens Borough—became a separate district after the beginning of state-wide registration.

Richmond Borough—became a separate district after the
beginning of state-wide registration.

Several other cities which originally fell into this catagory have since ceased to function as separate registration districts and are now within the state registration areas. In most cases, however, the records from those early periods are still on file in the cities concerned. Of special note here are Philadelphia, from 1860, and Pittsburgh, from 1870 (including Allegheny City, now a part of Pittsburgh, from 1882 to 1905). There was state registration in Pennsylvania from 1885, but the present Bureau of Vital Statistics dates from 1906. Albany, Buffalo and Yonkers, New York, also had their own registration offices prior to 1914 when they joined the state system.

In many states you may secure copies of vital certificates from either the state vital records office or from some local official; in other states you can get them only from the state office.

There are also a few states which have had their early vital records (from various sources) collected and indexed in their state libraries and/or archives and (sometimes) even published. If you happen to have ancestry in one of these you may get some real help from those records. The following states have such collections:

CONNECTICUT: "The Barbour Collection" (vital records compiled from church, cemetery and town records before 1850).

"The Hale Collection" (marriages, deaths and burials from cemetery inscriptions and newspapers (pre-Civil War).

DELAWARE: Birth records, 1861-1913 (with a card index for the same period); death records, 1855-1910 (with a card index to records from very early to 1888); index cards of baptisms, 1759-1890; and index cards of marriages, 1730-1850, are at the Hall of Records, Dover. These were mostly collected by the Clerks of the Peace in the counties.

MAINE: Vital records index, early to 1892. (The records are for only 80 towns, and only 17 of these have been published under authority of the Maine Historical Society.

Brides' Index to Maine Marriages, 1895-1953.

MARYLAND: Indexes are in the Hall of Records, Annapolis, for births, 1801-1877, and deaths, 1865-1880, for Anne Arundel County and some during the 1600's in Charles, Kent, Somerset and Talbot counties. There is also a card index to pre-Revolutionary marriages in Charles, Kent and Somerset counties and later marriages

in Anne Arundel, Caroline, Cecil, Dorches-
ter, Frederick and Prince George's counties
and a separate index for Baltimore County
marriages.

MASSACHUSETTS: From early to 1850. (Church, cemetery and town
meeting records for more than 200 towns
have been collected and published, mostly by
the New England Historic Genealogical Society,
Franklin P. Rice and the Essex Institute.

NEW HAMPSHIRE: Town records, many extending to the 1850's,
1860's and later, have been transcribed and
indexed in a special collection at the State
House in Concord. (There is a complete card
index to surnames.)

RHODE ISLAND: "The Arnold Collection of Vital Records" (1636-
1850) is published (in 21 volumes) and is
available in many libraries.

VERMONT: There is an index to vital records from early to
1870 and also an index to vital records from
1871 to 1908 at the Secretary of State's Office, Montpelier.

It is interesting to note that, of the states in the above list, all except
Delaware and Maryland are in New England. New England, as a whole, was
a leader in the keeping of vital records; but, as good as these collections
are, none of them is complete. The South and the middle-Atlantic states,
however, were generally much less record-conscious. As you leave New
England and go south, the further you go, as a general rule, the worse are
the vital records.

D. MARRIAGE AND DIVORCE RECORDS

Marriage records are, for the most part, available quite early in many
areas of the U.S., with such well-known exceptions as South Carolina which
did not have official marriage records until 1911. Most of these records
do not contain detailed genealogical data until recently; however, there are
also exceptions to this. During the earlier periods these records were
usually kept in the counties where the licenses were issued (the towns in
New England) and can be located there.

Divorce records follow much the same pattern as marriage records but
are not generally as early. Most of the records are in the counties where
the divorces were granted, but many states now have central filing of the
official divorce records. More is said about divorce records, their location and their use in Chapter Eighteen.

E. WRITING FOR THE RECORDS

When writing for copies of certificates you should be as brief as you can. This is not a matter of winning good will; it is just a matter of practicality. In the first place, busy public officials do not have time to read long letters; in the second place, your specific requests and desires may be overlooked in the body of a long letter; and in the third place, time is too precious to spend it writing verbiage that may only be confusing.

It is a good idea to tell your relationship to the person about whom you are inquiring as some vital statistics offices will supply records only to relatives. As far as possible the correct amount of money should be sent with your request. Personal checks should be avoided in favor of cashier's checks and money orders; some offices will not accept personal checks. You may also send cash if you like, but it is not recommended as a standard practice. It is impossible to prove that cash was sent and it is also more difficult to keep a good record of it.

When you request a copy of a certificate you should state all you know about the event or the record may not be found, but it is not necessary to give information about a person's _death_ when you are requesting his _birth_ certificate as we have seen some persons do. If you desire a death certificate the date of death is needed. (Note that there are a few exceptions to this rule depending upon the filing systems used in the various states. Most states file their records chronologically, but some have special indexes.) The specific place of death is not always important, but it may help registration officials determine if they are sending you the correct certificate. Correct names are important. You will appreciate this when you write for the death certificate of someone you know died on a certain date in a certain place, and the certificate cannot be found. The certificate is there all right but you sent the wrong name. This often happens with women. A remarriage you have forgotten, or about which you may not have known, can cause many difficulties. Also, any efforts to secure a death certificate of a married woman under her maiden surname will be disappointing.

A request for a birth certificate must include the names of parents, but parents' names are not quite so important in securing a copy of the death record or marriage record. However, they can be helpful if some other important data are unknown. Ages on death certificates fall into this same "helpful" catagory. If you do not have all pertinent names and dates it is still worthwhile to try to obtain a copy of the record. If it is found it will have even greater value for you. Vital records officials must have some information with which to work—and the more the better, so long as it is relevant to the request.

The following letter is a typical request for a death certificate, but remember that this example is only given by way of suggestion and will not fit every situation:

138 N. Westside Ave.
Haysbury,   Georgia
September 30, 1972

Section of Vital Statistics
State Department of Health
350 State Office Building
St. Paul, Minnesota 55101

Gentlemen:

    Please send me a copy of the death certificate of my great grandmother, Martha Black, who died June 7, 1928, in Cloverton, Pine County, at about age 59. Her father was Mendon Marshall and her husband was Braxton Black.

    One dollar ($1) is enclosed to cover your fee.

    Thank you for your help.

                              Sincerely yours,

            (signed)   Sidney   Orbeck

The dates in which the several states began registration of vital records are shown on Table 1.

IV. TOWN MEETING RECORDS

In most of New England vital information was recorded in the town meeting records. Typical of these are the ones of Chester, Vermont. You will note from the following extract that births and marriages were generally recorded much more faithfully than were deaths. You will also note that it was quite common to record the births of all the children in a family at one time, often several years after the actual dates of some of those births:

Jacob Chase of Chesterfield and Olive Wilson of Chester were Joined in Marriage Feb^ry 1st, 1792 by Daniel Heald Jus^t Peace

. . . .

October ye 3: 1792 then personally came before me the subscriber at my dwelling house in Chester John Chandler and Anna Tarlick Both of Chester and Said John Chandler Did then and there Say the following words /viz/ I take this wooman to be my weded wife and then Said Ann Tarlick Said Likewise I take this man to be my weded husband but nither of them took eatch other by the hand.

Daniel Heald Just. Peace

. . . .

Polly Ston Dafter of John Ston June by Lucy his wife born September ye 30 1773

Rhoda Ston Dafter of John Ston Juner by Lucy his wife born October 8th 1774

Sally Ston Dafter of John Ston Juner by Lucy his wife born Jany 4th 1777

Lucy Ston Dafter of John Ston June by Lucy his wife born Jany 4th 1779

John and Betsy Ston Son and Dafter of John Ston Juner by Lucy his wife born Sept 4th 1783

John Ston Son of John Ston June by Lucy his wife born July 28th 1784

Earl and Betsy Ston Son and Dafter of John Ston Juner by Lucy his wife born April 13th 1786

Ivanna Ston Dafter of John Ston Junr by Lucy his wife born June 2th 1788

Ivanna Ston Dafter of John Ston Juner by Lucy his wife born June 2th 1790 [15]

---

15. This family was recorded in the town meeting records in 1798.

. . . .

Calvon Here and Abner Here Sons of William Here by Merean
    his wife May 22 1788
Abner Here Departed this Life May 23 1788
Calven Here Departed this Life August 6 1788
Thomas Riggs Here Son of William Here by Merean his wife born
    July 13 1789
Aber[n] Here Son of William Here by Merean his wife born June
    29 - 1791
Stephen Here Son of William Here by Merean his wife born March
    22 - 1796

Though some of these town meeting records have been published and
others have been microfilmed, most of them must still be searched at the
town hall.

V. RECORD PROBLEMS

The main problems and limitations in the use of vital records by the
genealogist are as follows:

A. LIMITATION OF TIME

The greatest weakness, of course, is the limitation of time. Vital records are of no value for the periods not covered, but too often we imagine
greater limitations than actually exist. As already discussed, many gaps
<u>can</u> be bridged through efficient use of even relatively recent records.

B. LACK OF NEEDED INFORMATION

Another limitation is that it is frequently necessary to have quite detailed information in order to secure the records you need. Too often the
vital records office, because of the filing system employed, will request
the very information from you that you are trying to obtain. Some data always necessary, regardless of filing system, are:

    1. Name at the time of the event.
    2. Place of the event (at least the state). Many persons, when
they get older, go to live with their children, and it is sometimes difficult to find this information.
    3. Date of the event. (In all states it is necessary to have at least
an approximate time; some require the exact date.) Without this information on names, places and dates you really have nothing with which
to work, and the need for complete identifying data is even more acute

if the surname happens to be a common one.

4. For a birth record you must also have the names of the parents. For a marriage or death certificate those names are also helpful. (In any case the name of one parent is better than the name of neither.)

C. THE RELIABILITY QUESTION

There is always a reliability question on vital records which must be considered. On a marriage record an age or the name of a parent may be deliberately falsified for one reason or another. These same items of information might also be unintentionally misstated with just as serious an effect. With a death certificate you are at the mercy of the informant. If his connection to the deceased was close the data may be accurate, but often even those close to a person really know very little about him. The date and place of birth and the names of parents as given on the death certificate of an elderly person are strictly secondary evidence. You must also consider that even members of the immediate family who would otherwise furnish reliable data, when confronted with the shock of the death and the pressure of the situation, do not think as clearly as they should and the record suffers. (Note that this is also one reason why obituary notices are often inaccurate.)

D. EARLY FORMS

Some of the early forms used by the states before they entered the national registration areas left much to be desired (especially death records). Many of them called for only limited information of a genealogical nature. Texas is one such state. The early Texas death forms called only for the country of birth (and "U.S.A." doesn't really give you much assistance in research). This was the case until as late as 1927.

E. HANDWRITING

Handwriting is sometimes a problem. If you have trouble reading a prescription written by your family doctor you should have no difficulty imagining that a birth or death certificate filled in, at least partially, by that same physician might also be hard to read. Today these certificates are usually typewritten and death certificates are generally the responsibility of the funeral director, but these practices are both of relatively recent acceptance. Thus some of the old handwritten certificates hold many secrets, undecipherable by even the most adept. One advantage you have is that most registration offices make photocopies of their records when you request copies and do not attempt to interpret them for you. This gives you the opportunity to puzzle over the handwriting and study it to your heart's content to get the correct interpretation. You do not have to accept anyone else's say-so; and you may have clues in what you already know about the person that will lead you to a correct interpretation of the writing.

F. OTHER LEGIBILITY PROBLEMS

Other things are often responsible for illegibility also. Acts of God such as floods and fires take their toll. Mildew, poor quality ink and inferior grades of paper can render a record (or portions thereof) unreadable after a time and thus limit its genealogical value. Those record collections which have most often become the victims of improper care are the ones kept on the local (town or county) level. Elected public officials too often have no idea or feeling about the value of the records left in their custody; and among vital records, marriage records and those birth and death records kept before state-wide registration have suffered most. Overheated attics and musty basements have too long been used as repositories for the oldest and most valuable records.

Some states are passing legislation to bring these old records into a place where they can be properly cared-for and preserved. This is a step forward and should be encouraged by every genealogist and genealogical organization.

G. RESTRICTIVE LEGISLATION

Another, more recent, problem is that some states are enacting laws designed to restrict access to their vital records. Missouri is a good example of this. The law in that state provides that. . .

> The state registrar shall not permit inspection of the records or issue a certified copy of a certificate or part thereof unless he is satisfied that the applicant therefore has an interest in the matter recorded and that the information therein contained is for a research project, study, newspaper, radio, television, or other news media reports or reporting, or it is necessary for the determination of personal or property rights. The registrar may require an applicant to sign an affidavit reciting the grounds on which he seeks to acquire the information requested. His decision shall be subject, however, to review by the division or a court. . . . [16]

This is the law. It is quite restrictive, but the Director of Vital Records for the state advises that. . .

[16.] Revised Statutes of Missouri, Chapter 193.240.

If a person is interested in the record of a member of his family and will indicate his relationship to the person and... [will] furnish all available information such as the name of the person at the time of the event, the approximate address, and approximate year in which the event occurred... [the request will be given serious consideration]. [17]

Being aware of laws like this one can assist you immeasurably as you seek to secure copies of records pertaining to your ancestors.

It is plain that vital records are not without fault as a genealogical source, but the perfect record source does not exist. If you overlook vital records when they are available you are not doing the best research of which you are capable. In the interest of complete and accurate records your research must also be complete and accurate.

[17.] Letter from Charles L. Bell, Director of Vital Records, Missouri Divison of Health, dated May 7, 1969. Mr. Bell also advised in his letter that the term "research project" as used in the statute has been held to refer to a matter concerning the Public Health.

CHAPTER TEN

CENSUS RETURNS

There is probably no other single group of records in existence which contains more information about persons and families who lived during the 1800's than do the population schedules of the U.S. federal censuses. Though these population censuses are mostly unindexed, and only on <u>rare</u> occasions are families arranged alphabetically (in a few counties in some of the earlier years), their value is great. A census search can be laborious and very time-consuming as you must read name-by-name and page-by-page, but research on no American genealogical problem is complete until all pertinent census schedules have been searched.

I. WHAT IS THE CENSUS?

The first census was taken in the United States in 1790 as a result of a Constitutional provision that...

> Representatives and direct Taxes shall be apportioned among the several states which may be included with this Union, according to their respective Numbers... The actual Enumeration shall be made within three Years after the first Meeting of the Congress of the United States, and within every subsequent Term of ten Years, in such Manner as they shall by Law direct.... [1]

It is indeed a historical phenomenon for a country to set out in the document which formed it the means and method of taking a census, but, due to the very nature of this new government, it was a political necessity.

The first census did just what it was designed to do—it counted the population, but within limited age catagories by sex. However, it did go one step beyond this—it also listed the names of the heads of families—and through several decades the same basic pattern remained unchanged except that the age groupings became more minute. Since 1790 the federal census has been taken every ten years (as the Constitution provided) right up to the present time. As already mentioned, many of the early censuses

---

[1] United States Constitution, Article 1, Section 2.

contained a minimal amount of genealogical data; but, notwithstanding this fact, they have proven to be invaluable aids in painting a complete genealogical picture as well as useful tools to help locate and identify specific persons.

If you will study Charts 1, 2 and 3 and the reproductions of the various census schedule forms in Figures 1 through 9 very carefully you can gain an excellent knowledge of the various censuses and their contents. Any time you spend studying these will be well spent. In connection with these censuses you will note that there were no printed schedule forms for any of the censuses prior to 1830 though the form to be followed was prescribed in the various census acts. Because of this there is little uniformity in the early schedules. Presumably the persons taking the census, the marshals' assistants, provided their own paper except for the 1790 Census of Massachusetts where printed forms were used. The remaining 1790 enumerations were taken on papers ranging in length from four inches to three feet, and some were taken "in merchants' account books, journals, or ledgers; and others were bound with old newspapers, wrapping paper, or wallpaper."[2]

The greatest, and surely the most significant, changes in the census schedule forms (see glossary at the end of this chapter) came in 1850. The entire format of that census was altered from that used in previous years. Lemuel Shattuck of Massachusetts, probably America's greatest crusader in the vital registration and public health movement (see Chapter Nine) was the man chiefly responsible for the innovations of this and later censuses.

Shattuck had prepared a census for Boston in 1845 which had so impressed federal officials that they invited him to come to Washington in 1849 to help with plans for the 1850 U.S. census. Apparently he was almost solely responsible for the great improvements which were made. The most important change in this census was to make the individual, rather than the family, the primary census unit. Instead of describing an entire family on a single line as had been done in the earlier schedules, one line of the census was used to record information on each person.

As we discussed in the last chapter, Shattuck, against his better judgment, also introduced the practice of using the census enumerations to collect data on births, marriages and deaths. The population schedule forms allowed for a column asking "Married within the year?" (adding a column in 1870 to record month of birth for those born within the census year). There was also an additional "mortality schedule" seeking information on deaths (and the diseases which caused them) within the 12 months immed-

---

2. Katherine H. Davidson and Charlotte M. Ashby (comp.), Preliminary Inventory of the Records of the Bureau of the Census (Washington, D.C.: The National Archives, 1964), p. 99.

CHART 1—CENSUS CONTENT CHART (1790-1840)

CONTENT	1790	1800	1810	1820	1830	1840
Names of heads of families only	X	X	X	X	X	X
Number of free white males under 16 in family.	X					
Number of free white males 16 and over in family.	X					
Number of free white females in family (no age breakdown).	X					
Number of free white males and females (separately) in family, in age groups: under 10, 10-15, 16-25, 26-44, 45 and over.			X	X	X	
Number of free white males and females (separately) in family, in 5 year age groups under 20 years of age.					X	X
Number of free white males and females (separately) in family, in 10 year age groups, ages 20-99.					X	X
Number of free white males and females (separately) in family, 100 years of age and over.					X	X
Number of free white males in family ages 16-18.				X		
Number of all other free persons (including colored).	X	X(a)	X(a)	(a) X(b)	X(c)	X(c)
Number of slaves.	X	X	X	X(d)	X(e)	X(e)
Number of foreigners not naturalized.				X	X	
Number of deaf and dumb (white and colored enumerated separately).					X(f)	X(f)
Number of blind (white and colored enumerated separately).					X	X
Number of insane or idiotic (white and colored enumerated separately).						X(g)
Civil division of place of residence.	X	X	X	X	X	X
Number of persons engaged in agriculture.				X		X
Number of persons engaged in commerce.				X		X
Number of persons engaged in manufacturer. [sic]				X		X(h)
Number of persons empoyed in mining.						X
Number of persons employed in navigation of the ocean.						X
Number of persons employed in the learned professions and engineers.						X
Names and ages of pensioners for Revolutionary or Military Service.						X
Number of white males over 21 years of age who cannot read and write.						X
Total number of persons in household.					X	X

General note: All of the above catagories which refer to "number of persons" have to do with each household individually.

(a) Except Indians, not taxed.
(b) Free colored persons in age groups (under 14, 14-25, 26-44, 45 and over) by sex.
(c) Free colored persons in age groups (under 10, 10-23, 24-35, 36-54, 55-99, 100 and over) by sex.
(d) In age groups (under 14, 14-25, 26-44, 45 and over) by sex.
(e) In age groups (under 10, 10-23, 24-35, 36-54, 55-99, 100 and over) by sex.
(f) Whites only are in age groups (under 14, 14-24, 25 and over). Colored not divided by age.
(g) Those in public charge and those in private charge are separately listed.
(h) and the trades.

CHART 2---CENSUS CONTENT CHART (1850-1880)

CONTENTS	1850	1860	1870	1880
Name of every person whose usual place of abode (on June 1) was in this family.	X	X	X	X
Dwelling houses are numbered in order enumerator's visit.	X	X	X	X
Families are numbered in order of enumerator's visit.	X	X	X	X
Enumeration districts listed at tops of pages.	X			
Post office addresses listed at tops of pages.		X	X	X
Street addresses given in cities.				X
Age of every person at last birthday before census date (June 1).	X	X	X	X
Sex of every person.	X	X	X	X
Color of every person (white, black, mulatto).	X	X		
Color of every person (white, black, mulatto, Chinese, Indian).			X	X
Profession, occupation or trade.	X(1)	X(2)	X(3)	X(3)
Value of real estate owned by person.	X	X	X	
Value of personal estate owned by person.		X	X	
Place of birth (state, territory or country) of each person.	X	X	X	X
Place of birth (state, territory or country) of each person's father and mother (separately).				X
If person was married within the year previous to June 1.	X	X	X(4)	X
If person attended school within the year previous to June 1.	X	X	X	X
If person over 20 could not read and write.	X	X	X(5)	X(5)
If person was deaf and dumb, blind, insane, idiotic.	X(6)	X(6)	X(6)	X(7)
If person was a pauper or a convict.	X(6)	X(6)		
Month of the person's birth, if born within year prior to June 1.			X	X
If person's father or mother was of foreign birth (separate columns).			X	
If person was a male citizen of the U.S. age 21 or over.			X	
If person was a male citizen of the U.S. age 21 or over whose right to vote is denied or abridged on grounds other than rebellion or other crime.			X	
Relationship of each person to the head of the family.				X
Civil condition (single, married, widowed, divorced).				X
Number of months person was unemployed within year prior to June 1.				X
Sickness or disability, if person is sick or temporarily disabled (on date of the enumerator's visit).				X
Whether person was maimed, crippled, bedridden or otherwise disabled.				X

(1) All males over 15.
(2) All persons over 15, male and female.
(3) All persons regardless of age and sex.
(4) Gives the specific month.

(5) There are separate columns for whether the person can read and whether he can write.
(6) The correct word is written in blank space.
(7) There is a separate column for each item listed.

CHART 3—IMPORTANT CENSUS DATA

STATE	BECAME A TERRITORY	BECAME A STATE	FIRST AVAILABLE CENSUS	PERTINENT COMMENTS	MISSING CENSUSES								
					1790	1800	1810	1820	1830	1840	1850	1860	1870
Alabama	1817	1819	1830	Before creation of the State of Miss. in 1817 Ala. formed the E. half of the Miss. Terr. It had been a part of Ga. until 1802. That part of the state S. of the 31st parallel was in Spanish W. Fla. until 1812.			All. (as part of the Miss. Terr.)	All. (Census of some counties is in Alabama Historical Quarterly (Fall 1944, Vol. 6).					
Alaska	1912	1959	1880	Those censuses before territorial status were taken while Alaska was still a district.									
Arizona	1863	1912	1870	Ariz. was in N.M. Terr. from 1850-63. A portion in the S. was added by the Gadsden Prchs. in 1852 while still in N.M. Terr.									
Arkansas	1819	1836	1830	Ark. was in the La. Prchs. of 1803 and was part of the Mo. Terr. 1812-19 when Mo. first applied for statehood. The Ark. Terr. included the Indian lands in Okla.				All				Indian lands (Okla.) and Little River County.	
California		1850	1850	Spain controlled Calif. before 1822. From 1822-48 it was owned by Mexico.							San Francisco Co. Santa Clara Co. Contra Costa Co.		
Colorado	1861	1876	1870 (1860 Census of Arahoe Co. in Kan. Terr.)	The area now comprising Colo. included abt 50 million acres previously assigned to Utah and Kan., abt 10 million from the N.M. Terr. The Terr. of Jefferson was voted by the residents in 1859 but was never recognized by Congress.									

STATE	BECAME A TERRITORY	BECAME A STATE	FIRST AVAILABLE CENSUS	PERTINENT COMMENTS	MISSING CENSUSES								
					1790	1800	1810	1820	1830	1840	1850	1860	1870
Connecticut		1788	1790	One of the original 13 states. Fifth to ratify the Constitution.	All (reconstructed)								
Delaware		1787	1800	One of the original 13 states. First to ratify the Constitution.									
District of Columbia	1790	Became seat of govt. in 1800	(in Delaware vols)	Land area was taken from both Va. and Md. to form the district.		Incomplete	All (including Alexandria Co., now in Va.).						
Florida	1822	1845	1830	Fla., which early included parts of S. Miss. and Ala., had at various times belonged to Spain and Britain, was ceded to U.S. by Spain in 1819.								Hernando County	
Georgia		1788	1820	One of the original 13 states. Fourth to ratify the Constitution.	All (reconstructed)	All except Oglethorpe County.	All	Franklin Co. Rabun Co. Twiggs Co.					
Hawaii	1900	1959	1870	Ruled by native monarchs until 1893, was then a republic until 1898, then ceded itself to U.S.									
Idaho	1863	1890	1870	Originally a part of the Oregon Terr., 1848-53; Wash. Terr., 1853-63; became Idaho Terr. in 1863 including small parts of Mont. and Wyo. W. of the divide.									Kootenai County
Illinois	1809	1818	1820	Ill. was part of the N. W. Terr. (1787), became part of Ind. Terr (1800), thus remained until 1809. Original Ill. Terr. included area of present Wisc. and E. part of Minn.		All (as part of the Indiana Territory).	All except Randolph Co.						

STATE	BECAME A TERRITORY	BECAME A STATE	FIRST AVAILABLE CENSUS	PERTINENT COMMENTS	MISSING CENSUSES									
					1790	1800	1810	1820	1830	1840	1850	1860	1870	
Indiana	1800	1816	1820	Became part of the N.W. Terr. (1787). The Ind. Terr. as set up in 1800 included Ill., Wisc., W. Mich., E. Minn., with E. Mich. being added in 1803.		All	All	Daviess County Dearborn County	Wabash County					
Iowa	1838	1846	1840	Iowa was part of the La. Prchs (1803). Was in Mo. Terr. 1812-21, un-organized territory 1821-34, Mich. Terr. 1834-6, Wisc. Terr. 1836-8.										
Kansas	1854	1861	1860	Kan. was part of the La. Prchs (1803). Was in Mo. Terr. 1812-21, un-organized territory (Indian) 1821-54.									Arapahoe County	
Kentucky		1792	1810	Very early the Ky. area was considered part of Augusta Co., Va. Later (1584) part of Virginia Co. Pre-settlement Ky. called Fincastle Co.. Va. During time of early settlement it was called Kentucky Co., Va. (c. 1775-6). In 1776 it was divided into 3 counties—Fayette, Jefferson and Lincoln. Further divided into 9 counties in 1790. The early settlers called it Transylvania.	All. (Tax lists have been substituted.)	All. (Tax lists have been substituted.)							
Louisiana	1805	1812	1810	Part of the La. Prchs (1803). S. part of prchs lands became Orleans Terr. in 1804. La. was the major portion of this territory.			St. Landry and W. Baton Rouge pars. and some areas no longer in state.					Bienville Parish	

STATE	BECAME A TERRITORY	BECAME A STATE	FIRST AVAILABLE CENSUS	PERTINENT COMMENTS	MISSING CENSUSES								
					1790	1800	1810	1820	1830	1840	1850	1860	1870
Maine		1820	1790	This territory was annexed by Mass. in 1693 as York(shire) Co. and remained part of Mass. until 1820. In 1760 the one county was divided to fo;m three.		Part of York Co.	Part of Oxford County.	Washington County and part of Penobscot County.					
Maryland		1788	1790	One of the original 13 states. Seventh to ratify the Constitution.	Allegany County Calvert County Somerset County	All of Baltimore Co. except the City of Baltimore.			Montgomery, Prince Georges, St. Marys, Queen Annes, and Somerset counties.				
Massachusetts		1788	1790	One of the original 13 states. Sixth to ratify the Constitution. Included Maine until 1820.		Part of Suffolk County	All						
Michigan	1805	1837	1820	Part of the N.W. Terr. (1787). In 1800 the W. part of lower Mich. nd E. part of upper Mich. became part of Ind. Terr. In 1802 all of state was in Ind. Terr. and thus remained until 1805 when Mich. Terr. was created. Jurisdiction extended W. to the Miss. River, including Wisc. and E. Minn. (from 1818-36).									
Minnesota	1849	1858	1850 (There was also a special enumeration in 1857.)	In 1787 E. part of area became part of N.W. Terr. W. part was in La. Prchs of 1803. In 1800 E. part was in Ind. Terr.; 1818 in Mich. Terr.; 1836 in Wisc. Terr. Thus remained until 1849. Wisc. Terr. also included the W. part of the state. The Minn.									All originals missing except the counties alphabetically from Stearns to Wright. (State Hist. Soc. and Nat'l

STATE	BECAME A TERRITORY	BECAME A STATE	FIRST AVAILABLE CENSUS	PERTINENT COMMENTS	MISSING CENSUSES								
					1790	1800	1810	1820	1830	1840	1850	1860	1870
Minnesota (cont'd)				Terr. (1849) extended W. to the Mo. River including much of what later became the Dakota Territory.									Archives have copies of missing schedules.
Mississippi	1798	1817	1820	Originally claimed by Ga. Remained loyal to the Crown during Revolutionary War, but was taken over by Spain btw 1789-91. Held by Spain until 1798. All of the state S. of 31st parallel was in Spanish W. Fla. until 1812. In 1817 Ala. was separated from the Miss. Territory.			All	All (including Alabama).		Pike County		Hancock, Sunflower and Washington counties.	
Missouri	1812	1821	1830	N. part of the La. Prchs was made Mo. Terr. in 1812. Originally this territory included Ark., Iowa, Kan., Neb., and Okla.			All (in La. Terr.)	All					
Montana	1864	1889	1860 (in Neb. Terr.)	Extreme N.W. part of state was in Ore. Terr. 1846-53, Wash. Terr. 1853-63, Idaho Terr. 1863-4. Most of state part of La. Prchs(1803) in La. Terr. 1805-12, Mo. Terr. 1812-54, Neb. Terr. 1854-61, Dakota Terr. 1861-4.									
Nebraska	1854	1864	1860	Originally part of La. Prchs (1803). Part of Mo. Terr. 1812-20 (no settlers until 1823), unorganized territory 1820-34. In 1834 part of area was placed under jurisdiction of Ark., part under Mich., and part under Mo. When									

STATE	BECAME A TERRITORY	BECAME A STATE	FIRST AVAILABLE CENSUS	PERTINENT COMMENTS	MISSING CENSUSES								
					1790	1800	1810	1820	1830	1840	1850	1860	1870
Nebraska (cont'd)				Neb. Terr. was created it included parts of Colo., Mont., Wyo., and N. and S. Dakota (N. from the 40th parallel to Canada and W. from Mo. River to continental divide). Area was reduced to present size of state in 1861 with creation of Colo. and Dakota Terr.									
Nevada	1861	1864	1860 (in Utah Terr.)	Land ceded to U.S. by Mexico in 1848. From 1850-61 it was part of Utah Terr., except S. tip of state which was in N.M. Terr. 1850-63, before Ariz. Terr. was organized.									
New Hampshire		1788	1790	One of the original 13 states. Ninth to ratify the Constitution.		Parts of Rockingham and Strafford cos.	All	Grafton Co.; parts of Rockingham and Strafford cos.					
New Jersey		1787	1830	One of the original 13 states. Third to ratify the Constitution.	All	All	All	All					
New Mexico	1850	1912	1850	Land ceded to U.S. by Mexico in 1848, except for strip of land which Texas had claimed E. of the Rio Grande. When territory was created in 1850 it included Ariz. and part of Colo. (A small area in S.W. corner and a larger area now in Ariz. were added by Gadsden Prchs. 1852.)									
New York		1788	1790	One of the original 13 states. Eleventh to ratify the Constitution			Cortland County.						

STATE	BECAME A TERRITORY	BECAME A STATE	FIRST AVAILABLE CENSUS	PERTINENT COMMENTS	MISSING CENSUSES								
					1790	1800	1810	1820	1830	1840	1850	1860	1870
North Carolina		1789	1790	One of the original 13 states. Twelfth to ratify the Constitution. Included Tennessee until 1796.	Caswell, Granville, and Orange cos.		Craven, Green, New Hanover and Wake counties.	Currituck, Franklin, Martin, Montgomery, Randolph, and Wake counties.					
North Dakota	1861	1889	1860 (as the Dakota Terr.)	Area was originally part of the La. Prchs (1803). Later when Minn. Terr. formed in 1849 it included all of the area of N. D. as far W. as the Mo. River, but was left in unorganized territory in 1859 when Minn. was cut to its present boundaries. As Dakota Terr. was organized in 1861 it included both Dakotas and most of Wyo. and Mont. In 1864 Wyo. and Mont. separated to form Mont. Terr. A movement to divide the Dakotas began in early 1870's but was not legislated until 1889 when both became states.									
Ohio	1799	1803	1820	Ohio was originally part of the N.W. Terr. (1787) and was the first state carved out of this area. It began to function as a state in 1802.		All	All	Franklin and Wood counties					
Oklahoma	1890	1907		Okla. became part of the Ark. Terr. in 1819 but the relevant history dates from 1866 when the Indian tribes ceded the W. portion of their domain to the U.S. Land was not opened for white settlement until 1889.									

MISSING CENSUSES

STATE	BECAME A TERRITORY	BECAME A STATE	FIRST AVAILABLE CENSUS	PERTINENT COMMENTS	1790	1800	1810	1820	1830	1840	1850	1860	1870
Oklahoma (cont'd)				The Indian Terr. (abt the E. 1/3 of the present state and was not officially organized but remained under the jurisdiction of Ark. until statehood.									
Oregon	1848	1859	1850	Original Oregon Terr. embraced all of Wash. and Idaho, British Columbia to 54°40', and Mont. and Wyo. W. of the continental divide until cut to present size to become a state.									
Pennsylvania		1787	1790	One of the original 13 states. Second to ratify the Constitution.		Part of Westmoreland County	Parts of Bedford, Cumberland and Philadelphia counties						
Rhode Island		1790	1790	One of the original 13 states. Thirteenth to ratify the Constitution.									
South Carolina		1788	1790	One of the original 13 states. Eighth to ratify the Constitution.		Richland County		Clarendon County	Clarendon County	Clarendon County	Clarendon County		
South Dakota	1861	1889	1860 (as the Dakota Terr.)	Originally part of the La. Prcha (1803). When Minn. Terr. was formed (1849) it included all of the area of S. Dak. E. of the Mo. River, but this area was later left unorganized (1859) when Minn. was cut back to its present size. When the Dak. Terr. was created in 1861 it included both Dakotas and most of Mont. and Wyo. In 1864 Mont. and Wyo. separated to form the Mont. Terr., and in the early									

STATE	BECAME A TERRITORY	BECAME A STATE	FIRST AVAILABLE CENSUS	PERTINENT COMMENTS	MISSING CENSUSES									
					1790	1800	1810	1820	1830	1840	1850	1860	1870	
South Dakota (cont'd)				1870's a movement to form 2 Dakotas began, but no legislation to this effect was passed until 1889 when both were made states. Before the area E. of Mo. River was in Minn. Terr. it had been in the Wisc. Terr. (1836-49).										
Tennessee		1796	1820 (one county in 1810)	Tenn. was originally a part of N.C. In the early settlement period it was called Washington Co., N.C. The State of Franklin was formed in an effort to separate from N.C. but it was never recognized.		All	All missing except Rutherford County.	Anderson, Bledsoe, Blount, Campbell, Carter, Claiborne, Cocke, Grainger, Greene, Hamilton, Hawkins, Jefferson, Knox, McMinn, Marion, Monroe, Morgan, Rhea, Roane, Sevier, Sullivan, and Washington counties.						

STATE	BECAME A TERRITORY	BECAME A STATE	FIRST AVAILABLE CENSUS	PERTINENT COMMENTS	MISSING CENSUSES 1790	1800	1810	1820	1830	1840	1850	1860	1870
Texas		1845	1850	Texas belonged to Spain before 1822. In 1822 Mexico became sovereign. It belonged to Mexico until an independent republic was set up in 1836 by the settlers.								Blanco, Coleman, Concho, Duval, Edwards, Hardeman, Kimble, Knox, La-Salle, McCullock, McMullen, Tarrant, Taylor, Wichita, Wilbarger, Wilson cos.	Archer, Baylor, Concho, Edwards, Hardeman, Knox, Taylor, Wichita, and Wilbarger counties.
Utah	1850	1896	1850	Original territory included all of Nevada except S. tip. It also included W. Colo. and S. W. Wyo. (as far N. as the present Utah-Idaho border).									
Vermont		1791	1790	Prevented from being one of the original states by claims made on her territory by N.H. and N.Y. Fourteenth state.									
Virginia		1788	1810	One of the original 13 states. Tenth to ratify the Constitution. Included W. Va. until 1863; Ky. until 1792. Alexandria Co. was in the Dist. of Col. in the censuses of 1820, 1830 and 1840. The 1810 is missing.	All. (Tax lists have been substituted.)	All	Cabell, Grayson, Greenbrier, Halifax, Hardy, Henry, James City, King Wm., Lee, Louisa, Mechlenburg, Nansemond, Northampton, Orange, Patrick, Pittsylvania, Russell, Tazewell cos.						

STATE	BECAME A TERRITORY	BECAME A STATE	FIRST AVAILABLE CENSUS	PERTINENT COMMENTS	MISSING CENSUSES								
					1790	1800	1810	1820	1830	1840	1850	1860	1870
Washington	1853	1889	1860	In Oro. Terr. 1848-53. What later became Idaho Terr., with small sections of Mont. and Wyo., was included in Wash. Terr. from 1853-63.								Benton, Columbia, San Jaun, Snohomish and Stevens counties	Benton, Columbia, and San Jaun counties.
West Virginia		1863	1810 (in Va.)	Separated itself from Va. and was admitted to the Union during the Civil War.	All (part of Va.)	All (part of Va.)	Cabell, Greenbrier, and Hardy counties (in Va.)						
Wisconsin	1836	1848	1820 (in Mich. Terr.)	Was part of the N.W. Terr. (1787). In Ind. Terr. 1800-09, in Ill. Terr. 1809-18, in Mich. Terr. 1818-36. In the beginning the Wisc. Terr. extended W. as far as Mo. River and included what later became the Minn. Terr. and much of the Dakota Terr.		All (as part of Indiana Terr.)	All (as part of Illinois Terr.)						
Wyoming	1868	1890	1860 (in Neb. Terr.)	The area was mainly in the La. Prchs (1803). Later it was in Neb. Terr. 1854-61, Dakota Terr. 1861-4, Mont. Terr. 1864-8. The extreme W. part was in the Oro. Terr. 1848-53, Wash. Terr. 1853-63, Idaho Terr. 1863-68; and the S.W. corner was in Utah Terr. 1850-68.									

FIRST CENSUS OF THE UNITED STATES ___1790___

HEADS OF FAMILIES _____
                              (STATE)

_____
                              (COUNTY)

NAME OF HEAD OF FAMILY	Free white males of 16 years and upward, including heads of families.	Free white males under 16 years.	Free white females including heads of families.	All other free persons.	Slaves.
Town, city					

FIGURE 1——THE 1790 FEDERAL CENSUS

FIGURE 2—THE 1800 FEDERAL CENSUS
(Note that the same schedule form was also used for the 1810 census.)

CENSUS OF 1820

SCHEDULE OF THE WHOLE NUMBER OF PERSONS WITHIN THE DIVISION ALLOTTED TO. . . . .

Name of county, parish, township, town or city, where the family resides.

Names of heads of families.

Free white males:
Under 10 years of age
Of 10 and under 16
Between 16 and 18
Of 16 and under 26, in-cluding heads of families
Of 26 and under 45, in-cluding heads of families
Of 45 and upwards, in-cluding heads of families

Free white females:
Under 10 years of age
Of 10 and under 16
Of 16 and under 26, in-cluding heads of families
Of 26 and under 45, in-cluding heads of families
Of 45 and upwards, in-cluding heads of families

Foreigners not naturalized

Number of persons engaged in:
Agriculture
Commerce
Manufacture

Slaves:
Males:
Under 14 years
Of 14 and under 26
Of 26 and under 45
Of 45 and upwards
Females:
Under 14 years
Of 14 and under 26
Of 26 and under 45
Of 45 and upwards

Free colored persons:
Males:
Under 14 years
Of 14 and under 26
Of 26 and under 45
Of 45 and upwards
Females:
Under 14 years
Of 14 and under 26
Of 26 and under 45
Of 45 and upwards

All other persons,
except Indians not taxed

FIGURE 3——THE 1820 FEDERAL CENSUS

Department of Commerce
Bureau of the Census
CENSUS OF 1830.

SCHEDULE of the whole number of persons within the Division allotted to .... by the Marshal of the
District (or Territory) of ....

Name of county, city, ward, town, township, parish, precinct, hundred, or district

Names of heads of families

Free white persons, including heads of families

Males:
- Under 5 years of age
- Of 5 and under 10
- Of 10 and under 15
- Of 15 and under 20
- Of 20 and under 30
- Of 30 and under 40
- Of 40 and under 50
- Of 50 and under 60
- Of 60 and under 70
- Of 70 and under 80
- Of 80 and under 90
- Of 90 and under 100
- Of 100 and upwards

Females:
- Under 5 years of age
- Of 5 and under 10
- Of 10 and under 15
- Of 15 and under 20
- Of 20 and under 30
- Of 30 and under 40
- Of 40 and under 50
- Of 50 and under 60
- Of 60 and under 70
- Of 70 and under 80
- Of 80 and under 90
- Of 90 and under 100
- Of 100 and upwards

Slaves

Males:
- Under 10 years of age
- Of 10 and under 24
- Of 24 and under 36
- Of 36 and under 55
- Of 55 and under 100
- Of 100 and upwards

Females:
- Under 10 years of age
- Of 10 and under 24
- Of 24 and under 36
- Of 36 and under 55
- Of 55 and under 100
- Of 100 and upwards

Total

White persons included in the foregoing
- Who are deaf and dumb, under 14 years of age
- Who are deaf and dumb, of 14 and under 25
- Who are deaf and dumb, of 25 and upwards
- Who are blind
- Aliens—foreigners not Naturalized

11031

FIGURE 4—THE 1830 FEDERAL CENSUS

Department of Commerce
Bureau of the Census
CENSUS OF 1840.

SCHEDULE of the whole number of persons within the Division allotted to .... by the Marshal of the ....
District (or Territory) of ....

Name of county, city, ward, town, township, parish, precinct, hundred, or district	Names of heads of families	Free white persons, including heads of families																													Slaves														Number of persons in each family engaged in-	Pensioners for Revolutionary or military services, included in the foregoing	

(Free white persons — Males: Under 5 years of age; Of 5 and under 10; Of 10 and under 15; Of 15 and under 20; Of 20 and under 30; Of 30 and under 40; Of 40 and under 50; Of 50 and under 60; Of 60 and under 70; Of 70 and under 80; Of 80 and under 90; Of 90 and under 100; Of 100 and upwards. Females: Under 5 years of age; Of 5 and under 10; Of 10 and under 15; Of 15 and under 20; Of 20 and under 30; Of 30 and under 40; Of 40 and under 50; Of 50 and under 60; Of 60 and under 70; Of 70 and under 80; Of 80 and under 90; Of 90 and under 100; Of 100 and upwards. Slaves — Males: Under 10 years of age; Of 10 and under 24; Of 24 and under 36; Of 36 and under 55; Of 55 and under 100; Of 100 and upwards. Females: Under 10 years of age; Of 10 and under 24; Of 24 and under 36; Of 36 and under 55; Of 55 and under 100; Of 100 and upwards. Total. Pensioners for Revolutionary or military services: Name; Age.)

FIGURE 5——THE 1840 FEDERAL CENSUS

DEPARTMENT OF COMMERCE
BUREAU OF THE CENSUS
WASHINGTON

SCHEDULE 1.— Free Inhabitants in................, in the County of................, State of................
enumerated by me, on the.............. day of.............., 1850. .... Ass't Marshal

1	2	3	Description			7	8	9	10	11	12	13
			4	5	6							
Dwelling-houses numbered in the order of visitation.	Families numbered in the order of visitation.	The name of every person whose usual place of abode on the first day of June, 1850, was in this family.	Age	Sex	Color.—White, black or mulatto.	Profession, Occupation, or Trade of each male person over 15 years of age	Value of Real Estate owned.	Place of Birth, naming the State, Territory, or Country.	Married within the year.	Attended school within the year.	Persons over 20 years of age who cannot read and write.	Whether deaf and dumb, blind, insane, idiotic, pauper, or convict.

FIGURE 6—THE 1850 FEDERAL CENSUS

Page No.

SCHEDULE 1.—Free Inhabitants in _____ in the County of _____

State of _____ enumerated by me, on the _____ day of _____, 1860.

Post Office _____, Ass't Marshal.

Dwelling Houses—numbered in the order of visitation.	Families numbered in the order of visitation.	The name of every person whose usual place of abode on the first day of June, 1860, was in this family.	DESCRIPTION			Profession, Occupation, or Trade of each person, male and female, over 15 years of age.	VALUE OF ESTATE OWNED.		Place of Birth. Naming the State, Territory, or Country.	Married within the year.	Attended School within the year.	Persons over 20 years of age who can not read and write.	Whether deaf and dumb, blind, insane, idiotic, pauper, or convict.
			Age.	Sex.	Color. (White, Black, or Mulatto.)		Value of Real Estate.	Value of Personal Estate.					
1	2	3	4	5	6	7	8	9	10	11	12	13	14
1													
2													
3													
4													
5													
6													
7													
8													
9													
10													
11													
12													
13													
14													
15													
16													
17													

FIGURE 7—THE 186

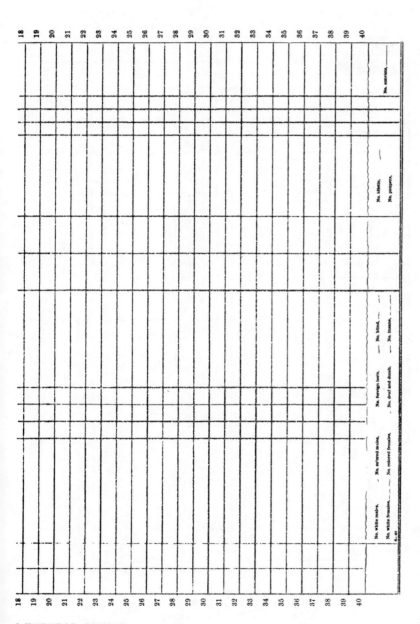

0 FEDERAL CENSUS

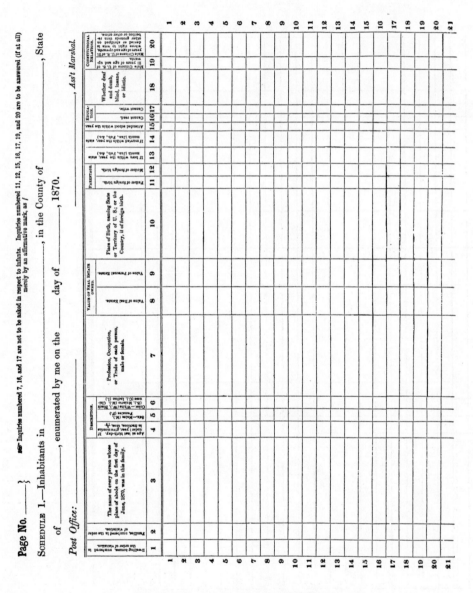

FIGURE 8——THE 1870 FEDERAL CENSUS

[7-296]

Page No.......................
Supervisor's Dist. No..........
Enumeration Dist. No...........

Note A.—The Census Year begins June 1, 1879, and ends May 31, 1880.
Note B.—All persons will be included in the Enumeration who were living on the 1st day of June, 1880. No others will. Children BORN SINCE June 1, 1880 will be OMITTED. Members of Families who have DIED SINCE June 1, 1880, will be INCLUDED.
Note C.—Questions Nos. 13, 14, 22 and 23 are not to be asked in respect to persons under 10 years of age.

SCHEDULE 1.—Inhabitants in ...., in the County of ...., State of ....

enumerated by me on the .... day of June, 1880.

....
Enumerator.

	In Cities					Personal Description.					Civil Condition.				Occupation.		Health.						Education.			Nativity.		
	Name of Street.	House Number.	Dwelling houses numbered in order of visitation.	Families numbered in order of visitation.	The Name of each Person whose place of abode, on 1st day of June, 1880, was in this family.	Color—White, W; Black, B; Mulatto, Mu; Chinese, C; Indian, I.	Sex—Male, M; Female, F.	Age at last birthday prior to June 1, 1880. If under 1 year, give months in fractions, thus: 3/12.	If born within the Census year, give the month.	Relationship of each person to the head of this family—whether wife, son, daughter, servant, boarder, or other.	Single, /.	Married, /.	Widowed, /. Divorced, D.	Married during Census year, /.	Profession, Occupation or Trade of each person, male or female.	Number of months this person has been unemployed during the Census year.	Is the person [on the day of the Enumerator's visit] sick or temporarily disabled, so as to be unable to attend to ordinary business or duties? If so, what is the sickness or disability?	Blind, /.	Deaf and Dumb, /.	Idiotic, /.	Insane, /.	Maimed, Crippled, Bedridden, or otherwise disabled, /.	Attended school within the Census year, /.	Cannot read, /.	Cannot write, /.	Place of Birth of this person, naming State or Territory of United States, or the Country, if of foreign birth.	Place of Birth of the Father of this person, naming the State or Territory of United States, or the Country, if of foreign birth.	Place of Birth of the Mother of this person, naming the State or Territory of United States, or the Country, if of foreign birth.
			1	2	3	4	5	6	7	8	9	10	11	12	13	14	15	16	17	18	19	20	21	22	23	24	25	26
1																												
2																												
3																												
4																												
5																												
6																												
7																												
8																												
9																												
10																												
11																												
12																												
13																												
14																												
15																												
16																												
17																												
18																												
19																												
20																												
21																												
22																												
23																												
24																												
25																												
26																												
27																												
28																												
29																												
30																												
31																												
32																												
33																												
34																												
35																												
36																												
37																												
38																												
39																												
40																												
41																												
42																												
43																												
44																												
45																												
46																												
47																												
48																												
49																												
50																												

NOTE D.—In making entries in columns 9, 10, 11, 12, 16 to 23, an affirmative mark only will be used—thus /, except in the case of divorced persons, column 11, when the letter "D" is to be used.
NOTE E.—Question No. 12 will only be asked in cases where an affirmative answer has been given either to question 10 or to question 11.
NOTE F.—Question No. 14 will only be asked in cases when a gainful occupation has been reported in column 13.
NOTE G.—In column 7 an abbreviation in the name of the month may be used, as Jan., Apr., Dec.

© U.S. GOVERNMENT PRINTING OFFICE 19[illegible]

FIGURE 9—THE 1880 FEDERAL CENSUS

iately prior to the date of the census. [3] This program was never quite what it was hoped it would be, yet this method of collecting national vital statis tics was not entirely abandoned until the 1910 census. [4]

II. WHERE ARE THE CENSUS RECORDS?

A. 1790 THROUGH 1880

The 1790 census—as much of it as is extant—has been indexed and published, and copies are available in many libraries throughout the U.S. Some of the 1790 schedules were destroyed and are not available. In this circumstance contemporary tax lists provide quite useful substitutes, though not so complete. Some of these tax list compilations have been published as "reconstructed" censuses.

Some other censuses have also been published in part by interested parties and agencies, but they are comparatively few. In 1966 the National Genealogical Society in Washington, D.C., undertook a project of transcribing and indexing the 1850 census. The society began by using Tennessee as a pilot project, hoping eventually to cover all states and territories included in that census. Each schedule was to be transcribed from microfilm by two persons, independent of each other. The results of these two transcriptions were then to be compared and differences rectified through use of the schedules in Washington. The project was abandoned in 1968 because of its great cost (even with volunteer labor), before the state of Tennessee was completed. (That state has since been completed.)

All of the census schedules, from 1800 through 1880, with the exception of those no longer in existence, are available for personal searching at the National Archives in Washington, D.C. However, constant use had a wearing effect on the original schedules and by the beginning of the present century the pre-1890 schedules had shown excessive damage. The older ones had also deteriorated with age. Though efforts were made to keep the old volumes repaired, it finally became necessary to withdraw the original schedules from public use and replace them with copies. The 1790 schedules were then published, as we have already mentioned, in the several volumes of Heads of Families at the First Census of the United States Taken in the Year 1790 (Washington, 1907-8, and since reprinted by both the Reprint Company, Spartanburg, South Carolina, and the Genealogical Pub-

---

3. For more information on vital statistics by enumeration see Chapter Nine.

4. United States. National Office of Vital Statistics, Vital Statistics of the United States 1950 (Washington, D.C.: U.S. Public Health Service, 1954), Vol. 1, p. 6.

lishing Company, Baltimore, Maryland). The 1800 through 1830 schedules were photostated and the photostatic copies were bound for use. This work began as a Civil Works Administration project in 1934 and was completed by the Census Bureau in 1939. Thus the pre-1840 schedules were retired from active public service.

Between 1936 and 1940 the Census Bureau microfilmed the schedules of 1840-1880 and retired the originals from use. The 1900-1940 schedules have also been filmed but neither the originals nor the films are open to public use. For the most part these copies were made from the original schedules, but some of the original schedules of 1860 and 1880 were damaged and pages in others were torn and faded. The damaged pages were removed and replaced in the bound volumes by photocopies. [5]

All of the decennial population censuses through 1880 are also available on microfilm at the LDS Genealogical Society, and some parts are in various libraries, genealogical societies, historical societies and agencies hroughout the country. Many libraries have the census schedules for their own states. One library, that of Washington State University at Pullman, has all available U.S. census microfilms. A valuable guide to the location of census microfilms and transcripts is Dr. Neil W. Franklin, "Availability of Federal Population Census Schedules in the States," National Genealogical Society Quarterly, Vol. 50 (1962), pp. 19-25, 101-109, 126; Vol. 51 (1963), pp. 16, 165-167. A supplement to these articles was prepared by Milton Rubincam and was published in Volume 51, pages 167-168.

During various sessions of Congress in the 1920's and 1930's, legislation was introduced in the House of Representatives to provide for the copying and publishing by the Bureau of the Census the names of heads of families in the 1800 through 1840 enumerations, but none of these bills ever passed Congress. [6]

B. MISSING CENSUS SCHEDULES

As we have said, part of the early schedules are missing for various

---

[5.] Davidson and Ashby, pp. 93-101.

[6.] Typical of this legislation was H.R. 5626 (70th Congress, First Session, 1927-8) introduced by Representative Andrew Jackson Montague (D) of Virginia. Montague introduced essentially the same bill in the First Session of the 73d Congress (1933, H.R. 4343) and in the First Session of the 74th Congress (1935, H.R. 1408). Also, Representative George Huddleston (D) of Alabama introduced a bill in the House during the First Session of the 70th Congress (1927-8, H.J. Res. 127) calling for the names of heads of families in the second, third and fourth (1800, 1810 and 1820) censuses to be published, but this bill failed too.

reasons. The most extensive losses are among the early censuses. It has been reported by some that the loss of the missing 1790, 1800 and 1810 schedules was the result of the fire in Washington set by the British during their siege of that city in the War of 1812, but this assumption is unfounded; the actual reasons are unknown. In fact, under the provisions of the Census Acts from 1790 through 1820, the population schedules were deposited in the U.S. District Courts where they were to be preserved by the clerks. It was by a resolution of May 28, 1830, that the District Court clerks were finally requested to forward the schedules for the first four censuses, then in their possession, to the U.S. Secretary of State.[7]

In 1849 the responsibility for the census was shifted from the State Department to the Interior Department with the creation of the latter, and all records were transferred to the new department. No inventories of the materials transferred have been found.

The earliest inventories of census holdings that have been located were made in 1865 and 1870, and comparison of these with later inventories suggests that many of the missing schedules, including 17 volumes of 1790-1820 censuses, were lost before 1895. Extensive efforts were made to locate the missing schedules, but the only thing that turned up was the 1830 schedules for the Western District of Missouri.

Apparently it was customary in the early times for both the State Department and the Interior Department to lend census schedules to agency officials and congressmen upon request, and it may be that some of the schedules were thus lost.

The inventory of 1895 cannot now be found but a comparison has more recently been made between the 1870 inventory and one made in 1903 and many discrepancies were noted—some apparently due to the binding and rebinding of the schedules. So it is really impossible to say how or when those missing early schedules were actually lost,[8] except that they were not casualties of the War of 1812.

Congress prescribed the process for getting census schedules into the hands of the federal government after they were taken. The 1790-1820 schedules were sent to Washington pursuant to the Congressional resolution of 1830. In 1830 and 1840 the marshals who took the censuses were required to make two copies. One of these was to be sent to the clerk of the District Court and the other to be sent to Washington. In 1850-1870 the assistants were to turn over their original enumerations to the clerks of the County Courts plus two copies "duly compared and corrected" to the marshals of the District Courts. The marshals were then to send one of these copies to the Secretary of the Interior in Washington and the other to the secretary of

---

7. Davidson and Ashby, p. 94.

8. Ibid., pp. 94-95.

the state or territory of which that District was a part.

Those census schedules which are missing from the National Archives collection, up through 1870, are indicated on Chart 3. In a few instances, because Congress required that duplicate copies be made, those which are not in the National Archives are in the states. There are no missing schedules in any of the censuses after 1870, according to Milton D. Swenson, chief of the Personal Census Service Branch of the Census Bureau, with one major exception—the 1890 census. [9] However, the censuses taken later than 1890 are not public records and their use is restricted.

C. THE 1890 CENSUS

Most of the 1890 schedules do not exist. A fire in the Commerce Department (note another new department) building on January 21, 1921, is to blame for this destruction. Though not all of the schedules were consumed in the blaze, most were so badly damaged that Congress authorized their disposal. Those persons who would blame Congress for the destruction of a large portion of this census are in error. After all, what can you do with a pile of ashes? Inasmuch as those ashes were once a census they could not be thrown away unless Congress gave its approval. This it did.

Sporadic schedules for some of the states do exist, and a card index to the names on those schedules has been prepared by the National Archives. This index, available on microfilm (National Archives microcopy No. M-496, 2 rolls), relates to schedules, arranged by state, for Alabama, the District of Columbia, Georgia, Illinois, Minnesota, New Jersey, New York, North Carolina, Ohio, South Dakota and Texas. The schedules are also available on microfilm but comprise only three rolls of 35 mm film. [10] The National Archives microcopy number for these is N-407.

The contents of these schedules include:

ALABAMA:	Perry County (Perryville Beat No. 11 an Severe Beat No. 8).
D.C.:	Q, R, S, 13th, 14th, 15th, Corcoran and Rigg Streets and Johnson Avenue.
GEORGIA:	Muscogee County (Columbus).
ILLINOIS:	McDonough County (Mound Township).
MINNESOTA:	Wright County (Rockford).
NEW JERSEY:	Hudson County (Jersey City).
NEW YORK:	Westchester County (Eastchester) and Suffolk County (Brookhaven Township).

---

9. Letter from Mr. Swenson, dated March 11, 1968.
10. Davidson and Ashby, p. 102.

FAMILY SCHEDULE—I TO 10 PERSONS.

		[7—556 b.]	Eleventh Census of the United States.
Supervisor's District No.			SCHEDULE No. 1.
Enumeration District No.			POPULATION AND SOCIAL STATISTICS.

Name of city, town, township, precinct, district, beat, or other minor civil division.) _____ ; County : _____ ; State : _____ ;

Street and No.: _____ ; Ward : _____ ; Name of Institution : _____ .

Enumerated by me on the _____ day of June, 1890.

_____ ,
Enumerator.

A.—Number of Dwelling-house in the order of visitation.	B.—Number of families in this dwelling-house.	C.—Number of persons in this dwelling-house.	D.—Number of Family in the order of visitation.	E —No. of Persons in this family.
INQUIRIES.	1	2	3	4	5
1	Christian name in full, and initial of middle name.					
	Surname.					
2	Whether a soldier, sailor, or marine during the civil war (U. S. or Conf.), or widow of such person.					
3	Relationship to head of family.					
4	Whether white, black, mulatto, quadroon, octoroon, Chinese, Japanese, or Indian.					
5	Sex.					
6	Age at nearest birthday. If under one year, give age in months.					
7	Whether single, married, widowed, or divorced.					
8	Whether married during the census year (June 1, 1889, to May 31, 1890).					
9	Mother of how many children, and number of these children living.					
10	Place of birth.					
11	Place of birth of Father.					
12	Place of birth of Mother.					
13	Number of years in the United States.					
14	Whether naturalized.					
15	Whether naturalization papers have been taken out.					
16	Profession, trade, or occupation.					
17	Months unemployed during the census year (June 1, 1889, to May 31, 1890).					
18	Attendance at school (in months) during the census year (June 1, 1889, to May 31, 1890).					
19	Able to Read.					
20	Able to Write.					
21	Able to speak English. If not, the language or dialect spoken.					
22	Whether suffering from acute or chronic disease, with name of disease and length of time afflicted.					
23	Whether defective in mind, sight, hearing, or speech, or whether crippled, maimed, or deformed, with name of defect.					
24	Whether a prisoner, convict, homeless child, or pauper.					
25	Supplemental schedule and page.					

TO ENUMERATORS.—See inquiries numbered 26 to 30, inclusive, on the second page of this schedule. These inquiries must be made concerning each family and each farm visited.

(10279—1,780,000.) 1 b   34

FIGURE 10——THE 1890 FEDERAL CENSUS
(front side)

NORTH CAROLINA: Gaston County (South Point and River Bend Townships) and Cleveland County (Township No. 2).

OHIO: Hamilton County (Cincinnati) and Clinton County (Wayne Township).

SOUTH DAKOTA: Union County (Jefferson Township).

TEXAS: Ellis County (J. P. No. 6, Mountain Peak and Ovilla Precinct), Hood County (Precinct No. 5), Rusk County (No. 6 and J. P. No. 7), Trinity County (Trinity Town and Precinct No. 2) and Kaufman County (Kaufman). [11]

The 1890 census was the only one (until 1970) to use a "family schedule"—a separate schedule for each family enumerated. (See Figure 10.) On the two sides of the schedule there was room to enumerate 10 family members. If the family was larger than that, two schedules had to be used.

There were also some Civil War Union Army Veterans' Schedules, taken in connection with this census, which are still available. These are discussed later in this chapter.

D. LATER CENSUSES—CONFIDENTIAL

The personal information from the 1900 and subsequent population enumerations can be furnished by the Bureau of the Census under special circumstances only. (See Figure 11 for a sample of the schedule form used in the 1900 census.) The Bureau can furnish census information to the person to whom that information relates and in some instances to the legal representative of that person upon presentation of a certified copy of the court order which appointed him. If the record sought relates to a deceased person the application must be accompanied by a certified copy of the death certificate and can be filed by anyone fitting one of the following descriptions:

1. A blood relative in the immediate family—ie., parent, child, brother or sister.
2. The surviving spouse.
3. A beneficiary with legal proof of such beneficiary relationship.

In all except the 1900 and 1920 schedules, [12] the exact address of the

---

11. United States. National Archives, Federal Population Censuses, 1790-1890 (Washington, D.C.: National Archives, 1966), p. 145.

12. It is necessary to know only the name of the state to locate families

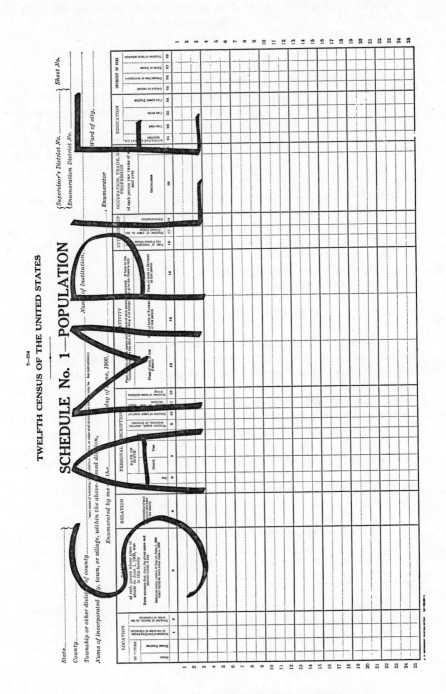

FIGURE 11——THE 1900 FEDERAL CENSUS

person's residence at the time of the census must be given. The name of the head of the household is also essential. If possible, the names of other family members should be given in order to remove all questions of identity. "Age Search" application forms (the forms required for such a search—form BC-600) and details for a search of these confidential censuses are available from the Personal Census Service Branch, Bureau of the Census, Pittsburg, Kansas 66762. Fees for such searches are subject to change but are (1972) $5 for an expedited search and $4 for a regular search in turn. [13]

As for the reasons behind these censuses being confidential (and hence so inaccessible, a letter of explanation was sent to the LDS Genealogical Society, dated January 12, 1960, by the Personal Census Service Branch which explains the government's position quite clearly. Following is a portion of that letter:

> The present official viewpoint of the Bureau is that at least an interval of 75 years or longer must elapse before consideration could be given to removing the confidential restrictions on the 1900 Census.
>
> On the occasion of each decennial census enumeration, assurances have been given that the information collected regarding any individual will not be disclosed and that it will be combined with similar information for other individuals to provide statistical totals. Presidential Proclamations have been issued prior to decennial censuses assuring the American people that the information given to the census enumerator would be confidential. Repudiation of this pledge would seriously reduce public confidence and would lead to doubts as to whether future legislation might make personal information available within a short period of time.
>
> The insurance of confidentiality of the information is an important element in securing reliable information from the public. We regularly receive information which the respondent would be unwilling to give to other agencies. If the confidence which people have in Census operations were to be shaken, the problems of getting reliable information and the cost of the censuses would be substantially increased. At the present time there are approximately 30 million persons who were living at

---

in the 1900 and 1920 censuses because they are indexed. However, the more specific your information, the better are your chances for success.

[13.] United States. Department of Commerce, "Your Name is Somewhere in the Census Records" (Form BC-628), (Pittsburg, Kan.: Bureau of the Census, 1967), pp. 2-3.

the time of the Census of 1900. Most of these people were living in the United States at that time and, presumably were included in that census. Some of them no doubt were living in institutions at the time of the census; others were living in unusual family arrangements which they may prefer not to be disclosed. The possibility that such facts would be revealed, even after a substantial period of years, might be a source of embarrassment to some families. In future enumerations, knowledge that this might occur could result in the withholding of correct information.

The 75-year limitation as expressed in this letter is a three-year extension beyond the "72-year ruling" made by the Director of the Census in a letter to the Archivist of the United States, August 26, 1952. In his letter he stated that the census schedules in the National Archives might be made available after a lapse of 72 years from the enumeration date for "legitimate historical, genealogical or other worth-while research," so long as the information was not used to the detriment of the persons therein enumerated. [14]

It is because of a provision in the Census Acts (Sect. 32 of 1909 Act; Sect. 33 of 1919 Act; and Sect. 18 of 1929 Act) authorizing the Census Director, "in his discretion, to furnish to individuals such data from the population schedules as may be desired for genealogical or other proper purposes" that the Census Bureau now furnishes information on a person's own enumeration as proof of age. A person making a personal application for information relating to himself does not constitute publication, and it has further been ruled that personal application releases the Census Bureau from the confidential restrictions of the law. [15]

Official thinking on removing the restrictions has apparently been altered since the previously-mentioned letters were written. In a letter to us dated December 14, 1970, Census Director George H. Brown stated:

> The censuses from 1900 on were conducted under laws which require that the records be maintained in a confidential status and do not provide for a lifting of the confidential restriction at any date. [Emphasis added.]

How long this will be the official position is impossible to predict, but it is not likely to change soon. Many countries have a 100-year restriction on census enumerations.

---

14. Davidson and Ashby, p. 98.
15. Ibid., pp. 96-99.

III. SPECIAL INDEXES

During the 1930's, under the auspices of the Works Projects Administration (WPA) as part of a Federal Works Project, names and other pertinent data on persons enumerated in the censuses of 1880, 1900 and 1920 were copied onto file cards. The cards for each of these censuses were alphabetically coded and filed by state under a system where all names sounding alike, regardless of spelling differences or errors (if they began with the same letter of the alphabet), would be interfiled. (This is called "Soundex indexing.") The cards contain complete family listings and families in these censuses can be more readily located than those in the other censuses.

The 1880 index (the only one of the three that has been made public) is not a complete index. It includes only those families or households with children ten years of age or below. When such a child was in a home where he was not a child of the head of the household a separate index card was made for him as well as a card for the family. This was true even when the child had the same surname as the family with whom he resided. The index is located in the National Archives, where it has been since 1964, and searches will be made in it by archives workers without charge, provided the required information is furnished on the state of residence and the family. (It is best to furnish as much information as possible for identification purposes.) If you desire a photocopy of the page of the census on which your ancestral entry is found, this will be made for a reasonable fee.

The LDS Genealogical Society also has a copy of this 1880 index on microfilm, and it can be used there in conjunction with the 1880 census films. Personal use of the index is helpful because it enables you to "look around" for your family and also to pick up other families of the same surname that may have been in the same locality or which may be of interest to you for other reasons.

To use the index you must encode the surname you wish to find and then look for the code number in the proper state, since all cards are filed by their Soundex codes under the separate states.

Should you have opportunity personally to use the index you will find that detailed instructions on how to use the Soundex system are included therewith. The system is based on the principle of assigning a numerical value to each of various consonant letters, letters having similar sounds being assigned the same code numbers. Each surname is then filed under the letter of the alphabet with which it begins and a three-digit number representing its consonant sounds. If there are not three codable letters in the name then zeros are added. If there are more than three then only the first three are considered. The initial letter of the surname is not coded and is used for filing only. As an example of how the system works let's look at the surname Greenwood which has a code of G653. The "G" comes from the initial letter, the "6" is the code number assigned to r, "5" is the code

A CARD FROM THE 1880 CENSUS INDEX

for n and "3" is the code for d. (E's, w's and o's are not codable.) Hence the number G653. Any variation of spelling or mispelling should, in theory, produce the same code number and be properly filed. However, one minor problem is that surnames like Garnett, Gerrand, Grant, Grende, Grund, Grimaud and Grimmett would also be coded as G653.

The Soundex code numbers are:

1 - b, p, f, v.
2   c, s, k, g, j, q, x, z.
3 - d, t.   .
4   l.
5   m, n.
6   r.

No code is assigned to a, e, i, o, u, y, w or h. And whenever two letters with the same code number are in immediate sequence the two are coded as one letter.

Many other projects in indexing and/or publishing census schedules have been attempted, and some of them completed, by individuals and by special-interest groups and organizations, mostly within the individual states. For example, the Illinois State Archives at Springfield has indexes to many of that state's early censuses, and the Indiana State Library at Indianapolis has card indexes to the 1820, 1830 and 1850 population schedules of that state. Connecticut has an index to its censuses, 1790-1850. (This is also on microfilm at both the National Archives and the LDS Genealogical Society.) There is also a type-script index to the 1850 population census of the Provisional State of Deseret (Utah Territory) at the LDS Genealogical Society.

Some of the federal population censuses which have been published or have published indexes include the 1830 and 1840 of Arkansas, the 1850 of California, the 1800 of Delaware, the 1830 and 1840 of Florida, the 1820 and 1840 of Georgia, the 1820 of Illinois, the 1820 of Indiana, the 1840 of Iowa, the 1800 of Kentucky (reconstructed from tax lists), the 1800 of Maryland, the 1820 and 1830 of Michigan, the 1820 and 1830 of Mississippi, the 1830 of Missouri, the 1850 of Tennessee (the National Genealogical Society project), the 1840 and 1850 of Texas and the 1800 of Vermont. Hundreds of such published census schedules and indexes for the individual counties are also known to exist.

One partial guide to these publications is Mary Marie Brewer, Index to Census Schedules in Printed Form (Huntsville, Ark.: Century Enterprises, 1969). This is a bibliography of published censuses and census indexes for the United States. Century Enterprises also issues a quarterly bulletin on published censuses in order to keep up to date.

In March 1971 the National Archives announced that it is preparing a

master list of published census indexes. An effort is also being made by
the National Archives to secure copies of all such indexes. The completion
and continuance of these projects should prove most useful to genealogists
and the work should be somewhat more complete than Miss Brewer's.*

IV. MILITARY SERVICE INFORMATION IN THE CENSUS

Two censuses—the 1840 and the 1890—included valuable information
about persons who performed military service. The 1840 census included
an enumeration of Revolutionary War pensioners of the federal government
and the 1890 census, as mentioned earlier, included a special enumeration
of Union Army veterans of the Civil War and the widows of deceased veterans.

In the 1840 census of pensioners there seems to be some omissions as
well as some men listed as pensioners who were not. The LDS Genealogical Society has prepared an index to the government publication of this pen-
sioner census, A Census of Pensioners for Revolutionary or Military Services (Washington, 1841). Both this list and the index [16] have been recently
published by the Genealogical Publishing Company in Baltimore.

The 1890 special enumeration is incomplete. Those 14 states and territories alphabetically from A through Kansas (and part of Kentucky) have
been lost. These schedules include the veteran's name (also the widow's
name if the veteran was deceased); his rank; company; regiment (or vessel);
enlistment and discharge dates; length of service in days, months and years;
post office address; nature of any disability, and other remarks. [17]

Both of these military service enumerations are useful tools which can
lead you to other genealogical records, but the 1890 veterans' schedules
have more useful features than their early cousin.

V. SPECIAL ENUMERATIONS AND STATE CENSUSES

In addition to the federal decennial censuses which we have discussed,
a few limited censuses were taken during the colonial period and several
states have taken censuses for various reasons. Also, the federal government has taken a few special censuses in some of the states between the

---

[16.] Census of Pensioners, A General Index for Revolutionary or Military Service (1840), prep. by The Genealogical Society of The Church of
Jesus Christ of Latter-day Saints, (Baltimore: Genealogical Publishing Co.,
1965).

[17.] Meredith B. Colket, Jr., and Frank E. Bridgers, Guide to Genealogical Records in the National Archives (Washington, D. C.: The National
Archives, 1964), pp. 8-9.

* See note at the end of this chapter.

regular enumerations. The exact nature and extent of the various colonial and state censuses is itself a complete study and will not be dealt with in this volume. For the present you should be aware of a little U.S. government pamphlet, State Censuses; an Annotated Bibliography of Censuses of Population Taken After the Year 1790 by States and Territories in the United States (Washington, 1948). This little booklet is now out of print but can be found in some libraries and government document depositories. Most colonial censuses have been published.

Special enumerations taken by the federal government are as follows:

1857: MINNESOTA TERRITORY. (This is in the National Archives in five printed volumes.)

1864: ARIZONA TERRITORY. (The Secretary of State in Phoenix has the originals. The National Archives has copies.)

1866: ARIZONA TERRITORY. (Photostats are in the National Archives.)

1867: ARIZONA TERRITORY (Mohave, Pima and Yuma counties). (Photostats are in the National Archives.)

1869: ARIZONA TERRITORY (Yavapai County). (Photostats are in the National Archives.)

1880: SPECIAL CENSUS OF INDIANS NOT TAXED, within the jurisdiction of the United States. The schedules show the name of the tribe, the Indian Reservation, the Agency, the nearest post office; the number in each household and a description of the dwelling; the Indian name, with its English translation, of every person in the family; his relationship to the head of the family; his marital and tribal status; his description; his occupation; health; education; ownership of property, and means of subsistence. (There are only four volumes in the National Archives:
> Vol. I and II: Indians near Fort Simcoe and at Tulalip, Washington, Territory.
> Vol. III: Indians near Fort Yates, Dakota Territory.
> Vol. IV: Indians in California.)

1885: COLORADO, DAKOTA TERRITORY, FLORIDA, NEBRASKA and NEW MEXICO TERRITORY. (This census was taken by the states and territories on a federal option and promise of partial reimbursement. The schedules are similar in form to those of 1880, and photostats of all except Dakota are in the National Archives. Nebraska and Colorado are also available there on microfilm. The Dakota census, with several counties missing, is located at Bismarck in the library of the State Historical Society of North Dakota.)

1907: OKLAHOMA (Seminole County). (This is not yet a public record.)

VI. MORTALITY SCHEDULES

Beginning with the 1850 census—the first to enumerate every person in the individual households—the persons in charge conceived the idea that a certain amount of useful vital (birth, marriage, death) information could be collected through the census medium. (See Chapter Nine.) This was the beginning of mortality schedules. A separate schedule was thus devised in compliance with an act of Congress. This schedule was for the purpose of collecting data about persons who had died during the census year. (See glossary of terms at the end of this chapter.) These mortality censuses exist for the years of 1850, 1860, 1870, 1880 and the limited census of 1885.

In 1918 and 1919 these schedules, with the exception of those for 1885, were removed from federal custody and each state was given the option of securing the ones relating to itself. Those not claimed by the states were given to the National Society of the Daughters of the American Revolution and were placed in the Society's library in Washington, D.C. Those original schedules held by the DAR are for the states of Arizona, Colorado, Georgia, Kentucky, Louisiana, Tennessee and the District of Columbia. Most, but not all, of these have been indexed by the DAR and some have been transcribed. Chart 4 shows the locations of the various mortality schedules with the exception of those connected with the limited census of 1885 (Colorado, Dakota Territory, Florida, Nebraska and New Mexico Territory). All of these 1885 schedules are in the National Archives except those for Dakota which are in the library of the North Dakota State Historical Society at Bismarck.

The mortality schedules comprise a valuable source and should not be overlooked. However, there are problems of which you should be aware. In the first place they represent the deaths in only one year out of every ten. There were four mortality schedules to cover deaths over a 31-year period (1849-1880). That would be roughly 13 per cent of the deaths, but the Public Health Service reports that the actual count fell far short of this. It estimated that in the mortality schedules for 1850, 1860 and 1870 only 60 per cent of the actual deaths within those 12-month periods were reported. [18] If our math is correct that means that less than eight per cent of the actual deaths for this 31-year period are in the mortality schedules. (These figures are probably slightly off because the 1880 schedules had a somewhat higher percentage of completeness.)

The form and format of the mortality schedules were changed from one census to the next, but basically...

[t]he information usually shown in the schedules includes the

---

18. United States. National Office of Vital Statistics, Vol. I, p. 7.

CHART 4—AVAILABILITY OF CENSUS MORTALITY SCHEDULES

STATE	YEARS	LOCATION OF ORIGINALS	LOCATION OF MICROFILM COPIES	LOCATION OF TYPESCRIPT COPIES	LOCATION OF INDEXES
Alabama	1850-1860-1870-1880	Department of Archives and History, Montgomery			
Arizona	1870 (Mohave Co. thru Yuma Co.)	NSDAR Library	NSDAR Library, National Archives		
	1880	NSDAR Library	NSDAR Library, National Archives		NSDAR Library
Arkansas	1850-1860-1870-1880	University of Arkansas, Fayetteville, Ark.	NSDAR Library, National Archives	(1850 is published)	
	1850-1860		Secretary of State, Little Rock, Ark.		
California	1850-1860	California State Library, Sacramento, Calif.			NSDAR Library
	1870	California State Library, Sacramento, Calif.		NSDAR Library	NSDAR Library
Colorado	1870-1880	NSDAR Library	NSDAR Library, National Archives		
Connecticut	1850-1860-1870-1880	Connecticut State Library, Hartford, Conn.	LDS Genealogical Society		
Delaware	1850-1860-1870-1880	Public Archives Comm., Hall of Records, Dover			
District of Columbia	1850-1860-1870-1880	NSDAR Library	NSDAR Library, National Archives		NSDAR Library
Florida	1850-1860-1870-1880	Dept. of Agriculture, Tallahassee, Fla. (?)			
Georgia	1850-1860-1870	NSDAR Library	NSDAR Library, LDS Genealogical Society, National Archives		NSDAR Library, LDS Genealogical Society
	1880	NSDAR Library	NSDAR Library, LDS Genealogical Society, National Archives	LDS Genealogical Society	NSDAR Library, LDS Genealogical Society
Idaho	1870-880	Idaho State Library, Boise, Idaho			
Illinois	1850-1860-1870-1880	Illinois State Archives, Springfield, Ill.			

STATE	YEARS	LOCATION OF ORIGINALS	LOCATION OF MICROFILM COPIES	LOCATION OF TYPESCRIPT COPIES	LOCATION OF INDEXES
Indiana	1850-1860-1870-1880	Indiana State Library, Indianapolis, Ind.		NSDAR Library (Jefferson Co. only)	NSDAR Library (Jefferson Co. only)
Iowa	1850-1860-1870-1880	Iowa State Historical Soc., Iowa City, Iowa			
Kansas	1860	Kansas State Historical Society, Topeka, Kan.		NSDAR Library	
	1870-1880	Kansas State Historical Society, Topeka, Kan.	NSDAR Library		
Kentucky	1850	NSDAR Library (Pendleton thru Woodford counties)	NSDAR Library National Archives		NSDAR Library LDS Genealogical Society
	1860-1870	NSDAR Library	NSDAR Library National Archives	NSDAR Library	NSDAR Library LDS Genealogical Society
	1880	NSDAR Library	NSDAR Library National Archives	NSDAR Library LDS Genealogical Society	NSDAR Library LDS Genealogical Society
Louisiana	1850-1860-1870	NSDAR Library	NSDAR Library National Archives		NSDAR Library LDS Genealogical Society
	1880	NSDAR Library	NSDAR Library National Archives		NSDAR Library
Maine	1850-1860-1870	Office of Vital Statistics, Dept. of Health and Welfare, Augusta, Me.	LDS Genealogical Society		
	1880	Office of Vital Statistics, Dept. of Health and Welfare, Augusta, Me.			
Maryland	1850-1860-1870-1880	Maryland State Library, Annapolis, Md. (?)			
Massachusetts	1850	State Archives Boston, Mass.	National Archives	NSDAR Library	NSDAR Library
	1860-1870	State Archives Boston, Mass.	National Archives		
	1880	State Archives Boston, Mass.			
Michigan	1850	Michigan Historical Comm. Lansing, Mich.	NSDAR Library	NSDAR Library	NSDAR Library
	1860-1870-1880	Michigan Historical Comm. Lansing, Mich.	NSDAR Library		

STATE	YEARS	LOCATION OF ORIGINALS	LOCATION OF MICROFILM COPIES	LOCATION OF TYPESCRIPT COPIES	LOCATION OF INDEXES
Minnesota	1850-1860-1870	Minnesota State Library, St. Paul, Minn.	National Archives (1870 only)	NSDAR Library LDS Genealogical Society	
	1880	Minnesota State Library, St. Paul, Minn. (?)			
Mississippi	1850-1860-1870-1880	Department of Archives and History, Jackson			
Missouri	1850-1860	Missouri State Historical Society, St. Louis, Mo.		NSDAR Library	NSDAR Library
	1870-1880	Missouri State Historical Society, St. Louis, Mo.			
Montana	1870-1880	Montana State Historical Society, Helena, Mont.	National Archives		
Nebraska	1860-1870-1880	Nebraska State Historical Society, Lincoln, Neb.			
Nevada	1860 1880	Nevada State Historical Society, Reno, Nev.			
	1870	Nevada State Historical Society, Reno, Nev.		NSDAR Library	NSDAR Library
New Hampshire	1850-1860-1870-1880	New Hampshire State Library, Concord, N.H.	LDS Genealogical Society		
New Jersey	1850-1860-1870-1880	New Jersey State Library, Archives and History Bureau, Trenton, N.J.	NSDAR Library		
New Mexico	1850-1860-1870	New Mexico State Historical Society, Santa Fe, N.M. (?)			
New York	1850	New York State Library, Albany, N.Y.		NSDAR Library (City of Buffalo only)	NSDAR Library (City of Buffalo only)
	1860-1870-1880	New York State Library, Albany, N.Y.			
North Carolina	1850-1860-1870-1880	North Carolina State Department of Archives and History, Raleigh, N.C.	National Archives		

STATE	YEARS	LOCATION OF ORIGINALS	LOCATION OF MICROFILM COPIES	LOCATION OF TYPESCRIPT COPIES	LOCATION OF INDEXES
North Dakota	1860-1870	North Dakota State Historical Society, Bismarck, N.D. (?)			
	1880	North Dakota State Historical Society, Bismarck, N.D. (?)		LDS Genealogical Society	
Ohio	1850-1860 1880	Ohio State Historical Society, Columbus, O.			
Oregon	1850-1860-1870-1880	Oregon State Archives, Salem, Oregon			
Pennsylvania	1850-1860-1870-1880	Pennsylvania State Library, Harrisburg, Pa.		NSDAR Library (Mifflin Co. only)	NSDAR Library (Mifflin Co. only)
Rhode Island	1850	Rhode Island State Library, Providence, R.I.			
	1860-1870-1880	Rhode Island State Library, Providence, R.I.		NSDAR Library	NSDAR Library
South Carolina	1850-1860-1870-1880	South Carolina Department of Archives and History, Columbia, S.C.	NSDAR Library National Archives		
South Dakota	1860-1870	South Dakota State Historical Society, Pierre, S.D. (?)			
	1880	South Dakota State Historical Society, Pierre, S.D. (?)		LDS Genealogical Society	
Tennessee	1850-1860	NSDAR Library	NSDAR Library National Archives	LDS Genealogical Society	NSDAR Library
	1880	NSDAR Library	NSDAR Library National Archives		
Texas	1850-1860-1870-1880	Archives Division, Texas State Library, Austin, Texas	National Archives		
Utah	1850-1860 1880	(?)	National Archives		
	1870	Texas State Library, Austin, Texas	National Archives		

STATE	YEARS	LOCATION OF ORIGINALS	LOCATION OF MICROFILM COPIES	LOCATION OF TYPESCRIPT COPIES	LOCATION OF INDEXES
Vermont	1850-1860	Vermont State Library, Montpelier, Vt.		NSDAR Library	NSDAR Library
	1870	Texas State Library, Austin, Texas	Vermont State Library		
	1880	Vermont State Library, Montpelier, Vt.	National Archives		
Virginia	1850 1880	Virginia State Library, Richmond, Va. (?)			
	1860	Duke University, Durham, N.C.	National Archives		
	1870	Virginia State Library, Richmond, Va. (?)	LDS Genealogical Society		
Washington	1860-1870-1880	Washington State Library, Olympia, Wash.		NSDAR Library	NSDAR Library
West Virginia	1860-1870-1880	State Department of Archives and History, Charleston, W. Va.			
Wisconsin	1850-1860-1870	Wisconsin State Historical Society, Madison, Wis.		NSDAR Library	
	1880	Wisconsin State Historical Society, Madison, Wis.			
Wyoming	1870-1880	State Law Library, Cheyenne, Wyo. (?)		NSDAR Library	

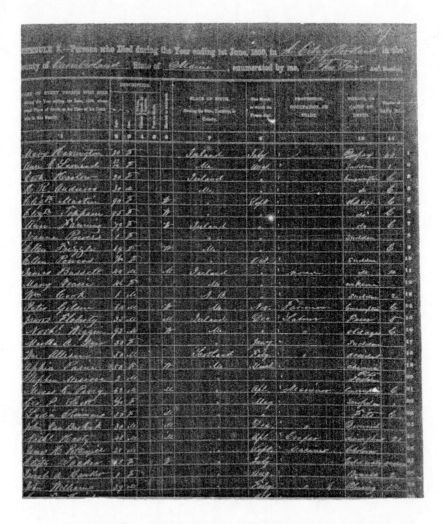

A PAGE FROM THE 1850 MORTALITY SCHEDULE, STATE OF MAINE

name of the person, his age, sex, state of birth, month of death and cause of death. The 1880 [and 1885] Mortality Schedules include also the state of birth of each parent of the deceased person, but the names of the parents are not given. The schedules are set up by county, but, where indexed, are indexed by the state as a whole. [19]

If you desire to use the schedules in the DAR library you should know that library personnel do not do genealogical research for patrons. Also, there are no facilities at the library for reproducing either the original schedules or the microfilm copies. For photocopies of entries in the mortality schedules write to the National Archives and Records Service, Washington, D. C. 20408, or visit or write other depositories as indicated in Chart 4. The DAR library is open to public use, however, so if you cannot visit there personally, your agent will be welcome.

It is interesting to note that the National Archives which once "disposed of" the mortality schedules is once again gathering copies to add to its collections.

VII. GLOSSARY OF CENSUS TERMS

The next chapter is devoted exclusively to helping you use the census; so, before we embark on that adventure, let's take a minute to familiarize you with some of the common census terms. The following list is adapted from a list published in the previously-cited inventory of the records of the Census Bureau. We think it will add to your understanding of census records. Some of these terms we have already used. [20]

ABSTRACT: The summary or aggregate of census results submitted by the assistant to the marshal or by the marshal to Washington.
ASSISTANT: The local census taker, 1790-1870.
CENSUS BUREAU: The Census Office, established 1902.
CENSUS DAY: The day set by law for the decennial enumeration to begin and the day for which certain census statistics were taken. The census days were as follows:
    1st - 4th Censuses, 1790-1820   First Monday in Aug.
    5th - 12th Censuses, 1830-1900   June 1.
    13th Census, 1910   April 15.

---

[19] "Federal Mortality Schedules in the NSDAR Library, Washington, D. C." (unpublished instruction sheet from NSDAR, 1967).

[20] Davidson and Ashby, pp. 139-141.

14th Census, 1920   January 1.
15th - 19th Censuses, 1930-1970   April 1.

CENSUS OFFICE: The temporary office set up for each decennial census before the permanent office, the Census Bureau, was established in 1902.

CENSUS YEAR: The 12-month period immediately preceding the census day for which certain census inquiries are made. This term was first used in the 7th census act (1850).

CIVIL DIVISION: An area over which a state or local government has jurisdiction and which, beginning with the 10th census (1880), was one of the bases for establishing enumerators' subdivisions.

DECENNIAL CENSUS: The population enumeration required by the Constitution to be taken every 10 years beginning in 1790.

DISTRICT: The enumeration area, often coterminous with a state or territory, over which a U.S. Marshal had jurisdiction, 1790-1870; also the smaller area assigned to a supervisor of the census beginning in 1880.

DIVISION: That portion of a district that was assigned to an assistant for taking the censuses, 1790-1840.

ENUMERATION: The population census required by the Constitution.

FAMILY SCHEDULE: The population schedules used only in 1890.

INTERDECENNIAL PERIOD: The time between decennial censuses.

MARSHAL: The judicial official who supervised the taking of the census in his judicial district, 1790-1870.

RECORDS: The term often used by the Census Office and the Census Bureau for all the census documentation except original schedules and published reports.

REGISTRATION AREA: A city in which an official registration of deaths or other vital statistics is maintained. Beginning with the 10th (1880) census, the Superintendent of the Census was authorized to obtain from such official records the statistics so maintained.

REPORTS: The term used for published census results.

RETURNS: A term often used interchangeably with schedules or completed questionnaires. Apparently the word returns, as used in the first census act, was interpreted by some assistants to mean abstracts or totals obtained from the schedules and by other assistants to mean the individual schedules themselves.

SCHEDULE: A completed census questionnaire.

SCHEDULE FORM: A blank census questionnaire.

SUBDIVISION: An enumeration area the boundaries of which are the limits of known civil divisions or are natural boundaries. The term was first used in the 7th (1850) census act.

NOTE: In 1972 the Gendex Corporation of Salt Lake City published The Census Compendium. This 420-page volume is a directory of the location of all known censuses (or substitutes) and census indexes. The volume is updated with quarterly supplements.

CHAPTER ELEVEN

USING CENSUS RETURNS

We have learned from experience that a student can memorize all of the essential data about a genealogical source but still not know how to use it. It is with that thought in mind that this chapter has been prepared. Our sole purpose here is to help you bridge the gap between theory and practice. In seeking this objective we will discuss the various benefits of census records as a genealogical source as well as the limitations. We will also provide examples of how the census schedules are used to solve some specific types of problems.

I. BENEFITS AND USES

A. 1790

The greatest benefit to the user of the 1790 census schedules is the fact that they are published and completely indexed. For example, if you know that your ancestor lived somewhere in Pennsylvania and was in the proper age range to be the head of a family at the time of this census, by checking the index to the Pennsylvania census you might discover his county of residence. Even if your ancestor's name proved to be common and you find eight or ten with the same name in various counties the census is still useful in that it at least limits the search to those few counties. Otherwise the entire 21 counties of 1790 Pennsylvania might need to be considered.

If your surname is at all common (at least 100 persons of that surname in the entire 1790 census) the geographic distribution of all persons of that surname, by state, is given in a special publication. [1]

The 1790 census has proven to be an excellent "finding tool." Even those published tax lists which have replaced the lost schedules in Delaware, Virginia, Kentucky (then part of Virginia), Georgia and the three missing

---

1. United States. Census Bureau, A Century of Population Growth From the First Census of the United States to the Twelfth, 1790-1900, (1909) (Baltimore: Genealogical Publishing Co., 1967 reprint).

counties of North Carolina (Caswell, Granville and Orange) are most useful in this function.

B. 1800-1840

Since the census schedules after 1790 are not generally indexed, they do not serve quite the same function—they cannot ordinarily be considered finding tools. It is possible to read all the census schedules within a state as a means of locating a family, but this action is usually taken as a last resort because of the mammoth size of such a task, especially in the more populous states. You must usually know the county of your ancestor's residence in order to locate him.

Many persons feel that there is little value in using the schedules before complete families were enumerated beginning in 1850. "Even after I find my family," they ask, "what do I have?" The truth is that if you can trace a family through these early censuses you can learn quite a bit. You will find some useful intelligence about movements in and out of an area, of deaths, of younger members of the family coming of age and becoming themselves heads of families. Nevertheless, you can get this information from the censuses only if you search all pertinent available schedules and if you search for all persons of your surname of interest. Information thus secured can also be a guide to the existence of other useful records relating to your family such as wills, marriage records, deeds, etc.

C. 1850-1870

The great value of these schedules lies in the fact that they enumerate complete households. The relationships which are implied between the members of these households provide some of the best circumstantial evidence available for the eventual proving of family connections. You cannot always safely assume what the relationship is between two persons in the same house, but at least you do have some basic information with which to work. An elderly person living with a family may prove to be a parent of either the husband or the wife. (The person's surname would often indicate which.)

Just as with the earlier censuses, if you search all the schedules pertinent to your problem and extract information for all persons of your surname(s) you can better understand the family, its movements, marriages, deaths, etc., as well as find clues to suggest the use of other records. It is essential that you copy all information relating to everyone of the surname into your research notes. This includes, also, complete families even when there is only one person of your surname in the household. Though you may not see the necessity for this at the time, we can promise that it is important. Nearly every genealogist has seen cases where important clues and even family connections have been passed over unnoticed when this has been neglected.

The movements of a family from one area to another and the length of time the family has lived in a certain locality can often be told from studying census enumerations. The states of birth as given for the children in the household are most helpful in this regard. Whether you can expect to find land deeds for a family can often be told by whether the census lists the person as an owner of real estate. (The censuses tell the value of real estate owned.) The value of real estate (and also of personal property in the 1860 and 1870 schedules) can be an indication of the social prestige and economic status of the family. Also, those who had extensive possessions were more likely to leave wills behind at their deaths and to be written of in local histories. And you can also tell whether children attended school and whether members of the family could read and write.

Since very few of them are indexed these censuses are definitely not general finding tools, but the fact that they are family-oriented—just as is genealogy—makes them invaluable.

D. 1880

The 1880 census is listed in a category by itself because it has some rather distinct differences from, and advantages over, its older brothers. However, everything we have said about using the earlier schedules also applies to the use of this one. The advantages (or differences) are as follows:

1. The partial index to this census, as discussed in Chapter Ten, makes it a useful finding tool.

2. The fact that the relationship of every person to the head of the family in which he lives is told makes family information much more authoritative than does the circumstantial evidence found in the households of the 1850, 1860 and 1870 schedules.

3. Alleged states (or countries) of birth for each person's father and mother are stated in this census.

And though these advantages are significant, to each of them we add a word of caution: They can be deceptive and work to your disadvantage if not properly understood. Consider:

1. The index is only a partial one, including only families with children ten years of age and younger.

2. The relationships given are to the head of the household only and not to other members of the household. There is no indication as to whether the head of the house has been married more than once and

whether his children are also the wife's children.

3. The states of birth which are listed for fathers and mothers are not necessarily correct. Some persons didn't even manage to get their own states of birth recorded correctly.

Sometimes the states of birth given for a child's parents can help you see if his father has been married more than once and which of his children belong to which marriage. For example, if the state of birth of the child's mother is different than the state of birth listed for the wife on that census then you have an obvious clue to the reality of another marriage. But, of course, this certainly is not a fool-proof formula. If a man had more than one wife and they were both (or all) born in the same state then there would be no clue.

II. LIMITATIONS OF THE CENSUS AS A GENEALOGICAL SOURCE

As with most records, many weaknesses in the censuses are self-evident. We have already discussed some of these but a listing and some further categorizing may prove useful.

A. LIMITATION OF TIME

The fact that there was no general census taken of the families in America until 1790 is a limiting factor. Other records must be used for the colonial periods. Also, in connection with this problem, we might mention the nature of census development—the earlier schedules do not contain nearly as much genealogical data as do the later schedules.

B. INCOMPLETENESS

At the taking of every American census there have been families missed due to a built-in "error factor"—the length of time allowed for the taking thereof. The act providing for the 1790 census allowed nine months for the marshals to complete their enumeration. This same length of time was allowed for all censuses until 1850 when the time was cut to five months. In 1870 it was reduced to one month. Any time an enumeration goes on over a period of time—even if it is only two or three days—it becomes more or less inaccurate for various reasons. Perhaps the most serious problem is that in a situation like that in early America, where the population was so very mobile, some families were missed completely and others were enumerated twice.

Also, the U.S. has never made use of "prior schedules," that is schedules to be left at the residence in advance of the enumeration to be completed by the head of the family. This is a practice used in nearly every European country and may or may not add to the validity of the census results, but they make it possible to take the entire census in a very short period of time (even one day). The 1970 U.S. census utilized a form which was mailed to families but this was the first move in that direction.

Another problem is that some families, especially in low-class, multiple-dwelling units (those made from large, old single-family units), are inadvertently bypassed because the enumerator (or the assistant) is not aware of their existence. And there are others missed also. Every genealogist has searched and searched for a family that "should have been there" —it was there in both earlier and later enumerations—but it was not to be found.

Under incompleteness we ought also to include those censuses for entire counties and even entire states which have been lost or destroyed.

C. INDIFFERENT ENUMERATOR (OR ASSISTANT)

In some instances incompleteness could be listed under this heading, but the census can be incomplete in spite of a conscientious census taker, so we give him the benefit of the doubt. However, there have been census takers who took the job only for what they could get out of it or because it was assigned to them by legislative act. Many of these persons were not well qualified and did not satisfactorily fulfill their obligations. Many of our census schedules reflect this because the instructions which the census takers received (or should have received) were not followed.

Some schedules list persons in a family by initials only. A few schedules list no places of birth. Sometimes families were not home when the census taker made his visit and neighbors were asked to give the information, or if the assistant was personally acquainted with the family he would complete the schedules to the best of his own knowledge. There were also times when young children in the family provided the "facts" for the census enumeration if no one else was at home.

Some census takers padded the population. Apparently reimbursed in proportion to the number of families enumerated, they listed many families twice in different parts of their schedules, sometimes varying the information slightly. Every genealogist has seen this type of double enumeration.

Before we go on, let us also say that most of the persons commissioned to take the census did a good job and the censuses they took represent their best and most conscientious efforts. Some were even over zealous, going well beyond the requirements made of them. A good case in point is provided by those census takers who listed counties of birth for all persons and not just states and countries.

D. INCORRECT INFORMATION GIVEN BY FAMILY MEMBERS

Often incorrect data, which resulted in inconsistencies in the records, were given to the assistants and enumerators by members of the family. Anyone who has read many censuses is aware of this problem. It manifests itself in almost any family that is traced through all available censuses. Inconsistent ages illustrate the problem best but names and places of birth also have some tendency to change from one census to the next. This is another reason why you should never stop after searching just one census, even though you think the family is complete. With this kind of problem the effect is the same whether the error was intentional or not.

E. LEGIBILITY

Too often the census schedules are difficult to read, and there are many reasons for this. Careless handwriting, unfamiliar abbreviations, the workings of time on poor quality inks—these are all familiar problems. The 1880 census, taken on such poor quality paper that it has not been able to withstand the ravages of time at all, was one of the first withdrawn from public use. [The originals are now in various non-federal depositories throughout the country as indicated on pages 130 and 131 of Katherine H. Davidson and Charlotte M. Ashby, Preliminary Inventory of the Records of the Bureau of the Census (Washington, D.C.: The National Archives, 1964).]

There are additional problems in reading microfilmed copies of the censuses. On some the photography was poor—under-exposure, over-exposure, etc. Others present special photography problems: Some of the writing was faded and simply did not photograph well. Another problem was found in the photographing of double-pages on single frames—since one page often stood higher than another it was impossible to get both into proper focus except near the center of the large bound volumes. This latter problem has now been solved, however, in the refilming of the 1850, 1860 and 1870 censuses on single-page frames by the National Archives. The difference is unbelievable! They are much more readable, not alone because everything is in focus, but also because the image is larger and the photography is better. The 1880 census was initially microfilmed on single-page frames.

Another problem with microfilms is that the filmer could inadvertently turn two pages at once. This has been known to happen so you should be alert to the possibility.

F. YOU MUST KNOW THE PLACE OF RESIDENCE

Because of lack of indexes it is generally necessary to know at least the county in which a family lived in order to find it in the census. This problem is especially acute in large cities where the census may include many volumes. In this case it is almost essential that you know the ward (or other geographic division) in which your family lived in order to complete a satisfactory search. Without this information a simple census search may take many days.

III. WHEN SHOULD THE CENSUS BE SEARCHED?

As we have said before, there is no immutable rule about sequence of searches. It all depends on the nature of the individual problem and your analysis thereof. The census schedules must always be searched in those problems which fall into the proper time periods, whether early or late.

By its very nature a census search will usually be one of the first searches you will need to make on a pedigree problem. And because of this it will frequently be necessary for you to read the same census again at a later date when further research has revealed other clues, such as the maiden surnames on female lines, etc. You should never hesitate to re-read a census if the need is indicated, but, on the other hand, you should be absolutely certain you are getting all you can on your first time through—not to do so is a very serious (and common) error.

A good example of what not to do is provided by the man who reads a census for one surname on his pedigree and then looks closely at his pedigree only to discover that he had two more lines in that same locality at the same time for which he ought to have been searching. There is no excuse for this kind of double-reading. You can look for two or three surnames in a census as easily as you can look for one. (However, if you make this mistake, do not hesitate to do what needs to be done—go ahead and read the census again. You probably will not make that same error again for a while.)

IV. EXAMPLES OF CENSUS USE

A. EXAMPLE NO. 1 (Note that this is not an actual case but is presented here only for purposes of illustration.)

Frank James Shears was, according to family records, born in Missouri about 1857. This is all we know of him until his marriage. He died in Arkansas in 1920. We do not know the names of his parents or anything about them, and we know nothing of any brothers and sisters.

SOLUTION: This is a problem where the census cannot be searched first. It is not a finding tool and, unless we can determine a specific place in Missouri there is little that can be done there. In this case, however, we would write to the State Bureau of Vital Statistics, State Health Department, Little Rock, Arkansas 72201, for the death certificate of Frank James Shears. This certificate should tell us the date and place of his birth and the names of his parents. (All of these data would be secondary evidence because of the time element.)

The death certificate (giving his death as December 2, 1920, at Rumly, Searcy County, Arkansas) is secured. It states as follows:

Date of birth:	April 15, 1856
State of birth:	Missouri
Father's full name:	Findley Shears
Mother's maiden name:	Unknown

This information helps but is not sufficient yet. An obituary printed in the local newspaper, however, shows that Frank J. Shears was born in Fulton, Missouri.

We now have sufficient data so that we can search the 1860 census schedule as soon as we learn from our gazetteer that Fulton, Missouri, is in Callaway County (founded in 1820). Even if the death certificate had not given his father's name this census search could still be made. In the search we would just look for all families named Shears (or Sheers, or Shares, etc.), but we do this anyway. It does help, however, if we know his father's name in case we find more than one child named Frank.

There are a number of places where we could find the 1860 census of Callaway County. In addition to some that we mentioned in the last chapter there are probably several libraries in the state of Missouri that have copies of Missouri censuses.

The 1860 census of Callaway County, Missouri, is searched and, among the various families found, was the following:

Findlay Sheers	28	Wagon maker	born Ky
Hulda "	29	housewife	" Mo
William "	6		" "
Frank "	4		" "
Alice A. "	2		" "
Jno F. "	8/12		" "

These results, of course, suggest the need for other censuses to be searched. Undoubtedly this couple was young enough to have more children, which indicates the necessity for searching both the 1870 and 1880 schedules if the family did not move away in the intervening years. If it did move it is important that its destination be determined and those censuses be searched.

A search of the 1850 census is also indicated by the results of our 1860 search. Since the eldest child of this couple is only six years old it is quite likely that Findlay and Hulda were not married until after 1850 and should hence be in the households of their parents in the 1850 census. However, we do not know Hulda's maiden surname so the search for her will have to wait. This is one of those situations where a later, second search of the census will be necessary after we have gathered more information.

The 1850 census of Callaway County, Missouri, revealed the following family:

Francis Sheers		48	farmer	born	Ky
Sarah	"	41		"	"
Findlay	"	17	farm hand	"	"
Sarah	"	14		"	"
William	"	12		"	Mo
Martha	"	7		"	"
Frank	"	5		"	"
Bethiah	"	3		"	"

[This family was also found in the 1860 census, but we didn't know who they were then as Findlay was not in the household. It's a good thing we copied all families of the surname.]

This 1850 census was very useful. It told a great deal about the "Sheers" family, including the approximate time of their migration from Kentucky to Missouri. As a result, the 1840 census of Callaway County was searched and also showed the Francis Shears family:

Francis Shears	1 male 30-40	1 female 30-40
	1 male 5-10	1 female 5-10
	2 males under 5	1 female under 5

Comparing these two censuses (the 1840 and the 1850) we see that there may be things that the 1850 census does not reveal about this family:

1. Where is the female in the 1850 census who was between 5 and 10 in the 1840 census? Did she die? Did she marry? Or wasn't she a member of the family? We cannot say at this point.

2. Where is the other male in the 1850 census who was under 5 in 1840? William is the only one in 1850 who would have been in that age group.

3. We might also ask about the large gap between the ages of William (12) and Martha (7) in the 1850 census. This suggests three possibilities:

a. One or more children may have died that were born during this period, perhaps the one unaccounted-for male from the 1840 census.

b. Francis Shears' wife may have died during this period of years and he did not remarry for three or four years, and hence had no children then. (She would have had to die following the 1840 census.) If this were the case, Sarah (in the 1850 census) would not be the mother of our Findlay Shears.

    c. There may have been no children born to the couple during this period. That wouldn't be too strange.

There is nothing to prove any of these possibilities now so we see that though the census is invaluable in supplying evidence to help us solve our problems, it does not provide all of the evidence we need. We must have further evidence from other sources.

B. EXAMPLE NO. 2

Family tradition indicates that the ancestor sought—the father of William Jasper Kerr—is named Joseph Kerr. William Jasper (born 1781) died on January 10, 1846, in Jefferson County, Iowa. His wife, Jemima, died there in 1842. William Jasper Kerr was supposedly born in North Carolina but tradition has it that he lived in Tennessee before coming to Iowa.

In a history of Jefferson County, Iowa, we read of one John Workman (born 1819 in Kentucky), an early resident of Jefferson County, who married in 1840 an Amanda J. Kerr, born in White County, Tennessee, on October 14, 1825. According to family records this Amanda J. was a daughter of William Jasper Kerr. This gave us a place to look in Tennessee.

The first step was to search and compare censuses in Jefferson County, Iowa, with those of White County, Tennessee, to see if we could find any correlation. The results of that search were as follows:

WHITE COUNTY, TENNESSEE—1820

Joseph Carr	3 males under 10	2 females 16-26
	1 male 26-45	

William Kerr	2 males under 10	1 female 26-45
	1 male 26-45	

(William Jasper would have been 39.)

WHITE COUNTY, TENNESSEE—1830

Joseph Kerr, Jr.	2 males 10-15	1 female 5-10
	1 male 20-30	1 female 15-20
	2 males 30-40	1 female 30-40
	1 male 50-60	

William Kerr	1 male 5-10	3 females under 5
	1 male 30-40	1 female 20-30
	1 male 50-60	

William Kerr, Sr. 2 males under 5   1 female under 5
                  1 male 5-10   1 female 10-15
                  1 male 10-15   1 female 15-20
                  1 male 15-20   1 female 40-50
                  1 male 40-50
                  1 male 60-70

(William Jasper would have been 49. William Kerr, Sr., is the only one with a male that age in his household. The older man living there might be either a father or father-in-law.)

WHITE COUNTY, TENNESSEE—1840

Levi J. Kerr   2 males under 5   1 female 15-20
                  1 male 15-20
                  1 male 20-30

William Kerr   3 males under 5   No females
                  1 male 5-10
                  1 male 15-20
                  1 male 40-50
                  1 male 60-70

(William Jasper would have been 59. The William who fits seems to be gone.)

JEFFERSON COUNTY, IOWA---1840 (This is the first census of the county as the county was created in 1839 from Indian lands.)

Henry Kuerr (?)   2 males 5-10   2 females under 5
                  2 males 20-30   2 females 20-30

William Kerr   1 male 5-10   1 female 5-10
                  2 males 10-15   1 female 10-15
                  1 male 15-20   1 female 20-30
                  1 male 20-30   1 female 40-50
                  1 male 50-60

(As we said, William Jasper would have been 59, and if you carefully compare this family with the family of William Kerr, Sr., in the 1830 census of White County, Tennessee, you will note a close correlation.)

Archibald Kerr   1 male 20-30   1 female under 5
                                       1 female 20-30

(William Jasper had a son Archibald whom this fits.)

On the basis of these censuses the move seems likely and this could be the family we seek; however, nothing can be proven by these censuses alone; additional evidence is needed.

Further evidence needed to help solve the original problem was found in a Revolutionary War pension file for a veteran (a spy) named Joseph Kerr who applied for and received a pension while living in White County, Tennessee, in 1833. He was born in 1760 in Chester County, Pennsylvania, (according to his application) and came to North Carolina with his parents as a child. It was in North Carolina that he served in the War. This might well be the man we seek but more evidence is needed to prove it. Perhaps he is the older man in William Kerr, Sr.'s, household in the 1830 census of White County.

These early censuses, even though they do not list names of individual family members, have provided some valuable evidence. This evidence should be considered carefully along with the other facts, but it cannot stand alone. It is insufficient to establish proof by itself.

C. EXAMPLE NO. 3

George Andrew Crossman and his wife, Lucy, came to the little mining town of Park City, Utah, in the 1880's; here they resided as faithful members of the Roman Catholic Church, prospered, saw children grow up and marry, and then they died. They came from somewhere in New York State —just where was not certain, though in more recent years the children consistently said it was "Haminville" (or "Hammondville," etc.). Though this seemed like good information, a definite problem arose when we could not identify such a place in New York State though we used supposedly-complete gazetteers of that state, even those published during the proper period of time. This made it impossible to trace the family in earlier periods because New York is quite a big place.

Since the Crossman family did not migrate to Utah until the 1880's and the children were quite young at the time, the answer to locating them in New York obviously lay in the use of the partial index to the 1880 census. The surname Crossman was encoded in accordance with the Soundex formula (see Chapter Ten) as C625 and was easily located in the New York index—not at any place the name of which even remotely resembled "Haminville"—but at Crown Point in Essex County (on lower Lake Champlain). The family was enumerated as follows:

Crossman,	George A.		27	Miner	born	N. Y.
"	Lucy E.	(wife)	21	Keeping house	"	"
"	Emma E.	(dau)	4		"	"
"	Cora A.	(dau)	3		"	"
"	Henry G.	(son)	1		"	"
Bennett,	Newell R.	(boarder)	21	Laborer	"	"

(The family was located on p. 4, Supervisor's District 7, Enumeration District 44, and we have omitted the information on the birth places of parents.)

Isn't this an easy way to solve an otherwise-difficult problem?

V. CONCLUSION

The census schedules can help us solve many genealogical problems, but they can also present problems if they are not properly used and interpreted.   They must be read scrupulously—if you overlook or misread important data the results may be disastrous and far-reaching because everyone will assume that you did a good job. No one ever really checks you out. In the name of science perhaps we should all be checked on more often than we are—and this ought especially to include checking on ourselves. We like the motto of the Royal Society of London: "Nullus in verba: we take no man's word for anything."

A guide to help minimize the human-error factor is found in the following rules for getting the most information out of the census schedules. These rules, written by E. Kay Kirkham, summarize (in part) our message in the last two chapters:

1. Note carefully the headings of the columns as given in the respective census enumerations.

2. A precaution should be given to watch for misinterpretation of the handwriting. Study it. Visualize the name that you are looking for in the handwriting as used. Watch for the unusual spellings that the name might have. It is best to watch for both the given name as well as the surname. Be thorough; every name listed should be deciphered, if necessary, at least enough so that you know it is not the name that you are looking for.

3. In searching for given names, and rarely surnames, watch carefully for abbreviations. Ex: X^r (Christopher), Eben^r, Danl, Saml, Nathl, Elea^r, Benj^m, Thos, etc.

4. Note carefully that it is very rare that every line on a page will not be used for the enumeration and a new locality is started at the top of a new page. It is very common to split the listings of a family between the bottom of one page and the top of the next without a second repetion of the family surname. The very name that you are looking for may be on the last line of a page. For thorough searching, this is very important.

5. A township census may be divided and not necessarily be in sequence in the enumeration. Incorporated cities will often be enumerated separately from township.

6. The utility of county histories and township maps cannot

be .. [overestimated] in studying a census report. It will save much time to know the township in which a city is found in order to eliminate the necessity of a complete county search of the census, or to concentrate on a search in a given part of a county.

7. Often a helpful analysis can be made by noting the birthpla es for the children of a family as well as the parents. By this means, with the children, an approximated date can be arrived at as to when the family went from one state to another or from a foreign country to the United States.

8. Don't fail to watch for the occurrence of the surname that you are looking for as being listed with another "head of family." Children are often located in this manner and quite often aged parents are listed with the family of a son-in-law or widowed daughter-in-law.

9. In a few eastern states some of the census reports before 1850 are arranged alphabetically. In searching these records watch carefully under the various spellings of the surname.

10. Remember that places named in the various census reports are the contemporary place-names for that census year. Period maps and county histories should be consulted for necessary details.

11. In the later census enumerations where the estate value is given, this may well be used as an indication that there might be a recorded will in the county seat for that particular person. This can be said with the assumption that the larger estates would likely be probated by the county courts.

12. In all cases of census searching the information in all columns should be entered in the notes. If for no other reason, a careful analysis of your problem may be assisted by such information at a later date. [2]

You must use the census returns and use them correctly. They are very important to your research.

---

[2] E. Kay Kirkham, The ABC's of American Genealogical Research (Salt Lake City: Deseret Book Co., 1955), pp. 65-68. By permission.

CHAPTER TWELVE

UNDERSTANDING PROBATE RECORDS
AND BASIC LEGAL TERMINOLOGY

I. DEFINITION AND BACKGROUND OF PROBATE RECORDS

All records which relate to the disposition of an estate after its owner's death are called probate records. These are many and varied in both content and value but, basically, they fall into two main classes:

    TESTATE
    INTESTATE

If a person died leaving a valid will we say he died <u>testate</u>, if not he died <u>intestate</u>. In most localities in America these records comprise, as a group, one of the most useful genealogical resources available.

Historically there has never been a time in America when men did not make wills or when the estates of those who failed to do so were not handled by a court, appointed for that purpose, to see that the legal heirs became the heirs in fact. In those colonies set up by British grant or dominion, English law and custom were meticulously followed. Thus the right of probate was never challenged.

Statutory probate law in America has developed as a state, rather than a federal, function; and laws do differ somewhat from one state to another. In general, however, especially so far as wills are concerned, anyone was free to make a will if he was of sound mind, of legal age and free from restraint. And, of course, anyone was free not to make a will and die intestate if he chose to do so.

II. CONTENT AND GENEALOGICAL VALUE

Some persons have died leaving no property of value and hence no record of probate. If you seek these persons in your research then probate records will have no <u>direct</u> value for you. Most persons in America, however, who have lived to adulthood, have left some type of estate to be administered and in the resulting records your searches can be quite rewarding. In fact you cannot completely write off the value of probate records even for those who died without property. They are often mentioned in probate records, especially wills, of others—sometimes as witnesses, sometimes as beneficiaries, sometimes as executors or trustees and sometimes just as innocent third parties (such as the person from whom something being bequeathed was acquired). Roughly half of the people in America, historically, have either left wills or have been mentioned in them.

The very nature of probate records recommends them as an invaluable genealogical source. They exist because of relationships, both family and social, between various persons. When a man makes a will it is because he wants those whom he loves—generally his family—to have the benefits of his worldly estate after his death. The laws set up to govern intestate estates are based on the same premise—members of the deceased's family are his rightful heirs. Thus the great value of probate records lies in their content, and those direct statements of relationship between persons found therein stand as powerful evidence in the genealogical "court."

Because more persons are involved than just those who made wills (testators) and those who died without so doing (intestates), the true value of probates is multiplied far beyond what you might ordinarily expect. Every person named therein and every relationship stated increases the value of the records. Probates are a family-oriented source, and families—complete families—after all are the keys to successful and correct genealogical research. They are what genealogy is all about.

In colonial and frontier America the proportionate number of persons who left wills was greater than we often imagine. This is because our American forebears were a land-and-property-minded people. Land was cheap and even those of humble circumstances could be land owners. Thus the proportionate number of wills is likely to be higher in rural and agrarian communities than in the larger cities and industrial areas where the majority of persons owned nothing of sufficient value to warrant the making of a will. Due to this factor, in those earlier periods of time when the population was nearly all rural and practically everyone owned land, and especially in those localities where few other records were being kept, we must depend heavily on probate records to help solve our pedigree problems. And, incidentally, they meet the challenge very well.

III. THE LIMITATIONS OF PROBATE RECORDS

We will say more about record problems later, particularly as they concern individual record types; however, at this point let us mention a few problems of a general nature. Though probate records are good they are not a perfect source, and the following points will illustrate where and why they fall short of that mark:

1. It is obvious that not everyone left a will and, as we have al-

ready said, for some persons it is impossible to find any kind of probate records. There would undoubtedly be more wills if everyone who intended to make one had gotten around to it.

2. All next-of-kin are not named in probate records, nor are spouses named in every case. In a will a person <u>usually</u> names his spouse and his <u>living</u> children as these are the ones who have a legal claim on his estate. If some of his children died leaving children ot their own, he <u>may</u> name them (his grandchildren) as they are his issue and thus legal heirs. Please note, however, the use of the words <u>usually</u> and <u>may</u> in the above statements; for what is <u>usual</u> is not sure, and what <u>may</u> be is even less certain. In fact there are many wills wherein no one is named directly but only by relationship--"my wife," "all my children," etc. And sometimes persons are named, but no relationships are stated.

In an intestacy your problem is usually even more difficult because in so many cases, until quite recent years, there were no statements in surviving probate documents as to the names and relationships of heirs.

3. To find places of residence of next-of-kin stated either in a will or in the proceedings of the court is rare in early probate cases. However, in the state of New York when a petition for probate or administration was filed with the court, that petition required a list of possible heirs, regardless of whether they were named in any extant will, plus their addresses. This practice dates back to about 1790 in New York. Petitions of this type are also common in some other states but not generally so early.

4. To find maiden surnames of female spouses of next-of-kin in probate records is almost unheard of, but very often you will find the names of sons-in-law and brothers-in-law.

5. Only occasionally in the records of the probate court can dates of death be found. However, any lack of these is usually not considered serious because the dates relating to the granting of probate, etc., establish an approximate time of death, <u>usually</u> considered sufficient for identification.

6. Not locating a person's place of residence at the time of his death will often be a barrier to your finding his probate record. A person will often live in a locality most of his life and then disappear about the time we expect him to die. Since we can find no record of probate we erroneously assume that there was no such record—that he died without one. It is more likely that he moved to another place, to live with one of his children, in his old age. He would die there and a probate record would be made and recorded in that jurisdiction. Since there are few master indexes on a state level it is usually necessary that you know the place of residence at death in order to find that probate record.

7. Probates are usually indexed within each jurisdiction (mainly county) but most of these indexes are only to testators (the persons who made the wills) and intestates and not to the beneficiaries or heirs. There are few exceptions.

The thing we need to remember is that probate records were not designed as a genealogical source but rather as a legal vehicle for settling estates in the most equitable manner and for protecting property rights. No original record was ever kept with genealogy as its prime objective. However, we must make the most of what we have available, and some of these records are very good, probate records being among the best.

IV. LEGAL TERMINOLOGY

Though it may appear otherwise, our purpose here is not to write a legal dictionary; but if we can help you gain an understanding of a certain amount of legal jargon you will be better equipped to understand probate records as a genealogical source and, for that matter, any other court records. The various types of probate records are not included here but are discussed in Chapters Thirteen and Fourteen. Many of the definitions of legal terms found in this chapter have been taken from, or are based on, the definitions published in Black's Law Dictionary, revised fourth edition (1968), copyrighted by West Publishing Company, St. Paul, Minnesota, and all rights are reserved. Any further reproduction of these legal definitions without consent of the copyright proprietor is prohibited.

ADMINISTRATION: Administration is a process, not a record. It involves the method of setting legal machinery to work in a particular probate case and the modes of operation until the estate is settled. This is necessary because the laws of descent and distribution are not self-executing. They must be carried out by the established judicial machinery. The term applies to both testate cases and intestacies since the term "execution" (q.v.) is not in common use. Administration normally involves the collection, management and distribution of an estate (q.v.) by the proper legal processes.

ADMINISTRATION CUM TESTAMENTO ANNEXO (C.T.A.): (Administration with will annexed)—This is an administration granted by the proper court when the decedent (q.v.) has left a valid will and (1) has failed to name an executor (q.v.), (2) has named an incapable person as executor or (3) the executor refuses to act. Such an administration is carried out as if by the executor.

ADMINISTRATION DE BONIS NON: Administration of any goods of a deceased person not already administered by a former administrator or executor (q. v.).

ADMINISTRATION DE BONIS NON CUM TESTAMENTO ANNEXO: Administration granted by the court when the executor of a will has died leaving a portion of the estate (q. v.) still unadministered.

ADMINISTRATION WITH WILL ANNEXED: See ADMINISTRATION CUM TESTAMENTO ANNEXO.

ADMINISTRATOR: A person appointed by the proper court to administer a deceased person's estate. He resembles an executor (q. v.), but is appointed by the court rather than by the deceased. He is bound to settle the estate strictly according to statute unless he is appointed with the will annexed. He must give security by entering into a bond with sureties.

ADMINISTRATRIX: A woman who administers an estate (q. v.).

AFFINITY: A relationship (or rather a connection) through marriage rather than by blood. See CONSANGUINITY.

ANCILLARY ADMINISTRATION: An administration granted in a state other than the state of residence at death. It is a subordinate administration and is an indication that the main administration has been granted in another state (the record will usually state where). If you find one of these it can be a very useful clue.

APPURTENANCE: Something which belongs to something else. In a land deed it might refer to rights-of-way, houses, barns, outbuildings, gardens, orchards, fences or anything else which belongs to the land.

ATTEST: To bear witness to something, as the execution (q. v.) of a will, and to affirm formally with your own signature that the document is genuine.

ATTORNEY: An agent or substitute, or anyone authorized to act in the stead of another. An attorney in fact is anyone appointed to act in a particular situation or transaction not of a legal nature. The bestowal of such authority is by a document called a power of attorney or letter of attorney (see Chapter Fourteen). An attorney at law is appointed to act in legal matters.

BENEFICIARY: A person for whose benefit a trust (q. v.) is created or who receives benefit from property. Those receiving by will are usually called beneficiaries.

BEQUEATH: To give personal property (q. v.) by will. Distinguishable from devise (q. v.) which relates to real property (q. v.).

BEQUEST: A gift of personal property by will.

BY THESE PRESENTS: See PRESENTS.

CHATTEL: A term for personal property which is more comprehensive than goods as it can include animate as well as inanimate properties. All interests in real property which are less than a freehold estate (q. v.)—as a lease—are also considered chattel. In early times chattel was also considered a synonym for slaves.

CHILD OF TENDER YEARS OF AGE: A child under 14 years of age.

COMMUNITY PROPERTY: Any property owned in common by both husband and wife as a kind of marital partnership. (In states where Spanish property law prevails all property procured by either spouse during the marriage is community property.) Arizona, California, Idaho, Louisiana, Nevada, New Mexico, Texas and Washington are community property states.

CONSANGUINITY: Blood relationship, either lineal or collateral. See AFFINITY.

CONSIDERATION: The price or motive, etc., in any contract.

CORPOREAL PROPERTY: Any property which can be seen and handled as opposed to INCORPOREAL PROPERTY which cannot, but exists only in contemplation. For example, a house is corporeal but the annual rents received from it are incorporeal. Some incorporeal property such as easements (q. v.) can be inherited and are appurtenant (q. v.) to the land.

COTENANCY: There are basically four types of joint ownership of land. One of these—community property—has already been discussed. The other three are:

1. Tenancy by the entirety. This is joint ownership of land by husband and wife with rights of survivorship. It is usually considered that the joint acts of both parties during their lives are essential to terminate the cotenancy. Most states do not recognize this type of estate today and most others no longer allow it unless created by specific language. This type of estate probably had its origin in the premise of the old common law which said that a man and his wife were one person (and that one was the man).

2. Joint tenancy. Joint tenancy is much like tenancy by the entirety but is not limited to husbands and wives and can be terminated by the individual acts (partition or sale) of any party. The parties have exactly the same interest arising out of the same instrument. The most important feature is the right of survivorship.

3. Tenancy in common. This is merely concurrent ownership by separate titles of undivided portions of the same real estate. There is no right of survivorship and each portion being held in fee simple (q. v.) by its owner is completely alienable. Any party may make moves to terminate the cotenancy.

COURT OF PROBATE: Any court having jurisdiction over the probate of wills, the grant of administration and the supervision of the management and settlement of estates of decedents (q. v.). In some states these courts have other names such as Court of the Ordinary, Surrogate Court, Orphans' Court, Circuit Court, Su-

FIGURE 1

RELATIONSHIPS AND DEGREES OF RELATIONSHIP

according to <u>CIVIL LAW</u> and CANON LAW

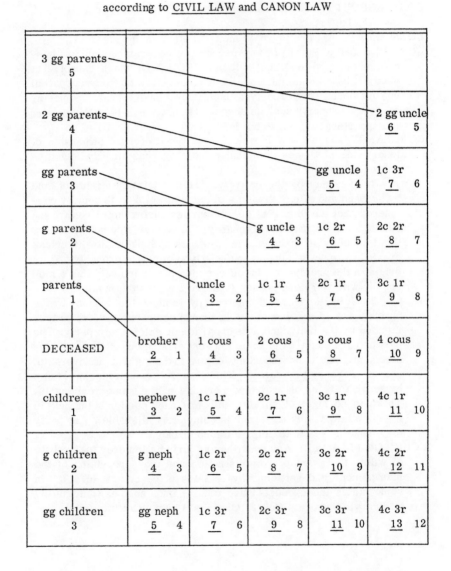

perior Court, District Court, County Court, etc.

CURTESY: The life estate to which a man is entitled under common law, upon the death of his wife, in the lands she possessed in fee simple (q. v.), provided they had children born alive. Curtesy has been greatly modified in most American jurisdictions where it is still recognized and is more like dower (q. v.)

CURTILAGE: The enclosed space of ground and buildings immediately surrounding a dwelling house or that land habitually used for family and domestic purposes.

DECEDENT: A deceased person, especially one who has recently died, testate or intestate.

DEGREE OF RELATIONSHIP: It has been erroneously assumed by some that relationship and degree of relationship mean the same thing. They are sometimes used interchangeably but degree of relationship is actually a legal term and does not state a specific relationship (i. e. , cousin, brother, second-cousin-once-removed, etc.) of one person to another. Degree simply means step and represents the distance between two persons who are related by blood. Under Canon Law (used in most states) two persons who descend from a common ancestor, but not one from the other (brothers, cousins, etc.) have collateral consanguinity (q. v.) and a degree of relationship of the same number as the number of generations the furthest is removed from the closest common progenitor. For example, an uncle and nephew are related in the second degree because the nephew is two generations from the common ancestor (his grandfather and his uncle's father). Two brothers are related in the first degree and first cousins are related to each other in the second degree, and so on. In lineal relationships (direct line) each generation is a degree. This means that both a man's parents and his children are related to him in the first degree. (Figure 1 shows degrees of relationship under both Civil Law and Canon Law. Those for the Civil Law are underscored.)

DEVISE: A gift of real property (q. v.) by will. See BEQUEATH.

DEVISEE: The person to whom real property is devised by will.

DEVISOR: A Testator who disposes of his real estate by his will. Broadly interpreted to mean anyone who makes a will.

DONEE: A person to whom lands are given in tail. See TAIL, ESTATE.

DONOR: The person who gives lands or tenements (q. v.) to another in tail. See TAIL, ESTATE.

DOWER: The lands and tenements to which a widow has claim (in life estate), after the death of her husband, for the support of herself and her children. Usually one-third in value of all lands which her husband has owned in fee simple (q. v.) at any time during their marriage. There is no dower in community property states, and statutes in some other states have provided other ways to look after the widow. See LIFE ESTATE.

DWELLING HOUSE: The house where a person lives with his family, including the curtilage (q. v.).

EASEMENT: A non-possessory right which a real property (q. v.) owner has (without profit) to the use of adjacent land, such as a water course or a way over the land.

EFFECTS: Personal property (q. v.) of any kind. Sometimes context will make this include real property (q. v.) also.

ENDOWMENT: Assigning or setting off the widow's dower.

ENFEOFF: To bestow a fee simple (q. v.) title in real property.

ESCHEAT: The reversion of property to the state when there are no qualifed heirs (q. v.).

ESTATE: The sum total or aggregate of a person's property. An estate is not a legal entity so it cannot sue or be sued though the term may be found in court records for the sake of convenience. A person might also be referred to as having an estate in certain lands; this refers to the nature and duration of this title [e. g. , fee simple (q. v.) estate, life estate (q. v.), etc.].

ESTATE TAIL: See TAIL, ESTATE.

ET UXOR: And his wife; a Latin term used in indexing and abstracting, often written simply as et ux.

EXECUTION: This usually means making or completing (the testator (q. v.) executes the will); however, it can also mean performing or carrying out (in which case the executor (q. v.) would execute the will —but the term usually preferred is administer.) Legally a document is executed when it is sealed and delivered (q. v.).

EXECUTOR: A person named by the testator in his will to see that the provisions of that will are carried out after his (the testator's) death. The term custodian and administrator may be used. If there is more than one person so named they are called coexecutors or joint executors.

EXECUTRESS. See EXECUTRIX.

EXECUTRIX: A woman named in a will to execute or administer it; also executress.

FAST ESTATE: See REALTY.

FEE: See FEE SIMPLE.

FEE SIMPLE: In American law, this is an estate in land which has the potential of lasting forever. The owner is entitled to the property to do with it as he wishes. He can convey it, devise it or let it descend to his heirs after he dies. It is total ownership though it can be subject to easements and restrictions. It is often designated by only the word fee or by fee simple absolute. (There are also defeasable fees but these are less common. Such estates are terminated by the happening of a specified precedent condition.)

FEE TAIL: See TAIL, ESTATE.

FEUDAL SYSTEM: Under a feudal system the sovereign owns all land. He subsequently grants his rights in the land to other persons whom we might call tenants-in-chief. These men in turn grant the right to the land to others, and this chain of subordination might go on and on. Feudalism means that the land is not owned by the person who appears to be its owner but is held by him from someone else. Those who hold the land have tenure in it and the types and forms of tenure vary—some free, some non-free—but most for some type of service to the lord. Military service was important in early centuries but in England was almost completely replaced by socage tenure which came to include all types of service except military (knight service), personal (sergeanty), religious (frankalmoin) and those of the most demeaning nature (villeinage). It included payments of money which we have called quit rents (q. v.).

The colonial grants in America were indeed feudal grants, and land tenure existed in America in a watered-down form throughout the colonial period (Its existence makes little difference to land records, however, because subinfeudation was not allowed once the property was in private hands.), but it was done away with by the various states once independence was gained.

FIEF: Something over which one has rights or executes control. Fief is seen only occasionally in early American (especially colonial) records and never in more recent records. Originally the term related to land held under feudal law on condition of rendering service to the proprietor (feud).

FIXTURE: A chattel attached to the land and usually becoming part of the realty (q. v.). A house is an appurtenance, but the cupboards built into that house are fixtures.

FOLIO: A leaf. In old records it was customary to number leaves rather than pages; hence a folio would be both sides of a leaf, or two pages. Occasionally you will find several pages numbered as one folio.

FREEHOLD ESTATE: An estate in land held for uncertain duration and for free tenure. There are four types: (1) fee simple absolute, (2) defeasable fee, (3) fee tail and (4) life estate (q. v.).

FRIENDLY SUIT: A suit brought by a creditor against an executor or administrator (being actually a suit by the executor or administrator against himself, in the name of the creditor) to compel the creditors of an estate to take an equal distribution of assets.

GOODS AND CHATTELS: The most comprehensive description of personal property.

GUARDIAN: A person who is invested with the right, and so charged, to manage the rights and property of another person, as of a minor or a person incapable of managing his own affairs for some reason (idiot, lunatic, spendthrift, habitual drunkard, etc.). A testamentary guardian is named in a deed or last will of the child's father. Otherwise the guardian is chosed by the election of the child (if over 14) or by appointment of the court (if the child is under 14).

GUARDIAN AD LITEM: A guardian appointed by the court to represent a minor or incompetent person in a particular suit only. This usually has little genealogical significance.

HEIR: A person who inherits or succeeds to the possession of property, through legal means, after the death of another, usually an ancestor. The term generally refers to cases of intestacy but is frequently used in a popular sense to designate any successor to property either by will or by law.

HEIRS AND ASSIGNS: Under common law these "magic" words were originally essential to any conveyance which granted a fee simple title. Though they are no longer necessary for that purpose in a deed or will they are still often used.

HEREDITAMENT: Anything capable of being inherited—real, personal, corporeal or incorporeal.

INCORPOREAL PROPERTY: See CORPOREAL PROPERTY.

INDENTURE: An agreement in which two or more parties are bound by reciprocal obligations toward each other and signed by both. Most deeds are not of this nature (though they may use that language) but are deeds poll, signed by only the grantor.

INFANT: Any person not of full legal age; a minor. Don't be confused by this term into thinking of only babes in arms. The person so designated may be six feet tall and weigh 200 pounds.

INSTRUMENT: Any formal legal document.

INTERMARRIAGE: A term used to indicate that the marriage contract was a reciprocal and mutual engagement by which each of the parties was "married" to the other. It has nothing to do with the parties being related to each other.

INTESTATE: The opposite to testate (q.v.). A person who dies without making a valid will. In an intestacy statutes provide for the distribution and disposition of the estate to the lawful heirs.

ISSUE: All lineal descendants of a common ancestor are his issue— not his children only.

ITEM: Also; likewise. The word was formerly used to mark the beginning of a new paragraph or division as in a will.

JOINT TENANCY: See COTENANCY.

LANDS, TENEMENTS AND HEREDITAMENTS: The most comprehensive description of realty (q.v.).

LATE: Defunct; existing recently but now dead.

LEASEHOLD: An estate in realty (q.v.) held under a lease.

LEGACY: Legacy and bequest (q.v.) are equivalent terms. A legacy amounts to a gift of personal property by will.

LEGATEE: A person to whom a legacy is bequeathed. However, the term is often used to describe anyone receiving property by will, whether real or personal.

LEGATOR: A person who makes a will and leaves legacies.

LIFE ESTATE: An estate that lasts only during the life of the person holding it, or for the duration of someone else's life. (This latter type is called a life estate per autre vie.) Often in a will a life estate is devised to the widow. A dower estate is also a life estate.

LITIGATION: A judicial contest or law suit.

MESSUAGE: A dwelling house (q.v.).

METES AND BOUNDS: When we speak of metes and bounds we are speaking specifically of the boundary lines and limits of a piece of land. They are defined by reference to natural or artificial monuments such as trees, roads, ditches, rivers, etc. This method of describing land boundaries was used exclusively before the passage of the Land Act of 1785 and the introduction of the Rectangular Survey system (q.v.). In those states not affected by that law this method of describing land continues in use. It is also used in connection with the Rectangular Survey system to describe a tract of land once a starting point is located within the system.

MINOR: See INFANT.

MOIETY: Half of anything.

MONEY: Money during the colonial period of America was mainly English or based on the English system of pounds (£), shillings (s) and pence (d). There are 20 shillings in a pound and 12 pennies in a shilling. Sometimes dollars are mentioned, but any similarity of these to our present dollar is purely coincidental. You will find mention of proclamation money also. This refers to the monetary system proclaimed by the legislative body of the particular colony. For a period in Virginia tobacco was used as legal currency because of the scarcity of precious metals, and the Dutch in New Netherland used beaver pelts (called simply "beavers") and wampum as media of exchange.

MOVABLE ESTATE: Personal estate or personalty (q.v.).

MOVABLES: Not quite equivalent to movable estate. These are personal property items which are attendant upon the owner and can be carried about from place to place. They include inanimate objects, vegetable products and animals which are in the possession, power and use of the owner.

NATURAL AFFECTION: Affection which exists naturally between near relatives and is usually regarded as good and legal consideration in a conveyance.

ORDINARY: In some states (Georgia and formerly South Carolina and Texas) this judicial officer has power invested by statute in regard to wills and other probate matters.

ORPHAN: A minor or infant who has lost both (or one) of his parents.

PARTITION: The dividing of real property among all cotenants according to their respective rights.

PER STIRPES: By roots and stocks. A Latin term used in the law of descent and distribution of estates. It indicates a method of dividing an intestate estate so that a group of children take only the share to which their deceased ancestor would have been entitled had he been living—acting as a group and not as individuals. Today the term "by representation" is in more common usage.

PERSONAL PROPERTY: See PERSONALTY.

PERSONALTY: Any personal or movable property; goods and chattels.

PRESENTS: It means literally "this document or instrument." In legal writing the term "by these presents" is used to designate the instrument in which the phrase itself occurs.

PROBATE: This term originally meant prove, especially proving that a will produced before the proper court as the "last will and testament" of a certain deceased person was, in reality, what it purported to be. In American law, however, you will find it used as an inclusive term to describe all matters over which a court of probate (q.v.) has jurisdiction.

PROBATE COURT: See COURT OF PROBATE.

PROGENY: Descendants of a common ancestor; issue (q.v.).

PROTHONOTARY: The chief or principal clerk who officiates in some courts.

PROVE: See PROBATE.

QUITRENT: A rent paid by the tenant of a freehold estate (q.v.) which discharges him from any other obligation or rents, usually just a token payment. Under the feudal system (q.v.) this was a payment to one's feudal superior in commutation of services.

REAL PROPERTY: See REALTY.

REALTY: Relating to land, as distinguished from personalty (q.v.). The term applies to lands, tenements and hereditaments (q.v.). Sometimes called fast estate.

RECTANGULAR SURVEY SYSTEM: A system of land survey adopted with the Northwest Ordinance of 1785 which provided that public lands be surveyed and described in terms of subdivision, section, township and range before settlement. See METES AND BOUNDS.

REGISTER OF WILLS: In some states this is an officer in the county who records and preserves all wills admitted to probate, issues letters of administration or letters testamentary, receives and files all accounts of executors and administrators, and acts generally as clerk of the court of probate (q. v.). (See Chapter Fourteen for a discussion of the various records.)

RELATIONSHIP: See DEGREE OF RELATIONSHIP.

RELICT: The surviving spouse when one has died, husband or wife. It specifies the relict of the united pair and not the relict of the deceased person.

SEALED AND DELIVERED: These words, followed by the signatures of witnesses, are the usual formula for attesting a conveyance. They indicate that the document is authenticated by the affixing of a seal and that the transaction is complete. Sometimes written: signed, sealed and delivered. (Most states today have abolished use of the seal.

SEISED: Used to express the seisin (q. v.) or owner's possession of a freehold (q. v.) or fee simple (q. v.) property. (Often spelled seized.)

SEISIN: The possession of a freehold (q. v.) or fee simple (q. v.) estate in land by having title thereto. (Often spelled seizin.)

SEPARATE EXAMINATION: The questioning of a married woman by a court official to acknowledge a deed or other instrument. This questioning is conducted out of the husband's hearing to determine if the wife acts of her own free will and not under the husband's compulsion in making the instrument.

SIGNED, SEALED AND DELIVERED: See SEALED AND DELIVERED.

STIRPES: The person from whom a family is descended. See PER STIRPES.

SURETY: A person who makes himself liable for another person's debts or obligations should the first default.

SURROGATE: In some states a judicial officer who has jurisdiction over probate matters, guardianships, etc. (New York and New Jersey).

TAIL, ESTATE: An estate which does not descend to heirs generally but rather to the heirs of the donee's (q. v.) body (his lawful issue) in a direct line as long as the posterity continues in regular order. Upon the death of the first owner without issue the estate is terminated. (For further explanation see Chapter Sixteen.)

TENANCY BY THE ENTIRETY: See COTENANCY.

TENANCY IN COMMON: See COTENANCY.

TENANT: A person who possesses lands or tenements by any right or title, either in fee simple (q. v.), freehold (q. v.), for life, for years, at will or otherwise. Usually the term is more restrictive in conotation and includes only those who hold the lands of other persons (called landlords), the term of tenancy usually being fixed by lease.

TENEMENTS: The word refers literally to anything held by tenure (q. v.) but is often applied only to houses and other buildings.

TENURE: Occupancy or tenancy.

TESTABLE: Capable of making a will.

TESTAMENTARY: Pertaining to a will.

TESTAMENTARY GUARDIAN: See GUARDIAN.

TESTATE: A person who dies leaving a valid will; the opposite of intestate (q. v.). To die leaving a valid will is to die testate.

TESTATOR: A person who leaves a will in force at his death.

TESTATRIX: A woman who dies leaving a valid will.

THESE PRESENTS: See PRESENTS.

TO WIT: Namely; videlicet (viz.).

TRACT: A lot, piece or parcel of land of any size.

TRUST: The legal right or title of property held by one person for the benefit of another who has an equitable title thereto.

TRUSTEE: The person who holds and administers a trust estate.

UXOR: A wife. See ET UXOR.

VALID: Legally binding.

VOID: Having no legally binding effect.

WILL CONTEST: Any kind of litigated controversy concerning the eligibility of a document for probate. It is not related to the validity of the will's contents (see Chapter Thirteen).

YOUNGER CHILDREN: A term used in English conveyances and somewhat applicable in colonial America with reference to settlements of land. It signifies all children not entitled to the rights of the eldest son, who held the right to succeed to the estate of his ancestor under laws of primogeniture. It includes daughters who may be older than that son.

V. THE PROBATE PROCESS

Under the assumption that the more you know about the legal processes which bring a probate record into existence (within limits of course) the more value they will have for you, let us explain a few details about probate law.

A. THE PHILOSOPHY OF PROBATE

The general rule is that all property which a person owns or is entitled to when he dies can be disposed of by a will, subject to the payment of debts and other obligations. A competent testator, subject to certain restrictions, can dispose of his property in any way he desires. [1] He can leave it to his

---

1. Under the old common law, when a man died, one-third of his es-

children and his relatives or he can leave it to strangers. Any restrictions to this rule are prescribed by state statute since the power to make a will is statutory and not a natural (or absolute) right.

Historically, under common law, a married woman has been considered incompetent to make a will of real estate (even with her husband's consent) unless they had previously entered into an antenuptial contract or agreement (see Chapter Fourteen) to preserve that right. A woman could, however make a will (or testament) of personal property with her husband's consent. A widow or unmarried woman could do as she pleased.

In more recent years, with the adoption of the Married Woman's Property Statutes, women generally have had the same probate rights as men.

The above are basic rules; however, there are a few exceptions to them, including:

1. The widow's dower was usually preserved for her and took precedence over any devise of realty in her husband's will unless she elected to accept the provisions of the will in lieu of dower or unless she had already forfeited dower claims by antenuptial agreement. There are a few states where the widow gets both dower and devised property.

2. There are some states (Arizona, California, Idaho, Louisiana, Nevada, New Mexico, Texas, Washington) where property acquired by husband or wife during their marriage is regarded as community property and is the equal property of both so that neither can devise the interest of the other. (Community property law comes from Spanish property law and not from English common law. There are variations of the law from one state to another.)

3. Posthumous children (those born after the death of the father) who are not provided for in the will usually take of the estate as though the parent had died intestate. In some states if the parent had no children at the time the will was drawn and children were later born to him, the will is deemed revoked unless it makes provisions for such children.

4. Living children who are not provided for in the will are usually allowed to take of the estate as heirs, unless it appears that their omission from the will was intentional. [It is interesting to note that most Canadian provinces make no provision in their probate law for any unnamed children (see Chapter Twenty-three).]

5. Several states will invalidate a will when the testator leaves his property for charitable purposes at the exclusion of his wife and

---

tate went to his wife (dower), one-third to his issue and one-third he could dispose of as he wished.

children unless the will is made a specified time (often more than one year) before the testator's death.

6. There are also states which do not allow a will made in favor of a mistress and illegitimate children at the exclusion of the testator's wife and his legal children.

B. LEGAL REQUIREMENTS

We mentioned earlier that a will could generally be made by any person of sound mind and legal age who was free from restraint. Let's look briefly at the requirements in each of these areas:

1. OF SOUND MIND: There is really no immutable rule as to what "of sound mind" means, but in general it does not require perfect mental sanity, and often a person may not be completely sane on all subjects yet have the capacity to make a will. The following quotation, though old, provides a good definition.

If the testator is able, without prompting, to summon before his mind, on the same occasion, and hold there for a reasonable time the nature of the business about which he is engaged, the persons who might naturally be the objects of his bounty and his relations to them, the kind and extent of the property to be disposed of, and the scope and effect of the disposition which he is about to make, he will be considered to have sufficient mental capacity to make a valid will....

It is not necessary that the testator know the number and the condition of his relatives, or that he should be able to give an intelligent reason for giving or witholding from any of them; nor that he should remember the names of absent relatives; nor that he should know the precise legal effect of the provisions which he makes in the will. [2]

Claims that the testator was not of sound mind are one of the most common reasons for challenging the validity of a will.

2. OF LEGAL AGE: Legal age is somewhat easier to define than mental soundness. The age when a person becomes legally competent to make

---

[2.] Charles E. Chadman (ed.), Chadman's Cyclopedia of Law (Chicago: American Correspondence School of Law, 1912), Vol. VII, pp. 34, 35. (We have chosen an old source because in genealogy we are dealing with old records. In this area of the law, however, time has wrought few changes.)

a will varies considerably from state to state. In more than half of the states it is now legal to make a will by age 18 (some earlier), but historically this has not been so. The most common "legal age" for making a will has been 21, though a few states have allowed persons younger than this to make wills (actually testaments) of personal property.

3. FREE FROM RESTRAINT: In order for a will to become void by restraint or undue influence, such restraint must destroy the free agency of the testator.

> Mere solicitations, however importunate, do not of themselves constitute undue influence, neither does honest persuasion, appeals to affection or gratitude, or to the ties of kindred, or for pity for future destitution; neither do fair and flattery speeches when not accompanied by fraud. To be sufficient the influence must amount to coercion or fraud, and must have overcome the free agency, or free will, of the testator. [3]

The acts which consititute undue influence or restraint may vary with each case. Often undue influence constitutes fraud, as has been suggested. This is a little easier to define and deal with. A will becomes invalid if:

> a. The testator was fraudulently induced to sign a will which he believed to be another.
> b. The testator was deceived as to the content of the will he signed.
> c. A legacy was given to a person who fraudulently assumed a character not his real one.
> d. There have been any fraudulent impositions on the testator. (Only fraud by a beneficiary gives grounds for contest.) [4]

However, in cases where fraud is claimed, it must be proven.

There is judicial machinery provided for the settlement of probate matters (whether there is a will or not), and because of legal requirements, probate matters cannot be settled apart from that machinery. When we know more about the nature and function of that machinery then the records devolved by the process become a more valuable tool for locating and identifying ancestors. In most states probate law is of English origin, with some modification by statute, but a few states settled by the French and Spanish—notably in the South and West—have statutes somewhat colored by

---

3. Ibid., pp. 50-51.
4. Ibid., pp. 46-47.

French and Spanish law. In Louisiana the probate law is of French-Roman origin and has only gradually yielded to the influence from outside. Anytime you use probate records you will find it helpful to understand the basics of probate custom and law in the state where your problem is. Thorough research may depend upon it.

CHAPTER THIRTEEN

WHAT ABOUT WILLS?

A will is just a wish or a desire, but in legal terminology it is specifically that declaration of a person's wishes or desires concerning the disposition of his property that becomes mandatory after he is dead. The
form of a will is not significant legally so long as it is properly executed
and does not become effective until after the death of its maker.

A will, when it operates upon personal property, is sometimes called
a testament, and sometimes, when it operates on real property, is called a
devise, but the more popular appelative of an instrument embracing both
real and personal property is last will and testament. For the sake of our
discussion we shall simply refer to all such documents as wills.

You will encounter many different kinds of things in wills. Some wills
are even humorous (though they may not have seemed so to the families of
those who made them). One that seems to be a favorite of lawyers was
made by a banker. It reads, in part:

> To my wife, I leave her lover, and the knowledge that I
> wasn't the fool she thought I was. To my son I leave the pleas-
> ure of earning a living. For twenty-five years, he thought that
> pleasure was mine. He was mistaken. To my daughter, I leave
> one hundred thousand dollars. She will need it. The only good
> piece of business her husband ever did was to marry her. To
> my valet, I leave the clothes he has been stealing from me. To
> my partner, I leave the suggestion that he take some other clever
> man in with him at once if he expects to do any more business. 1

Some wills are very long—others are very short. The longest will on
record was made in America by a Mrs. Frederica Cook in the early part of
this century. It contained 95,940 words and comprised four bound volumes.
The shortest known valid will merely says, "vse zene" (the Czech for "All
to wife"). It was dated January 19, 1967, in Langen, Hesse, Germany. A

_____

1. Joe McCarthy, "To My Wife, I Leave her Lover," This Week Magazine (September 26, 1965), p. 12. By permission.

will reading only "All for mother" was probated in England in 1906. [2]

I. KINDS OF WILLS

Though a will is a specific kind of document there are different kinds of wills, in addition to the regular every-day will, which you will see in your quest for forebears. Let's look at some of the more common ones quickly, in alphabetical order. Some of these definitions have been taken from, or are based on, the definitions published in Black's Law Dictionary, revised fourth edition (1968), copyrighted by West Publishing Company, St. Paul, Minnesota, and all rights are reserved. Any further reproduction of these legal definitions without consent of the copyright proprietor is prohibited:

CONJOINT WILL: See JOINT WILL.

HOLOGRAPHIC WILL: A will written, dated and signed in the testator's own handwriting. There are some differences in the statutes from one state to another but these do not generally require witnesses. They are sometimes called olographic wills.

JOINT WILL: When two or more persons make a will together and each of them signs it, it is called a joint will. Such wills are usually executed to make testamentary disposition of joint property or of separately-owned property to be treated as a common fund. Joint wills are sometimes called conjoint wills. They were especially popular with the Dutch in New Netherland because they protected their children from the orphan masters.

NUNCUPATIVE WILL: A nuncupative will is one declared or dictated by the testator. Such wills can usually dispose only of personal property (in limited amount) and are valid only for persons in their last sickness, persons overtaken with sudden illness or soldiers and sailors in actual service (combat). They are valid only if given before sufficient witnesses (numbers vary—usually two or three) and if they are reduced to writing within a limited time period (usually six to twelve days). No special form is required in a nuncupative will, but it must appear that the testator intended his words to amount to his will and that he desired the persons present to bear witness that what he said was his will. They are not allowed in some states.

The nuncupative will of Joseph Killgore was recorded in court as follows:

---

2. From The Guiness Book of World Records by Norris and Ross McWhirter, © 1968 by Sterling Publishing Co., Inc., New York 10016. By permission.

Memorandum. That on the Thirtieth Day of April last past, we the Declarants being at the House of Joseph Killgore late of York dec.^{d} when the Said Joseph was Sick on his Bed, when he had with him Mr John Frost writing his Will, and to our best discerning the Said Joseph was of Sound and disposing Mind and gave express Directions to the Said Frost with respect to the Disposition of his real Estate, but as to his personal, he then Said that it was his Will that (it being so Small) It was not worth while to put it into his Will, But that John Should have his moveable Estate except a Coat and Jacket to a grandson and Son of his Daughter, and the Said Joseph then and there declared that the above was his Will relating to his personal Estate, and desired the Declarants to bear Witness to it accordingly, or Words to that Effect.

In Witness whereof we have hereunto Set our Hands this fifteenth Day of May Anno Domini 1764.

John Frost
Gilbert Warren
her
Jane X Hasty
mark

York ss. York May 13, 1764.

Messrs John Frost Gilbert Warren and Mrs Jane Hasty the above Declarants personnally appearinge Severally made Oath the Truth of the above to which they have Subscribed,

Before. Danl Moulton, Jus. Peac

York ss.

At a Court of Probate held at York May 15, 1764

The above Instrument being presented to me under Oath as the nuncupative Will of Joseph Killgore above named dec.^{d}. I do hereby approve and allow the Same, and do commit the administration of the personal Estate of the Said Dec.^{d} above mentioned to his Son John Killgore to be administered according to the Direction of the Said Will.

Jer. Moulton. Judge

OLOGRAPHIC WILL: See HOLOGRAPHIC WILL.

UNOFFICIOUS WILL: A will made in disregard to natural obligations of inheritance is called an unofficious will.

UNSOLEMN WILL: An unsolemn will is one in which no executor is named. It will require that an administrator cum testamento annexo be appointed by the court.

While we are talking about wills let's also talk about codicils. A CODICIL is not a special kind of will, yet it deserves mention here because it is a supplement or an addition to a will that may explain or modify, add to or subtract from, qualify or alter, restrain or revoke the provisions of the will itself. It is a document which actually becomes a part of the will as it is made with the same solemnity, and it supersedes the will wherever it differs therefrom. There is no limit to the number of codicils that can be added to a will so long as they are properly executed. The late P.T. Barnum died leaving a 53-page will with eight codicils. [3]

Zachariah Gilson added the following codicil to his will. It is quite typical:

> I Zachariah Gilson of Westminster in the County of Windham & State of Vermont do this 19th day of June in the year of our Lord Christ [sic] make and publish this codicil to my last Will and Testament in manner following that is to say, I give to my beloved Annah Gilson, the whole of her wearing apparel of every description for her to dispose of at her own election. I also give unto my daughter Uceba Bewster the sum of ten dollars to be paid in one year after my decease and furthermore I give unto my youngest daughter Lois Gilson - the sum of twenty four dollars to be paid within two years after my decease. And it is my desire that this my present Codicil be annexed to and made a part of my last Will and Testament to all intents and purposes. In Witness where of I have hereunto set my hand and seal the day and year above written.
>
> Signed, sealed published and declared by the above named Zachariah Gilson as a codicil to be annexed to his last Will and Testament in presence of

> John Sessions ⎫   (signed) Zachariah Gilson
> Hannah Foster ⎬
> Sally White ⎭

---

3. McCarthy, p. 12.

II. PROVING THE WILL

Let's ride along now and observe the steps taken by a typical will as it goes through the process of being probated—from the time it is made until the estate is completely settled.

1. The first step is the making and proper execution of the will. When a person decides that he wants his estate divided in a different manner than is provided for by statutes of descent and distribution in his state of residence then he must make a will. Step-children for whom the testator may wish to provide ordinarily have no rights as heirs in an intestacy. Or, some children may have already received their portions. Or, the testator may not wish to leave equal inheritances to all of his children but rather to show special favor to one or more for some reason. Or, specific pieces of real estate or specific items of personalty may be earmarked for a certain child. There are innumerable situations which would bring a will into existence.

When the will is made all formalities which the law requires must be followed. Generally this means that the will must be in writing, it must be signed, it must be acknowledged before competent and qualified witnesses who must so attest with their signatures, and in a few states it must be sealed. (The seal, which was such a commonplace thing in earlier years, has now been largely abolished.)

A typical, modest and relatively short will was made by Skinner Stone in 1764:

> In the Name of God Amen.
> I Skinner Stone of Berwick in the County of York & Province of the Massachusetts Bay in New England yeoman, being of sound mind and Memory tho weak in Body, expecting shortly to put off this Body, do commit the Same to the Earth to be buried with decent Burial at the Discretion of my Execut^x hoping for a glorious Resurrection to Immortality, and my Soul into the Hands of God who gave it. Begging ye Pardon of all my Sins and the Salvation of my Soul thro the Merits and Mediation of the Lord Jesus Christ, and with Respect to what worldly Estate God hath been pleas'd to bless me with I dispose of it in manner and Form following Viz^t
> Imp^r I give and bequeath unto my beloved Wife Judith Item. the whole of my Estate real and personal for her Use & Improvem^t and for her to dispose of by Sale if She see Cause therefor, Provided she take Care for and be at the Charge of the Education & Support of Such of my Children as are here named vizt William Gabriel Jude Abigail & Patience till they come of age, or Shall be otherwise So disposed of at the Discretion of my Said Wife as

not to Stand in Need of any assistance from her, excepting what of my Estate is otherwise disposed of as hereafter mentioned.

Item. I give to my beloved Son Jonathan Stone five Shillings lawful money to be paid by my Executrix.

Item. Such part of my Estate as may remain undisposed of at the Decease of my Said Wife Jude, I give and bequeath to my five children above named viz.: William Gabriel Jude Abigail and Patience to be equally divided amongst them.

And I do hereby constitute and appoint my Said Wife Jude Stone the Sole Executrix of this my last Will & Testament And do hereby revoke and disannul all former Wills and Testaments whatsoever, and do confirm and declare this & this only to be my last Will and Testament.

In Witness whereof I have hereunto Set my Hand & Seal this 20th Day of March in the Year of our Lord One thousand Sevene Hundred and Sixty four.

Signed Sealed & delivered by y.ᵉ Said	his
Skinner Stone to be his last Will &	Skinner X Stone
Testam.ᵗ in presence of	mark
John Morse, Paul Stone	

After the will is properly made a codicil may be added at any time before the testator's death if correctly executed, or a new will can be drawn if this is desired. Any new will automatically voids its predecessor; so, quite strictly speaking, the last will and testament (properly executed) is the only one of value (legally).

2. The second step is the death of the testator. If there is any action which can be taken prior to his death then the instrument is not actually a will regardless of how it is worded or what its maker may have called it. The only exceptions to this would be: (a) A document which was a combination will-something else or (b) a conditional will which depends upon the occurrence of some uncertain event.

It is understood that the rights of devisees and beneficiaries under a valid will become vested property rights immediately upon the death of the testator but not one minute before.

3. However, before those vested rights become possessory, certain other steps are essential. The next step is that the will must be presented for probate before the proper authority to show that it is what it claims to be—i.e., the last will and testament of the decedent. The executor or some other person must present the will upon his own oath before the proper court. (In all of the states there are special courts for the probating of wills but they are not all called by the same name. More is said about these

courts, their names and their jurisdictions later in this chapter.)

The will is ordinarily brought before the court of proper jurisdiction to be probated by the filing of a written application or petition for probate. In more recent years, in the states which require them, these applications have proven to be invaluable genealogical documents as they must include names of all next-of-kin of the testator, relationship or degree of relationship to him (with ages of minors) and post-office addresses.

4. The next step is the admission of the will to probate by the court. Usually a time for a hearing is set and notice of this fact is published (sometimes directly to all interested parties and sometimes in a newspaper, or both, depending on state statute.) If no one comes forward to contest the will at the hearing then it is considered that there is no contest and it is ordinarily admitted to probate on the testimony of one of the witnesses whose signature attested its validity. Even in the case of contest the testimony of only one witness is sufficient if he can show due execution.

Should all subscribing witnesses be dead or incompetent or beyond reach of the court, the will can still be proven by other witnesses with only slightly more difficulty.

Having passed all of the necessary requirements, the will is admitted to probate and letters testamentary (legal authorization to proceed) are granted to the executor by the court.

5. Upon admission to probate and upon payment of a small fee the will is recorded or registered by the court. In the modern probate court this often takes place by the photographic process, but historically wills have been recorded by a clerk copying them verbatim in longhand into a "Register" kept by the court. It has not always been a legal requirement in most states that a will be thus recorded, but the advantages have generally been great enough so that most wills were recorded. In most states (before photographic registration) the copy of the will which was submitted for probate was also filed with the court in a special file (or dossier) together with all other papers relating to the probate case in question. This is in addition to the registered copy. Even those that were not recorded can usually be found here.

In addition to the recording (or registering) the will is usually indexed at the same time so that it can be found later, if necessary. In most states today all documents filed with the court during the probate process are registered and indexed. Most courts make a direct index—that is, an index to testators only—but occasionally you will also find a reverse index which has been kept. These, when available, are a most useful research tool. A reverse index is an index to the beneficiaries of the wills.

6. Next the executor, with court authorization, proceeds to settle the

estate as the will has stipulated, dividing to the respective beneficiaries according to the testator's instructions. Unless the will specified to the contrary, the executor must be bonded and he must adhere to the will's directions implicitly. Once probate has been granted by the court the only variations allowed from the will are in the settlement of all just debts and obligations and in setting-off the widow's dower (where applicable).

During the process of the administration of the estate an inventory must be taken and an appraisal made of the property. The appraisal is usually accomplished by the executor petitioning the court to appoint appraisers. There may also be a sale (by public auction) as part of the administration.

7. Many states also require the execution of a decree of distribution (or similarly-titled document) to be completed by the executor, through the court's authority, to show how the distribution has been completed. This document is issued and recorded by the court as the final document in the probate proceedings and is often (again depending upon state statute) recorded in both the probate court and with local land records. In the probate court it signifies that the executor has completed his job and in the recorder's office (land records), in those states which require it, it stands as proof to the world that title has passed. These documents generally do not go back a long way historically, but they are valuable as far as they go.

If the executor happened to die before his responsibility was discharged (and this may have been either before or after the death of the testator), or if he renounced his right, the court would appoint another in his place to carry out the provisions of the will as if he (the replacement) had been named executor himself. This person is called the administrator (de bonis non) cum testamento annexo (or with will annexed). Such an appointment is made by a special court order and is also registered in the court along with the motion requesting the appointment.

III. THE CONTESTED WILL

One genealogical benefit of probate records is the fact that the average man tries to get everything he thinks he has coming, and often a little bit more if he thinks he can. If he isn't left what he feels is enough by the will or if he is omitted completely, he will probably look for grounds upon which the will can be contested—usually that the testator was not of sound mind, that the will was made under restraint or undue influence, that it was not properly executed, or that some essential statutory requirement had not been met by the will's provisions. The following news story illustrates a typical case:

KANSAS COURT HEARS UTAHN'S 'WILL' CASE

Phillipsburg, Kan. ——The case of a Salt Lake City man who is contesting his uncle's will was continuing Thursday before District Judge William B. Ryan.

George T. Hansen Jr., president of the Hyland Oil Corp. of Salt Lake City, is seeking to have the will of the late Dane G. Hansen, who left a fortune estimated at $9 million, declared invalid.

The Salt Lake City man was left $10,000 under terms of the will. The elder Hansen left $1 million for a family trust fund and the remainder of his estate to a foundation for charitable, educational and scientific purposes.

The younger Hansen alleges his uncle was not competent when the will was signed. Hansen died Jan. 6, 1965, and his will was admitted to probate Feb. 12, 1965. He was 82 when he died of cancer.

Hansen was a bachelor and accumulated his wealth as an oil producer and a highway and bridge contractor.

Two witnesses to the will signing testified Tuesday that Hansen was mentally competent when he signed the document Nov. 2, 1964. A third witness, Dr. A. E. Cooper of the Norton County Hospital staff, was expected to testify Wednesday....[4]

Remember that not everyone has the legal right to contest a will. Only those who have an interest in the estate, and only then if they would receive more through laws of intestate succession than through the administration of the will.

When a will is contested a lawsuit ensues with the executor as the defendant. (He is, of course, the natural defender of the will.) Some states require that all interested parties must be parties in the suit, plaintiff or defendant, and this includes husbands of female heirs. Thus the names of all these persons will be in the complaint. (They are called indispensable parties.)

The proceedings and documents resulting from such a suit can be genealogical gold mines. When Philip Ryon died in Clark County, Kentucky, in the 1850's, his will was contested by some of his children. Philip had been twice married, leaving families by both wives. However, when he died at a good old age the will he left behind specified that all of his worldly goods were to go to his second wife and the children of that marriage. The descendants of the first wife contested the will, presented their evidence, and

---

4. The Deseret News (March 25, 1966), p. 12C. By permission.

thus provided a skeleton record of the descendants of Philip Ryon. The contention was that Philip, in his old age, was not of sound mind and that he acted under undue influence from family members. (And, incidentally, the contestants won the case.)

Though very few wills are ever contested, when that has happened to a will of your ancestor it is important for you to know of it. Learning of the contest poses no special difficulties however and the existence of the contest and the records arising therefrom are usually quite easy to ascertain. The procedure differs from one state to another, but the will itself will be registered just as if there had been no contest, and there will often be a notation of the contest. In the book of registered wills this notation might be made following the recording of the will itself where information about probate is usually given. Here you may or may not get a direct reference to the location of the record of the contest.

The foregoing approach is pretty typical of most old records which the genealogist will be searching, but there are other procedures, especially in more recent times. There may be a notation in an index or a special register kept by the court clerk. In many states the clerk of the court will keep a special register in which is a separate page for each action filed with the court. On that page each instrument filed with the court for recording is listed, thus by looking at the page for any particular probate action you could tell immediately if the will had been contested and be guided to the proper documents by page references. The clerk (or his deputy) maintains an index to this register so the whole procedure is very simple. This is only one example of the way such records are sometimes maintained, but the use of this principle with slight variations is common. The whole procedure is controlled by state statute.

A will is always contested in the court of original probate jurisdiction, but the final judgment of that court is appealable through regular appellate channels. Such appeals are very, very rare, but they do happen. Ordinarily, however, you won't get any more information from the appellate court record than you got from the trial court because no new facts can be added to a case on appeal. The record is sent up just as it developed in the trial court and it becomes a part of the records of that court as well as being a record of the probate court. There will also be an opinion written by the appellate court which might be of interest to you, but it will give you no more genealogical data than did the record of the trial court.

Sometimes other records (such as land records) suggest that there may have been a probate contest. Deeds often state that the grantor received the land he is selling as a result of such and such suit. You never want to pass up a clue like that. Even family tradition may tell you of conditions which would make a law suit probable; do not overlook them. A man who has married several times and left families by all of his wives could easily create such a condition if there were any hard feelings between the various families or any inequities in his will. (More is said about courts and their records in Chapter Eighteen.)

IV. THE VALUE OF WILLS

We have been talking a lot about the legal details involved in probating a will, now let's look at the fruits of these legal details and what they mean —in specifics—to you as a genealogist.

A. RELATIONSHIPS

As we mentioned earlier, perhaps the most significant quality of a will is the fact that it usually states some pretty specific relationships—direct statements by a person who ought to know. Nothing is more critical in genealogical research than how people are related to each other. Names, dates and places mean little unless relationships are established. Other records do not always give this type of direct evidence.

B. TIME PERIOD

We have also mentioned this before, but again let us stress that you can often find wills and other probate records for persons in America in periods and places when there are few other records. And most of these are reasonably accessible for research.

C. VALUES THAT ARE NOT SO OBVIOUS

The above are the more obvious values of wills; now let's look at some which might be less apparent:

1. A will often gives clues to former places of residence. For example, the will of Samuel Wheelwright (Vol. I, p. 69, York County, Massachusetts) tells where he previously owned some land:

> ... Item I do give and bequeath unto Hester my beloved Wife... all the rent which was dew to me from my land at Crofts in the County of Lincoln in England until the time it was sold by Mr. Ed^W Loyde....

2. When a name is common, legacies mentioned in a will can sometimes be traced to prove actual connections. If you find three contemporaries named Samuel Black living in the same locality, wills can often help prove (or disprove) parentage. You may find a William Black giving 200 acres of a certain description to his son Samuel. Once this information is

known you will need to locate the conveyance whereby one of the three Samuels sold that identical 200 acres.   If you can positively identify the seller you have your answer, one way or the other.

3.   A will may also give you an idea about the existence of other records. A man may mention his religious affiliation in his will, which could lead you to church records—often the specific parish or congregation.   His profession is usually indicated in his will, either directly or indirectly.   If he owned land this is a clue to search land records.   If he has extensive property, financial means or social status (usually quite obvious in the will) printed sources may be available that tell something about him.   Sometimes previous military or naval service is also indicated in a will.

4.   Wills and other probate records also provide information on when the death occurred--sometimes the exact date.   In some cases this is essential for identification.

5.   Often the persons who are named as executors or who sign as subscribing witnesses are relatives, and a careful study of records relating to these persons may lead to more information on your ancestors.   However, a person who receives by a will cannot legally sign as a witness to it.

V. RECORD PROBLEMS

In the last chapter we discussed some rather general weaknesses of probate records as a genealogical source; now let's look at some specific problems of wills and consider a few examples without too much rehashing of what we have already said.

Of course every will does not have problems, and all problems are not the same from one will to the next.   Some of the more common difficulties are:

A. INCOMPLETE LISTS OF FAMILY MEMBERS

A man may omit the names of one or all of his children from his will and neglect to tell his wife's name since "everybody knows."   If children are previously deceased, especially if they died as children rather than adults, there is no good reason why they should be mentioned in the will.   If a child dies as an adult he may be named in his parent's will because he left a wife and children to receive his portion.   If he had died intestate they would have been heirs to that portion.

Children who have already received their inheritances are sometimes left unmentioned by the wills of their parents, and children who may have been disowned may also be unnamed, but these two circumstances did not always cause an omission of the child's name. Statutes differ, but most states have laws which deal with this problem in some way. Many states allow a child to be omitted only if the intent of the parent to do so is clearly expressed in the will, unless there is evidence that the child was provided for outside the will or that substantially all of the estate was left to the child's other parent. The purpose of all such statutes is to protect the child from being negligently overlooked, and statutes to protect the rights of children born after the will has been executed are especially common. Laws to protect the rights of children mistakenly believed to be dead are also common. Most statutes protecting these pretermitted children, as they are called, provide that the child is to take of the estate as if the parent had died intestate.

B. INCONCLUSIVE RELATIONSHIPS

This problem is better illustrated than described, so let's take as an example the will of Francis Champernoun (York County, Massachusetts, Vol. 1, p. 55), probated December 25, 1687, which we also used as an example in Chapter Two.

> ... I give and bequeath & confirm unto my Son in Law Humphrey Elliot & Elizabeth his now wife... the other part of sd Island... Item I give and bequeath unto my Son in Law Robert Cutt my daughter in Law Bridget Leriven my daughter in Law Mary Cutt and my daughter in Law Sarah Cutt... all that part of three hundred acres belonging unto me lying between broken Neck and Ye land formerly belonging to....

Is it clear to you how all of these persons are related? If it is then you see something here that we do not. We are left to speculation as it seems quite unlikely that they are all children-in-law of the testator, especially in view of the girls' surnames.

C. NO RELATIONSHIPS

Again let's go to an example to illustrate the problem. This one is from the will of Jeremiah Willcocks (Pasquotank County, North Carolina, Vol. 34, p. 44, probated in July Court 1754):

> ... I give and bequeath to my son Stephen Three hundred acers of land,...
> ... [Some other land to be sold to a certain party] and if not I leave it to my Two Daughters Sarah and Ruth...
> I give to <u>Elizabeth Wakefield Living in Virginia</u> Two Cows

and one calf Called Blossom & Pyde and all the Rest of my Cattle to be Equally Devided Between my wife and my Three children...
        I Leave my Loving wife Elizabeth all the Remainder of my house hold goods.... [Emphasis added; see Figure 4, Chapter Two.]

Who is this Elizabeth Wakefield "Living in Virginia" that Jeremiah makes a beneficiary of his estate? We certainly cannot tell from his will. Perhaps other evidence will help.

D. WIFE AND CHILDREN NOT RELATED

If a man has married more than once it is seldom mentioned in his will. This means that the wife named in his will may or may not be the mother of the children named, and you have no way of telling. Also, if you know she is the mother of only part of the children, it is hard to know which ones. In a situation like this it is often impossible, just on the basis of evidence found in the will, to determine if there is even a problem.

E. OTHER PROBLEMS

There are other common difficulties which you will encounter as you use wills in your research. These will include spelling, nicknames, handwriting and legal jargon, but most of these can be solved by the conscientious genealogist. There are no general solutions other than those already given; beyond this, each problem must be studied and solved on its own merits.

VI. FINDING AND USING WILLS

A. ORIGINAL AND REGISTERED WILLS

Most wills in the United States are registered and filed in the counties where they were probated (at the testator's place of residence) though some states have other jurisdictions. The courts may be called by different names but their responsibilities are the same, as they are all concerned with probate.
        The present names of the courts and the limits of their jurisdiction in the several states are as follows:

ALABAMA: County Probate Court.
ALASKA: Superior Court of the Judicial District.
ARIZONA: Superior Court in the County.
ARKANSAS: County Probate Court.

CALIFORNIA:	County Superior Court.
COLORADO:	District Court in the county (except in Denver City and County which has a Probate Court). There are 22 judicial districts.
CONNECTICUT:	Probate Court in the district. (The state is divided into more than 100 probate districts with most large towns, and many smaller ones, having their own probate districts.) When the original counties were formed in 1666 probate was a responsibility of the County Court. (All extant original county and early district probate files are at the State Library where a complete index from 1641 has been made. There is a microfilm copy of both the files and the index at the LDS Genealogical Society.)
DELAWARE:	County Registers' Court. (Though this court has probate jurisdiction, all probate records, and card indexes to them, are in the Hall of Records, Dover.)
D. C.:	Probate Court, as a division of the District Court. (There are some transcripts in the National Archives, 1801-88, but originals are obtainable by addressing the Register of Wills and Clerk of the Probate Court, U.S. Courthouse, Washington, D.C.)
FLORIDA:	County Judge's Court.
GEORGIA:	County Ordinary Court.
HAWAII:	Circuit Court of the Island.
IDAHO:	District Court in the county. (On January 11, 1971, county Probate Courts were absorbed by the District Courts.) There are seven judicial districts.
ILLINOIS:	Circuit Court in the County. (There are 21 judicial districts.)
INDIANA:	County Probate Court has exclusive jurisdiction in Marion, St. Joseph and Vandenburgh counties. In Allen, Madison and Hendricks counties the Superior Court has exclusive jurisdiction. In all other counties the Circuit Court in the county has jurisdiction. However, in Bartholomew, Elkhart, Grant, Lake, LaPorte and Porter counties the Superior Court and the Circuit Court have concurrent jurisdiction.
IOWA:	District Court in the county. (There are 18 judicial districts.)

KANSAS: County Probate Court.

KENTUCKY: County Court.

LOUISIANA: District Court in the parish (county equivalent), and in Orleans Parish the Civil District Court. (There are 31 districts outside of Orleans Parish.)

MAINE: County Probate Court.

MARYLAND: County Orphan's Court. (All Maryland probates— in fact all official records—prior to 1788 are at the Hall of Records, Annapolis, as per state statute. Many other records since that time are also filed there for safe keeping at the discretion of county officials.)

MASSACHUSETTS: County Probate Court.

MICHIGAN: County Probate Court.

MINNESOTA: County Probate Court.

MISSISSIPPI: County Chancery Court.

MISSOURI: County Court.

MONTANA: District Court in the county. (There are 18 judicial districts.)

NEBRASKA: County Court.

NEVADA: District Court in the county. (There are eight judicial districts.)

NEW HAMPSHIRE: County Probate Court. (All probate records before 1771 were kept in the provincial capital; those between 1735 and 1771 have been published. Transcripts of these early records are in the State Archives Room in the Library of the New Hampshire Historical Society, Concord.)

NEW JERSEY: Surrogate of Probate Division, County Court. (This supersedes the County Orphan's Court.) All New Jersey wills proved before 1901 have been filed in the State Library, Bureau of Archives and History, Trenton, since 1964. (Thirteen volumes of will abstracts, 1670-1817, have been published and are completely indexed.) And all original probate records since 1901 are filed with the Clerk of the Superior Court, Probate Section, State House Annex, Trenton.

NEW MEXICO: County Probate Court.

NEW YORK: County Surrogates' Court. (Historically the County Clerk had custody of probate records, except in counties with more than 40,000 population, which have had a Surrogates' Court since about 1846. Today every county has a Surrogates' Court.)

NORTH CAROLINA: County Superior Court. (All prior to 1760 were kept on a colony-wide basis, and some were recorded by the Secretary of the Province as late as 1780.)

NORTH DAKOTA: County Court.

OHIO: County Probate Court.

OKLAHOMA: County Court.

OREGON: Circuit Court in the county in Clackamas, Columbia, Douglas, Jackson, Josephine, Klamath, Lake, Lane, Linn, Marion, Multnomah, Polk, Tillamook, Umatilla and Yamhill counties; District Court in the county in Benton, Clatsop, Coos, Curry, Deschutes, Hood River, Lincoln, Wasco and Washington counties; and County Court in all other counties.

PENNSYLVANIA: County Register of Wills. (Orphans' Courts have been established in 19 of the 67 counties, but even in these the Register of Wills is the Clerk of the Orphans' Court.)

RHODE ISLAND: Town Probate Court.

SOUTH CAROLINA: County Probate Court. (Until 1785 all were probated at Charleston.)

SOUTH DAKOTA: County Court.

TENNESSEE: County Probate Court in Shelby and Davidson counties; County Common Law and Chancery Court in Dyer County; County Chancery Court in Hamilton County; and County Court in all other counties.

TEXAS: Generally in County Court, but some larger counties have Probate Courts.

UTAH: District Court in the county. (There are seven judicial districts.)

VERMONT: District Courts. (The districts in the North are the same as the counties, but in the six southern counties of Addison, Bennington, Orange, Rutland, Windham and Windsor there are two districts per county.) A copy of each will is also recorded in the town clerk's office in every town where real property devised in the will is situated.

VIRGINIA.   County Circuit Court, except in incorporated cities (see Chapter Eighteen), which have their own Corporation Courts. In Richmond there is a City Chancery Court (north of James River) and a Hustings Court (south of the river). In Norfolk the City Law and Chancery Court, Circuit Court and Corporation Court have concurrent jurisdiction. In Roanoke the City Law and Chancery Court, Circuit Court and Hustings Court have concurrent jurisdiction.

WASHINGTON: County Superior Court.

WEST VIRGINIA: County Court.

WISCONSIN: County Court. (It has branches, and probate is usually handled by only one branch.)

WYOMING: District Court in the county. (There are seven judicial districts.) [5]

Except where indicated otherwise (with very few exceptions), the courts listed above have custody of the probate records. The main exceptions are states like Delaware, New Jersey, North Carolina, South Carolina, etc., where older records are being transferred from the courthouses to state archives and libraries.

As mentioned earlier, in addition to the recording of probate records in the courts of probate, some states also require that certified copies of decrees of distribution, affidavits or heirship, probate decrees and even wills be registered with the custodians of land records and recorded by them as proof of title when land is devised.

Some genealogical libraries, such as the LDS Genealogical Society, are also interested in these records and are taking steps to see that they are preserved. The above-named society has energetic microfilming programs going on in counties of several states and probate records, with their indexes, are a "must" source to its microfilm operators. That society also cooperates with many of the states' archives and other agencies in their microfilming projects. It also buys copies of many records which have already been filmed. The society does not claim to have all, or even most, of the available probate records, but its holdings are significant and should be checked by those who have access to them.

---

5. Martindale-Hubbell Law Dictionary, 100th ed. (Summit, N. J.: Martindale-Hubbell, Inc., 1968), Vol. V (by permission) and correspondence with various court officials.

B. PUBLISHED WILLS AND ABSTRACTED WILLS

We indicated in our jurisdictional descriptions that some probate records have been published and are available in book form in various places. The quality of these publications varies considerably and is hard to explain in a general statement. However, we recommend that if the originals (or films thereof) are available they should be used.

Some parties have also undertaken the task of making abstracts (abbreviated extracts with only essential data) of wills and publishing them. These should be used with extreme caution though some are quite accurate.

A few years ago while doing some research on a problem in Woodford County, Kentucky, we had occasion to use some typescript will abstracts which proved quite interesting. With this particular problem we also had access to microfilms of the original wills. In the abstract of the will of one George Blackburn, Sr., in 1817, were listed the following beneficiaries:

1. Wife Prudence
2. Son-in-law William White
3. Daughter Mildred White
4. Son Churchill J.
5. Son Jonathan
6. Daughter Harrett
7. Daughter Margaret Kinkade
8. Daughter Maria
9. Son Edward
10. M. B. George
11. Daughter Nancy Bartlett

As we read the microfilm copy of the original will we found the following beneficiaries listed. (Compare the two lists.):

1. Wife Prudence
2. Son-in-law William White
3. Daughter Mildred White
4. Son Jonathan
5. Son Churchwill J.
6. Son George Blackburn, Jr.
7. Daughter Margaret Kinkiad
8. Son Edward M.
9. Daughter Nancy Bartlett
10. Son William B.
11. Daughter Elizabeth Peart
12. Daughter Mary Holloway

Do you see any differences? Well, that is why it is best to use the originals. We humans are too prone to err. It was especially interesting in this case to note that the two persons which the abstracter listed as "Daughter Harrett" and "Daughter Maria" were actually named as negro slaves in the will and were being bequeathed to George's wife Prudence. You need abstracts like this one as much as Custer needed more Indians at the Little Bighorn.

C. TO FIND THE WILL—INDEXES

If you want to secure a copy of a will by correspondence, from a microfilm or in any other way, it is essential that you know the jurisdiction that originally produced and recorded that will. Once you determine the proper jurisdiction, you will find that most wills are indexed and can be searched quite easily. As we have already said, the direct indexes (to testators) are usually the only ones you will find. The approach that various jurisdictions use to make these indexes varies, but you can understand most of them quite easily because their basis is usually alphabetical.

Though they are not common, reverse indexes (to beneficiaries) will occasionally be found. (Most of those we have seen are in North Carolina.) These should never be overlooked. Consider an example of a reverse index and how it can be used to help solve a pedigree problem:

You know that the wife of Simion Hendricks is named Mahala, and that's about all you know concerning her. A reverse probate index, during the proper time period and in the locality where the family lived, shows that a Mahala Hendricks was named in the will of Shadrack Plant. Upon finding the will you discover that Plant named "my daughter Mahala Hendricks, wife of Simion." This may or may not be your Mahala, but the possibilities are obvious. Much depends on how many Simion Hendrickses there are with wives named Mahala.

Following is an extract of a portion of a page from the reverse index to wills in the Superior Court of Guilford County, North Carolina:

Name of Devisees	from	Name of Devisors	Date when Probated		Record of Wills	
					Book No.	Page
Cobb Susan		Cobb John	Aug	1846	C	252
John		"				
Christian		"				
Clapp Delilath		Hoffman Cathrine	Aug	1846	C	253
Clapp John R.		Clapp George	Aug	1846	C	254
Barbara H.		"				
Jacob		"				
Clapp Eve		Clapp Jacob	Nov	1846	C	256
Joshua		"				

Name of Devisees	from	Name of Devisors	Date when Probated		Record of Wills	
					Book No.	Page
Cobble Mary		Coble Abraham	Feby	1847	C	263
Roddy		"				
Louisa		"				
Cathrine		"				
Letitia		"				
Adaline		"				
Caulk Elizabeth		Caulk Hannah	Feb	1847	C	265
Hannah		"				
Clendenin Jenny		Donnell Robert	May	1847	C	274
Betsy Ann		"				
Cox Isaac		Mendenhall Moses	Aug	1847	C	277
Rachel		"				
Cain Andrew		"				
Sarah		"				

VII. THE IMPOSSIBLE DREAM

All would agree that one of the most difficult problems in American genealogy is to find the specific place of your ancestor's origin in the Old World. Sometimes this can be accomplished through probate records. Let's take an example to show what we mean:

Your immigrant ancestor dies and leaves a will in America. In that will he says something like Francis Champernoun did in his will, proved in 1687 in York County, Massachusetts (now Maine):

... To my grandson Champernoun Elliot, son of Humphrey Elliot all ye lands of Right belonging unto me or that may belong unto me either in Old England or in New England not by me already disposed of. ...

The happening of significance is that a man died in America leaving land in England. That property cannot pass through probate in American courts but must be probated in England. But where is the property? The will doesn't say and English probate jurisdictions are pretty complicated before 1858. Still it might not be too difficult since the Prerogative Court of Canterbury (PCC) in London claimed probate jurisdiction over the estates of most persons who died outside of the country regardless of where in England their property may have been, and the record of this probate may be located in that court. Since the probate records of the PCC are all available it might not be too difficult to find out where that land was and perhaps Francis's place of origin. The LDS Genealogical Society has these records all on microfilm along with calendars (indexes) and act books.

CHAPTER FOURTEEN

THE INTESTATE——MISCELLANEOUS PROBATE
RECORDS——GUARDIANSHIPS

I. THE INTESTATE AND THE PROBATE PROCESS

The process of settling an estate is somewhat different when the decedent left no valid will behind at his death than when there is a will. In effect, when the intestate dies, the state makes his will for him; statute dictates completely the formula for settling his estate and distributing his property among the heirs.

Too often we think that the record of settlement of an intestacy is of little value (and sometimes this may be true) but there are frequently occasions when the intestacy creates records of equal or greater value than the settling of a will. Especially when the estate is large, relatives come from out of nowhere. People never heard of before claim inheritance rights in the estate, but before any of them can collect a cent they must first prove the validity of their claims, and such proof must be recorded in probate court. A case came into court about 35 years ago in Pennsylvania when a woman died intestate leaving an estate worth more than $17,000,000. Before final settlement was reached 26,000 persons claimed to be relatives and more than 2,000 hearings were held in probate court over a 16-year period, resulting in 115,000 pages of testimony. [1] True, this case is extreme, but the principle applies in estates of even much smaller size.

In some courts, records of intestate probates are separated from the wills, while in other courts all probate records are recorded in the same books. It is not uncommon to find master probate indexes listing all documents on file for each probate case. Where they exist these indexes can save you much time and energy, and their existence signals the fact that all probate records, and not just wills, are recorded in the registers of the probate court.

Just as we surveyed the steps involved in the process of probating a will let us also survey the process, from beginning to end, for probating an

---

1. Joe McCarthy, "To My Wife, I Leave Her Lover," This Week Magazine (September 26, 1965), p. 14.

Petition for Administration.   #5018.   Republican Job Printing House, Columbus, Wis

State of Wisconsin, Columbia County.

In the Matter of the Estate
or
Samuel Stahl _____ deceased.

To the County Court of Said County:

The petition of *Mary E. Grover, Wm E. Stahl and Winfield S. Stahl* of the *Residences as hereinafter stated*, ~~in the County of~~ and ~~State of~~ respectfully represents:

That *Samuel Stahl* died at the *village* of *Lodi* in the County of *Columbia* and State of *Wisconsin* on the *7th* day of *February*, 1904, intestate as petitioners believe, and being at that time an inhabitant of said County of *Columbia* residing at the *village of Lodi aforesaid*.

That said deceased left personal estate to be administered within this State, the value of which does not exceed *Thirty five hundred* dollars, and real estate within this State, ~~consisting of his~~ homestead, worth about *Fifteen hundred* dollars, the annual rents and profits of which do not exceed *one hundred* dollars, as petitioners believe; and that said deceased left *no* debts known to your petitioners ~~amounting to about~~

That said deceased left surviving *him* next of kin and heirs at law as follows, viz:

No widow. Children as follows: Benjamin F Stahl of Portland Oregon; Harriet Jane Tallman of Bancroft, Iowa; Mary E. Grover of Portland Iowa, P.O. Burt Iowa; Joseph C. Stahl, of Marysville, Washington; Almira M. Davidson of Marysville Washington; William E. Stahl of Burt, Iowa; Winfield S. Stahl of Bancroft, Iowa; and Grand children as follows: Guy F Streeter of West Bross, Minn.; John Burt Streeter of Lake Arthur La; Lovie Streeter of Pocahontas, Iowa; Winfield S Streeter of Lake Arthur, La.; Wesley Streeter of Winnebago City, Minn.; George Streeter of Lake Arthur La; Eugenia Streeter of Pocahontas, Iowa; Leo Streeter of Winnebago City, Iowa; Claire Streeter of Pocahontas, Iowa; the last three named are minors, and are children of Catherine Streeter deceased, and Samuel Burnett of Wausau, Wis. son of Sibbel Burnett and Louise A. Burnett deceased

That your petitioners ~~are children~~ of said deceased. Wherefore, your petitioners pray that administration of the estate of said deceased be granted unto *Winfield S. Stahl of Bancroft, Iowa* or some other suitable person.

Dated, *February 10th*, 1904.

Mary E. Grover
Wm E. Stahl
Winfield S Stahl

STATE OF WISCONSIN, } ss.
COLUMBIA COUNTY.

Mary E. Grover Wm E. Stahl and Winfield S. Stahl being duly sworn, on oath say that *they are* the petitioners above named; that *they have* heard read the above and foregoing petition, and know the contents thereof, and that the same is true to *their* own knowledge, excepting as to matters therein stated on information and belief, and as to those matters *they* believe it to be true.

Subscribed and sworn to before me this *10th*

Mary E. Grover
Wm E. Stahl
Winfield S Stahl

L.D. Waters
Notary Public

FIGURE 1—A PETITION FOR PROBATE
(This is a very informative document. Compare it with the Assignment illustrated in Figure 2. They relate to the same estate.)

Assignment of Real Estate   PFEIL'S PRACTICAL PRINTING, PORTAGE, WIS.

At a _____ term of the County Court in and for the County of Columbia in the State of Wisconsin, held at the Probate Office in the City of Portage, on the ___3rd___ Tuesday of _November_ A. D. 191_9_, being the _18²_ day of _____ said month, _and on the 4th day of said term, to wit, on Nov. 21st 1919._

Present, _Hon A P Kellogg_ County Judge.

IN THE MATTER OF THE ESTATE

OF

Samuel Stahl Deceased.

Whereas _Samuel Stahl_ of _Lodi_ in said County, died intestate on the ___7ᵗʰ___ day of _Feb_ 19 _04_, and _his_ estate has been fully and finally settled by and under proper proceedings in this Court, all _his_ debts and the expenses of administration paid, and _his_ personal estate fully accounted for and assigned to the persons entitled thereto: whereby the real estate owned by said deceased at the time of _his_ death can now be assigned in accordance with law.

And Whereas, It has been established to the satisfaction of this Court, that said deceased left _him_ surviving _no_ widow and _seven_ and only _such_ children viz: _Benjamin F. Stahl, Harriet Jane Tallman, Mary E. Grover, Joseph E. Stahl, Almina A. Davidson, William E. Stahl, and Winfield S. Stahl_; _nine grandchildren, children of a deceased daughter Catherine Streator, Frank, Guy F. Streator, John Burt Streator, Lewis S. Streator, Winfield S. Streator, Wesley Streator, Geo. S. Streator, M. Jean Streator, Leo Streator and Ralph C. Streator_; _one grand child, child of a deceased daughter Louise A. Burnett, to wit: David Burnett; that said Benjamin F. Stahl died during the administration of said estate..._ _leaving him surviving ... two widow Mary E. Stahl and ... children to wit: Janette Lewis Roberts, Lizzie May Roberts, John E. Stahl, Loyal C. Stahl, Mary B. Robinson, ... a child, who are the heir and only heirs at law and entitled to said real estate._

It is Therefore Ordered, Adjudged and Decreed, That all the real estate owned by said deceased at the time of _his_ death be and the same is assigned to said _Harriet Jane Tallman, Mary E. Grover, Joseph E. Stahl, Almina A. Davidson, William E. Stahl and Winfield S. Stahl children, to each the undivided one ninth thereof; To Guy F. Streator, John Burt Streator, Lewis S. Streator, Winfield S. Streator, Wesley Streator, Geo. S. Streator, M. Jean Streator, Leo Streator and Ralph C. Streator, to each the undivided one ninth thereof; To David Burnett the undivided one ninth thereof; To Janette Lewis Roberts, Lizzie May Roberts, John E. Stahl, Loyal C. Stahl, Mary B. Robinson, Ellen a Roberts, and Benjamin W. Stahl, the undivided one ninth thereof; subject to dower of ... in common and undivided, share and share alike,_ to have and to hold the same to _them and_ heirs and assigns forever, but subject to the dower and homestead rights therein of _Mary E. Stahl, widow of Benj. F. Stahl_

widow of said deceased.

By the Court _A F Kellogg_
County Judge.

Dated _Nov. 24 1919._

FIGURE 2—DECREE OF DISTRIBUTION (ASSIGNMENT OF REAL ESTATE)
(This document relates to the same estate as the Petition for Probate in Figure 1. Note that circumstances have changed somewhat in the years between the two documents.)

intestate estate:

1. There is, of course, no case until after the person dies, and for the case to be intestate the person who dies must leave no valid will behind. No court can acquire jurisdiction unless there is proof of death.

2. Probate proceedings are usually set in motion by a petition from some person interested in the estate, showing the fact and nature of his interest, being filed in the proper court. This petition, usually called an application for letters of administration or a petition for probate also tells that the death has taken place, that the decedent died intestate and that property within that court's jurisdiction (and sometimes additional property) was left to administer. The amount of the property must be stated, and, in more recent years, the names and relationships of those persons who may be entitled to share in that property must be given.

The person most often claiming the right of administrator has been the surviving spouse or the next-of-kin. In the case of a wife surviving her husband she often claims her right to administration (as a co-administratrix) in connection with the next-of-kin. When there are several next-of-kin in the same degree of relationship, the court usually has power to select the most suitable. In appointing an administrator, the court usually follows certain guidelines; that is, a sole administration is preferred to a joint one, males are preferred to females, residents are preferred to non-residents, unmarried women are preferred to married women, whole-blood relatives to those of half blood, those more interested in the estate to those less interested, etc. Those with no interest in the estate cannot petition to be appointed as administrators. If there are no next-of-kin claiming the right of administration, creditors usually will have claim.

3. When the court receives a petition a hearing is set and notice is given to all interested parties, either by direct notice or by publication, or both, depending upon state statute. The purpose of the hearing is to establish proof of the claims of the petition. This done, administration is granted and letters of administration (see the list of terms later in this chapter) are issued. The administrator now has authorization to proceed.

In some states the minimum size of an estate which requires administration is set by statute, and in other states there is no such statutory limitation, though there must usually be some assets to justify an administration grant. This is why we find no trace of probate records for some of our ancestors.

The administrator, once named, must give bond for the faithful performance of his administration[2] as required by statute before the actual letters of administration can be issued.

4. Once the above details have been taken care of, the administrator

---

2. See definitions of terms in Chapter Twelve.

can begin his task. He must distribute the assets and real property and disburse the monies of the estate according to statute, first paying all just debts and obligations against the estate. One important duty which he must perform as part of his administration is to make a complete inventory of the assets of the estate and file it with the court where it too is recorded and indexed. In most states the court will appoint appraisers to ascertain the true value of the estate. Failure to make an inventory is generally considered a breach of the administrator's bond.

5. The administrator keeps an accurate record of everything he does as part of his administration as he must make an account thereof periodically, usually on a yearly basis (if his job takes that long). At the termination of his trust he must make a final account in any event. These accounts are recorded in the court and filed there. The final account (or settlement) must be accepted by those interested in the estate and can be disputed by them.

6. In some states, and especially in more recent years (so don't expect to find these in very many old records), a decree of distribution is issued by the court at the completion of the administration, as with the testate estate, to show proof of title. This document finally and officially vests the title to the decedent's property in his heirs. It is often (again depending upon state law) recorded in the local land records when real estate is administered, as well as in the probate court. The document is called by various names in different places. Such terms as decree of heirship, probate decree, assignment of real estate, order of distribution, probate assignment, decree of distribution, certificate of devise, as well as others, are not uncommon. However, they all serve the same basic purpose.

The great value of these records lies in the fact that they show exactly how the estate was divided and who got what. Often these can be better genealogical sources than wills because they always name names and they cannot omit any living legal heirs. Law requires that all documents created during the process of probate be filed and/or recorded in the court.

7. Should the administrator be relieved of his duties before they are completed, either by death or for any other reason (perhaps even at his own request), the court will choose a successor. This person is called an administrator de bonis non. His job is to complete the work of the first administrator in the settlement of the estate.

II. MISCELLANEOUS PROBATE RECORDS

There are many other kinds of probate documents besides wills, as our discussion has already indicated. Some deal with testate estates, some with intestate estates and some with both. Let's look at some of the more important ones in a little more detail. Many of these definitions are taken from, or are based on, the definitions published in Black's Law Dictionary, revised fourth edition (1968), copyrighted by West Publishing Company, St. Paul, Minnesota, and all rights are reserved. Any further reproduction of these legal definitions without consent of the copyright proprietor is prohibited:

ACCOUNT (or ACCOMPT): The administrator of an estate is sometimes required by statute to make a periodic (often once a year) report of his administration. And at the end of his trust he must make a final account. (See also SETTLEMENT.) These accounts are a record of the activities associated with settlement of the estate. The following is typical:

> The account of Elizabeth Hodsdon of her admin[ion] of the Estate of her late Husband John Hooper the third late of Berwick in the County of York dec[d] Intestate. The Said Accomptant chargeth herself with y[e] person[l] Estate of S[d] Dec[d] as p[r] Invent[y] £ 21"13"— And prayeth an Allowance of the following Articles of Charge viz[t]
>
> To paid for Letters of Admin[ion] Inventory & c................... £—"12"—
> To a Tourney to exhibit y[e] Inventory and give Bond for Admin[ion]........ —"10"—
> To so much due to y[e] appriz[rs] for their services.................... —" 9"—
> To p[d] for Swearing Apprizers....... —" 1" 2
> To so much for 3 Bondsmen to y[e] Admin[x] 1 Day themselves & Horses and Expense each 4/.......... —"12"—
> To p[d] Doct[or] Parsons for Visits & Medicins p[r] Rec[t]............ —"12"—
> To p[d] Hall Jackson £ 17,17. N. Hampsh[r] old Ten[r]........... —"17"10
> To Eben[er] Thomson to get a War[t] of Apprizem[t]................. —" 3"—
> To D[o] to a Scribe for drawing this acco[t]. —" 1" 4
> To Sundries allowed y[e] Widow as necessarye for Life.................... 14"08"10
> To Admin[x] time attending the Apprizers 1 Day.................... —" 2"—
> Probate Fees on this acco[t]..... —" 6"—
> Due to Marg[t] Norson for nursing y[e] Admin[x] in y[e] lifetime of the Said Intestate.................... 3"—"—
> _____
> £ 21"15" 2

Errors excepted   Eliz[a] (her mark) Hodsdon

York Ss. At a Court of Probate held at York July 12, 1763.
Elizabeth Hodsdon above named made Oath that the
above account is just and true. Ordered that She be allowed twenty one pounds fifteen Shillings and two pence
out of the Said Estate in full discharge thereof.

Jer[a] Moulton, Judge

ADMINISTRATION BOND: A bond (q.v.) posted by the person selected
as administrator of an estate to ensure that his administration will
be satisfactorily accomplished.

ANTENUPTIAL CONTRACT: Though an antenuptial contract or agreement is not a probate document, it does have substantial effect on
the probate proceedings whenever it exists. It is a contract made
between a man and a woman before their marriage wherein property rights of one or both are determined, secured and delineated.
Such contracts have usually been made by persons who have been
previously married and who want to preserve their properties and
wealth for the issue of their previous unions in case of their own
deaths, rather than to each other. Such contracts, in probate
court, have precedence over laws of descent and distribution. They
have been quite common, especially in states with community property laws and with the Dutch in New Netherland. [3]

ASSIGNMENT OF DOWER: This is the document by which a widow's
dower is assigned to her as part of the administration. There are
many different terms used to describe this document in various
states but they all boil down to the same thing. Often it is called
a dower division, the setting off of the dower, and sometimes
merely the widow's dower. Ordinarily there is not a lot of genealogical data in this kind of record, but occasionally you will find an
accompanying plat (a map of the land) showing complete division
of the estate to all the heirs. The assignment of Mercy Cloutman's
dower provides a typical example:

York Ss.   Lebanon June 20, 1763.
We the Subscribers being appointed by
the hon[ble] Jeremiah Moulton Esq[r] Judge of Probate for
Said County to divide and set-off to Mercy Cloutman
Widow of John Cloutman late of Said Lebanon dec[d] In-
testate one third part of the real Estate of the Dec[d] We

---

3. There is an example of an antenuptial contract in Chapter Sixteen.

have attended that Service, and have Set off to the Said
Mercy one third part of the Said Estate on the following
Manner, Eight Acres of Land in the Lot originally
granted to John Cartice, jun^r in Said Township. N.
Seven in the first Range of the Home Lots which Lot y^e
Said Cloutman purchased of one Samuel Rounds begin-
ning at the highway leading between the first and Second
Range of Lots and extending Eastwardly the wedth of
the Lot thirty two Rods which contains Eight Acres and
is bounded Northerly by a Lot granted to Richd Cutt
Esqr and Southerly by a Lot granted to Crisp. Brad-
bury and is Forty Rods in Breadth. As Witness our
Hands.

> Joseph Farnam
> Philip Doe (his mark)
> Paul Farnam

York Ss

> At a Court of Probate held at York July 11, 1763
> The within Instrument being presented to me un-
der Oath for my Approbation. I do hereby approve and
allow of the Same as the Division of the Widow's Dower
in the Estate of John Cloutman Dec^d And do order that
ye Same be assigned to her accordingly —

> Jer^a Moulton Judge

BOND: An instrument with a sum of money affixed as a penalty, binding the parties to pay that sum if certain acts are not performed.
If the obligation is properly discharged then the penalty is void.
In probate matters the administrator whom the court appoints to
settle the intestate estate and the executor of the testate estate
must both be bonded. Often the bondsmen (sureties) for a bond of
this type are relatives of the administrator or the executor, thus
providing another research clue when the going gets tough.

CAVEAT: (Let him beware.) A caveat is a formal notice given to the
court by an interested party to suspend a proceeding until he can
be heard. This power is often used to prevent temporarily a will
from being probated or administration from being granted. In such
a case it is usually an attack on the validity of the will or administration. This is the document required by many states for contesting a will.

DECREE OF DISTRIBUTION: As mentioned earlier, the decree of distribution is the final instrument issued in a probate case. By it
the heirs receive actual title to the property of the deceased. In
earlier periods in some localities this was sometimes called a

division. Other names have also been applied, as previously mentioned. The following decree of distribution was made in Nevada County, California, in 1904:

In the Matter of the Estate of William D. Woods,
    deceased.   Decree of Distribution of Estate.
    W. J. Woods, the Executor of the will of Wm. D. Woods, deceased having on the 21st day of July 1904 filed in this Court his final a/c and petition, setting forth among other matters that his accounts are ready to be finally settled, and said estate is in a condition to be closed, and that a portion of said estate remains to be divided among the devisees of said deceased, said matter coming on regularly to be heard this 1st day of August 1904 at 10 o'clock A M the said executor appearing by his counsel, Chas. W. Kitts, Esq. this Court proceeded to hear said final account and said petition for distribution; and it appearing that said executor has collected the sum of $50 and has expended the sum of $431.50 as such; that he has paid the legacies provided in said will to M. B. Townsend, E. M. Shaw and the heirs of J. A. Holman, deceased; that he waives his commissions as executor; waives repayment of the sums he has paid exceeding the amount collected by him and has settled on his own account with Chas. W. Kitts, as his attorney, and that said account is in all respects just and true. It is hereby ordered that the same be and the same is hereby settled, allowed and confirmed.
    This court proceeded to the hearing of the petition, and it appearing to the satisfaction of this court that the residue of said estate, consisting of the property hereinafter particularly described, is now ready for distribution, and that said estate is now in a condition to be closed. That the whole of said estate is separate property. [California is a community-property state.] That the said William D. Woods, died testate, in the county of Nevada, Cala., on the 22nd day of Feby 1904 leaving him surviving, his son, W. J. Woods, a resident of Grass Valley, Cala., his daughter Matilda B. Townsend of said City of Grass Valley, his Daughter E. M. Shaw a resident of Bakersfield all of the age of majority and S. A. Holman, Jr., A. J. Holman, L. E. Holman, M. W. Holman and W. H. Holman, children of his deceased daughter, Julia A. Holman deceased.

That since the rendition of his said final account nothing has come into the hands of said executor, and nothing has been expended by said executor as necessary expenses of administration; and that the estimated expenses of closing said estate will amount to the sum of nothing. That the said W. J. Woods is entitled to the whole of the residue after paying to said Matilda B. Townsend, E. M. Shaw legacies of $100 each, and to the heirs of said Julia A. Holman a legacy of $100, all of which have been paid.

Now on this, the 1st day of Aug 1904, on motion of Chas. W. Kitts Esq., counsel for said executor it is hereby ordered, adjudged and decreed, that the residue of said estate of William D. Woods, deceased, hereinafter particularly described, and now remaining in the hands of said executor and any other property not now known or discovered, which may belong to the said estate, or in which the said estate may have an interest, be the same is hereby distributed as follows, to wit: The "Woods Ranch" consisting of the W 1/2 of N.W. 1/4 of Section 27 and the south east quarter of the north east quarter of Section 28 Tp 16 N.R. 8 E.M.D.M. containing 89 ac and being the whole of said legal sub divisions, save such portions as have been conveyed by said testator.

All that portion of lot 3 in Blk 15 in the City of Grass Valley, Nevada Co., Cala., as per map of said City of Grass Valley, made by Saml Bethell in 1872, fronting 50 ft on Carpenter Street, bounded south by Perdue's lot and thence extending back easterly 100 ft.

That part of lot 3 in block 15 aforesaid, bounded north by Main Street; east by west lines of lots of Pattison, Clemo & Wesley and Carpenter St.; on south by Grass Valley Townsite.

Lot 6 in Sec 27 Tp 16 NR 8 EMDM.

Done in open Court, this 1st day of Aug 1904.

F.T. Nilon, Judge

Filed August 1st 1904

F.L. Arbogast, Clerk

By A.J. Hosking, Deputy Clerk.

State of California,

ss.

County of Nevada.

DEED OF PARTITION: See Chapter Sixteen.

DEPOSITION: A deposition is not strictly a type of probate record but belongs to all types of court proceedings. It is the written testimony of a witness on certain questions, not taken in open court but intended for use in a court action. In a case where a will is being contested, depositions may be taken from friends, neighbors, family, etc., on the mental soundness of the testator (or whatever) and presented to the court (sometimes admissible as evidence). Depositions are made under oath in response to questions posed usually by the opposition. A court official is in charge of the taking of the deposition.

DISCHARGE: See RELEASE.

DIVISION: See DECREE OF DISTRIBUTION.

DOWER: See ASSIGNMENT OF DOWER.

FINAL SETTLEMENT: See SETTLEMENT.

INVENTORY: An inventory is a detailed list of all the goods and chattels of the decedent, made usually by the administrator or the executor of the estate. Genealogically the inventory gives us a glimpse into the personal life of the decedent—his occupation, his wealth or lack of it and the nature of the times in which he lived. In the absence of other probate records the inventory can also give some indication of the approximate time of death—a must in many problems. The inventory of William Gowen's estate tells his occupation and also indicates that he was not a man of affluence:

> A true Inventory of the Estate of William Gowen late of Kittery in ye County of York Mariner dec^d taken by us the Subscribers October 8th 1763. Shown to Abigail Gowen Widow and Admin^x of Said dec^{ds} Estate vizt.

To 1 feather Bed & Furniture.	£ 6"10"—
One Ditto and Furniture.	6"10"—
To 1 Desk 40/. a Trunk 10/. a Chest 6/.	2"16"—
A round Table 13/. two Small Ditto 6/.	—"19"—
2 Small old Chests 2/. a Spinning Wheel & Real 4/.	—" 6"—
12 old Chairs 10/. 2 old Bibles & Sunday Small Books 10/.	1"—"—
2 old Tramells grate from Toaster and Spit.	—"12"—
a Small p^r old handjrons fireslice & Tongs.	—" 9"—
Ironing Box & Heaters 6/. old narrow ax 1/6.	—" 7" 6

a Coffee Mill 5/. three old
   pewter Dishes 6/. . . . .   —"11"—
12 old pewter Plates 6/. 2 old
   Basons 2/6. . . . .   —" 8" 6
4 pewter Porringes 3/6. old earthen
   Ware 6/. . . . .   —" 9" 6
Some old glass Bottles and Caps. . .   —" 5"—
2 Small looking Glasses 5/. 1 D^{o}
   3/. 5 old Candlesticks 2/. . . . .   —"10"—
a marking Iron & Hammer 1/6. . . .   —" 1" 6
a warming pan 12/. Six old
   maps 3/. . . . .   —"15"—
4 old casks 4/. Some old Knives
   & Forks 1/. . . . .   —" 5"—
2 old Razors 1/. old Cutlash 8^{d}. . . .   —" 1" 8
two potts and Ten Kettle and frying
   pan 14/. . . . .   —"14"—
old Skimmer and flesh Forks 1/.
   3 old Tubbs 2/4. . . . .   —" 3" 4
                                          ———————————
                                          £ 23"14"—

> James Gowen
> Japhet Emery
> Joseph Goold

York Ss.   Decr 31, 1763.

Abigail Gowen within named made Oath that ye Sever^{l} articles mentioned in the within Inventory are all ye Estate belonging to ye Said Dec^{d} that has come to her hands, and that if any thing more here after appear, She will give it into ẏ^{e} Reg^{er} office. The apprizers being Sworn.

> Jer: Moulton Judge

LETTERS OF ADMINISTRATION: This is the document (singular) issued by the probate court which authorizes the administrator of an intestate estate to function in that assignment. The following example is a document commonly referred to as an "administration" but is actually a combination letters of administration, bond and inventory:

Letters of Administration granted to Elizabeth Littlefield on the Estate of Nathan Littlefield deceased she produceing in Court An Inventory of the said Estate and John Barrett was bound in Eighty pounds bond To

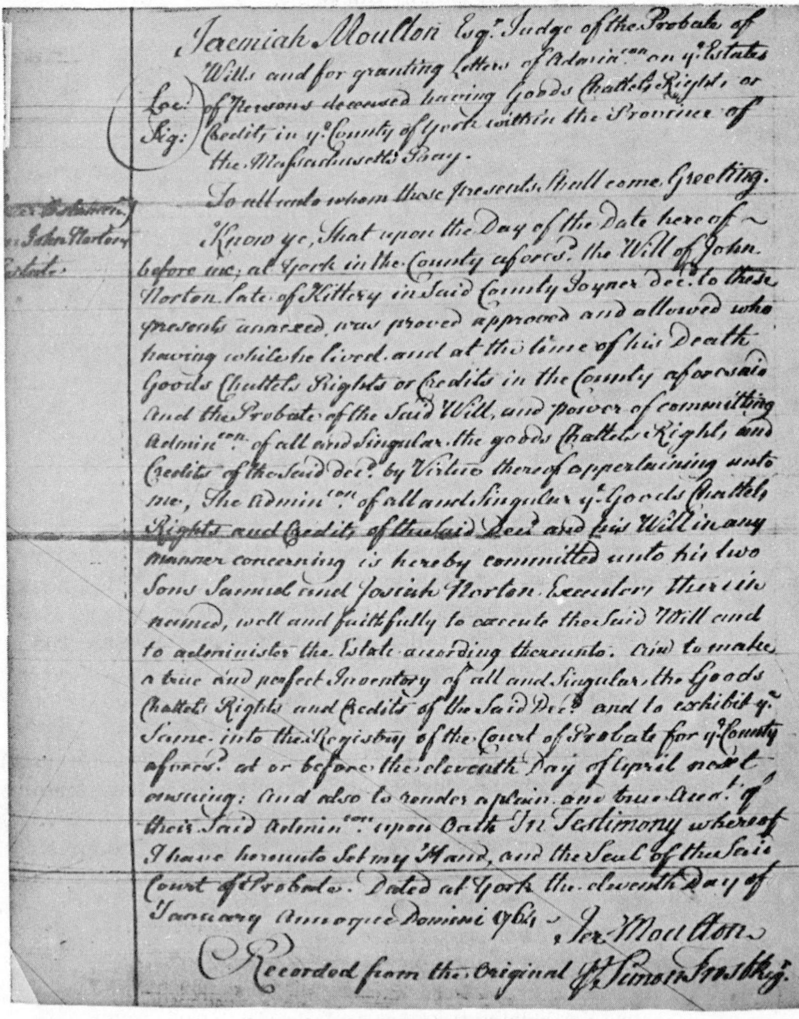

Loc. Sig:

Jeremiah Moulton Esqr. Judge of the Probate of Wills and for granting Letters of Admincon on ye Estates of Persons deceased having Goods Chattels Rights or Credits in ye County of York within the Province of the Massachusetts Bay.

To all unto whom these presents shall come Greeting.

Know ye, That upon the Day of the date hereof before me, at York in the County aforesd. the Will of John Norton late of Kittery in said County Joyner decd. to these presents annexed, was proved approved and allowed who having while he lived and at the time of his Death Goods Chattels Rights or Credits in the County aforesaid And the Probate of the said Will, and power of committing Admincon. of all and Singular the goods Chattels Rights and Credits of the said decd. by Virtue thereof appertaining unto me, The Admincon. of all and Singular ye Goods Chattels Rights and Credits of the said Decd. and his Will in any manner concerning is hereby committed unto his two Sons Samuel and Josiah Norton Executors therein named, well and faithfully to execute the said Will and to administer the Estate according thereunto. And to make a true and perfect Inventory of all and Singular the Goods Chattels Rights and Credits of the said Decd. and to exhibit ye Same into the Registry of the Court of Probate for ye County aforesd. at or before the eleventh Day of April next ensuing: And also to render a plain and true Accot. of their said Admincon. upon Oath In Testimony whereof I have hereunto Set my Hand, and the Seal of the said Court of Probate. Dated at York the eleventh Day of January Annoque Domini 1764 — Jer. Moulton

Recorded from the Original Pr Simon Frost Regr.

LETTERS TESTAMENTARY

our soveraigne Lord the King his Heires and successors
that she the Said Elizabeth Littlefield shall administer
according to Law.

	£	S	d
Imprimis [4] Wearing cloaths-----------	3	00	00
Ip. Bed and bedding----------------	04	00	00
Ip. Some household goods-------------	01	00	00
Ip. 2 guns 2 pistols: 1 sword and amunition--------------------	03	00	00
Ip. 2 oxen and Two Steeres-----------	12	00	00
Ip. 1 Cow and Calfe----------------	03	00	00
Ip. 2 yearling--------------------	02	00	00
Ip. 1 Heyfor 2 year old-------------	01	10	00
Ip. 1 Horse---------------------	02	00	00
Ip. 1 sow and 9 pigs---------------	03	00	00
Ip. 3 yds Searge------------------	01	10	00
Ip. Board and Shingle nayles---------	01	10	00
Ip. Sheeps Wool------------------	00	10	00
Ip. to one quart pt of a p^r of Logging wheels--------------------	00	10	00
Ip. to Steel traps-----------------	01	00	00
	40	10	00

The prmisses abovesd were apprized th 13th of March
1688 by us here subscribed

Sam^{ll} Wheelwright
Jonath Hamonds

LETTERS TESTAMENTARY: An executor of a will has no legal authority, even though the will names him, until authorized by the probate court.   The court authorization—letters testamentary—is
equivalent to the letters of administration issued by the court to
the administrator of an intestacy.

MARRIAGE SETTLEMENT: See ANTENUPTIAL CONTRACT.

PETITION: An application, in writing, to the court for an exercise of
judicial power in a matter which is not the subject of a suit.   The
would-be-administrator or executor petitions the probate court to
grant him letters of administration or letters testamentary.

RECEIPT: A receipt is merely a written acknowledgement that goods
or property have been received.   In some states it is not uncommon
to find them recorded in the probate court.   Such receipts give the
acknowledgement of heirs that they have received their full portions of the estate and then discharge the executor or administra-

---

[4.] A Latin term meaning first or in the first place.

tor from further responsibility in their behalf. An example, from the records of York County, Massachusetts (now Maine), follows:

> Know all men by these presents that we Samuel Whitmore and Mary his Wife of Gorham in the County of Cumberland do acknowledge to have rec^d in full of Joel Whitney of Gorham in the County aforesaid Three pounds twelve Shillings in full for our Part & Portion in the Estate of Abel Whitney late of Gorham deceas'd We do hereby acquit exonerate and discharge the Said Joel his Executors and admin^{rs} from every part and parcel thereof. In Witness whereof we have hereunto Set our Hands and Seals ye 28th Day of January Anno Domini 1765.
>
> Ammos Whitney } { Sam^{ll} Whitmore
> Zebulon Whitney } { Mary Whitmore

RELEASE: There are many kinds of releases but two are significant here. The first is accomplished when an heir releases his expectency interest to the source thereof. The second conveys one person's rights or interest to another person who also has an interest in the same estate. For example, children might release certain rights in their deceased father's estate to their widowed mother. This document is sometimes called a <u>discharge</u>. It may be recorded in the land records since it acts more as a conveyance than a devise. Both types require fair consideration. An example we used in Chapter Two illustrates the second type:

> Know all men by these Presents that we William Bryer Shipwright Richard Bryer Weaver Andrew Haley husbandman and Mary his Wife Caleb Hutchins Caulker and Sarah his Wife Joseph Hutchins Weaver and Elizabeth his Wife William Willson Weaver and Eadah his Wife John Haley Husbandman & Hephzib^a his Wife all of Kittery in the County of York in the Province of the Massachusetts Bay in New England and William Tapley Taylor of New Hampshire & R [sic] his Wife Do forever acquit exonerate and discharge our Father in Law Benjamin Hammond of Kittery & Province afors^d and our Mother Sarah Hammond lately call'd Sarah Bryer from the Demands of us or our or either of our Heirs and unto any part of the Cattle or Household Goods or moveable Estate of our hon^d Father William Bryer late

of Kittery afores^d dec^d and We the Subscribers that have receiv'd of our Mother Sarah Hammond any part of the moveable Estate above mentioned We do hereby promise to return the Same to our Mother Sarah Hammond on her Demand. Furthermore we the Subscribers Do by these Presents promise and engage to let our Mother above named have and improve one third part according as the Law directs of the Land or Lands that was the Estate of our Father William Bryer as aforesaid during her natural Life.

In Witness whereof we have hereunto Set our Hands and Seals this 31st Day of January Anno Domini 1738/9.

Saml Haley	Andrew Haly
her	Caleb Hutchins
Elizabeth X Dill	Joseph X Hutchins
mark	William Willson
Witnesses for Wm Tapley	John Haley his
Andrew Haley	William Bryer X
Caleb Hutchins.	mark
	his
	William X Tapley
	mark

RENUNCIATION: A renunciation, sometimes called a disclaimer, is a refusal to accept a testamentary transfer or a transfer by will. At common law an heir (one who took property by inheritance from an intestate) could not renounce.

SALE BILL: A sale bill is a record made of the goods and properties sold at public sale by the executor or administrator of the estate. The record is usually quite complete, listing items sold, buyers and prices. Relatives often buy many of the articles offered at such sales and a thorough study of the record may provide useful clues to identities. However, you cannot expect to find conclusive genealogical proof in a sale bill by itself. Following is a sale bill from the records of Lancaster County, Virginia:

November 3^d 1795. Memo^{dum} of goods sold belonging to the estate of Newton Brent decd.

1 tenant Saw · · · · To Wm Gibson· · · · · ·	£ 0 . 12 .	0
7 walnut chairs. . . . .William Kirk.	0 . 9 .	0
1 gun. . . . . .James Pollard. . . .	1 . 5 .	0
1 do. . . . . John Thrall.	· 0 . 3 .	0
1 sword. . . . . .Thomas James. . . .	0 . 3 .	0
1 whip saw. . . . . . . .Capt. Gibson.	1 . 3 .	6

3 planes . . . . .Thomas Lawson. . .	0 .	4 .	0
1 small box of tools. .Thomas Short.	0 .	4 .	0
parcel planes. . . . . . Tarpley George. . . .	0 .	4.	3
1 bead plane. . . . . . John Flowers.	0 .	1 .	0
1 red bull. . . . . . . Wm Eustace.	2 .	10 .	0
1 pied cow & calf. . . Wm Eustace.	1 .	14 .	0
1 cow & calf w horns. capt Gibson.	1 .	15 .	0
1 cow & calf. . . . . . .John Hunt.	1 .	15 .	0
1 cow. . . . . Wm Eustace.	2 .	0 .	0
1 Heifer. . . . . Vincent Brent.	1 .	8 .	6
1 small bull. . . . . . . Wm Eustace.	1 .	3 .	0
1 do do . . . . . . John Thrall.	1 .	8 .	6
1 do do . . . . . . Henry Palmer. . . .	1 .	6 .	0
5 first choice sheep. .Tho[S] Jaines.	1 .	16 .	0
5 2nd do do . . do do	1 .	3 .	6
5 3rd do do . .Vinson Brent.	0 .	16 .	6
			£ 24 .	4 .	9

At a court held for Lancaster county on the 21st day of
February 1797   This account of the sale of part of the
estate of Newton Brent decd was returned and ordered
to be recorded —

Teste. Henry Towles cl. curia

SETTLEMENT: The settlement (or final settlement) is the instrument
which itemizes the expenses of the estate, showing how the monies
were disbursed to settle the financial obligations thereof. It indicates total assets after such settlement and all that remains is
the final distribution. This is frequently called the final account.

TESTAMENTARY BOND: This is a bond (q. v.) posted with the court
by the executor of a will guarantying a proper administration of
the estate.

WARRANT: A warrant is a court order. In probate cases some state
statutes require a warrant to precede nearly every action of the
probate court. A warrant may be issued prior to the assignment
of the widow's dower, prior to the taking of the inventory, prior to
the settlement or prior to almost any other action in which the probate court has interest. Genealogically the warrant does not often
give any more information (and often less) than the record of the
event which it fathered.

III. GUARDIANSHIPS

A. COURT JURISDICTION

Guardianships are very closely related to probate records and the probate process. The reason for this, as you know, is that when the decedent is survived by minor children, such children are not considered capable by law of managing their own persons or properties. Hence a guardian must be appointed. In some courts the records arising out of guardianship matters are kept in the probate record books, while in other courts these records are kept in separate registers. But, regardless of this, in most states they are handled by the same courts.

The following list shows the courts where guardianship matters are controlled in the several states. As you use it be aware that in most states the jurisdiction is in the county of the child's residence rather than the guardian's. This generally makes the records easier to locate and use as a genealogical source.

ALABAMA:	County Probate Court (but administration of guardianships may be removed to the County Chancery Court).
ALASKA:	State Superior Court.
ARIZONA:	Superior Court in the county.
ARKANSAS:	County Probate Court.
CALIFORNIA:	Superior Court in the county.
COLORADO:	District Court in the county. (The Juvenile Court has jurisdiction in Denver.)
CONNECTICUT:	Probate Court in the district (see Chapter Thirteen).
DELAWARE:	County Orphans' Court (for minors); County Chancery Court (for all others).
D. C.:	Probate Division of District Court.
FLORIDA:	County Judge's Court.
GEORGIA:	County Court of Chancery.
HAWAII:	Circuit Court of the Island.
IDAHO	District Court in the county (see Chapter Thirteen).
ILLINOIS:	Circuit Court in the county.
INDIANA:	Court that has probate jurisdiction in the county (see Chapter Thirteen).
IOWA:	County Probate Court.
KANSAS:	County Probate Court.
KENTUCKY:	County Court.
LOUISIANA:	District Court in the parish (county equivalent) and, in Orleans Parish, the Civil District Court. (Guardianship is called tutorship.)
MAINE:	County Probate Court.
MARYLAND:	County Equity Court. (The County Orphans' Court may also appoint the guardian for a minor entitled to property in an estate.)

MASSACHUSETTS: County Probate Court.
MICHIGAN: County Probate Court.
MINNESOTA: County Probate Court.
MISSISSIPPI: County Chancery Court.
MISSOURI: County Probate Court.
MONTANA: District Court in the county.
NEBRASKA: County Court.
NEVADA: District Court in the county.
NEW HAMPSHIRE: County Probate Court.
NEW JERSEY: County Surrogate's Court. (In cases of dispute the
                    County Court must order the Surrogate to act
                    and in cases of incompetency the County Court
                    and the Superior Court have jurisdiction.)
NEW MEXICO: Either in County Probate Court or in District
                    Court in the county.
NEW YORK: County Surrogate's Court.
NORTH CAROLINA: County Superior Court.
NORTH DAKOTA: County Court.
OHIO: County Probate Court.
OKLAHOMA: County Court.
OREGON: Court having probate jurisdiction in the county (see
                    Chapter Thirteen).
PENNSYLVANIA: County Orphans' Court.
RHODE ISLAND: Probate Court of the town (with right of appeal to
                    Superior and Supreme Courts).
SOUTH CAROLINA: County Probate Court.
SOUTH DAKOTA: District Court in the county.
TENNESSEE: Both County Court and County Chancery Court.
TEXAS: County Court and County Probate Court (with right
                    of appeal to the District Court).
UTAH: District Court in the county.
VERMONT: Probate Court in the district (see Chapter Thir-
                    teen).
VIRGINIA: Courts of Equity (see Chapter Eighteen).
WASHINGTON: County Superior Court.
WEST VIRGINIA: County Circuit Court (in Chancery) has authority
                    with some concurrent jurisdiction in the ap-
                    pointment of guardians lying in the County
                    Court.
WISCONSIN: County Court.
WYOMING: District Court in the county. [5]

------

5. Martindale-Hubbell Law Directory, 100th ed. (Summit, N.J.: Martindale-Hubbell, Inc., 1968), Vol. 5 (by permission) and correspondence
with various court officials.

The guardianship records which are kept under the jurisdiction of the court of probate are more likely to be indexed and easier to use, but this is not always the case. You will find vast differences in the availability of these records which apparently have nothing to do with the jurisdictions in which they are kept (i.e., the differences have nothing to do with the nature of the jurisdictions).

B. THE VALUE OF GUARDIANSHIP RECORDS

There are various kinds of situations in which guardianship records may have been kept. First, you ought to be aware that it is not always necessary for the parents to be deceased for guardianship records to exist. There are many instances where children are left legacies (often by a grandparent or other relative) and their own natural parents are appointed as special guardians of property and rights which such a legacy may involve. In some states, however, statutes prohibit natural parents from being guardians in such situations; other states allow them to be co-guardians.

You may find a guardian ad litem being appointed to represent the minor child or the incompetent person in a specific law suit, but seldom is there great genealogical value in such an appointment in and of itself. The suit itself may provide useful information, however.

Another type of situation which you may encounter in your research which would suggest the necessity of investigating guardianship records is when you find a young person who comes of age, marries and secures property in a locality, and there is no indication of a connection to persons of an earlier generation. Often the reason for this lack of connection is that his parents died when he was young. Never hesitate to check guardianship records when you find a situation like this. They may hold the answer to your problem.

There are several kinds of records and varying kinds and amounts of information which these records can give you if you are alert to them. The first document made in a guardianship case is the appointment. Then the guardian must be bonded, and then he must make an inventory. Throughout the term of the guardianship he must make periodic accounts to the court showing all his activities in relation to his charge. Then, as the guardianship terminates, either by the child coming of age or by the death or marriage of the child, a final account (or settlement) must be filed with the court.

The information found in these records will vary, but there are a number of things that are quite consistent. For one thing, there is usually a difference in how the guardian is chosen depending upon the age of the child. The general rule is that if the infant is under 14 the court has full authority to name his guardian (usually giving preference to relatives), but if he is 14 or older he can nominate his own guardian subject to court approval.

Sometimes just this small detail can give you an idea of the age of the child. If the guardian was named by the parent in his last will (a testamentary guardian) then the matter is settled, but it will be noted in the record of the appointment. The final account filed at the termination of the guardianship is sometimes even more useful in determining the child's age because this usually took place when he arrived at legal age.

Very often you will also find apprenticeship records for orphan children, especially in the earlier periods of time.

Other items of information often found in guardianship records will include the names of the natural parent(s), the name of the guardian and the name(s) of the child(ren). Sometimes descriptions of real property are also given in these records and can be useful identification aids.

Following is a document wherein the court named Samuel Jefferds as testamentary guardian of Bartholomew Jefferds, the son of yet another Samuel:

Jeremiah Moulton Esq.ʳ Judge of the Probate of Wills & c. for and within the County of York within the Province of the Massachusetts Bay.

To Samuel Jefferds of Wells in Said County yeoman Greeting. Trusting in your love and Fidelity I do by these presents, pursuant to the Power & authority to me granted in and by an Act of the General Assembly of the Said Province nominate & appoint you to be Guardian unto Bartholomew Jefferds a Minor and Son of Samuel Jefferds late of Wells afores.ᵈ Clerk dec.ᵈ who has chosen you to the Said Trust, with full Power & authority to ask demand Sue for recover receive & take into your Custody all & Singular Such part & portion of Estate as recrues to him in Right of his S.ᵈ Father or which by any other way or Means whatsoever doth of Right appertain or belong to him; and to manage employ & improve the Same for his best profit & advantage; and to render a plain & true Acco.ᵗ of your Guardianship upon Oath, so far as the Law will charge you therewith when you Shall be lawfully required, and pay & deliver Such & so much of the Said Estate as shall be remaining upon your Acco.ᵗ the Same being first examined & allowed by the Judge of Probates for the time being unto the Said Minor when he Shall arrive at full age or otherwise as the Said Judge or Judges by his or their Decree or Sentence pursuant to Law Shall limit & appoint.

In Testimony whereof I have hereunto Set my Hand & Seal of the Said Court of Probate. Dated at York the fifth Day of April Anno Domini 1763.

Jer: Moulton

[Emphasis added.]

We hope you didn't accept at face value what we said about the foregoing guardian being named as a testamentary guardian. That is not altogether clear. It all depends on what is the antecedent of "who has chosen you..." If this clause referred back to "Samuel Jefferds late of Wells afores^d dec^d." then that assumption is correct, but if it referred back to "Bartholomew Jefferds" then it would tell us that Bartholomew was 14 or older and thus nominated his own guardian subject to court approval. Very confusing isn't it?

The LDS Genealogical Society has some guardianship records for some localities on microfilm, but holdings there are not extensive. Never assume that because such records are not in that library that they do not exist, even in areas for which the society has extensive microfilm collections of other records.

IV. CONCLUSION

As we conclude our discussion of probate records let us re-emphasize that in most localities in America these records comprise one of our most important sources (as a group) of genealogical data. They deal with families and family relationships—the very meat of genealogy. And they exist in places and for times in which few other records are available.

As a genealogist you would do well to gain a thorough understanding of probate records and then to use them knowledgeably.

CHAPTER FIFTEEN

GOVERNMENT LAND: COLONIAL AND AMERICAN

I. BACKGROUND

As we begin our discussion of land records let us say at the outset that it is rare to find complete basic genealogical data in them. Land records are not the type of source which you will find filled with names, birth dates, birth places, names of parents, etc., that identify and set apart one person from all others. Certainly some of this information can be found in some land records, but it is most uncommon to find all essential genealogical evidence in land records by themselves. Land records are not a perfect genealogical source; however, as a whole they comprise one of the most important sources for research in American genealogy.

There are three factors which make land records important to the American genealogist:

1. Just as we said in our discussion of probate records, the early American was land-minded. Land was inexpensive and readily available, so most persons owned some. Hence, in early America and, in fact, until well into the nineteenth century, nearly every male who lived to maturity can be found in the land records. Nowhere in the modern world has this been true quite to the extent that it has in North America. And any record which includes most of the population has to be an important source.

2. Land records exist from the very beginning of the first permanent settlements in America and are frequently one of the few records in existence for early settlement periods. Their very existence in periods when there were few other records makes them valuable far beyond what their ordinary content might suggest.

3. The third factor which makes these records so valuable is unique to those land records which result from private land transactions. We will discuss this in greater detail in Chapter Sixteen but, basically, it is that the older the records the more genealogical data (especially concerning relationships) they contain. How different this is from the pattern followed by most genealogical sources.

There are many different kinds of land records arising out of many different kinds of situations. The main situations which produce useful land records are:

1. When a government conveys land to an individual.
2. When individuals deal in land, conveying it to one another.

Land transfer in America has gone through five important phases (overlapping somewhat in time period):

1. In the beginning all land was claimed by the British Crown. Because of this the first phase was for the Crown to make grants to the colonies. Such grants (or charters) were made between 1606 (Virginia) and 1732 (Georgia).

2. The second phase was for the colonies to transfer the land to the individual colonists or settlers. This phase, of course, lasted only through the colonial period, so the time period was from about 1607 until the Revolutionary War. The various methods involved in transferring the land are discussed in some detail later.

3. The third phase began when the United States became a sovereign power after winning independence from Mother England. It involved the transfer of land from various foreign powers and from the individual colonies (now states) to the federal government. This began in 1780 when New York and Connecticut ceded certain lands to which they held claim to the federal government and ended in 1867 with the purchase of Alaska from Russia. This phase made the federal government (we the people) a land owner, thus creating public land (or public domain). The entire nation was not a part of this public domain, however. The 13 original states plus Kentucky, Maine, Tennessee, Texas, Vermont and later West Virginia retained state ownership and control of the ungranted public lands within their boundaries and are called state-land states.

4. The transfer of the land from the federal government to private individuals was the fourth phase. This was accomplished by various means as we shall discuss later in this chapter. It began with the Land Ordinance of 1785 and ended, for all practical purposes, with the Taylor Grazing Act of 1934.

5. The fifth phase is probably the most significant to the genealogist. It involves all land transactions between individual parties and is under the direction of the county (most common) or some other local government entity. This phase began as soon as individuals were given the right to hold land (see phase 2) and has continued uninterrupted to the present.

Let's look now at the details of phases 2 and 4 and see what value lies within the records when a government transfers land to private parties. We will look at phase 5 in Chapter Sixteen.

II. LAND FROM THE COLONIAL GOVERNMENT

A. THE LAND-GRANT PROCESS

When a government, under English common law, gives land to an individual it is called a land grant, and a record is made of the transaction. Title to the land so granted is transferred by the issuance of a patent or letters patent. In the colonial period of American history the individual colonies, either by authority from the Crown or by the authority which they held under their charters, could make such grants to their settlers. Such a transfer was actually a state deed of real estate from the government to the individual and was for a specified tract of land rather than for land in general. A small consideration was usually involved, sometimes in cash or commodity in the form of a quitrent. [1] Quitrents were not imposed in New England (except in early Maine and New Hampshire) nor in Dutch New York and were completely eliminated during the Revolutionary War.

Several records resulted from early colonial land grants. Let's look now at the grant process and at those records:

1. The first step in the land-grant process was the filing of an ENTRY (sometimes called a petition or application) by the person seeking the grant. The entry was filed with the colonial governor. Though you will find some of these colonial land entries recorded, many of them were probably never considered of enough importance to make a permanent record since they had nothing to do with the actual land title.

2. Upon approval of the entry a WARRANT was issued for the land. A warrant is an order, and in this case it was a directive, for the "laying-out" of the lands to be granted. It was sometimes issued directly to the applicant by authority of the governor or the Crown to be surrendered by him (the applicant) at the office of local land jurisdiction where the warrant was to be carried out. This procedure was not followed in all colonies but, in

---

[1.] The quitrent was a small fee paid as a rent for a special purpose. In its true usage under feudal law it was paid on property by a freeholder in lieu of feudal services. In America some colonies set up a quitrent system as a means of buying tenure on proprietary grants. Having such rents due did not prevent one from having freehold title—as good a title as anyone else had.

those where it was followed, most of the warrants were recorded and preserved at the office where they were surrendered. The applicant was ordinarily given the right to specify the land he wanted "laid out."

3. Next the land was surveyed and measured to meet the requirements
of the entry and warrant, and then a PLAT (sometimes called a <u>survey</u>) of
the land was made. A plat is a map of the tract, often showing its location
in relation to land held by others and having an accompanying written description with metes and bounds. Many plat (or survey) books and other
records of these have been preserved, but again all colonies did not follow
this same procedure.

The descriptions were very specific, but quite different from the Rectangular Survey system descriptions used later in the public domain. The
following description is from a plat for 50 acres made in behalf of William Smith in Giles County, Virginia, and is typical:

> ... 50 acres... assigned to him... in the county of Giles on
> the South side of East River and bounded as followeth, To wit,
> Beginning at a beech on the bank of the River running thence
> 54° W 54 poles [2] to 4 Spanish oaks on the top of a hill S 66° E 34
> poles to two white oaks on the side of a hill S. 31° E 28 poles to
> two white oaks East 20 poles to two white oaks N 31° E 36 poles
> to a Sugar tree and Spruce Pine on a cleft of rocks N. 14° W 39
> poles to down the clefts and crossing the River to a large Sedar
> tree thence up the River with the meanders thereof and binding
> thereon 129 poles to the beginning variation three degrees East.

4. Some colonies also issued LICENSES to land grant applicants. A
license, in this sense, was a document which granted permission to the
applicant to take up certain lands—usually a specifically described and surveyed tract. The colonies that used land licenses often preserved lists of
the licensees with descriptions of the lands.

5. Now the grantee was ready to take possession of his land and the
PATENT could be issued and recorded. Through the patent, title was secured. Everything done previously had fulfillment in the issuance and recording of the patent. The patent itself was sometimes nothing more than
a brief statement of confirmation; it was documentary evidence of title to
land and is probably the land-grant document most often preserved.

Technically, there is no one document type which can be called a land

---

[2.] A pole is equivalent to a rod (16 1/2 feet or 5 1/2 yards).

grant. The grant was not a document but a process and often involved several documents as we have already pointed out. However, it is not unusual to find documents entitled "grants." Typical of these is the "grant," in 1643, to Francis Littlefield from Sir Ferdinando Gorges, Lord Proprietor of Maine before the entire colony was annexed by the Massachusetts Bay Colony. You will note that this is little more than a deed from Gorges' agent and deputy governor to Littlefield. The document is actually a patent:

> To all to whome theise presents shall come greeting know yee that I Thomas Gorges Deputy Governor of the province of Mayne by vertue of Authority from Sr fferdinando Gorges Knight Lord Proprietor of the said province for divers good causes & considerations me thereunto moveing have In the behalfe of the said fferdinando Gorges given granted & confirmed & by theise pnts do give grant & confirme unto ffrancis Littlefield of Wells in the county of Somersett the elder ffifty Acres of Land scituate Lying & being in Wells aforesaid adioning the land of Edmond Littlefield on the Easter side thereof containing twenty poles in breadth towards the sea & soe up into the Mayne Land till ffifty acres be compleated wth all the Marsh ground lyeing betweene the said land & the Sea wall to contayne twenty pole likewise in breadth and eight acres or thereabouts to be taken in Egunquick Marsh to have & to hould the aforesaid land & all & singular the primises wth the appurtenances unto the said ffrancis Littlefield his heirs & assignes for ever to the only use & behoofe of the said ffrancis Littlefield his heires & assignes for ever more, yeilding & paying for the prmises yearely unto the said Sir fferdinando Gorges his heires & assignes two shillings & six pence on the Nine & twentieth day of September And I the said Thomas Gorges doe hereby depute Edmund Littlefield to be my lawful attorney in the behalf of the Said Sr fferdinando Gorges to enter into the prmises or into pte thereof in name of the whole & to take possesion therof & after seisin & possesion so taken to deliver possesion & seisin of the prmises unto the said ffrancis Littlefield in witness whereof I the said Thomas Gorges have hereunto sett my hand & seale the ffourteenth Day of July Anno Dmi 1643.

> Tho Gorges Deputi Govrnor

> Sealed Signed & Delivered
> in the presence of
> Roger Guarde
> George Puddinton

> Veareable & quyet possession taken & given to ffrancis Littlefield of all pts & prtlls of land & marshs wth the ap-

urtenances mentioned in the
Deed

By me Edmund Littlefield

B. HEADRIGHT GRANTS

One special type of grant was known as a HEADRIGHT GRANT. This was not unlike other grants except in the consideration involved. Some of the colonies, in order to attract settlers, granted land to those who paid the passage fare for someone to come to the colony from the Old World. One man could pay the passage for several persons (often as his indentured servants) and would thus be granted so much land (initially 50 acres) "per head"—hence the term headright grant. Some of the records of these grants have been published in various forms. One example is Mrs. Nell M. Nugent's abstracts of the Virginia headright grants between 1623 and 1666 under the title of Cavaliers and Pioneers, Vol. I (all published), 1934, (Baltimore: Genealogical Publishing Co., 1963 reprint).

C. NON-GRANT TRANSFERS

All of the lands which passed from the colonies to the individual owners were not as a result of grants. Another means of transfer was by cash sale. These became increasingly popular during the eighteenth century. Often persons and companies with considerable capital bought huge tracts at bargain prices. Many of these owners never personally set foot in the colonies but were content to sit back in England and collect the rents from their tenants. Also, in those colonies which were established under proprietary grants (Delaware, Maryland, Pennsylvania, the Carolinas and early Maine and New Hampshire) the Lord Proprietors collected rents annually (through their agents or deputies) and RENT ROLLS were religiously maintained— one copy in the county and a duplicate copy to be sent to the Lord Proprietor.

During the Revolutionary War most states seized the proprietary and Crown lands and sold them along with confiscated Loyalist properties.

D. VALUE OF GRANTS AND ASSOCIATED RECORDS

To the genealogist there is a great deal of value in the records discussed here—other than just historical interest. All of them contain valuable data on names, dates and places which can help us put wandering ancestors in specific places at specific times and can provide other useful clues essential to genealogical investigation—even clues to connections between individuals and families. Do you think there might be any connection between Francis Littlefield and Edmund Littlefield in the land patent we looked at a few moments ago?

III. AFTER THE REVOLUTION

A. INITIAL LEGISLATION

After the War of Independence the state-land states continued to grant their previously-ungranted lands just as in their parent colonies. There is little difference in the records in these states before and after the war.

The main difference in records after the war was due to the creation of the public domain. Making the federal government a land owner fostered a completely different brand of land record—records of transfer from the federal government (all of us) to the private individual (one of us).

As we said earlier, the enactment of the Northwest Ordinance of 1785 signaled the start of these new records. The objective of the ordinance was to get the land settled quickly and to form new states. It provided:

1. That the land should be purchased from the Indians prior to settlement.

2. That land should be surveyed and laid out in townships and sections (Rectangular Survey system based on meridians and baselines) before settlement.

3. That the first tracts surveyed would be drawn by lot for military bounties which had been promised earlier.

4. That remaining tracts should then be offered for sale at public auction in township and section-size units.

5. That certain lands would be set aside for educational purposes.

6. That absolute (or fee simple) title would be transferred with all lands.

A second Northwest Ordinance in 1787 specifically provided that if a land holder died intestate his widow would receive one-third of the land (in fee simple) and the remainder would descend to his children in equal portions. It also provided that wills and deeds had to be duly proved and recorded within one year or would be invalid. This ordinance also made both resident and non-resident land owners subject to taxation, but exempted all government land from taxes.

B. RECTANGULAR SURVEY SYSTEM

Many have asked what the Rectangular Survey system involves, so let's explain it as simply as we can. First of all, when the public land system was adopted by Congress it was specified that two lines should be run through the territory to be surveyed—a base line running east and west and a meridian line running north and south, to intersect each other at right angles. Townships were then surveyed from the point of this intersection.

6	5	4	3	2	1
7	8	9	10	11	12
18	17	16	15	14	13
19	20	21	22	23	24
30	29	28	27	26	25
31	32	33	34	35	36

FIGURE 1
NUMBERING AND DIVIDING THE SECTIONS OF A TOWNSHIP

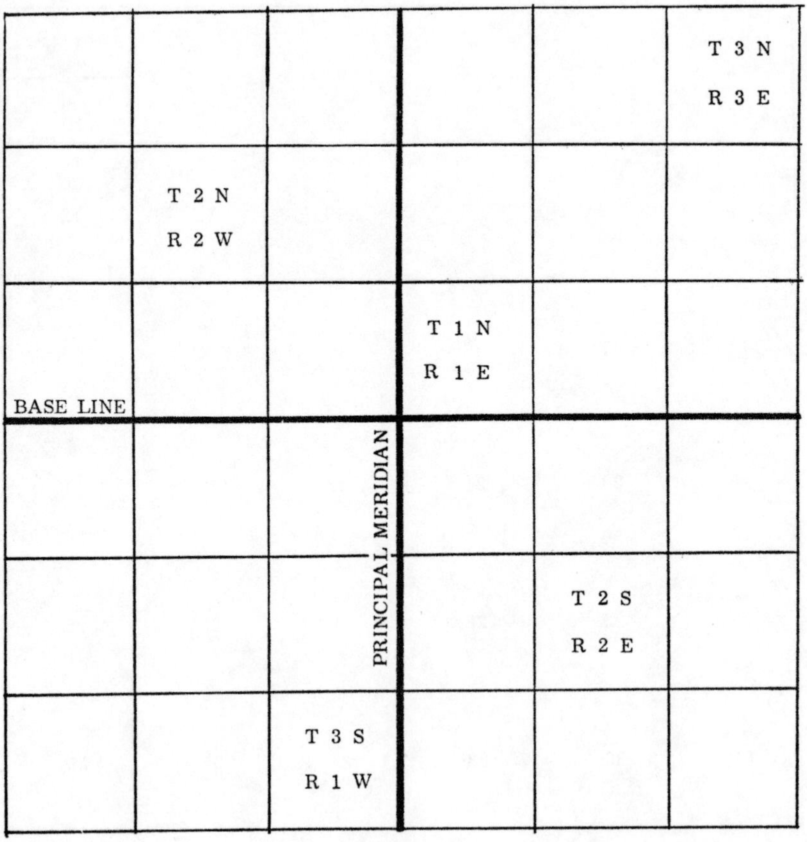

FIGURE 2
NUMBERING TOWNSHIPS AND RANGES FROM THE BASE LINE
AND THE PRINCIPAL MERIDIAN

Each township is six miles square (36 square miles) and is subdivided into 36 sections of 640 acres (one square mile) each, and all townships are numbered with reference to the baseline and meridian line. They are numbered from the base line north and south and from the meridian line east and west; however, in east or west numbering they are referred to as ranges. For example, the township situated three townships (ranges) west of the meridian line and four townships south of the base line is described as being Township 4 south, Range 3 west (or T 4 S R 3 W).

The sections are divided by running lines through their centers north and south as well as east and west. The divisions are called half sections and quarter sections. A quarter section can also be subdivided but this was not part of the original survey. Figures 1 and 2 illustrate the system.

IV. HISTORY OF LAND ENTRIES IN THE PUBLIC DOMAIN

Early in the American Revolution the Continental Congress authorized each private and noncommissioned officer to receive a bounty of $50, 50 acres of land and a new suit of clothes for his service. Various states, in addition to the promises of the Continental Congress, authorized bounty land for Revolutionary veterans and preserved tracts in their western territories to make good their pledges. A good example of this is the Western Reserve, a section of land in northeastern Ohio which Connecticut reserved to grant to her veterans when she ceded her western lands to the federal government in 1786. Later on, bounty land was also granted to soldiers for their service in the War of 1812, the Indian wars and the Mexican War.

The first act passed by the U. S. government for military bounty land in the public domain was in 1812. These bounties were situated in special districts in Arkansas, Illinois and Missouri and were non-transferrable. Four very important acts were passed between 1847 and 1856. The Act of 1847 provided for soldiers who served for at least one year in the Mexican War. The Act of 1850 extended this bounty to all War of 1812 veterans and Indian wars veterans. The Act of 1852 extended benefits to officers as well as enlisted men and made all benefits assignable. And the Act of 1855 (amended in 1856) included every soldier (or his heirs) who had served at least 14 days in any war since (and including) the Revolution. These acts were unique because they offered bounty as a reward to soldiers who had already served rather than as an inducement for enlistment as had been done by all previous legislation.

All of these acts provided that a warrant for a quarter section (160 acres) of land, located on any part of the surveyed public domain, would be granted to those who qualified. Scrip was issued which could be exchanged for title at any public land office or could be (and usually was) sold. [3]

---

[3] Roy M. Robbins, Our Landed Heritage: The Public Domain 1776-1936 (Lincoln: University of Nebraska Press, 1962), pp. 156-157.

As a result of the Land Ordinance of 1785 the federal government sold land in 36-section townships (23,040 acres) and in sections (640 acres) for a minimum of $1 per acre payable within one year. A new ordinance in 1796 raised the minimum price to $2 per acre, and another in 1800 reduced the minimum size of a sale tract to 320 acres (a half section). The 1800 ordinance also allowed for four payments over a five-year period, but this extension of credit encouraged speculation and the system proved unsuccessful.

A new ordinance in 1820 did away with credit sales, reduced the minimum size of a sale tract to 80 acres (one-eighth section) and lowered the minimum price to $1.25 per acre. Land was sold under this act until 1908.

In 1830 the first preemption act was passed by Congress, in an alliance between South and West, which allowed any settler (or squatter) on the public land who had cultivated a tract in 1829 to buy it (up to 160 acres) for $1.25 per acre. This was merely a pardon to those who had illegally settled. Once such a step had been taken it was difficult to reject demands for similar action later on, so for a time the act was renewed nearly every time Congress convened.

Following the financial panic of 1837, after much debate by government officials, a new act was passed in 1838 allowing any settler on the public domain, who was either over 21 or the head of a family, who was living on the land when the act was passed and who had been there for four months preceding the act, to have all the benefits granted in the Act of 1830. Preemption became a major issue in the Presidential campaign of 1840 (Harrison over Van Buren) and the act was again renewed by Congress.

In 1841 a permanent preemption act was passed which allowed anyone who was the head of a family (including widows) or over 21 who was a U.S. citizen or who had declared intention to become one, [4] to stake a claim on any tract up to 160 acres and then buy it from the government for $1.25 per acre. Certain lands including reservations, school lands, certain Indian lands, land already selected for townsites, mineral and saline lands, land within incorporated towns and lands already granted for various reasons were not open to preemption.

In 1854 another act made public land available for 12 1/2 cents per acre if it had been on the market for 30 years, and in some remote areas other measures were taken to lure settlers. In the territories of Florida, New Mexico, Oregon and Washington donation land grants were given by the federal government to those who would settle there. East Florida was extended this privilege in 1842 to attract men to protect the territory, and any man over 18 or the head of a family who took up permanent residence was entitled to 160 acres of free land.

[4.] Aliens could make claims under all earlier preemption acts.

The next donation land act was passed in 1850 for the Oregon Territory. This act granted a "donation" of free land—320 acres to each single man and 640 acres to each married man—to anyone who had settled on the land before December 1 of that year. This act required four years of continued residence on the land and cultivation thereof, but in 1853 the residency requirement was cut in half. In 1854 another act extended the same donation land benefits to the Washington Territory which had been divided off the year previous. Both acts expired in December 1855.

On July 22, 1854, just three days after passage of the Washington Donation Land Act, donation privileges were extended to the New Mexico Territory. This act (10 Stat. 208) provided that donation claims could be changed to cash purchases for $1.25 per acre. The New Mexico act did not expire until 1883.

In essence these donation land experiments were a limited trial of the principle of homesteading before the latter became a national policy. [5]

After the secession of the southern states, who had opposed the homestead principle, cash sales and preemptions were largely replaced by homesteads. Under the Homestead Act of 1862 a settler could gain title to public lands without monetary consideration (except for a small filing fee) by meeting a five-year residency requirement and cultivating and improving the land. Any person who met the age and citizenship requirements of the Preemption Act of 1841 could homestead up to 160 acres (quarter section) of public land. However, this law did not completely eliminate either direct cash sales or preemptions.

A provision in the Homestead Act allowed the homesteader to commute his homestead entry to a cash entry for $1.25 per acre after six months' residence and improvement of the land if he desired. Union Army and Navy veterans (anyone who had served 14 or more days during war time) were considered automatically to meet the age requirement. Anyone who had borne arms against the government or had given aid to its enemies was excluded, but only until January 1, 1867.

Many changes were made by various bills in Congress and an act passed in 1872 made it possible for all Civil War veterans with at least 90 days' service to apply that service, up to four years, toward the five-year homestead residency requirement.

Acts passed in 1879 and 1880 made it possible to commute a preemption claim to a homestead claim and vice versa should the claimant so desire. The privileges and guarantees were the same. Preemption was finally repealed by Congress in 1891 with the provision that claims initiated before passage of the repeal could be completed.

Later bills provided for larger homesteads (320 acres) in the West on

---

5. Robbins, pp. 153-154.

certain non-irrigable lands (Act of 1909) and for three-year homesteads (Act of 1912). Stock raising—primarily grazing—homesteads of 640 acres were specified in the Act of 1916.

Another type of grant was the <u>Private Land Claim</u>. This was merely an acknowledgement of title by the federal government to those who owned or **had** been granted land by a foreign government before the U. S. became sovereign in the area concerned. These claims covered a broad period of time and extensive portions of the public domain—from Missouri to California to Wisconsin to Alabama. Portions of 15 states were involved.

The Taylor Grazing Act of 1934, as amended, closed most of the public domain to entry, and grazing lands were left to be held by public ownership under control of the Interior Department, and in 1935, by Presidential order, all public lands were closed to individual entry.

V. LAND ENTRY RECORDS FROM THE PUBLIC DOMAIN

We have introduced various kinds of land entries and, as would be expected, most records of these land entries have been preserved. They were housed in the General Land Office and, when that office was discontinued, the records were sent to the National Archives. Most land entry records for the public domain are in this collection, but a few are still in land offices in the individual states.

The records in the National Archives are as follows:

A. CREDIT ENTRY FILES

As indicated earlier, most of the land sold by the federal government between the passage of the Land Act of 1800 and the Act of 1820 was on five years' credit for a minimum of $2 per acre. The Credit Entry Final Certificates which were issued on all completed purchases are the most important records in this file, but you will also find an occasional Assignment filed with the certificates, along with other records.

All final certificates filed before the Act of 1820 are called "Credit Prior Certificates" and those filed after that date (under relief legislation) by those who had begun payment before the act was passed, but had not finished, are called "Credit Under Certificates."

Both types of final certificates normally show...

... the name of the entryman; the place of his residence as given at the time of purchase; the date of the purchase; the number of acres in the tract; the description of the tract in terms of subdivision, section, township and range; a summary of the payments made; and a citation to the record copy of the patent in the

Bureau of Land Management. [6]

In addition to the records in the National Archives, the Bureau of Land Management in Washington, D.C., has five volumes of indexes for tract books from the Ohio land offices at Canton (Woolster); Chillocothe; Cincinnati; Marietta and Zanesville; and Steubenville. [7]

B. CASH ENTRY FILES

Beginning with the Act of 1820 most land sold by the government was for cash at a minimum of $1.25 per acre. The Cash Entry Files are arranged at the National Archives under the names of the individual land offices, but there is a master card index to the cash entries for Alabama, Alaska, Arizona, Florida, Louisiana, Nevada and Utah.

An individual file contains an application for a tract, a receipt for money and a Final Certificate which authorized the claimant to secure a patent. In cases where the land was claimed by preemption, the preemption proof may also be in the file. If the tract was entered as a homestead but commuted to a cash entry, the Homestead Entry File is included.

Ordinarily the most valuable document in a Cash Entry File is the Final Certificate. It...

... shows the name of the entryman; the place of his residence given at the time of the purchase; the description of the tract in terms of subdivision, section, township, and range; the number of acres in the tract, the date of the patent; and the volume and page of the record copy of the patent in the Bureau of Land Management... The testimony of claimant in a preemption proof shows the name of the claimant, his age, his citizenship, the date of his entry on the tract, the number and relationship of members of his household, and the nature of the improvements on the tract. [8]

All preemption entries were for cash and are therefore in these files. Cash Entry Files cover the period from 1820 to 1908, but the records of ·ll land offices do not cover the entire period as many were opened at much later dates.

------

[6]. Meredith B. Colket, Jr., and Frank E. Bridgers, Guide to genealogical Records in the National Archives (Washington, D.C.: The National Archives, 1964, p. 106.

[7]. Ibid., p. 106.

[8]. Ibid., p. 106.

C. DONATION ENTRY FILES

The Florida Donation files are mainly for 1842 through 1850 and are of varying degrees of completeness, depending on the extent to which title was perfected in the land. If the claimant completed the five-year residency requirement, his file—a complete one—contains a Permit to Settle, an Application for a patent, a Report by the land agent and a Final Certificate authorizing him to obtain a patent. All files that include Final Certificates are indexed in a master card index.

Regarding the information in these records, Colket and Bridgers state:

> A permit to settle shows the name of the applicant, his marital status, the month and year he became a resident of Florida, and a description of the land in terms of subdivision, section, township, and range. An application for a patent shows the name of the applicant, a description of the land, the date of the patent, and the volume and page number of the recorded copy of the patent in the Bureau of Land Management. [9]

The Donation Entry Files for Oregon and Washington are filed separately in the National Archives and those for each state are divided into two series—one for completed entries and one for those not completed. Both the Oregon and Washington files are indexed. An alphabetical list of the Oregon claims has also been published serially in the Genealogical Forum of Portland, Oregon under the title of "Index to Oregon Donation Land Claims."

All completed files contain a Notification on the Settlement of Public Land and a Donation Certificate. A...

> ... notification on the settlement of public land shows the description of the land in terms of subdivision, section, township, and range; the name of the entryman; the place of his residence at the time of notification; his citizenship; the date and place of his birth; and, if married, the given name of his wife and their date and place of marriage. A donation certificate shows the name of the entryman, the place of his residence, the description of the land, the date of the patent, and the volume and page number of the recorded copy in the Bureau of Land Management... [10]

---

9. Ibid., p. 107.
10. Ibid., p. 108.

The New Mexico Donation Entry Files are apparently non-existent as neither the National Archives, the New Mexico State Land Office nor the Land Office of the Bureau of Land Management in Santa Fe has any knowledge of the location of these records. [11]

D. MILITARY BOUNTY LAND ENTRIES

Also in the National Archives are records of both the Virginia and the U.S. bounty land warrants surrendered at the various land offices for acreage in the public domain or for scrip certificates which could be used to purchase land. All except the War of 1812 warrants were assignable and most were assigned (i.e., sold).

The Virginia military bounty land warrants are indexed in one manuscript volume at the National Archives entitled "Virginia Military Warrants, Continental Line, Alphabetical Index to Warrantees (vol. 30)." The names of these warrantees have also been copied onto cards which have been filed in a consolidated bounty land warrant index. The names are also in Gaius M. Brumbaugh, Revolutionary War Records, Vol. I (all published), 1936, (Baltimore: Genealogical Publishing Co., 1967 reprint), pp. 323-525.

These Virginia bounty land warrant records themselves show...

... such information as the name of the warrantee; the name of the patentee; the location of the land in terms of lot, quarter section, township and range; and the date of the patent. Some files show the dates and places of death of the warrantees, the names of their heirs and the places of their residence. [12]

Because of sales the warrantee and the patentee were often different persons, and there is an index to patentees in a manuscript volume at the National Archives entitled "Virginia Military Land Patent Index (vol. 34)." This index also tells the name of the warrantee and the location of the entry file, in addition to the name of the patentee.

As you know, much of Kentucky was settled as a result of Revolutionary War bounty land warrants from the Virginia Line, and Willard R. Jillson, Old Kentucky Entries and Deeds, 1926, (Baltimore: Genealogical Publishing Co., 1969 reprint), pp. 313-392, is a record of these warrants.

Bounty Land Entries (other than the Virginia warrants) are filed and indexed in various series at the National Archives. They are discussed in some detail in Chapters Twenty-one and Twenty-two. Let it suffice here

---

11. Letter from Gayle E. Manges, Field Solicitor, Santa Fe Field Office, United States Interior Department, February 28, 1969.

12. Colket and Bridgers, pp. 110-111.

for us to mention briefly those warrants issued for unspecified public land as a result of the various Congressional acts between 1847 and 1855. (These acts, as we said earlier, were different from all prior legislative acts in that they were passed to reward those who had already served rather than to induce men to enlist.) Nearly all of these warrants were sold by their recipients.

Most of the files contain no genealogical data about the warrantee except in the unlikely case that he died while still in possession of the warrant. In such an instance the file would contain the names and places of residence of his heirs. All patentees are identified and the location of the land is shown. The files are arranged by year of the basic Congressional act, thereunder by the number of acres awarded, and then chronologically by warrant number. Applications for these bounty land warrants are arranged alphabetically in two series at the National Archives—one series for those with Revolutionary War service and one for those with later service. Locating the application enables you to locate the applicant's file. [13]

No bounty land warrants were issued after passage of the Homestead Act in 1862. Veterans were instead given special consideration under the various homestead acts as we have already discussed.

E. HOMESTEAD ENTRY FILES

The Homestead Entry papers are filed in the National Archives under the names of the individual land offices, usually in two separate series— one series for those who completed their entries and the other for those who did not. These files cover 1863 to 1908. A completed file includes...

... the homestead application, the certificate of publication of intention to make a claim, the homestead proof consisting of two witnesses and the testimony of the claimant, and the final certificate authorizing the claimant to obtain a patent; and also, when appropriate, a copy of naturalization proceedings or a copy of a Union veteran's discharge certificate. [14]

Regarding the information contained in these records, Colket and Bridgers further explain:

A homestead application shows the name of the entryman, the place of his residence at the time of application, the descrip-

---

13. Ibid., pp. 90, 115.
14. Ibid., p. 108.

tion of the tract, and number of acres in the tract. The testimony of claimant on a homestead proof shows a description of the tract; the name, age, and post office address of the claimant, the date the patent was issued, and the volume and page number of the recorded copy of the patent in the Bureau of Land Management... A copy of naturalization proceedings relating to a naturalized citizen or an alien who had declared his intention of becoming a citizen shows such information as the name of the immigrant, the date and port of his arrival, and the place of his birth. [15]

Homestead entries which were commuted to cash entries are in the Cash Entry Files and include all previously-completed homestead papers.

F. PRIVATE LAND CLAIM ENTRIES

The National Archives has records of private land claims relating to parts of 15 states: Illinois, Indiana, Michigan and Wisconsin (all originally in the Northwest Territory); Alabama and Mississippi (both originally in the Mississippi Territory); Louisiana and the Missouri Territory states of Arkansas, Iowa and Missouri (all originally part of the Louisiana Purchase); Florida (originally the Florida Cession from Spain); and Arizona, California, Colorado and New Mexico (states in and adjacent to the southwestern territory ceded to the U.S. by Mexico). [16]

The records arising out of various private land claims vary with both time period and territory. Some of the available records include certificates of survey, surveyors' reports, Congressional reports, board of commissioners' reports, journals, claims papers, certificates of confirmation and maps. Many of these records are indexed but do not seem to have exhaustive genealogical data in them.

G. LAND ENTRIES SINCE 1908

All land entry records between July 1, 1908, and December 31, 1950, are filed in the National Archives in one numerical series, regardless of entry type. Colket and Bridgers describe these records:

Each file shows the name of the patentee; the place of his residence; the description of the tract in terms of subdivision, section, township, and range; the date of the patent; and the

---

15. Ibid., p. 108.
16. Ibid., pp. 116-117.

number of the file, which is also the number of the record copy of the patent in the Bureau of Land Management... Additional information in the file depends upon the type of land entry...

Files relating to land entries that have been cancelled, relinquished, or rejected during this period have been retained in part by the Federal Records Center, Alexandria, Virginia, and in part by the Bureau of Land Management. [17]

The records in the National Archives are available through the use of a card index located at the Bureau of Land Management.

VI. TEXAS

Earlier in this chapter we mentioned that Texas is not in the public domain even though it has no connection with the original states. At the time Texas was annexed in 1845 Texans considered themselves independent, though Mexico did not agree. (After the battle of San Jacinto in April 1836, Mexico had no actual control over Texas though such was never admitted.) Because of the unique situation of annexing an independent republic, special agreements were made in regard to control of public land and the state's responsibility for her own debts.

Prior to the time when Texas entered the Union she proposed that the U.S. pay her $10,000,000 public debt in return for title to her public lands. The Congress rejected this arrangement on two occasions. The third time annexation came before Congress Texas agreed to assume responsibility for her own public debt if she could retain title to her public land. This proposal was accepted as the condition of annexation. [18]

To help you appreciate the situation of Texas land, let's look at her land history. In 1820 Moses Austin left Missouri for Texas where he made an agreement with the governor that he could bring 300 families into the state. He died shortly after arriving back in the U.S. and left his son, Stephen F. Austin, to fulfill the agreement.

Young Austin brought the first settlers into the Brazos Valley in December 1821 only to learn that his father's agreement with the governor needed also to be ratified by the Mexican Congress. This was not finally achieved until 1823. Under the agreement Austin allowed each of the 300 families one labor (177 acres) for farming and 74 labors (13,098 acres) for stock raising. This made one sitio or one square league (13,275 acres) for each settler. He charged only 12 1/2 cents per acre to cover expenses of administration

---

17. Ibid., p. 127.

18. Letter from Jerry Sadler, Commissioner of Texas General Land Office, Austin, Texas, February 18, 1969.

and settlement.

By September 1824 there were 272 families who had received grants from Austin, and at about the same time he was given permission to bring another 300 families from the United States.

About this same time—March 1825—Mexico passed a Colonization Act under which it contracted empresarios to bring in families who, upon coming, would receive a league of land (4428 acres) by paying $30 in three installments. If an empresario brought in 100 families he would be entitled to five leagues of grazing land and five labors of farming land for himself. However, Austin's colonies still proved the more popular; the empresarios were really no competition.

Most of the pioneers coming into Texas were Americans, chiefly from Missouri, Tennessee and Kentucky. By 1830 there were some 20,000 Americans in Texas.

Later, after the battle of San Jacinto, when America was recovering from the financial crash of 1837, the Republic of Texas offered every family that would settle in her boundaries 1280 acres of free land. This gift proved very popular despite unsettled conditions and threats from Mexico. Hence Texas grew rapidly in population as she continued to grant her land under this liberal policy, a policy which continued even after annexation.

All of these Texas land grants are filed at the State Land Office in Austin.

VII. OTHER STATE-LAND STATES

Just because the land in the 13 original states, and a few others closely allied thereto, was not placed in the public domain is no indication that all available land in those states had already been granted. This, of course, is quite untrue since many of these states—especially the newer ones—had considerable ungranted lands. The individual states, however, rather than the federal government, were in exclusive control of those lands.

There were many land grants issued by these states. In fact the process was not essentially different from what it had been in the colonies. So far as records are concerned the procedure varied from one colony to another (or from one state to another). Some, both before and after the Revolution, preserved land-grant records with the deeds and other local land records. Others, such as Georgia, Maryland, Massachusetts, Pennsylvania, Tennessee and Virginia, kept their land-grant records in state land offices.

CHAPTER SIXTEEN

LOCAL LAND RECORDS

Local land records are those which are the result of the fifth phase of American land transfer as indicated in the last chapter. They are the records of land transactions between individual parties under the jurisdiction of a local governmental unit, most often the county. As you use the records of such transactions the first two basic terms you will need to know are GRANTOR and GRANTEE. In a land conveyance the seller is called the grantor and the buyer is called the grantee.

I. LAND TITLES

Let's briefly discuss the nature of land titles as a basis for a better understanding of land records. We have already mentioned many of the terms related to land titles in earlier chapters, but we need to look at them again purely in the context of land records.

The best title a person can hold in real property is called FEE SIMPLE. In America fee simple has always meant that the estate would potentially last forever and descend to one's heirs if he died intestate, or it could be devised by will, or that the owner could sell it (or any part of it) any time he chose to do so. The chief obstacles preventing fee simple from being absolute ownership are:

1. The provisions in our land law which say that an estate will escheat (see Chapter Twelve) to the state when there are no heirs. This is a carry-over from feudal law.

2. The right of eminent domain which gives the government the right to take private lands for public purposes upon payment of just compensation.

There are many kinds of estates less than fee simple and most of these, with some limitations, can also be sold by the title holder and sometimes be left to his heirs or devisees. These include LIFE ESTATES, ESTATES TAIL (or FEE TAIL), ESTATES UPON CONDITION, ESTATES FOR YEARS and ESTATES FROM YEAR TO YEAR (or ESTATES AT WILL), plus a few others. All of these types of estates are less than absolute. Though some give greater portions of the complete title than others, none is fee simple except certain estates upon condition.

A LIFE ESTATE merely entitles the holder to possess title to the property during the period of his own life or the life of some other specified person (life estate per autre vie). A dower estate is a life estate but we will talk more about that later. Also, we find some persons selling their lands in their old age, usually to their children or other relatives, and preserving a life estate for themselves. Thus they dispose of their fee simple estate before their deaths without being uprooted from the "old homestead." After the death which terminates a life estate the future interest which has been created becomes possessory.

In ESTATE TAIL the ownership is not absolute because of the limitation on the holder that he cannot convey more than a life estate (his own life) in the property but, upon his death, it will descend to some particular class of heir only, usually the heirs of his body (forever). Most estates tail are created by wills, but not all of them. Should the line and the posterity entitled to tail cease the estate would terminate and the property title would revert (in fee simple) to the estate from which it was created. Tails can be either general, special, male or female. Today they are not legal in most states because they make land inalienable. If the language of an instrument would create an estate tail, different jurisdictions react in different ways.

An ESTATE UPON CONDITION is based upon the happening of some uncertain event. It can be created by such an event (and may be fee simple), it can be enlarged (again perhaps fee simple) or it can be terminated. The condition must be valid and must not violate good morals or public policy. Many states have put time limits on conditions which cause forfeiture because the law abhors a forfeiture for they tend to make land inalienable.

Many estates upon condition are created by wills. An example of such an estate is provided by the provision which a man makes in his will to provide for his widow by leaving her certain lands "during the space of her widowhood." If she remarried her estate in that land would terminate and title would revert to the estate from which it came, that of the deceased husband (unless such a provision was ruled to be against public policy).

An ESTATE FOR YEARS usually exists by virtue of a lease. It exists by contract for a definite and specified time period, the length of which is not significant. Such an estate usually exists by virtue of the payment of an interest or rent, but not always.

Closely related to an estate for years is an ESTATE FROM YEAR TO YEAR. It extends for an unspecified period upon the mutual agreement of the parties. It is sometimes referred to as an estate at will and is very common. The period may be less than a year—even from week to week or from month to month, depending on how rent is reserved.

All of the above types of estates are less than fee simple except as stated and can affect the records which are kept. Let's look now at some of the record types that have arisen out of private land ownership.

II. TYPES OF LAND RECORDS

Some of the records which we list here will not be new to you, or even new to our discussion; many were introduced when we discussed probate records. However, as we mentioned at that time, land and probate records are generally recorded in different places. We have duplicated only to clarify and not to confuse, so don't be confused by our tactics.

Many of the definitions found in this chapter have been taken from, or are based on, the definitions published in Black's Law Dictionary, revised fourth edition (1968), copyrighted by West Publishing Company, St. Paul, Minnesota, and all rights are reserved. Any further reproduction of these legal definitions without consent of the copyright proprietor is prohibited. The records are as follows:

ABSTRACT OF TITLE: An abstract of title is a condensed history of the title to a piece of real estate. It should include a summary of every conveyance of the property, all restrictions and express easements, and a statement of all liens or charges against it. It will often include maps, platts and other aids. In most localities abstract offices have been set up by individuals or corporations who will, for a fee, furnish an abstract of the title to any real estate in the jurisdiction. In some places the accuracy of the abstracts is guaranteed; in other places it is not. In any case the abstract is not a complete record, but it can serve as an (expensive) index to the original records. The description of the land (by subdivision, section, township and range) is essential in locating a title at the various title and abstract offices as tract indexing is used (see the discussion on indexes at the end of this chapter).

AGREEMENT: There are various things upon which two (or more) parties can agree which might be recorded in land records. The term simply implies that the parties have given mutual assent to a particular matter which might change some of their rights or obligations. A typical example might be the agreement made between George Litzinger and his wife Elizabeth (of the first part) and John Boardley and Isaac Perryman (second part) in Baltimore County, Maryland, March 31, 1802. They signed an agreement which would...

> ...keep and leave open an alley on the west side
> of the brick house now occupied by the said Boardley
> of the width of three feet and running back of the depth
> of thirty six feet from King Tamany street which alley

shall be for the use and benefit of the said parties their heirs or assigns provided always and... that the said George Litzinger and Elizabeth his wife their heirs or assigns shall have the privilege and benefit of building over the said alley against the west wall of the said brick house at least thirteen feet from the surface of the earth without the least trouble or interruption of the said Perryman and Boardley their heirs or assigns....

An agreement is similar to a contract yet the term is a broader one.

ANTENUPTIAL CONTRACT: This is a contract which a man and his bride-to-be execute wherein the property rights of one or the other or both are delineated. Such agreements are usually made prior to a second marriage and are often for the purpose of securing certain properties for the children of the former union(s), though this is not always the case. So far as we know, these settlements are found in the records of most states but are especially prevelant in states with community property laws and were also common among the Dutch in New Netherland. The following antenuptial contract provides for the inheritance rights of the bride-to-be and her daughter by a former marriage:

This indenture made this thirteenth day of June... one thousand eight hundred and one between Patrick Bennet of... Baltimore,... Maryland of the one part Elizabeth McCay of the same place... of the second part and James Bennet of the same place... of the third part WHEREAS a marriage is agreed upon... to be shortly... solemnised between... Patrick Bennet and Elizabeth McCay Now this indenture WITNESSETH that ... Patrick Bennet in consideration of the... intended marriage and of the personal estate which... Elizabeth McCay stands possessed of and which... Patrick Bennet will be entitled to and also for... the sum of five shillings... to him... paid by James Bennet... before the sealing... of these presents the receipt whereof is hereby acknowledged hath... transferred and set over ... unto... James Bennet... all that... parcel of ground... on Fells Point... plat... number two... TO HAVE AND TO HOLD the said... parcel of ground ... unto James Bennet... until said marriage shall take effect... and immediately after the solomnization thereof to the use of Patrick Bennet... during his nat-

ural life and from immediately after the decease of...
Patrick Bennet in case... Elizabeth McCay shall survive him to the use of... Elizabeth... in the name of a
Jointure [1]... and will... pay... unto Ann Alley the
daughter of... Elizabeth McCay by a former marriage
... five hundred dollars... at... the age of twenty one
years or day of marriage... and the said Elizabeth
McCay doth... agree... to accept... the provision before made for her... for her Jointure in lieu... of all
such dower... at common law which she... might... be
entitled to out of... any freehold lands whereof...
Patrick Benet... shall be seized... in case... Patrick shall... die intestate....

These are also called antenuptial agreements, antenuptial
settlements and marriage settlements.

ASSIGNMENT: In most cases the assignments you will find recorded
in land-record books have to do with the assignment of certain property rights such as the unexpired term of a lease or life estate,
but also include the assignment of all types of property rights. It
is not uncommon to see trusts and mortgages involved in assignments.

BILL OF SALE: We are sure that you are already aware that a bill of
sale is a statement indicating a transfer of ownership by sale, and
that it is certainly not ordinarily a land record. However, bills of
sale, especially those involving the buying and selling of slaves,
were frequently recorded in the land-record books.

CONTRACT: A contract is an agreement made between two or more
persons to do something for their reciprocal benefit. The law
recognizes a duty therein and it is enforceable under the law. A
contract for the sale of land is made prior to the making of the deed
and is completely fulfilled with the delivery of the deed. In such
a contract the seller is called the vendor and the buyer is called
the vendee. These documents are seldom recorded.

CONVEYANCE: See DEED.

DEED: The deed (or conveyance) is our main consideration in a study
of local land records. It is the document by which title in real
property is transferred from one party to another. There are dif-

---

1. Jointure is an estate conveyed to the wife in lieu of dower. In establishing it the husband secures for his wife a freehold estate to take effect
upon his decease and to continue during her life (again a life estate but not
limited to one-third of the real property as is dower).

ferent types of deeds but the most common type is the <u>deed in fee</u>
which conveys a fee simple title. It is usually referred to simply
as a <u>deed</u> and that is how we shall refer to it. Other significant
types of deeds are discussed separately under their various titles.
(Note especially WARRANTY DEED and QUITCLAIM DEED.)

DEED IN TRUST: See TRUST DEED.

DEED OF DIVISION: See PARTITION.

DEED OF GIFT: See GIFT DEED.

DEED OF PARTITION: See PARTITION.

DEED OF RELEASE: This is a document which is executed by a lien
    holder once the lien, mortgage (deed of trust in many states) or
    other encumbrances have been paid. It returns the complete title
    to its owner. This is sometimes called a <u>release</u> (q. v.), but it is
    usually quite different from the document ordinarily referred to as
    a release.

DEED OF TRUST: See TRUST DEED.

DEPOSITION: We mentioned depositions under probate records, but let
    us define the term again. A deposition is a written testimony of a
    witness to a certain matter. Such a testimony is not taken in
    open court but may be used there (under certain conditions) and
    must be properly authenticated by the court official in charge of
    taking it. It is taken under oath. Depositions were often taken to
    verify land titles and to help settle matters of land dispute because
    boundary markers were often removed or destroyed and surveys
    were sometimes inaccurate or based on incorrect reference points.
    The following deposition, which was one of several taken relative
    to the same matter, is typical of those you might find recorded
    with the local land records:

> A deposition of Nicholas Frost aged about Sixty
> yeares, or thereabouts, This deponent Sayth that about
> sixteen or seaventeen yeares since, Thomas Crockett
> had possession of a necke of Land in Spruse Cricke,
> lying on the North Side of the cricke, against the field,
> he now hath. His possession was had by falling tymber
> & clearing ground, and made preparation to build an
> house upon the Sd Land, & further Saith not, Taken upon
> oath before me Nicholas Shapleigh this 30th of the 4th
> 1658.

DIVISION: See PARTITION.

DOWER RELEASE: See RELEASE OF DOWER.

GIFT DEED: This is a deed whereby real property is transferred with-
    out normal consideration. Usually such deeds transfer real estate

from a parent to his offspring, but there is no rule about that. The consideration is often stated as: "... the natural love and affection which I bear towards my son _____ and for other valuable consideration..." An example follows:

> Know all men by these presents, that I Richard Kirle of Kittery in the County of Yorke, as well for my natural affection & parentall Love wch I bear to my well beloved Son in law, Samuell Knight of s^d Towne & County, as allso for diverse others good Causes & Considerations, me at present especially moving, have freely given & granted, & by these presents do give & grant to s^d Samuell Knight Six Acres of Land being part of a Town Grant of fiveteen Acres of Land, lying & being in Kittery, s^d Knight Part shall begin at the Great Cove, & so run sixty eight Pole next to the Land, which is now Remonicks Land, and such breadth, as makes up the forementioned Summ of Acres - To have & to hold all & singular the s^d six Acres of Land to s^d Knight, his Heires, Executors, Administrators, & Assignes forever to their own proper Use & Behoof, freely and Quietly without any matter of Challenge or claim, or demand, of me the s^d Kirle, or of any other person or persons w^{t}soever for me, in my name, by my cause, meanes, or procurement, and without any money or other thing to be yeilded and paid, unto me s^d Kirle, my Heires, Executors or Assignes, And I the said Kirle all the s^d Land to the s^d Knight his Heires, Executors, Administrators, & Assignes, to the use aforesaid against all People doth Warrant & defend by these presents, And farther Know that the s^d Kirle, hath put s^d Knight in peaceable and Quiet Possesion of the s^d Land, at the delivering & Sealing of the presents, as wittnesse my hand Seale this twenty seventh day of July one thousand, six hund, & seventy six.
>
> Signed Sealed & delivered in
> the presence of us
>   his
> John ✝ Green   (signed) Richard Kirle
>   marke
> Thomas Spinney,

LEASE: An agreement which creates a landlord-tenant relationship is called a lease. Because it transfers an estate in real property it is very much like a deed and all rights of each party are defined within it. Though the document itself is much like a deed in its format the title transferred is less than fee simple and its duration is usually specified. The estate which one holds under such an instrument is referred to as <u>leasehold</u> or as an <u>estate for years</u>.

LETTER OF ATTORNEY: See POWER OF ATTORNEY.

LIEN: A lien is not a land record but should be mentioned because it does relate thereto. It is a claim by one party upon the property of another for security in the payment of a debt. In some (most) states mortgages (q.v.) do not create legal title but are merely liens against the property.

MARRIAGE SETTLEMENT: This can be either an <u>antenuptial contract</u> (q.v.) or a similar postnuptial contract.

MEASUREMENTS OF LAND: As you read old land records you may come across land measurements which are not familiar to you, so let's look at a few of the most common units of measurement which you will encounter:

ACRE: 43,560 square feet, 160 square rods.

CHAIN: 66 feet or 22 yards (100 links).

FURLONG: 660 feet or 220 yards (10 chains).

LINK: 7.92 inches. (There are 25 links in a rod and 100 links in a chain.)

MILE: 5,280 feet (80 chains, 32 rods or 8 furlongs).

PERCH: 5 1/2 yards or 16 1/2 feet; also called <u>rod</u> or <u>pole</u>.

POLE: 5 1/2 yards or 16 1/2 feet; also called <u>perch</u> or <u>rod</u>.

ROD: 5 1/2 yards or 16 1/2 feet; also called <u>pole</u> or <u>perch</u>.

ROOD: As a measurement of length this varies from 5 1/2 yards (rod) to 8 yards, depending on locality. It was also used sometimes to describe an area equal to 1/4 acre.

MORTGAGE: A mortgage is a conditional transfer of legal title to real property as security for payment of a debt. It is much like a deed in its form, but if the conditions prescribed therein are met (the debt is paid) the conveyance becomes void. Actual legal title is transferred by this deed to the mortgagee under common law and he has the right to possess the land. In many states, especially in more recent times, the common law rule of mortgages has been altered and no title is transferred; it is regarded rather as a <u>lien</u> (q.v.) upon the property.

PARTITION: When two or more persons hold real estate as cotenants (such as the undivided property left them in a probate settlement) and they wish to divide that property among them, a partition or deed of partition is made and recorded. It shows the separate parts taken by each. No additional title is taken or conveyed by any party to such an instrument but a joint title is divided into separate titles. This is sometimes called a <u>division</u>.

PETITION: We discussed petitions when we discussed probate records, but they are also very common in land records. A petition is a request made to a court for action in a matter not the subject of a suit. A good example is provided in the petition recorded in Land Book No. 1 in Kossuth County, Iowa, and made by the administrators of the estate of Thomas Gallion in 1882:

> The petition of E. S. Streeter & J. H. Grover administrators of the Estate of Thomas Gallion of Kossuth County - Iowa respectfully shows to this court That the said Thomas Gallion died on or about the 19th day of August 1881 in said county, leaving an estate to be administered upon. Your petitioners were duly qualified administrators of his estate and letters of administration were issued to them on the 30th day of Sept. 1881 which has never been revoked.
>
> Your petitioners duly made and returned a true inventory of all the personal property, book accounts &c of the said deceased on the 14th day of October 1881.
>
> They also published due notice of their appointment as administrators and notified all parties who were indebted to the estate by such publication to pay the debts due the estate, and all creditors to present their claims duly verified for allowance and payment—all of which will more fully appear by a referance to the papers on file in the clerks office.

> The amount of property which has come into
> the administrators hand is valued at $414.66
> The amount which has been paid out for debts
> and expenses of administration $ 69.00
> The amount set aside to the widow as exempt
> from execution as provided by Law $381.16
> The amount debts due from the estate $300.00
> The necessary expenses of administration in
> the future $ 50.00
> Total amount due when the estate will be
> settled $419.00
> The above said decedent died possessed in fee of a certain tract of land containing eighty acres situated in Kossuth County Iowa described as follows to wit the South half of South west quarter of sec thirty-six (36) in Township # Ninety seven (97) North of range # twenty Eight (28) west of 5th P. M. Iowa.

The whole of which estate was acquired by him since his marriage. Also the following are the names and ages of the devisees of the deceased to wit.

— Jane Gallion widow of Deceased   age 64
Thomas S. Gallion son of Deceased   "   40
John Gallion   " "   "   "   38
Maggie Stahl daughter of Deceased   "   35
James Gallion son   "   "   "   33
W. J. Gallion   "   "   "   "   30
Robert Gallion "   "   "   "   25

Your petitioners therefore allege that the personal estate in the hands of the petitioners is insufficient to pay the debts, and the allowance to the family and expenses of administration and that it is necessary to sell the whole or some of the real estate for that purpose.

Wherefore your petitioners pray that an order be made by said court directing all persons interested in said real estate to appear before said Court at such time as it may appoint to show cause why an order should not be granted to your petitioners to sell so much real estate as shall be necessary.

And that after a full hearing of this petition and examinations of the proofs and allegations of the parties interested due proof of the publication of a copy of said order to show cause &c an order of sale be made authorizing your petitioners to sell so much, and such parts of the real estate as said Court shall Judge necessary or beneficial or that such or farther order May be necessary in the premises.

(signed) E. S. Streater
(signed) J. H. Grover.

POWER OF ATTORNEY: When a person is unable to act for himself in a certain matter and appoints another to act for him, the document by which he does so is called a power of attorney or letter of attorney. The person thus appointed becomes an attorney in fact in the performance of specified acts. If a man who lives in Iowa inherits property from his grandfather who died in North Carolina and he wishes to sell that property he may make a power of attorney to his brother (or anyone else he chooses) who lives much closer, authorizing him to act as his agent in selling the property. As long as he is acting within the limits specified in the power of attorney the closer brother can do all things as if he were actually the Iowa brother. John Cox made such a document in 1810:

Know all men by these presents that I John Cox, of
Knox County and state of Kentucky have made ordained
Constituted & appointed, and by these presents do make
ordain Constitute & appoint Samuel Cox Jun[r] my true &
Lawful attorney, for me & in my name, but For my use
to do perform & Transact all my Business In the State
of Virginia To make a deed of Conveyance To a Certain
tract of Land Lying in Grayson County in the State of
Virginia it being the Same Which Robert still Sold as
agent for me To a Certain William Byers, To Collect
all money or Moneys which may be due me and to Transact any other Business Which may be Necessary for my
wellfare and Well Standing in the Said State of Virginia
and what ever Lawful act my said attorney may do or
Cause to be done for me and in My Name I do by these
presents ratify and Confirm, in witness where of I have
here unto set my hand and affixed my seal this 28th day
of August 1810.

Teste   his
Nathan Cox   John ✖ Cox
Richard Cox   mark

QUITCLAIM DEED: A quitclaim deed is an instrument by which a person releases all title, interest or claim which he may possess in
certain real properties without making any warrants thereto. (He
merely conveys all he has.) The title or claim released is <u>not</u>
<u>necessarily</u> a valid one, but on many occasions it is the instrument
of a valid conveyance of land. One example of a situation which
might produce a quitclaim deed would be an error in a land survey.
When the error is corrected the party affected by it often makes a
quitclaim deed releasing all claim to the paper title which he held
before the correction.

RELEASE: A release is a document by which a person gives up, to another, his right to something in which he has a just claim. Such a
conveyance must be, under common law, to a person who has either
possession or interest in the property. It does not constitute a
cancellation of rights but must be supported by lawful consideration.
A cotenant of undivided lands can transfer his rights to another cotenant by a release. (There is an example of a release in Chapter
Fourteen.)

Releases are sometimes erroneously confused with <u>assign-</u>
<u>ments</u> (q. v.). They are also quite different from <u>deeds of release</u>
(q. v.) in most jurisdictions.

RELEASE OF DOWER: We discussed the nature of dower briefly under probates, but it might be worth while to review a couple of essential points here just to show why such a document exists. Dower, of course, is the right (to a life estate) which the widow has in the real estate of her deceased husband under the common law, but the thing that is significant is that any property which he has procured in fee simple during their marriage is subject to her dower claim. This means that even though a man sells "Blackacre" his widow can come back after his death, even if it has been 50 years since the sale, and legally claim dower in it. Consequently, when a person bought a piece of land he was usually pretty careful to see that the wife of the grantor signed the deed or executed a release of her dower rights. Through such she relinquished all claims. Though genealogically it may tell no more than her name, the release of dower, by giving that name, provides evidence which may sometimes be found in no other place.

Releases of dower will ordinarily not be found in public domain states but there are exceptions. It was more common in these states for the wife to sign the deed.

RELEASE OF MORTGAGE: See DEED OF RELEASE.

SURRENDER: A surrender as a land record is much like a deed in its form and involves the yielding or giving up of a lease (an estate for years) before its term is expired. It is not an abandonment but is made with the mutual consent of both parties.

TAX RECORDS: Through the years tax records have been widely recognized as an important genealogical source. When many of the early census schedules were lost they were replaced (reasonably well) by contemporary tax lists. Others have been published separately; and many others have been microfilmed. In some places, during the early periods, you can follow your ancestors through the tax lists almost as if they (the lists) were a yearly census. We will look later at how these records provide data to help solve pedigree problems.

TRUST DEED: In most states where you find trust deeds recorded in the land records you will find that they are a type of mortgage. They operate by placing the title to real property in one or more trustees to secure the payment of a debt. For example, the State of Maryland passed early legislation allowing the legal title to the property of certain insolvent debtors to be transferred to trustees in behalf of the creditors. The instrument of such a transfer was referred to as a <u>deed in trust</u> or trust deed. Though the approach may be slightly different, these records are not unlike those which may be found in several other states and in the District of Columbia. The arrangement under which such a trust is established allows the property to be sold in case of default and for the appli-

cation of net proceeds to the payment of debts, turning all surplus
back to the debtor.

WARRANTY DEED: A warranty deed is perhaps the most important
and common type of deed. Thereby the grantor warrants (by covenant) the title of the property he sells; and should the title become
faulty because of paramount claims against it, or for any other
reason, the grantor (or his heirs) may be sued on the warranty.
See also DEED.

You will also find other kinds of documents, including various court
orders (decrees) and miscellaneous probate instruments, recorded in land-
record books in various localities. Some states, as we mentioned in Chapter Thirteen, even require the filing of certain final papers of probate with
the custodian of local land records to be recorded by him as proof of title.
The important thing is for you not to be too fussy about what you find in land
records; just use what you find there. In all states the recording acts provide that most any document may be recorded upon payment of the proper
fee. And most documents affecting land titles are recorded as a measure
to secure those titles.

III. USING LAND RECORDS

We have used up a great deal of space in defining and describing, but we
have said little about the value of land records. And knowing all about them
is not very helpful if they contain nothing of value.

Our earlier observation about land records being among the best sources
for American genealogical research is true. Land and probate records are,
in fact, the American researcher's "bread and butter," and what we said
about the general value of land records in Chapter Fifteen is especially true
of those land records which arise from private ownership. When you consider that a large percentage of your American ancestors were probably
land owners, that good land records exist right from the beginning of most
of the early permanent settlements in America and that the older records
uniquely contain much more genealogical data than their modern counterparts, then you can begin to comprehend the significance of this much-over-
looked genealogical source.

A. RELATIONSHIPS

You already know that local land records contain the names of men's
wives, a very useful tool in their (the men's) identification, but did you know
that these records also contain many other statements of relationship?
Someone has suggested that statements of relationship (other than husband
and wife) are found in about 10 per cent of the early American deeds—and

the earlier the better.   Our experience tells us that this figure is probably about right, but in some localities the percentage is somewhat higher— much depended upon the scribe and upon local custom.   But regardless of what the percentage might have been, the important thing is that if any possibility at all exists of your finding a relationship in a deed which will help in solving a genealogical problem, you ought to be ready and willing to search for that deed.   There are many such possibilities.

This brings us back to an old theme—one we hope is indelibly stamped on your memory by now—that you must search the records for everyone of your surname (including spelling variations).   Remember that in this business of finding relationships in records you cannot determine beforehand what you are going to find.   You cannot afford to pick and choose if you want to be successful in research.

To illustrate some of the possibilities let's look at a few representative samples from deeds of Baltimore County, Maryland.   One of the most helpful of all deeds is the one where joint heirs in an estate (cotenants) combine as grantors to sell their property.   Consider the following example:

> This Indenture made this twenty fifth day of April in...
> Eighteen hundred and one between Ignatius Diggs and Charlotte
> his wife formerly Charlotte Weaver and Lewis Weaver of Balti-
> more County of the one part and Joshua Jones of the Same County
> of the other part WHEREAS Daniel Weaver by his last Will and
> Testament bearing date the 22^d March 1797 did devise and be-
> queath as follows....
>
> [The deed then goes on to quote part of the will in which Dan-
> iel Weaver named his son Daniel Weaver, daughter Elizabeth
> Hesson and daughter Charlotte Weaver.]... WHEREAS the said
> Daniel Weaver [the son] after having Complied with the Condi-
> tions aforesaid departed this life intestate leaving the aforesaid
> Charlotte and Lewis TOGETHER with Elizabeth Hesson now the
> Wife of Benjamin Morrison and John Weaver now under age his
> heirs and legal representatives. Now this Indenture WITNESS-
> ETH that the said Ignatius Diggs and Charlotte his wife and Lewis
> Weaver for... three hundred and eighty five Dollars....

This is as far as we need to go.   There is a lot of good relationship in-formation in that deed even though the relationships between all persons are not completely clear.   Relationship data like this are often found in deeds where there are co-grantors.   Now let's look at another deed:

> This indenture made this twenty second day of September in
> the year of our Lord one thousand eight hundred and one by and
> between Andrew Boyd the Elder of the City of Baltimore of the

one part and Elizabeth Boyd and Mary Boyd of said City and
daughters of the Said Andrew Boyd of the other part.... [James
P. Boyd signed as a witness.]

The foregoing is a deed of gift, and a quite unusual one at that—it has
co-grantees. Here's another interesting deed:

> This indenture made the thirtieth day of May in the year of
> our Lord eighteen hundred and one between John Hollins of the
> city of Baltimore in Baltimore County and state of Maryland
> Merchant Samuel Smith of the same County and State Esquire
> and Margaret his wife William Patterson of the same County and
> State Esquire and Dorcas his wife William Lee Forman of the
> same City County and State Merchant and Jane his wife and Jo-
> seph Spear of the same City County and State Merchant and Bar-
> bara his wife which said Margaret Smith Dorcas Patterson Jane
> Forman and Barbara Spear are the daughters of William Spear
> deceased late of Baltimore County and State aforesaid Merchant
> of the one part and Martin Eichelberger of the same City County
> and State Merchant of the other part WHEREAS by a decree of...
> chancellor of the said State of Maryland made in a cause depend-
> ing in the High Court of Chancery of the said State between Eph-
> raim Robinson and other Plaintiffs and Mary Spears heir of John
> Spear deceased defendant bearing date the first day of July in the
> year seventeen hundred and ninety-nine it was by the said Chan-
> cellor... adjudged ordered and decreed that the before named
> John Hollins be and he was thereby appointed trustee for making
> sale of the real estate late of the said deceased or so much there-
> of as would be necessary for the payment of his just debts....
> by public auction... and whereas the said Children of the said
> William Spear deceased and Sisters of the said John Spear also
> deceased and their respective husbands have agreed to join with
> the said John Hollins as trustee... In the conveyance....

A document much better than this one might be hard to find.

Also, well buried in land records are relationships of persons who are
neither grantor nor grantee. These, of course, are much harder (in fact
often impossible) to find, but their value cannot be denied. Consider the
following:

> THIS INDENTURE made this Sixteenth day of June in... one
> thousand eight hundred and one Between John Tolley Worthington
> of Baltimore County and State of Maryland of the one part and
> Caleb Merryman of the said County and State of the other part

WHEREAS William Ridgley of John by his deed of indenture bearing date the thirteenth day of April in... One thousand Seven hundred and Ninety five and recorded among the Land records of Baltimore County Court in Liber WGN⁰ TT folio 73 for the Considerations therein mentioned did Convey unto the said John Tolley Worthington... all that part of a tract called Well's mannor... in the County aforesaid which was devised to the said William by the last Will and Testament of his father John Ridgley late of Baltimore County deceased....

This deed tells us the relationship between William and John Ridgley but, as good as it is, would be almost impossible for the Ridgley researcher to find since it would not be indexed under either name.

B. PLACES

In addition to their giving relationships, deeds and their cousins are also useful because of the places of residence they state for both grantors and grantees. In all of the instruments from which we have just quoted you will note that this was true and that information is of value. However, it is usually of even greater value if the party you seek is from a place other than where the deed was recorded. If, for example, the grantee buys property before he moves into the county, the deed tells his immediate origin and facilitates an extension of research. And if the grantor sells his land after moving away, the deed will tell where he has gone and will expedite your search for him and his family in later records.

C. PROVING CONNECTIONS THROUGH LAND DESCRIPTIONS

Very often in genealogy we trace a pedigree back to a situation where an ancestor has one or more contemporaries with his same name and it is impossible, on the face of it, to distinguish one from the other in existing records. In circumstances like this, land descriptions can provide evidence to help solve the problem under certain circumstances. The technique is quite simple if the approach fits the situation. Let's look at the approach.

You tackle the problem in conventional fashion--i.e., you work from the known to the unknown gathering data on all persons of the surname. If you can do this the process will not be complicated and will not involve any special kind of research, but can be easily handled during the evaluation and tabulation of your research findings.

Not every genealogical problem can be solved through this approach. In fact it can work only when two specific conditions are present:

1. There is a positive identification of your ancestor at the time

he disposes of the land.

2. There is a direct statement of relationship—preferably a lineal relationship—between your ancestor and someone else in the instrument giving him (i.e., your ancestor) title to the land.

You must know that your ancestor owned land and that he disposed of it by a deed (or will) in which you positively identify him as grantor. (There must be <u>no</u> possibility of this person being his like-named counterpart.) You may identify him by the name of his wife—this is very common—or by his signature or mark, or by some other means. Regardless of method, that identification is essential.

The more deeds of this nature you find the better will be your chances for success. You must note very carefully the description of the lands being sold. (This is quite easy where the Rectangular Survey system was used but more difficult where land was described by metes and bounds unless the tracts were given specific names.)

Next you must find the instrument by which this tract of land was acquired by your ancestor. If the land was acquired from a relative and a statement of relationship between your ancestor and that relative is given, you are in luck. Any relationship thus stated increases your chances for solving the problem—but of course we prefer lineal connections. Sometimes you may find the land in question devised to your ancestor in his father's (or other relative's) will, and wills serve our purposes here as well as do deeds.

It all boils down to this: If you find your ancestor, John X, selling 100 acres of land of the same description as William X sold to his son John 16 years earlier, you have a pretty good case. This can be tricky though, because sometimes tracts are divided or combined with other tracts when they are sold.

IV. USING TAX RECORDS

There are varying kinds of tax records—in fact you will seldom find two exactly the same—but they can generally be divided into three main types:

1. Real property tax records.
2. Personal property tax records (primarily livestock and slaves).
3. A combination of the above two.

All of these are good but those which show records of persons taxed for personal property often have an advantage because they pick up persons established in the community but who own no land. Persons who owned little of anything may not be found in any of these lists.

Depending on locality and time period, taxes on real property usually

FIGURE 1—KENTUCKY TAX LISTS

Name	Land (acres)	County	Water course	In whose name entered	In whose name surveyed	In whose name patented	White males over 21	Blacks over 16	Total Blacks	Horses and mares	Value of land per acre	Valuation Total	chn. 4-14	chn. 7-17
1819:														
Cobb, William							1			1		$40		
Elisha							1			2		$90		
Asa							1			1		$40		
John	100	Owen	Eagle	Phillips & Young	same	same	1			3		$500		
1820:														
Daniel							1			1		$40		
Cobb, Thomas	100	Owen	Eagle	H. Marshall	same	same	1	1	1	4		$1,000		
William							1			1		$50		
John	100	Owen	Eagle	Phillips & Young	same	same	1			2		$500		
1821:														
Cobb, Asa							1			2		$80		
William							1			1		$50		
Elisha							1			1		$40		
Daniel							1			1		$30		
							1			1		$30		
							1			1		$60		
							1			1		$40		
John	100	Owen	Eagle	Phillips	same	same	1		1	2	4	$500		
Thomas	100	Owen	Eagle	Marshall	same	same	1	1	1	4	5	$1,050		

Name	Land (acres)	County	Water course	In whose name entered	In whose name surveyed	In whose name patented	White males over 21	Blacks over 16	Total Blacks	Horses and mares	Value of land per acre	Total valuation	Chn. 4-14	Chn. 7-17
1822:														
Cobb, William							1			2		$70	3	
Asa							1			1		$30		
Elisha							1			1		$65	1	
Thomas	100	Owen	Eagle	Marshall	same	same	1	1	1	4	2	$1,050	4	
Daniel							1			1		$40	3	
1823:														
Cobb, Asa							1			2		$60		
Elisha							1			1		$50		
Daniel							1			1		$50		
William							1			1		$100		
Thomas	100	Owen	Eagle	Marshall	do	do	1			4		$1,250		
John							1							
1824:														
Cobb, Thomas	100	Owen	Eagle	Marshall	do	do	1			4		$1,200		
William							1			1		$80		
Elisha							1			1		$50		
Asa							1			1		$75		
Daniel							1			2		$80		
1825:														
Cobb, William	100	Owen	Eagle	Weaver	same	same	1			1	3	$540		
Daniel							1			2		$150		
Asa							1			1		$100		
Elisha							1			3		$150		

Name	Land (acres)	County	Water course	In whose name entered	In whose name surveyed	In whose name patented	White males over 21	Blacks over 16	Total Blacks	Horses and mares	Value of land per acre	Total valuation	chn. 4-14	chn. 7-17
1825 (cont'd):														
Cobb, Thomas	100	Owen	Eagle	Marshall	same	same	1			5	3	$1,450		
same	300	Owen	Stevens	May & Co.	same	same	1			5		$950		
1826:														
Cobb, Thomas	100	Owen	Eagle	Weaver	same	same	1			2		$100		
Elisha	100			Weaver	same	same	1			2		$325		
William	100			Weaver			1			1		$65		
Asa	100						1			1		$40		
Daniel	100						1			2		$330		
1827:														
Cobb, William	100	Owen	Eagle	Marshall	do	do	1			4		$750		
Thomas	100	"	"	Weaver	do	do	1			1		$200		
Elisha	100	"	"	"	do	do	1			2		$280		
Daniel	50	"	"	Asburn	do	do	1			2		$350		
John	27	"	"	May & Co.	do	do	1			2		$200		
same	97 1/2	"	"	Weaver										
Asa		"	"		do	do								
1828:														
Cobb, John	102	Owen	Eagle	May & Co.	do	do	1			2	3	$356		
Elisha	100	"	"	Weaver & c	do	do	1			1	2	$250		
Thomas	100	"	"	Marshall	do	do	1			4	6	$750		
Daniel	100	"	"	Weaver	do	do	1			1	2.50	$280		
Asa	107	"	"	"	do	do	1			2	2	$239		

Name	Land (acres)	County	Water course	In whose name entered	In whose name surveyed	In whose name patented	White males over 21	Blacks over 16	Total Blacks	Horses and mares	Value of land per acre	Total valuation	chn. 4-14	chn. 7-17
1829:														
Cobb, Asa	97 1/2	Owen	Eagle	Weaver	do	do	1			2	2	$750	3	
Elisha	100	"	"	"	do	do	1			2	2	$250	3	
Daniel	60	"	"	Marshall	do	do	1			2	5	$350	4	
Thomas	100	"	"	Weaver	do	do	1			4	5	$660	3	
William	100	"	"	"	do	do	1			4	3	$460	4	
1830:														
Cobb, Elisha	100	Owen	Eagle	Weaver	do	do	1			2	2.50	$300		
Daniel	60	"	"	"	do	do	1			2	5	$350		
Asa	106	"	"	"	do	do	1			1	2.50	$310		
William	100	"	"	"	do	do	1			3	5	$625		
1831:														
Cobb, Elisha	100	Owen	Eagle	T. Weaver	do	do	1			3	2.50	$350		
Daniel	60	"	"	"	do	do	1			2	5	$360		
Asa	106 1/2	"	"	"	do	do	1			1	2.50	$300		
William	100	"	"	"	do	do	1			3	5	$600		
1832: Tax list is missing														
1833: Tax list is missing														
1834:														
Cobb, Asa	106	Owen	Eagle	Weaver	do	do	1			2	2.50	$325		
Elizabeth	40	"	"	"	do	do				1	3	$150		

Name	Land (acres)	County	Water course	In whose name entered	In whose name surveyed	In whose name patented	White males over 21	Blacks over 16	Total Blacks	Horses and mares	Value of land per acre	Total valuation	chn. 4–14	chn. 7–17
1834 (cont'd):														
Cobb, Elisha Jr							1			1		$10		
Daniel	100	Owen	Eagle	Weaver	do	do	1			2	5	$560		
Elisha	100	"	"	"	do	do	1			3	3	$410		
1835:														
Cobb, Asa	106	Owen	Eagle	Weaver	do	do	1			2	3	$390		
Daniel	100	"	"	"	do	do	1			3	5	$600		
Elisha	100	"	"	"	do,	do	1			4	3.50	$500		
Elizabeth	95	"	"	"						1	2	$270		
Elisha Jr							1			2		$30		
1836:														
Cobb, Elisha	100	Owen	Eagle	Weaver	do	do	1			3	5	$700		
Daniel	100	"	"	"	do	do	1			3	6	$730		
Elizabeth	40	"	"	"	do	do				1	25	$1,050		
Asa	106	"	"	"	do	do	1			2	3	$458		
Elisha Jr	100	"	Richland	Weaver	do	do	1			1	3	$330		
1837:														
Cobb, William	100	Owen					under age			1	2	$260		
Elisha Sr	950	"					1			5	5	$1,493		
Daniel	50	"					1			5	19	$1,200		
Elizabeth	100	"								1	8	$850		
Asa	156	"					1			1	6	$1,061		
Elisha Jr	100	"					1			1	2	$260		

Name	Land (acres)	County	Water course	In whose name entered	In whose name surveyed	In whose name patented	White males over 21	Blacks over 16	Total Blacks	Horses and mares	Value of land per acre	Total valuation	chn. 4-14	chn. 7-17
1838: Tax list is missing														
1839:														
Cobb, Asa	206									3	5	$1,030		
Danl	157									2	6	$942		
Elisha Sr	168									2	6	$1,008		
Danl F.	100									2	3	$300		
Wm	100									2	3	$300		
Elisha Jr	140									2	2.50	$350		
1840:														
Cobb, Elisha Sr	100	Owen	Eagle				1					$753		2
Asa	205	"	"				1					$940		3
Daniel F.	100	"	Elk				1					$275		
Daniel	155	"	Eagle				1					$1,670		
Elisha Jr	140	"	"				1					$323		1
William	100	"	Elk				1					$375		
1841:														
Cobb, Elisha Sr	110	Owen	Eagle				1			4		$744		3
Asa	207	"	"				1			3		$990		5
William	100	"	Elk				1			2		$350		
Daniel	155	"	Eagle				1			2		$1,076		1
Daniel F.	100		"				1			2		$275		
Elijah							1			1		$50		
Elisha Jr							1			1		$40		1

show the amount of land; its location (including on what watercourse); the persons in whose name it was originally entered, surveyed and patented; and its value.

All states did not keep good early tax records so this will not be a source you will use on every problem, but you need to keep it in mind. Let's look at Kentucky where some of the best tax lists were kept in early periods. Figure 1 illustrates the value of these records. For the illustration we have chosen the surname Cobb and followed it through 23 years of tax schedules in Owen County. Note carefully the nature of the information and the knowledge which can be gained when you consider everyone of the surname, every year, over a long period of time. (In this case we have actually stopped before we would have ordinarily.)

We know that these records leave many questions unanswered, but when other records—such as deeds, probates, marriage records, etc.—are used in conjunction with this information you can tell quite a lot about the persons involved.

Tax lists are usually kept in columnar form as you can observe, but we cheated a little and put everything on one standardized form. The forms of the actual schedules vary somewhat from year to year as witnessed by some of the blank spaces left on our form. Also, you should know that some of these lists have other minor columns which our form has omitted. As you study our example you will observe that there is nothing spectacular about tax lists. They just contain good basic data which might somewhere, sometime, provide the clues you need to help solve a genealogical problem.

V. LAND-OWNERSHIP MAPS

Another useful source for some time periods and some localities is old county land-ownership maps. In 1967 the Geography and Map Division of the Library of Congress in Washington, D.C., had some 1,449 pre-twentieth century land-ownership maps from 1,041 different U.S. counties. Most of these are counties in the northeastern states, north central states, California, Texas and Virginia and comprise in total nearly one-third of all American counties. About seven per cent of these maps are of pre-1840 vintage and about 24 per cent were published between 1840 and 1860. About 38 per cent were published between 1860 and 1880 and approximately 30 per cent between 1880 and 1900. [2]

These maps antedate county platbooks and topographical surveys of the U.S. Geological Survey, and scales vary from 1:3,960 to 1:600,000. Seventy-six per cent have scales larger than 1:100,000. [3] In most cases the

---

[2.] Richard W. Stephenson (comp.), Land Ownership Maps (Washington, D.C.: Library of Congress, 1967), pp. vii-viii.

[3.] Ibid., pp. vii-viii.

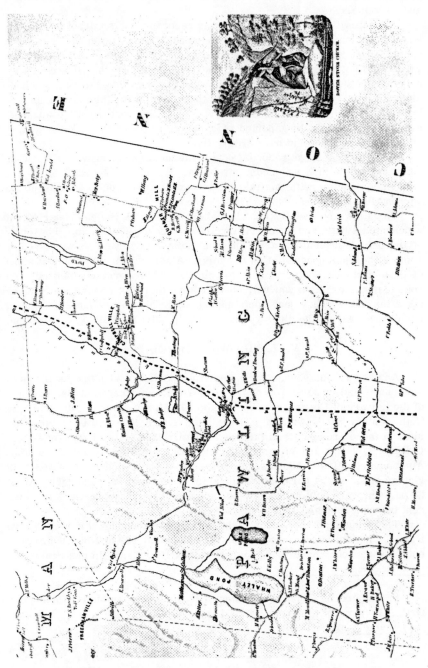

FIGURE 2—LAND OWNERSHIP MAP FOR PART OF DUTCHESS
COUNTY, NEW YORK (1:42,240—1850—J.C. SIDNEY).

names of land holders at the time the map was made are recorded directly on the map. Thus their genealogical value is quite obvious (see Figure 2).

Reproductions of most of these maps (usually photostats) are available from the Photoduplication Service, Library of Congress, Washington, D. C. 20540, for a small reproduction and mailing fee. Rates lists and cost estimates are furnished upon request. Payment must be made in advance on all orders for photoduplicates.

As a guide to the land-ownership map holdings of the Library of Congress, Richard W. Stephenson of the Geography and Map Division has compiled a checklist of the library's nineteenth century county maps in a small booklet as indicated in footnote number 2 in this chapter. The booklet is available from the Superintendent of Documents, U. S. Government Printing Office, Washington, D. C. 20402, for 70 cents.

VI. AVAILABILITY OF LAND RECORDS

Now that you have become more familiar with the value and use of local land records, let's look quickly at the problems of availability.

A. LOCATION

In most states land records are under county jurisdiction, but there are too many exceptions for us to give that as a standing rule. Following is a list of the courts and custodians of these land records in the several states. The record is always made in the jurisdiction where the land in question happens to lie:

ALABAMA:	Probate Judge of county.
ALASKA:	Recorder of judicial district.
ARIZONA:	County Recorder.
ARKANSAS:	County Recorder. (County Circuit Clerk is ex-officio recorder.)
CALIFORNIA:	County Recorder.
COLORADO:	County Recorder.
CONNECTICUT:	Town Clerk.
DELAWARE:	County Recorder of Deeds. (Use is restricted to attorneys at law, but the LDS Genealogical Society has all deed books up to 1850 on microfilm.)
D. C.:	Recorder of Deeds (6th and D Streets, N. W.).
FLORIDA:	Clerk of County Circuit Court.
GEORGIA:	Clerk of County Superior Court.
HAWAII:	Registrar of Conveyances, Honolulu.
IDAHO:	County Recorder.

ILLINOIS: County Recorder of Deeds (in counties over 60,000 population) and County Clerk (in counties of smaller population).

INDIANA: County Recorder.

IOWA: County Recorder of Deeds.

KANSAS: County Clerk has transfer books recording all transfers before deeds can be recorded by the County Register of Deeds.

KENTUCKY: County Clerk (also called Clerk of County Court).

LOUISIANA: Recorder of Mortgages and Register of Conveyances in the parish. (The Clerk of the Court is ex-officio Register and Recorder except in Orleans Parish.)

MAINE: Register of Deeds in the county, in all but Aroostook and Oxford counties. (In Aroostook County there is a Northern Registry District at Fort Kent and a Southern Registry District at Houlton. In Oxford County there is a Western Registry District at Fryeburg and an Eastern Registry District at South Paris.)

MARYLAND: Clerk of the Circuit Court for the County. (In Baltimore County it is the Clerk of the Superior Court.) All land records for Maryland before the federal Constitution was ratified in 1788 are in the Hall of Records, Annapolis. There are also many records right up to the twentieth century housed at the Hall of Records, but this is purely at the discretion of county officials and not because of law. Some of these records were housed in the State Land Office at Annapolis but that office was recently abolished and the records transferred to the Hall of Records.

MASSACHUSETTS: The Registry of Deeds in the county, except for five counties which have more than one registry office. (Berkshire County has a Northern District at North Adams, a Middle District at Pittsfield and a Southern District at Great Barrington. Bristol County has a Northern District at Taunton and a Southern District at New Bedford. Essex County has a Northern District at Lawrence and a Southern District at Salem. Middlesex County has a Northern District at Lowell and a Southern

District at Cambridge. Worcester County has a Northern District at Fitchburg and a Worcester District at Worcester.) You need to be acutely aware of dates of creation of various counties and districts.

MICHIGAN: County Register of Deeds.

MINNESOTA: County Register of Deeds.

MISSISSIPPI: Clerk of the Chancery Court in the county. (In the district if the county is divided.)

MISSOURI: Recorder of Deeds in the county.

MONTANA: County Clerk and Recorder.

NEBRASKA: Register of Deeds in the county. (In counties of less than 16,000 the County Clerk is ex-officio Register.)

NEVADA: County Recorder.

NEW HAMPSHIRE: Town Clerk.

NEW JERSEY: County Register in counties that have them (Camden, Essex, Hudson, Passaic, Union). County Clerk in other counties. All land records prior to 1800 are in the State Library, Bureau of Archives and History, Trenton. A few later ones are also there.

NEW MEXICO: County Recorder. (County Clerk is ex-officio Recorder.)

NEW YORK: County Clerk (except in New York, Kings, Queens and Bronx counties where they are in custody of the Register of the City of New York).

NORTH CAROLINA: County Register of Deeds.

NORTH DAKOTA: County Register of Deeds.

OHIO: County Recorder.

OKLAHOMA: County Recorder of Deeds. (County Clerk is ex-officio Recorder.)

OREGON: County Clerk (except in Linn, Marion and Umatilla counties where it is the County Recorder; Lane and Washington counties where it is the Director of Records and Elections; Hood River County where it is the Department of Records and Assessment; and Multnomah County where it is the Department of Records and Elections, Recording Division).

PENNSYLVANIA: County Recorder of Deeds.

RHODE ISLAND: Town and City Clerks (except City of Providence has a Recorder of Deeds).

SOUTH CAROLINA: Register of Mesne (pronounced mean) Conveyances or, if none, the Clerk of the County Court. (All prior to 1785 were recorded at Charleston.)

SOUTH DAKOTA: County Register of Deeds.

TENNESSEE: County Register of Deeds.

TEXAS: County Clerk.

UTAH: County Recorder.

VERMONT: Town and City Clerks.

VIRGINIA: County Circuit Judge (unless the property is in a city and a Corporation Court has jurisdiction). A special situation exists in Richmond where the Chancery Court of that city has jurisdiction north of the James River and the city's Hustings Court south of the River. (See Chapter Eighteen for further information on courts and jurisdictions in Virginia.)

WASHINGTON: County Auditor.

WEST VIRGINIA: Clerk of the County Court.

WISCONSIN: County Register of Deeds.

WYOMING: County Clerk. [4]

In those New England states of Connecticut, New Hampshire, Rhode Island and Vermont where land records are kept in the town it is important in tracing a family to search the records of all towns of interest including "parent" towns in the period before any newer towns were divided off. This is essentially the same principle you follow when you search the records of parent counties in other states.

You should also know that the LDS Genealogical Society has quite extensive collections of local land records on microfilm. These records are a "must" source whenever county records are filmed, so if you have access to that library's collections, check the card catalog for holdings in the localities of your problems.

There are a few situations where restrictions have been put on the use of land records and the public cannot have direct access to them. The Delaware State Legislature passed a bill a few years ago which restricted the direct use of land records to attorneys at law. Laws like this one are a direct affront to the right of access to public records. It would not surprise us if such laws, if tested, would be found unconstitutional. Often the careful researcher can still gain access to these records if he makes ap-

_____

4. Martindale-Hubbell Law Directory, 100th ed. (Summit, N. J.: Martindale-Hubbell, Inc., 1968), Vol. V (by permission) and correspondence with various court officials.

plication to the resident judge before visiting the county courthouse.

B. INDEXES

You will find that most local land records are well indexed, both by names of grantors and by names of grantees. (Usually these are separate indexes but they are sometimes combined.) Thus you can generally put your hand on records pertaining to your ancestors without a great deal of difficulty. There are a few limitations in these indexes but you can learn to live with them. Some of the main limitations are:

1. If there is more than one grantor (or grantee) the index often refers only to the one named first in the instrument. The fact that there are other parties involved is sometimes indicated by merely putting et al. in the index after the name of the first party.

2. If a trustee, a guardian, an attorney, an executor, an administrator, a commissioner or any other legal agent (including those court representatives who sell land for tax purposes) acts as the grantor in a deed in behalf of your ancestor, you will not usually find your ancestor's name in the index but will more likely find the name of the legal representative (if only we knew who he was, or even that such a sale had taken place!).

3. Most indexes are not strictly alphabetical but are usually alphabetical only by the first letter or two of the surname, then alphabetical by the first letter of the given name, then chronological. In any case it will generally be necessary for you to go through the entire index of the initial letter of your ancestor's surname to find all entries relating to that surname.

4. In most localities record custodians have developed master indexes to land records. These master indexes are especially easy to use because they eliminate the need for checking multiple volumes to find a few entries, but you should be aware that many of these master indexes are incomplete. Therefore, if you have access to the individual volumes and if they are indexed, it is a good idea to check them. Many master indexes were compiled from the indexes to individual volumes, and it is easy for an indexer inadvertently to skip entries.

5. A few states in the public domain (Iowa is a good example) have no direct indexes to the parties of land transactions, but rather all land records are indexed according to tract. Under this type of index a line or column is assigned to conveniently-sized tracts (maybe a section, quarter-section, platted block or lot). In such cases it is necessary to know the subdivision, section, township and range (or block number) in order to find

York s.s. Registry of Deeds. LEDGER INDEX OF RECORDS, from January 1, 1760, to December 31, 1895, inclusive.

GRANTOR	GRANTEE	Kind of Instrument	BOOK	PAGE	Date of Record
Lock **Locke**					
William G.	Wentworth Mark F.	Wty	292	549	Dec. 24 1866
	Bartlett Mary F.	Q.C.	311	447	Mar. 12 1869
	Rockingham Ten lots Bar Bk.	Mort.	335	316	Apr. 8 1871
	Young Samuel L.		338	657	19 1872
	Locke James W.	Ded.	405	480	Oct. 25 1886
William J.	Litchfield Elizabeth B.	Q.C.	256	180	Jan. 5 1855
William W.	Locke Lydia A.	Wty	318	103	July 16 1869
	John J.		327	473	Sept. 16 1872
	John A.	Q.C.	328	547	
	Rockingham Ten lots Bar Bk.	Assignt	346	136	Sept. 4 1874
	Eulana George G.	Wty	349	334	Dec. 14 1875
	Portsmouth Bar Bk.	Mort.	362	168	Mar. 7 1878
Woodbury	Dixon Oliver	Wty	340	520	June 8 1874
			365	367	June
Lockhart					
Lucy O.	Litchfield David	Q.C.	324	109	Apr. 21 1871
	Thomson William S.		346	441	Jan. 22 1874
William S.	Litchfield David		324	109	Apr. 21 1871
	Thomson William S.		346	441	Jan. 22 1874
Locklen					
Thomas W.	Cotton Jeremiah	Q.C.	210	482	Feb.
Lombard					
Abby	Bacon W. W.	Assignt	292	549	Dec.
	Adams George W.				

A GRANTOR INDEX TO LOCAL LAND RECORDS

the records. These indexes are an asset to those who examine land titles, but they pose problems for the genealogist.

Sometimes these survey descriptions of a man's land are given in a biographical sketch as found in a county history. The petition by the administrators of Thomas Gallion's estate in Kossuth County, Iowa, which we used as an example earlier in this chapter was located in this way.

In many states there are several other indexes in addition to those for grantors and grantees. In order to cover land records completely all such indexes should be checked. In Idaho, for example, 27 separate indexes are required by statute.

You must use the indexes. In spite of their shortcomings they are good and they provide easy access to most land records. If you do not have personal access to the records, do not be afraid to write to a record custodian and ask him to check an index for you; but be sure your requests are reasonable and that you are willing to compensate him for the time he spends in your behalf.

In its microfilming program the LDS Genealogical Society always films indexes when it films the land records. If you have access to these films you will find them easy to use—just as easy as reading the same indexes at the courthouse. And again we remind you that when you use indexes you must consider every possible spelling of the name you seek.

CHAPTER SEVENTEEN

ABSTRACTING WILLS AND DEEDS

We have already spent considerable time discussing the importance of taking adequate research notes and of getting all available information on everyone of the surname. Let's talk now about how best to accomplish this feat—how to get the required information from the records into your notes in a meaningful and readily-usable form without omitting anything of significance.

It sounds quite simple, but when you get down to bare facts there are some obstacles—it is often difficult to tell what is important and what is not. Your experience will teach you best, but perhaps some carefully thought-out suggestions can be of assistance while you are gaining experience.

I. ABSTRACT VS. EXTRACT

In Chapter Six we introduced abstracts and extracts but didn't really say much about relative values, so let's look at them now in a little more depth. First let's define our terms: ABSTRACT means to summarize or abridge or to take essential thoughts only. In Chapter Sixteen we mentioned Abstracts of Title, and from the above definition it should be clear why they are so called. Contrast this term with EXTRACT which means to copy, usually signifying that the material or item being copied is copied in its entirety, though perhaps taken from a larger work, as one will is taken from a book of wills or one biographical sketch from a book of such sketches. TRANSCRIBE also means to copy but _any_ copy or reproduction is referred to as a transcript or transcription.

Most records need to be extracted. Census schedules, vital certificates, church register entries, tax lists, immigration records, passages from books, etc., etc., all fall into this catagory. With these records an extract is essential to proper analysis. But wills, deeds, most other court records and early military pension and bounty land warrant application papers can and should be abstracted.

This chapter deals with the abstracting of land and probate records. It is especially important that we learn how to abstract them because we often find hundreds of documents in one locality relating to our surnames.

There is so much in these records that is nothing more than legal gobbledy-gook that it is folly to waste time copying it; and to do so can even cause us problems. It adds unnecessary bulk to our research notes and increases the amount of time needed for evaluation since we must go through this re-dundant verbiage to ferret out essential facts.

Some say it is best to make a verbatim extract of every pertinent rec-ord you find or, still better, get a photocopy of every record. They argue that such copies ensure that you have all the information you need and that it is correct. The argument is valid; however, if you are careful and pre-cise in your abstracting you can have the same assurance without the added time, effort or expense. Most genealogists who argue for the complete copy are searching for specific individuals only in their research and not for everyone of the surname—definitely the wrong approach.

The only universal rule about abstracting that we can offer is this: GET ALL THE ESSENTIAL FACTS. Don't try to be too brief, and when you are not sure if something is important, copy it. It is better to get too much information than not enough. As you gain experience your ability to discern will become more acute.

One measure you can take to help assure that the information you put into your abstract will not be misinterpreted is to keep everything in the first person, just as it is in the document. If a man says in his will: "I leave to my son John such and such property...," you should use the same pronouns he used—and be consistent in this throughout.

Some genealogists like to make abbreviated abstracts, copying only dates, names and relationships from wills; and names, dates, considerations (price) and relationships from deeds. These brief abstracts may be all right on rare occasions, but they cannot ordinarily be classified as good research notes. It is much easier to make errors when you are looking only for those limited items of information. A good case in point is the ab-stract of George Blackburn's will in Chapter Thirteen where the abstracter went through picking out names and consequently listed two unrelated per-sons—Negro slaves—as children in the family, and then missed some of the actual children.

As you do your research—if you intend to do good, reliable work—you must make fairly detailed abstracts (depending on the record). The only requirement is that you follow our rule: Get all the essential facts!

II. THE NATURE OF THE ABSTRACT

Every abstract you make must fit naturally into your note-keeping sys-tem, and there must be a notation on your research calendar of every rec-ord you search. Every abstract must include a complete reference to its source by locality, volume (or book or liber, etc.) and page (or folio)—and also serial numbers of microfilms where appropriate. It must also clearly state the type of record and must include all dates important to the document—the date made and the date recorded for a deed, and the date made and the date probated (sometimes date recorded) for a will.

Some persons have prepared forms for abstracting different types of records. These are fine, especially for the beginner who may wonder what is significant and what is not; however, you must be careful of these because some valuable information in the records may not fit the form.

We prefer not to use these forms for abstracting wills and deeds, not because they are bad, but mainly because they require more space and add bulk to our note file. (Usually only one deed or one will is abstracted on one page of notes when the forms are used, while you are not limited to this extent otherwise.) If this doesn't bother you, you may want to develop and use some type of form.

A. ABSTRACTING DEEDS

Whether you use a form or not there are certain basic data which must be abstracted. In addition to the complete locality, the dates and the source information we indicated earlier, you should consider the following eight items as being essential to a deed abstract:

1. The parties of the deed—the grantor(s) and the grantee(s).
2. The places of residence of those parties.
3. The consideration involved—the price paid and the terms.
4. A description of the land—including size (acreage) and location. (If metes and bounds were used this might include a relationship to a water course or other body of water, or a road, and/or connection to the lands of other persons, and/or a brief history of the title of that land, and of the beginning of the metes and bounds, such as "Beginning at a sweet gum tree on the shore of William's Bay at the corner of the land belonging to Matthew Quick...," and the name of the tract, should it have one—as in Maryland. In the public domain states the description will usually be in terms of subdivision, section, township and range.)
5. Miscellaneous information. (This catagory is the most difficult to define because you never know what you are going to find in a land record. Relationships, of course, would be significant. These may be relationships of any type and between any persons—not just between the grantor and grantee. A deed may also include special terms, restrictions or privileges that are significant. A man may have sold land and preserved a right-of-way through the land he sold. Or he may have even reserved a small corner where the family burial plot was located. Anything else of value you must determine from the record itself.)
6. The names of witnesses—exactly as they appear. (Today deeds

do not have witnesses but rather acknowledgements by notaries.)

    7. The signature(s) of the grantor(s). (Though you do not find actual signatures in the land-record books, it is often helpful to know whether a man signed his own name or whether he used a mark, and this _is_ indicated in the deed books.)

    8. Any release of dower by the wife of the grantor. (Such releases are often recorded immediately following the deeds to which they pertain—but not always.)

B. ABSTRACTING PROBATE RECORDS

As you abstract probate records there are nine items you ought to consider in addition to the type of document, the source and locality reference and the essential dates. They are:

    1. The name of the testator—the person who made the will.

    2. Any additional description of the testator—such as place of residence, occupation, inferences of age or state of health, etc.

    3. All persons named in the will should be listed in the order named, in direct connection with...

    4. Any relationships stated for those persons to either the testator or to each other, and...

    5. The essentials of the bequests and devises made to these persons. (This should include any land descriptions, names of Negro slaves, amounts of money and all other property of consequence.)

    6. Miscellaneous information. (Again this is a difficult catagory to define because wills are just as unpredictable as are deeds. But usually any special explanations, restrictions or privileges might fall into this classification.)

    7. The name(s) of the executor(s) and any relationships or connections which are stated between him (them) and the testator.

    8. The names of witnesses—exactly as they appear.

    9. The signature of the testator. (As with deeds it is often useful to know whether a man signed his name or made his mark. This may be evidence that would help support a connection sometime. And though the wills in the registers are not the originals and do not show the original signatures, they do indicate a mark if it was used, and marks were usually duplicated from the original documents.)

Now that we have discussed the essentials of abstracting deeds and wills, let's look at some actual documents and the abstracts of them. The deeds abstracted here were recorded in Washington County, Virginia, and the wills in Guilford County, North Carolina.

III. ABSTRACTS OF DEEDS

A. EXAMPLE NO. 1

DEEDS OF WASHINGTON COUNTY, VIRGINIA—BOOK 11 (1831-1834), PAGE 6.

This Indenture made this first day of November in the year of our Lord one thousand eight hundred and thirty one Between Jacob Lynch commissioner appointed for the purpose by the County Court of Washington of the one part and Andrew Shannon of the County of Washington and State of Virginia of the other part: Whereas in a suit in chancery depending in the County Court of Washington aforesaid wherein Andrew Shannon is Complt and Hannah Warsham, David S, Joseph, Jonathan M. Warsham and Jesse Lee & Edith his wife, widow and heirs of William Warsham deceased, John & Joseph Warsham, Eliza and Robert Warsham children & sole heirs of Robert Warsham Jr dec^d, Thomas Warsham, Jeremiah Warsham, The children and heirs of Beary Warsham, decd, the children & heirs of Jefferson W. Warsham, dec, John, Maria, Polly, George, and the other five children of Patsey Smith dec^d & Tobias Smith her husband, William Mackey & Ruth his wife, being all heirs of Robert Warsham the elder deceased are defendants, it was on the 18th day of May 1831 adjudged ordered and decreed that Jacob Lynch who is hereby appointed Commissioner for the purpose do convey to the Complt all the lands in the bill mentioned, except the portion of Lee & wife and the interest therein of Polly Rockholds heirs according to the partition between the Complainant and Lee and wife which is hereby affirmed, with covenants of special warranty against himself and his heirs: and the Complt be forever quieted in the possession and enjoyment of the lands hereby decreed to be conveyed: Now therefore This Indenture Witnesseth: That the said Jacob Lynch for and in consideration of the promises Doth hereby grant, bargain & sell unto the said Andrew Shannon and his heirs, the tract of land above mentioned which according to the plot filed among the papers in said suit in Chancery contains one hundred and fifty three acres 135 3/4 poles, and is bounded as followeth to wit Beginning at two Spanish oaks and poplar N 43° W 78 poles to a black oak, N. 53° W 140 poles to two white oaks & a black oak N. 53° E 160 poles to a double Socerwood & a white oak S. 39° E 88 poles to a Spanish oak and Sugartree 39° 23' E. 144.2 poles to a stake on the patent line S 63° 40' W 54 poles to the Beginning excepting such interest az the heirs of Polly Rockhold dec^d may have therein with all its appurtenances. To Have and To Hold the above described tract of land with all its appurtenances unto the said Andrew Shannon and his heirs forever. And the said Jacob Lynch for himself and his heirs doth covenant with the said Andrew Shannon and his heirs that he the said Jacob Lynch and his heirs, the said tract or parcel of land, except az before excepted, unto the said Andrew Shannon and his heirs against all claim which said Lynch or his heirs, hath acquired thereto under the decree aforesaid will warrant and forever defend In Witness whereof the said Jacob Lynch hath hereunto subscribed his name and affixed his seal the day & year first written.

(signed) Jacob Lynch

[no witnesses signed]

This Indenture of bargain and seal was acknowledged in the clerks office of Washington County on the 11th day of November 1831 before David Campbell clerk of the said County by the said Jacob Lynch as his act and deed and admitted to record.

Not only does the above deed challenge the ability of the abstracter, it also suggests that court records in Chancery will hold some valuable information on the Warsham family. The sad part about a record like this one is that the researcher looking for records of the Warsham family may never find it because it is indexed with Jacob Lynch as grantor. (This is one of the problems with indexes to land records which we discussed in the last chapter.)

Now let's see if we can make an abstract:

DEEDS OF WASHINGTON CO, VA—BK 11 (1831-4) P. 6.

Deed from JACOB LYNCH, Co. Commissioner, to ANDREW SHANNON of Wash. Co.—result of suit in Chancery 18 May 1831 in which sd. SHANNON was complt. and the defend's were: "HANNAH WARSHAM, DAVID S., JOSEPH, JONATHAN M. WARSHAM & JESSE LEE & EDITH HIS WIFE, WIDOW & HEIRS OF WILLIAM WARSHAM DECD, JOHN & JOSEPH WARSHAM, ELIZA & ROBERT WARSHAM CHN & SOLE HEIRS OF ROBERT WARSHAM JR DECD, THOMAS WARSHAM, JEREMIAH WARSHAM, THE CHN & HEIRS OF BEARY WARSHAM, DECD, THE CHN & HEIRS OF JEFFERSON W. WARSHAM, DECD, JOHN, MARIA, POLLY, GEORGE, & OTHER 5 CHN OF PATSEY SMITH DECD & TOBIAS SMITH HER HUSBAND, WILLIAM MACKEY & RUTH HIS WIFE, BEING ALL HEIRS OF ROBERT WARSHAM THE ELDER DECD."—By court order LYNCH to transfer all lands mentioned in bill except portion of LEE & wife & interest of POLLY ROCKHOLD'S HEIRS according to partition btw SHAN-

NON & LEE—plot of tract filed with papers in suit—53 acres, 135 3/4 poles—Beginning at 2 Spanish oaks and poplar...—(adj. land holders and identifying topographic features not named)—no witnesses signed—(signed) Jacob Lynch—1 Nov 1831—Ack. & recd: 11 Nov 1831.

You will note that we have used several abbreviations in this abstract, but that names are not abbreviated unless they are abbreviated in the record being abstracted. They are always copied exactly as they are found. You will note also that we have done a lot of capitalizing. This makes the abstract a lot easier to use and the data therein a lot easier to tabulate. You can underline with similar effect. Without additional evidence some of the relationship information in this deed could be very easily misinterpreted. In cases like this you should do as we have done and copy the information verbatim rather than try to interpret it. (Anything copied verbatim is put in quotation marks.) By following these procedures you can save yourself a lot of headaches and questions later when you begin to analyze your notes.

B. EXAMPLE NO. 2

DEEDS OF WASHINGTON COUNTY, VIRGINIA—BOOK 11 (1831-1834), PAGE 289.
    This Indenture made this 23^d day of July 1833, Between James Mobley of the one part and Peter Mayo of the other part, both of Washington County, Virginia: Witnesseth that the said James Mobley for and in consideration of one dollar to him in hand paid, doth bargain and sell unto the said Peter Mayo and his heirs the following property To wit, two negro boys, one named William about 13 years old, and one named Mark about ten years old, being slaves left him Mobley by his father John Mobley dec^d To Have and To Hold said property unto said Peter Mayo and his heirs against the claims of all persons whomsoever. In Trust: Nevertheless, that if the said James Mobley or his heirs, shall on or before the 23^d day of July 1834 will and truly pay or cause to be paid unto James C. Hayter the just and full sum of three hundred dollars with interest from this day which is justly due him, together with the expense of drawing and recording this Indenture, then this Indenture to be void. And in further Trust that if said James Mobley or his heirs shall fail to pay the said sum of three hundred dollars with interest on or before the 23^d day of July 1833 [sic] then it shall be lawful for the said Peter Mayo or his heirs, executors or administrators to proceed to sell the above described property at public sale, to the highest bidder for ready money, having advertised the time

and place of sale twenty days by putting up an advertisement for that purpose for that space of time at the front door of the Courthouse in Washington County, and out of the proceeds of said sale to pay said Hayter whatever may be due him of the debt aforesaid the expense of drawing and recording this Indenture, the expense of sale and six per cent to said trustee for his trouble, and the overplus if any to said James Mobley or his heirs, and if the property should not pay the debt, he promises to pay the balance and binds his heirs thereto In Witness whereof said parties have hereunto set their hands and seals this day and year first above written.

(signed) James Mobley
(signed) Peter Mayo

[no witnesses signed]

At a court continued and held for Washington County the 23^{d} day of July 1833.

This Indenture in trust between James Mobley of the one part and Peter Mayo of the other part, was acknowledged in court by the said Mobley and Mayo as their act and deed and ordered to be recorded.

As you note from reading it, the above instrument is a trust indenture and was made to ensure the payment of a debt. (It is not a deed because it does not deal with real estate, but it is nevertheless recorded in the deed registers.) If, and when, that debt is paid then this indenture becomes void. Now let's abstract it:

DEEDS OF WASHINGTON CO. VA—BK 11 (1831-4) P. 289.

In trust from JAMES MOBLEY to PETER MAYO, both of Wash. Co.—for $1—2 negro boys, William, age 13, & Mark, age 10—slaves left to MOBLEY by HIS FATHER JOHN MOBLEY, DECD—to secure payment of $300 debt owed by MOBLEY to JAMES C. HAYTER, due 23 July 1834—if debt not pd property to be sold at public sale by MAYO to pay debt—no witnesses signed—(signed) James Mobley, Peter Mayo—23 July 1833— Ack. & Recd: same day.

C. EXAMPLE NO. 3

DEEDS OF WASHINGTON COUNTY, VIRGINIA—BOOK 12 (1834-1837), PAGE 45.

This Indenture made this 30th day of January in the year of our Lord one thousand eight hundred and thirty between Joseph Warsham and Nancy his wife of the County of Washington and

State of Virginia of the one part and John Hacket of the said County and State of the other part Witnesseth that the said Joseph Warsham & Nancy his wife for and in consideration of the sum of _____ current money of the United States to them in hand paid, the receipt whereof is hereby acknowledged do grant bargain and sell unto the said John Hacket a certain piece or parcel of land, lying and being in the County of Washington on the waters of the North fork of Holstein and in the rich Valley being part of two surveys one of 190 acres patented to John McHenry & one of 50 acres patented to Job Crabtree, and bounded as follows, to wit, Beginning at a Sugar tree and Bucheye Sapling on the South line of the said 50 acre survey thence for a division line between said Hackett and Warsham N 9 1/2° W. 61 poles to two Buckeye saplings and a Stake in a rich hollow N 45° W 38 poles to a white oak dogwood and Maple Sapling N 66° 27 poles to a white oak and Dogwood N 3° E 17 poles crossing the creek to a white oak at the mouth of a cave near where a beech stood a corner of the 190 acre survey and with a line thereof S 75° W 90 poles to a white oak and maple N. 84° W 7 poles to a white oak thence leaving said lines S 17° E 39 poles to a Locust bush on the top of a hill S 28 1/2° E 110 poles to a dogwood and small buckeye bush N 55° E 52 poles to the Beginning containing fifty four acres be the same more or less with all its appurtenances.   To Have and To Holde, the said piece or parcel of land with all its appurtenances unto the said John Hacket and his heirs to the sole use and behoof of him the said John Hacket and his heirs forever.   And the said Joseph Warsham and Nancy his wife for themselves and their heirs do covenant with the said John Hacket and his heirs that they the said Warsham & wife and their heirs, the said piece or parcel of land with all its appurtenances unto the said John Hacket and his heirs against the claims of all persons whomsoever, shall Warrant and will forever defend.   In Witness whereof the said Joseph Warsham & Nancy his wife have hereunto subscribed their names and affixed their seals, the day and year first above written.

signed sealed and delivered   (signed) Joseph Warsham
in presence of [no witnesses   (signed) Nancy Warsham
named].

Washington County, to wit,

We Joseph C. Trigg and Tobias Smith justice of the peace of the county aforesaid in the state of Virginia do hereby certify that Nancy Warsham the wife of Joseph Warsham parties to a certain deed bearing date on this 30th January 1830 and hereunto annexed personally appeared before us in our County aforesaid and being

examined by us prively and apart from her husband and having
the deed aforesaid fully explained to her she the said Nancy Warsham acknowledged the same to be her act and deed and declared
that she had willingly signed sealed and delivered the same and
she wished not to retract it given under our hands & seals this
30th January 1830.

(signed) Joseph C. Trigg
(signed) Tobias Smith

At a Court held in Washington County the 27th day of October
1834 This Indenture of bargain & sale between Joseph Warsham
& Nancy his wife of the one part and John Hacket of the other part
was acknowledged in Court by the said Warsham as his act and
deed and together with the certificate of the acknowledgment of
the said Nancy made thereto ordered to be recorded.

There is nothing unusual about this deed. It is probably very much like
most deeds you will find for your ancestors and presents very few problems
for the abstracter. Your abstract might look something like this:

DEEDS OF WASHINGTON CO, VA—BK 12 (1834-7) P. 45.
    Deed from JOSEPH WARSHAM AND WIFE NANCY of Wash.
Co. to JOHN HACKET of Wash. Co.—for (price not stated)—
tract in Wash. Co. on N. fork of Holstein [sic] in the rich Valley,
part of 2 surveys (one of 190 acres patented to JOHN McHENRY
& one of 50 acres patented to JOB CRABTREE), "Beginning at a
Sugartree and Buckeye sapling on S. line of said 50 care survey..."—54 acres—no witnesses signed—(signed) Joseph Warsham, Nancy Warsham—Certif. of acknowledgement made by
Nancy—30 Jan 1830—Recd: 27 Oct 1834.

D. EXAMPLE NO. 4

DEEDS OF WASHINGTON COUNTY, VIRGINIA—BOOK 12 (1834-
1837), PAGE 40.
    This Indenture made this tenth day of October in the year of
our Lord one thousand eight hundred and thirty one Between
Isaiah Austin heir at Law of James Austin deceased of the county
of Washington of the one part and John Austin of Atkens Tennessee of the other part Witnesses that the said Isaiah Austin the
father and heir at law of James Austin deceased for and in consideration of the sum of two thousand dollars current money of
the United States to him in hand paid, the receipt whereof is
hereby acknowledged doth grant bargain and sell unto the said

John Austin two several tracts of land adjoining each other lying and being in the County of Washington on the waters of the middle fork of holston river, One which was conveyed to the said James by deed bearing date the 4th of October 1823 executed to him by James Edmondson and William Buchanan executors of William E. Buchanan deceased bounded as follows to wit, Beginning on two white oaks and dogwood N. 16 1/2^O West 88 poles to a white oak and hickory North 1^O East 54 poles to a white oak & Black oak on the side of the knob, South 54 1/2^O West 136 poles North 62 1/2^O West 36 poles South 29 1/2^O West 58 poles South 66° West 146 poles to a black oak on the great road South 57° East 120 poles to a white oak, South 12 1/2^O East 36 poles to a hickory and dogwood North 62° East 114 poles to the Beginning containing two hundred acres be the same more or less. Also one other tract conveyed to the said Isaiah Austin by James Edmondson bounded az follows to wit Beginning at three chestnut oaks on a ridge on said Edmondsons line thence with the same S 27° E 70 poles to two white oaks corner to same S 5° E. 16 poles to a white oak and black oak corner to James Austins land, thence with Austins line S 57° W 136 poles to two hickories and white oaks N 70° W 36 poles to a maple on the side of a Knob S 32° W 58 poles to a white oak S 65° W 76 poles to a stake on said James Austins line thence with Benjamin Sharps line N 37° W 14 poles to a white oak and two hickories Thence N 50° E 122 poles to two white oaks & ash by a swamp thence N 45° E 180 poles to the Beginning. containing ninety five acres with all its appurtenances: To Have and To Hold the said tracts or parcels of land with all their appurtenances unto the said John Auston and his heirs to the sole use and behoof of him the said John Austin and his heirs forever. And the said Isaiah Auston for himself and his heirs doth covenant with the said John Austin and his heirs that he the said Isaiah Auston and his heirs the said tract or parcels of land with all appurtenances unto the said John Auston and his heirs against the claims of all persons whomsoever, shall and will forever defend. In witness whereof the said Isaiah Auston hath hereto subscribed his name and affixed his seal the day and year first above written.

Signed sealed & delivered
in presence of   Isaiah X (his mark) Austin
    John H. Fulton
    John C. Cummings
    Bev R. Johnston
    Charles S. Bekem

At a Court held for Washington County the 27th day of October 1834 This Indenture of bargain & sale between Isaiah Austin of the one part and John Austin of the other part was proved in court by the oath of John H. Fulton, Beverly R. Johnston and Charles S. Bekem three of the subscribing witnesses thereto to be the act and deed of said Isaiah and ordered to be recorded:

There is the deed; here is an abstract of it:

DEEDS OF WASHINGTON CO, VA—BK 12 (1834-7) P. 40.
Deed from ISAIAH AUSTIN, FATHER & HEIR AT LAW OF JAMES AUSTIN, DECD of Wash. Co. to JOHN AUSTIN OF AT-KENS, TENN. (both names sometimes spelled AUSTON in the deed)—for $2,000—2 tracts adj. each other on middle fork of Holston River—1 conveyed to sd JAMES AUSTIN by JAMES ED-MONDSON & WILLIAM BUCHANAN, EXORS OF WILLIAM E. BUCHANAN, "Beginning on two white oaks and dogwood..." on the great road (200 acres)—other conveyed to ISAIAH by JAMES EDMONDSON, "Beginning at 3 chestnut oaks on a ridge on sd EDMONDSON'S line..." adj. JAMES AUSTIN'S land & sd EDMONDSON AND BENJAMIN SHARP (95 acres)—witnesses: JOHN H. FULTON, JOHN C. CUMMINGS, BEV(ERLY) R. JOHNSTON, CHARLES S. BEKEM—(signed) Isaiah X (his mark) Austin—10 Oct 1831—Recd: 27 Oct 1834.

E. EXAMPLE NO. 5

DEEDS OF WASHINGTON COUNTY, VIRGINIA—BOOK 12 (1834-1837), PAGE 366.
This Indenture made this first day of December 1835 between Amelia Conn Sen[r] and Amelia Conn Jr. both of Washington County Virginia. Witnesseth that the said Amelia Conn S[r] for & in consideration of the natural love and affection which she bears unto her daughter the said Amelia Conn Jr. & for the further consideration of one dollar to her in hand paid hath granted given bargained & sold to the said Amelia Junior thirty two acres of the tract of land on which she the said Amelia Conn Sr at the present resides to include the dwelling house & spring and to be laid off in convenient form, To Have and To Hold the same unto the said Amelia Conn Jr. & her heirs forever. But the said Amelia Sr reserves to herself the right to the possession and exclusive enjoyment of the said land and premises during her natural Life at the termination of which the said Amelia Conn Junr or her heirs shall be entitled to enter upon the same In

witness whereof the said Amelia Conn Senr hath set her hand &
seal the day and year first above written.

Attest

David Parks   Amelia IE (her mark) Conn
John Melton
John Parks

This Indenture of bargain & sale between Amelia Conn Sr of the
one part and Amelia Conn Jr of the other part was proved in the
Clerk's office of Washington County on the 2nd day of March 1836
before David Campbell Clerk of the said County by the oath of
David Parks one of the subscribing witnesses thereto to be the
act & deed of said Amelia Senr. At a court held for Washington
County the 22^d day of August 1836——
It was proved in Court by the oath of John Parks another witness
thereto to be the act & deed of said Amelia Senr—And at a Court
continued and held for said county the 23^d day of August 1836—
It was further proved in Court by the oath of John Melton another witness thereto to be the act & deed of said Amelia Senr
and ordered to be recorded.

And the abstract:

DEEDS OF WASHINGTON CO, VA—BK 12 (1834-7) P. 366.

Gift deed from AMELIA CONN SR TO HER DAU AMELIA
CONN JR, both of Wash. Co.—for love and affection & $1—
32 acres of tract where AMELIA SR now resides, including
dwelling house & spring, to be laid off—AMELIA SR reserves
right of possession during natural life—witnesses: DAVID PARKS,
JOHN MELTON, JOHN PARKS— (signed) Amelia IE (her mark)
Conn—1 Dec 1835—Recd: 23 Aug 1836.

Now that we have illustrated the abstracting of various land records
let's look at the mechanics involved in abstracting wills.

IV. ABSTRACTS OF WILLS

A. EXAMPLE NO. 1

WILLS OF GUILFORD COUNTY, NORTH CAROLINA, BOOK A
(1771-1813), PAGE 37.

Whereas Thomas Cox of Richland Creek in Guilford County
and North Carolina yeoman being but weak in body but in perfect
mind and memory and taking into consideration the certainty of

death and ye uncertainty of life hath thought good to make order and appoint this my last will and Testament in manner and form following revoking and disr---tling all manner of will or wills before by me made this only to be my last will and Testament.

Imprimis [first]—I commit my soul to Almighty God who gave it me and my body to be decently buried by my brother Solomon Cox and William Wierman who I appoint my Executors to see the accomplishment of this my last Will and Testament and make full satisfaction for all funeral charges and other Worldly debts every where to be paid. ——

I leave and give to my beloved wife a fether bed & bed cloaths a side sadle and bridle and the third part of all the remainder part of my personal estate excepting only such particular artickels as are herein hereafter mentioned and given to particular persons.

I leave and give to my son Thomas one hundred acres of land including the improvements whereon I live to him his heirs and assigns forever—I leave and give to my son Joshua one hundred acres of land to be laid of for him on the South side of the aforesaid tract and joining Solomon Cox's land to him his heirs and assigns forever. I leave and give my son Daniel one hundred acres of land to be laid of for him on the west side of my son Thomas' land to him his heirs and assigns forever. —I leave and give my son John one hundred acres of land to be laid of for him on the North side of my son Thomas' land to him his heirs and assigns forever. —I leave and give to my son Abner all the remainder part of my lands to be laid of for him where it should be most suitable to be valuable. —I leave and give my daughter Sarah a fether bed. —I leave and give my daughter Martha a fether bed to be made of the benefits of my improvements, and it is my will and desire that my wife shall live with my son Thomas on his place if she so wishes so long as she lives single—and I leave and give to my son Thomas ten pounds prock money—and it is my will and desire that my children have larning at least to read and write. —I leave and give to my son Abner fifteen pounds prock money—and I leave the remainder part of my personal estate to be equally divided among all my children—and it is my will that my sons shall possess every one his part of my estate at the age of twenty one years and that my daughters shall everyone possess her part at the age of eighteen years—and it is my will that if any of my sons do not live to the age of twenty one years that then his or their lands shall be sold to the highest bider of his brethren and the price thereof be equally divided amongst his brethren—and it is my will that if any of my children do not live to the years above ordered to possess their estates at that then his heirs or their personal estate shall be equally divided amongst the living ones.

Signed and sealed in the
presence of   (signed) Thomas Cox
    Wm Garner
    Stephen Hussey (jurat)
    John Kenworthy   North Carolina, Guilford County,
                            November Court 1771. Then the
                            within last will & Testament of
Thomas Cox was proved in open court by the oath of Stephen Hussey one of the subscribing witnesses thereto and motion ordered to be recorded. Then Solomon Cox and William Wierman (who by the Testator were left Executors of the within will) came into court and qualified as such &c.

The abstract of Thomas Cox's will should look something like this:

WILLS OF GUILFORD CO, N. C. — BK A (1771-1813) P. 37.
    WILL OF THOMAS COX, Richland Creek, Guilf. Co, Yeoman—weak in body—Exors: MY BROTHER SOLOMON COX & WILLIAM WIERMAN.
To my BELOVED WIFE (NOT NAMED)—certain personal property.
To my SON THOMAS—100 acres including improvements whereon I now live.
To my SON JOSHUA—100 acres on S. side of aforsd tract—adj. SOLOMON COX.
To my SON DANIEL—100 acres on W. side of SON THOMAS.
To my SON JOHN—100 acres on N. side of SON THOMAS.
To my SON ABNER—all the remainder part of my lands.
To my DAU SARAH—fether bed.
To my DAU MARTHA—fether bed.
MY WIFE to live with my SON THOMAS as long as she is single (if she desires).
To my SON THOMAS—10 pounds prock[lamation] money.
To my SON ABNER—15 pounds prock money.
ALL MY CHN shall learn to read and write.
Remainder of personal estate divided equally among chn.
SONS to possess their part of estate AT AGE 21, and DAUS AT AGE 18.
If son dies before 21 land to sell to highest bidding brother, price equally divided amongst his brethren.
If any child die before of age, personal estate divided equally to

others.

Witness: WM GARNER, STEPHEN HUSSEY, JOHN KENWORTHY.
(signed) THOMAS COX.
Not dated—Proved: Nov Crt 1771.

The way we have abstracted this will takes a little more space than it would have if we had just listed one item right after the other with only dashes between, as we did with the deeds. You can do it the other way, but this form makes for easier tabulation.

B. EXAMPLE NO. 2

WILLS OF GUILFORD COUNTY, NORTH CAROLINA—BOOK A (1771-1813), PAGE 224.

This first day of February in the year of our Lord one thousand eight hundred and fourteen I Robert Lamb of the State of North Carolina and County of Guilford: being sound in health of bodday minde and memmory do make this my last will and testament at the same time revoking all former wills made by me, declaring this to be my last will & Testament.

Firstly—I give and bequeath unto my three sons namely Samuel, Simeon and John Lam all the lands that I have previously put them in possession of together with there stock and every spicice of property that I have heretofore given them.

I also give and bequeath unto my four daughters and my grand daughter namely Elizabeth White Deborah Hoggatt Ester Hodson Ann Reynolds Margate Balilen each and every of them the whole property which I have heretofour given them.

I allso give and bequeath unto my beloved wife all my household furniture together with all the live stock which I am now in possesion of the same to be subject to hir use and benefit during hir natureal life and at hir death the same to be devided eaqually between my three sons my four daughters and my grand daughter as above named--and lastly after my just debts are paid I give and bequeath all the rezidue of all my estate what eaver and whearever to my eight children as above named equally devided between them and at the same time. I appoint my friend Zino Worth and do impower him to act as the Executor of this my last will and Testament to which I have hereunto set my hand and affixed my seal the day and date above mentioned.

Daniel Worth (Jurat)

Benjamin Hall   Robert X (his mark) Lamb

For probate &c. of the foregoing Will—see min. Doc. No. 4, page 409.

There is the will; now let's abstract it:

WILLS OF GUILFORD CO, N.C.--BK A (1771-1813) P. 224.
    WILL OF ROBERT LAMB of Guilf. Co—in good health.
To my 3 SONS SAMUEL, SIMEON & JOHN LAM—all lands and
    property I have previously given them.
To my 4 DAUS AND MY G DAU ELIZABETH WHITE, DEBORAH
    HOGGATT, ESTER HODSON, ANN REYNOLDS, MARGATE
    BALILEN—property I have heretofore given them.
To my BELOVED WIFE (NOT NAMED)—all household furniture
    and livestock now in my possession, during her natural
    life—at her death to be divided among my 3 SONS, 4 DAUS
    AND G DAU.
All residue to my 8 CHN, above named, equally.
Exor: My FRIEND ZINO WORTH.
Witness: DANIEL WORTH, BENJAMIN HALL.
(signed) ROBERT X (his mark) LAMB.
Dated: 1 Feb 1814—No date of probate given ("FOR PROBATE,
    ETC., SEE MINUTE DOCKET #4, P. 409.")

You noticed that the above will suggests the use of another record. And you would make a serious mistake here if you failed to look up the court record (minute docket) where the information about the probate of this will is recorded. We have also inserted commas between some names in this abstract, but this is done only when their placement is obvious.

C. EXAMPLE NO. 3

Some other types of probate records contain very little genealogical data yet are significant in other ways. Consider, for example, the account of the administrator of his activities in probating an estate. Names and dates are significant, but often little else. Here is an example:

SETTLEMENTS OF ESTATES, GUILFORD COUNTY,   NORTH
CAROLINA, 1844-1853, PAGE 104.
MAY Term 1846
  : May 15th 1846—We the undersigned Justices of the Peace in aforesaid County having met at the house of James S. Watson Admr of Eleanor Watson Dec[d] in pursuance of an order of Court to us directed proceeding to settle with said Admr and find as follows:
        Dr. to amount of Sales $198.57
            Vouchers
[Immediately following is a long list of accounts, the names

of which are probably, but may not be, without significance. Because of this factor, it is usually desirable at least to make an abstract of the foregoing and then list the names.] In this account the names were:

M. D. Smith, Washington Donnett, Walter McConnel, Saml Nelson, Francis Obriant, Catharine Clark, L. W. Doakes, Rev. John A. Gritter, DR. L. W. WATSON, James R. McLean, Sarah Mathews, Mrs. Dick.

[These names may provide some clues to connections with other persons when considered with other evidence.]

(signed) F. Shaw J. P.
(signed) E. Denny J. P.

All information in this chapter is given only as a suggestion. We are not trying to dictate the form or content of your abstracts, but are merely suggesting that your abstracts, though brief, must be complete enough to meet the demands of thorough scientific research. We hope that our suggestions and examples will be helpful and will expedite your research. But, above all, your notes must be both complete and correct, because these records (land and probate records) are the "bread and butter" sources of American genealogy. Usually the information is limited so you are going to need all the information that is there—the way that it is there.

CHAPTER EIGHTEEN

COURT RECORDS

To some it may seem strange that we include an entire chapter on court records since many of the records already discussed have been court records of one type or another—notably land, probate and guardianship records. However, other types of court records are also valuable genealogically and deserve our attention.

The story is told of a man who was going down the highway and stopped to help a lady motorist whose car had stalled. When he asked what the trouble was, she replied that she thought something was wrong with the clutch. The man went around and lifted the hood and, after looking inside, went back to report that the motor had fallen from its mounts and was lying on the ground beneath the vehicle. Her reply (in all seriousness): "Thank goodness it wasn't the clutch."

Somehow this woman got the idea that there were only certain things that could go wrong with her car, and if the problem was not one of those then it was of little consequence. The beginning genealogist often falls into the same trap as he tells himself that only certain records are of value and that others are not worthy of serious consideration. However, when he happens to need those other records—when they fit his problem—they are of great importance.

It has been our experience that court records, as a catagory, are among the most important records in existence and yet are seldom used. When court records exist for your ancestor, or when you find a situation which suggests their probable existence, you had better take heed.

I. BACKGROUND AND DEFINITION

Court records, as we will discuss them in this chapter, are the records of actions on civil matters. Roughly, court records are divided into two catagories—criminal (public) [1] and civil (private). We will not discuss criminal court records except to define them and to state that there is con-

---

1. Other forms of public law, of little concern to us here, include Constitutional, administrative and international law.

siderable overlap of criminal and civil records in most courts. Criminal actions deal with the bringing of public offenders to justice. Crimes are defined and punishments are established by statute. Civil actions deal with the protection of individual rights and, generally speaking, every civil action has two parties (plaintiff and defendant) opposed to each other for the recovery of a right or the redress of a wrong.

Extensive records are maintained by the courts. Every writ, affidavit, complaint, answer, summons, subpoena, judgment, injunction, petition, motion, deposition, pleading, sentence, order, decree, and all proceedings and testimony of every case are detailed in the courts' records and filed in systematic order. The extent and volume of these records is almost unbelievable to the layman.

II. THE AMERICAN COURT SYSTEM

It is impossible, in the space we have here, to explain the intricacies of the American court system, but we can give you an idea of the nature of the system. There are two sources of court control—the federal government and the individual states. The federal government, in addition to the U.S. Supreme Court, controls the U.S. Courts of Appeals set up in the circuits and the U.S. District Courts (and some others which we will not discuss). The federal District Courts, which often include whole states as districts, have jurisdiction over all admiralty and maritime causes, all bankruptcy proceedings, most criminal cases indictable under federal laws and many civil matters.

The courts set up under state statute differ from one state to another and, of course, are subject to structural change at the will of the several state legislatures. For example, the 1969 Idaho Legislature passed such "court reform" legislation (S.B. 1112, effective January 11, 1971). One thing that may be confusing to those trying to distinguish between state and federal courts is that many of the courts have the same names. Several of the states have District Courts and several others have Circuit Courts, but these are of inferior state jurisdiction. They usually include several counties, but in New England some states have several districts in each county.

Every state has a Supreme Court, but every Supreme Court is not the same. In most states the Supreme Court is a court of final appeal, but in a few (as in New York) it is a court of general original jurisdiction which may possess some appellate jurisdiction. Some states have County Courts with ordinary civil jurisdiction, limited criminal jurisdiction, appellate jurisdiction of justices of the peace or magistrates, as well as jurisdiction over probate and guardianship matters. In other states courts of various other names perform these functions. In many states you will find Circuit Courts; others have Inferior Courts, and still others have Superior Courts. Some states may have all of these. Some states have Justice-of-the-Peace Courts and others have Magistrate Courts, both of which are courts of limited original jurisdiction. Some have special Juvenile Courts with jurisdiction over neglected and delinquent children. Some have Family Courts and some have Small Claims Courts, etc., etc., etc. Every state has its own system, and you have to get used to the idea that what is called a District Court in Nebraska is a Superior Court in Massachusetts and a Supreme Court in New York.

III. A MISCONCEPTION

The LDS Genealogical Society and other organizations have filmed some court records besides those already discussed in previous chapters—mainly court minutes, dockets [2] and court orders—but only on rare occasions do they film the court files themselves (and in some localities where minutes, dockets, etc., have been filmed, not even all of these). Many researchers have gotten the impression that these films represent all court records available in the localities from which they come—a serious error to make. These films generally represent only a small portion of the available court records.

We are not saying that these filmed court records have no value, because some are extremely useful. Court dockets and minutes are especially good, [3] and usually contain things such as judgments, decrees, commissioners' reports and resolutions and various other court actions. Entries vary all the way from the simple notation that the action has been continued (carried over) until a later date, to the detailed account of the actions of an administrator in a probate matter. Some of these minutes and dockets are also indexed, which makes them quite easy to use. Those who have done microfilming in these records have been more inclined to film some types of court records than they have others. The minutes, dockets and court orders are bound and easily accessible while loose files are more difficult to work with (besides their prodigious volume).

In a few cases, as with the judgments of the Maryland Court of Appeals, some quite extensive court records have been filmed but, generally speaking, those records designated as court "record books" and court "orders"

---

2. Dockets are brief chronological abstracts of court actions and judgments prepared by the court clerk. In many states the law requires that these be indexed also.

3. If you have ancestry in North Carolina never overlook the old minutes of the County Superior Courts, a few of which are on film, and the old Courts of Pleas and Quarter Sessions, which are almost completely microfilmed. In some states lists of pending equity cases—called lis pendens—have also been filmed and have some genealogical value.

have only limited value.

You must never hesitate to write to the court where you have indication of the existence of valuable court records pertaining to your ancestors; this may be the most intelligent move you could make on your problem.

IV. RECORDS OF INTEREST

It will be helpful for us to examine some specific types of court actions and the records arising therefrom; however, we will first lay a basic foundation in the nature of court records and give some general jurisdictional helps. We will then look more specifically at divorce records and records of citizenship and naturalization. These are of special interest to a great many genealogists.

A. BACKGROUND OF CIVIL ACTIONS (LAW AND EQUITY)

At common law the terms equity and chancery (which are synonymous) are used to describe one type of court proceeding and the term law is used to describe another type of court proceeding. Equity means "justice" and relates to impartial justice between two parties whose claims (or rights) conflict. Except where bound by common law (i.e., legal precedent), judicial discretion may be exercised and traditionally there is no right to jury trial.

In an action at law one seeks to recover monetary damages for injuries to himself, his property, his pocketbook or his reputation, while in a suit in equity he seeks to compel someone to do something (specific performance decree) or to stop doing or refrain from doing something (injunction). Equity courts handle matters of divorces, foreclosures of liens, receiverships, partitions, trusts, real property controversies (with lis pendens), etc.

Two of the most important types of actions at law are founded in contract and tort. A tort is a wrong or injury arising out of the law, not associated with a contract but involving a legal duty, a breach of that duty and injury as a result of the breach. It involves injury to one's person (including his reputation and feelings) or his property. Assault, battery, trespass, misrepresentation, defamation and negligence are common torts.

Concerning the early history of American civil actions (equity actions especially) one legal writer wrote during the first part of this century:

> The American colonies were settled during the most influential period of the chancery court in England, and it, along with other serviceable institutions of the mother country, became engrafted on the judicial system of the various colonies. In most of them the equity powers were exercised by the royal governor in conjunction with his council, while in Rhode Island, during the colonial period, the assembly acted as a court of chancery.

In all of the colonies, except Pennsylvania, the chancery existed as a distinct tribunal from the common law courts. In Pennsylvania equity was administered by the law courts and, according to the procedure of the common law, until the middle of...[the nineteenth century]. When the colonies became states, they either established separate courts of equity, presided over by chancellors, or conferred the equity powers upon the ordinary law courts with a provision for its exercise according to the forms and procedure of chancery....

... The American states and territories may be divided into three groups as regards the method followed of administering equity jurisprudence. These are:——

First. Those states in which separate courts of chancery are maintained, and law and equity are administered by distinct tribunals under different modes of procedure. In this group the chancery court is copied after the Court of Chancery in England, and is similar as to powers and jurisdiction. This group...[has historically included] Alabama, Delaware, Mississippi, New Jersey and Tennessee.

Second. Those states in which law and equity are still administered in their distinct and appropriate forms, but by the same court. The boundaries between the two as to jurisdiction being jealously guarded, and the chancery jurisdiction not ceasing because the statutes confer the same powers on law courts. The most important member of this group... [has been] the federal government of the United States, comprising the various federal courts, which follow[ed] the system uniformly and are not influenced by state legislation. The states... [which have historically belonged] to this group are Arkansas, Florida, Georgia, Illinois, Maine, Maryland, Massachusetts, Michigan, New Hampshire, New Mexico, Pennsylvania, Rhode Island, Vermont, Virginia and West Virginia.

Third. This group includes the states and territories which have adopted the Civil Code. In these the distinction between actions at law and suits in equity is abolished, and all relief is said to be administered through the uniform procedure of civil action. The effect of this is not, however, to abolish entirely the distinction between law and equity, though affording a common method of administration. The fundamental principles of equity are regarded, and it is even quite common to refer to actions involving equity principles as equitable actions, as distinguished from law actions. The abolition of the distinction between suits in equity and law as made by the Codes does not allow of the bringing an action not previously cognizable either in law or equity. [4]

Since Mr. Chadman did his writing most states have changed their court systems, especially in the adoption of a system (which Chadman calls "the Civil Code") to combine equity and law matters into one type of civil action. You should be aware, however, that many of the states have only recently adopted this approach and that many of the Atlantic seaboard states (and a few others) have clung religiously to the old common law and equity definitions and procedures. In those states a person could not bring a simple action to set aside a contract or to force compliance with it or recover damages because of its breach. He would instead bring an action in <u>covenant</u> (to recover monetary damages), or <u>debt</u> (to recover a specific sum for a contract breach), or <u>assumpsit</u> (to recover damages if the agreement was not under seal), or <u>detinue</u> (to recover specific chattels rightfully taken but wrongfully retained), or <u>replevin</u> (to recover specific chattels unlawfully taken). A damage suit (tort action) would be either in <u>trespass</u> (for monetary damages), <u>trover</u> (for damages to property or goods by interference or improper detention) or <u>deceit</u> (damages due to any injury committed deceitfully).

Most states, though they have combined law and equity under the "civil action" title, still maintain a distinction between the two. Let's look at the individual states and see how they <u>presently</u> consider these actions. At the same time we will also point out the courts which have jurisdiction, as you must know these in order to find the records.

ALABAMA:	Distinction is maintained between law and equity actions, but both are now under jurisdiction of the CIRCUIT COURTS in the counties.
ALASKA:	No distinction in the form of action exists. The SUPERIOR COURT (in matters less than $3,000) and the DISTRICT COURTS have jurisdiction.
ARIZONA:	No distinction in the form of action exists. The SUPERIOR COURT in the county has jurisdiction.
ARKANSAS:	Law and equity actions are handled by separate courts. The County CHANCERY COURTS

[4.] Charles E. Chadman (ed.), <u>Chadman's Cyclopedia of Law</u> (Chicago: American Correspondence School of Law, 1912), Vol. 8, pp. 185-187. (The reason we have used a source so old is to capture the true historical background and significance of the American legal system. Obviously much information in such sources is now out of date but the history does not change.)

have equity jurisdiction and the CIRCUIT COURTS in the counties have jurisdiction in actions at law.

CALIFORNIA: Though a distinction between legal and equitable rights is preserved there is only one form of action. The County SUPERIOR COURTS have jurisdiction.

COLORADO: There is no distinction between legal and equitable actions though traditional equity grounds are necessary in cases of equity. The DISTRICT COURTS in the counties have jurisdiction, and in counties with over 300,000 population (Denver), the County SUPERIOR COURT has jurisdiction in claims from $500 to $5,000.

CONNECTICUT: There is no distinction in the form of action between law and equity matters. The SUPERIOR COURT in the counties has jurisdiction, with jurisdiction also lying concurrently in the County COURTS OF COMMON PLEAS in some claims between $250 and $15,000.

DELAWARE: There is a strict distinction between equity and law actions in Delaware. The CHANCERY COURT in the counties has jurisdiction in equity matters, and the SUPERIOR COURT in the counties has jurisdiction in actions at law.

D. C.: Equity and law actions are not distinguished. The COURT OF GENERAL SESSIONS (under $10,000) and the U.S. DISTRICT COURT for the District of Columbia have jurisdiction.

FLORIDA: Florida makes no distinction between equity and law actions. The CIRCUIT COURTS in the counties have jurisdiction.

GEORGIA: Georgia maintains the distinction between law and equity, but both are under the jurisdiction of the SUPERIOR COURTS in the counties.

HAWAII: There is no distinction between equity and law actions. Jurisdiction lies in the CIRCUIT COURTS.

IDAHO: There is no distinction between equity and law actions. Jurisdiction lies in the DISTRICT COURTS in the counties.

ILLINOIS: There is no distinction between actions in equity and actions at law. The CIRCUIT COURTS in the counties have jurisdiction.

INDIANA: All distinction between equity and law actions has been abolished. The CIRCUIT COURTS in the counties have jurisdiction, except that in some counties with SUPERIOR COURTS there is concurrent jurisdiction between the two.

IOWA: Civil actions are distinguished as equitable or ordinary, but both are under the jurisdiction of the DISTRICT COURTS in the counties.

KANSAS: There is no distinction between equity and law actions. The COUNTY COURTS (up to $1,000) and the DISTRICT COURTS in the counties have jurisdiction.

KENTUCKY: There is no distinction between equity and law actions. The QUARTERLY COURTS in the counties (up to $500) and the CIRCUIT COURTS in the counties have jurisdiction.

LOUISIANA: There has never been any distinction between equity and law actions in Louisiana. The DISTRICT COURTS in the parishes (counties) have jurisdiction.

MAINE: No distinction exists between law and equity actions. The STATE DISTRICT COURTS (up to $10,000) and the SUPERIOR COURTS in the counties have some concurrent jurisdiction.

MARYLAND: There is a distinction made between law and equity actions, but the CIRCUIT COURTS in the counties have jurisdiction of both.

MASSACHUSETTS: The distinction between law and equity actions is preserved, but both are under the jurisdiction of the SUPERIOR COURTS in the counties.

MICHIGAN: There is no distinction between equity and law actions. The CIRCUIT COURTS in the counties have jurisdiction.

MINNESOTA: All distinctions between equity and law actions have been abolished. The DISTRICT COURTS in the counties have jurisdiction.

MISSISSIPPI: A strict distinction of actions is maintained. The CHANCERY COURTS in the counties have jurisdiction in equity matters and the CIRCUIT COURTS in the counties have jurisdiction in law matters.

MISSOURI: Distinction between equity and law cases is preserved though both are under jurisdiction of the CIRCUIT COURTS in the counties.

MONTANA: There is no formal distinction between actions in equity and actions at law though traditional equity grounds must be shown in equity cases. The DISTRICT COURTS in the counties have jurisdiction.

NEBRASKA: The distinction between equity and law actions has been abolished. The DISTRICT COURTS in the counties have jurisdiction. (Some MUNICIPAL COURTS have jurisdiction in claims up to $2,000.)

NEVADA: The distinction between equity and law cases is preserved, but both are under jurisdiction of the DISTRICT COURTS in the counties.

NEW HAMPSHIRE: The distinction between equity and law cases is preserved, but both are under jurisdiction of the DISTRICT COURTS (up to $1,500) and the SUPERIOR COURTS in the counties.

NEW JERSEY: Formal distinctions between equity and law actions have been abolished though equitable action is still brought through the Chancery Division of the court. The SUPERIOR COURT in the counties has jurisdiction in two separate divisions—Law and Chancery. Historically these were two separate courts.

NEW MEXICO: The distinction between equity and law cases has been abolished. Jurisdiction lies in the DISTRICT COURTS in the counties.

NEW YORK: Distinction between equity and law cases has been abolished. The STATE SUPREME COURT has original jurisdiction; and the COUNTY COURTS (up to $6,000), DISTRICT COURTS (up to $6,000), and the CIVIL COURT OF THE CITY OF NEW YORK (up to $10,000) have limited jurisdiction.

NORTH CAROLINA: The distinction between equity and law cases has been abolished. The DISTRICT COURTS in the counties (up to $5,000) and the SUPERIOR COURTS in the counties have jurisdiction.

NORTH DAKOTA: No distinction exists between equity and law actions. The COUNTY COURTS (up to $1,000) and the DISTRICT COURTS in the counties have jurisdiction.

OHIO: Distinction between equity and law cases, in name and form, have been abolished, but operation and function of the court varies. The COURTS OF COMMON PLEAS in the counties have jurisdiction.

OKLAHOMA: The distinction between equity and law cases has been abolished. The COUNTY COURTS (up to $1,000) and the DISTRICT COURTS in the counties have jurisdiction. (The COURTS OF COMMON PLEAS have concurrent jurisdiction with the District Courts in Tulsa and Oklahoma counties.)

OREGON: There is a distinction between law and equity actions, but both are under the jurisdiction of the CIRCUIT COURTS in the counties. The DISTRICT COURTS in 21 counties have jurisdiction if claims are under $2,500.

PENNSYLVANIA: The distinction is maintained between equity and law actions, but the COURTS OF COMMON PLEAS in the counties have jurisdiction of both. (In Allegheny and Philadelphia counties, the COUNTY COURTS have jurisdiction in claims under $5,000.)

RHODE ISLAND: There is no distinction between equity and law actions. The DISTRICT COURTS (up to $1,000) and the SUPERIOR COURT in the counties have jurisdiction.

SOUTH CAROLINA: The distinction between equity and law actions is abolished. The COUNTY COURTS (limited) and the CIRCUIT COURTS (called COURTS OF COMMON PLEAS when thus convened) in the counties have concurrent jurisdiction.

SOUTH DAKOTA: Equity and law cases are distinguished by the court though differences in form do not exist. Both are under jurisdiction of the COUNTY COURTS (up to $1,000) and the CIRCUIT COURTS in the counties.

TENNESSEE: Equity and law cases are separate though the two courts which handle them have some concurrent jurisdiction. Equity matters are in the jurisdiction of the CHANCERY COURTS in the counties and actions at law are in the jurisdiction of the CIRCUIT COURTS in the counties.

TEXAS: All distinction between equity and law cases has been abolished. The COUNTY COURTS and the DISTRICT COURTS in the county have jurisdiction, depending on the county.

UTAH: A distinction is made between equity and law matters though they may be administered in the same action and are both within the jurisdiction of the DISTRICT COURTS in the counties. (In the county seats, the CITY COURTS have jurisdiction in claims up to $1,000.)

VERMONT: There is a strict distinction between law and equity cases in Vermont. Equity cases are under the jurisdiction of the CHANCERY COURTS and law actions are under the jurisdiction of the DISTRICT COURTS (up to $5,000) and the COUNTY COURTS.

VIRGINIA: Distinction between law and equity matters is maintained, but both are administered by the same courts. The CIRCUIT COURTS in the counties ordinarily have jurisdiction, but cities have CORPORATION COURTS with civil jurisdiction. (See the section on Virginia court records at the end of this chapter.)

WASHINGTON: There is no formal distinction between law and equity actions. The COUNTY SUPERIOR COURTS have jurisdiction.

WEST VIRGINIA: There is no distinction between law and equity actions. The CIRCUIT COURTS in the counties have jurisdiction.

WISCONSIN: There is no distinction between law and equity actions. The CIRCUIT COURTS in the counties have jurisdiction.

WYOMING: The distinction between law and equity matters is defunct. The DISTRICT COURTS in the counties have jurisdiction. [5]

The records arising out of civil actions are ordinarily indexed by both plaintiffs and defendants. Many of them contain useful clues and background on the persons involved, and in some instances they contain direct evidence on genealogical problems. Addresses, dates, etc., for the parties involved are always given.

---

[5] Martindale-Hubbell Law Directory, 100th ed. (Summit, N. J.: Martindale-Hubbell, Inc., 1968), Vol. V (by permission) and correspondence with various record custodians.

B. DIVORCE RECORDS

We talked briefly about divorce records in Chapter Nine but, because they are essentially court records, we feel it appropriate to discuss them further here. Many wonder about the genealogical value of divorce records because they do not understand them, but if the couple who sought the divorce had children, the names and ages of those children are usually given in the court records (though not on the certificate). Dates of birth (or ages) of both parties, state or country of birth of both parties, the date and place of the marriage, plus the date and grounds for the divorce itself are also given.

In most states the court having authority to grant divorces is the court which has control over other equity matters. There are only a few exceptions to this. Following is a list of the courts having jurisdiction in divorce cases in the several states. The records are ordinarily kept in these courts and, in most cases, are open to public use:

ALABAMA:	Circuit Court in the county.
ALASKA:	Superior Court. (There are four districts.)
ARIZONA:	Superior Court in the county.
ARKANSAS:	County Chancery Court.
CALIFORNIA:	County Superior Court.
COLORADO:	District Court in the county.
CONNECTICUT:	Superior Court in the county.
DELAWARE:	Superior Court in the county.
D. C.:	Court of General Sessions.
FLORIDA:	Circuit Court in the county.
GEORGIA:	Superior Court in the county.
HAWAII:	Circuit Court.
IDAHO:	District Court in the county.
ILLINOIS:	Circuit Court in the county.
INDIANA:	Circuit Court in the county or Superior Court in the county (depends on the county).
IOWA:	District Court in the county.
KANSAS:	District Court in the county.
KENTUCKY:	Circuit Court in the county.
LOUISIANA:	District Court in the parish (county).
MAINE:	Superior Court in the county.
MARYLAND:	Circuit Court in the county.
MASSACHUSETTS:	County Probate Court and Superior Court in the county have concurrent jurisdiction.
MICHIGAN:	Circuit Court in the county.
MINNESOTA:	District Court in the county.
MISSISSIPPI:	Chancery Court in the county.

MISSOURI: Circuit Court in the county.
MONTANA: District Court in the county.
NEBRASKA: District Court in the county.
NEVADA: District Court in the county.
NEW HAMPSHIRE: Superior Court in the county.
NEW JERSEY: District Court in the county.
NEW MEXICO: District Court in the county.
NEW YORK: County Court.
NORTH CAROLINA: Superior Court in the county.
NORTH DAKOTA: District Court in the county.
OHIO: Court of Common Pleas in the county.
OKLAHOMA: District Court in the county and Superior Court in
                     the county have concurrent jurisdiction.
OREGON: Circuit Court in the county.
PENNSYLVANIA: Court of Common Pleas in the county.
RHODE ISLAND: Family Court in the county. (The Family Court
                     was created in 1961. Before that year divorces
                     were handled by the Superior Court in the
                     county.)
SOUTH CAROLINA: County Court. (Divorce was not legal in South
                     Carolina until 1949.)
SOUTH DAKOTA: Circuit Court in the county.
TENNESSEE: Circuit Court in the county and Chancery Court in
                     the county have concurrent jurisdiction.
TEXAS: District Court in the county.
UTAH: District Court in the county.
VERMONT: County Court.
VIRGINIA: Any court with equity jurisdiction (usually County
                     Circuit Court, but cities also have courts
                     with jurisdiction—see the section on Virginia
                     at the end of this chapter).
WASHINGTON: Family Court (a department of the County Superior
                     Court).
WEST VIRGINIA: Circuit Court in the county, except in those coun-
                     ties where Domestic Relations Courts have
                     been established.
WISCONSIN: County Court and Circuit Court in the county have
                     concurrent jurisdiction (except in Milwaukee
                     where Circuit Court has sole jurisdiction).
WYOMING: District Court in the county. [6]

---

6. Ibid., Vol. V (by permission) and correspondence with various record custodians.

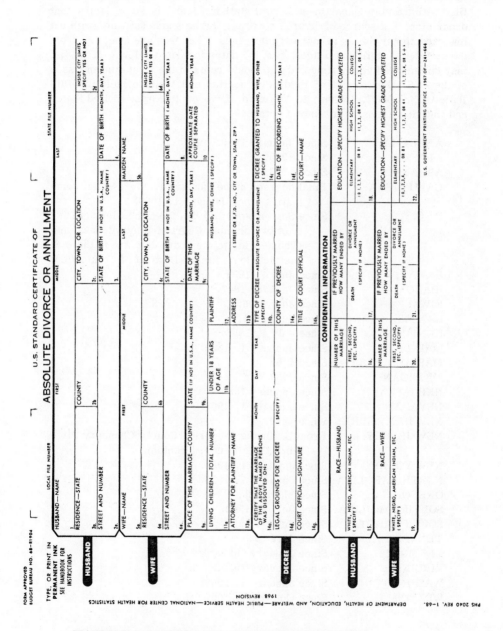

STANDARD CERTIFICATE OF DIVORCE OR ANNULMENT
(Certificates with this format are in current use in many states.)

In addition to the records of divorces kept in these courts many states have legislation which requires that a copy of the divorce certificate also be filed with the state department of vital statistics, and in some states that department is a source of divorce records, but as a general rule (with but few exceptions) this is in more recent years. Records are available from the state vital statistics offices from the dates indicated below. (This list may be amended at any time and you should refer to the most current issue of the U.S. Department of Health, Education and Welfare bulletin—PHS Bulletin No. 630C, "Where to Write for Divorce Records, United States and Outlying Areas," for current data):

ALABAMA:	Since January 1950.
ALASKA:	Since 1950.
ARKANSAS:	Since 1923.
CALIFORNIA:	Final decrees since January 1, 1962; initial complaints since January 1, 1966.
D. C.:	Since September 16, 1956, from the Clerk of District of Columbia Court of General Sessions. (Those prior to the above date are in the U.S. District Court for the District of Columbia.)
HAWAII:	Since July 1, 1951.
IDAHO:	Since January 1947.
IOWA:	Since July 1906.
KANSAS:	Since July 1951.
KENTUCKY:	Since July 1, 1958.
MAINE:	Since January 1, 1892.
MASSACHUSETTS:	Since 1952.
MICHIGAN:	Since 1897.
NEBRASKA:	Since January 1909.
NEVADA:	Since January 1, 1968.
NEW HAMPSHIRE:	Since 1880.
NEW JERSEY:	From beginning (Superior Court, Chancery Division, State House, Trenton).
NEW YORK:	Since January 1, 1963.
NORTH CAROLINA:	Since January 1, 1958.
OREGON:	Since May 1925.
SOUTH CAROLINA:	Since July 1, 1962.
SOUTH DAKOTA:	Since July 1, 1905.
TENNESSEE:	Since July 1945.
VERMONT:	Since January 1860.
VIRGINIA:	Since January 1918.
WASHINGTON:	Since January 1, 1968.
WISCONSIN:	Since October 1, 1907

WYOMING: Since May 1941. [7]

Some other states have state-wide filing of divorce records but do not issue certified copies of the decrees. Most of these offices will verify information for you and will forward inquiries and requests to the appropriate courts. These states include:

COLORADO: Has index, except for 1940-1967.
CONNECTICUT: Since June 1, 1947.
DELAWARE: Since March 1932.
GEORGIA: Since June 9, 1952.
ILLINOIS: Since January 1, 1962.
LOUISIANA: Since 1946.
MARYLAND: Since January 1961.
MISSISSIPPI: Since January 1, 1926.
MISSOURI: Since July 1948.
MONTANA: Since July 1943.
NORTH DAKOTA: Since July 1, 1949.
OHIO: Since 1948.
PENNSYLVANIA: Since January 1946.
RHODE ISLAND: Since January 1962.
UTAH: Since 1958. [8]

Divorce records are ordinarily indexed and, as we said earlier, they are public records in most states so they are quite easy to procure and use. However, there are some states, such as New York, where divorce records are open only to the parties of the action, but these are the exception and not the rule. All that is usually necessary to secure copies of these records is to write to the proper court giving the names of the parties of the divorce action and the approximate year thereof. Often the name of one party—usually the plaintiff—is sufficient. There will be a fee—likely somewhere between $1 and $3—but the amount varies considerably, even within some of the states.

C. CITIZENSHIP AND NATURALIZATION MATTERS

1. Background. Naturalization is the granting of citizenship rights to aliens as if they were native-born. Article 1, Section 8, Clause 4, of the U.S. Constitution authorized the formulation, by Congress, of a "uniform

---

[7]. "Where to Write for Divorce Records, United States and Outlying Areas" (Washington, D.C.: U.S. Public Health Service, 1968).

[8]. Ibid.

Rule of Naturalization," and beginning in 1790 Congress began to enact legislation to control the naturalization of aliens to citizenship.

During the colonial period there were few naturalizations of citizens. Only Europeans (from the continent) were not already considered as citizens because of the British control of the colonies. Since that time, however, naturalization of aliens in America has generally been handled in the courts and much of our present naturalization policy is based on some of the earliest Congressional acts. Of course there have been many modifications, but the policy has generally been consistent.

Prior to the enactment of the Fourteenth Amendment in 1868, all citizenship was said to be in the state and not in the nation. In some places the process of becoming a citizen (during the early periods) was quite simple. The immigrant merely signed a statement of allegiance as he came off the ship. Because of this we have listed some of the early books of citizenship lists as immigration lists (in Chapter Twenty). In reality that is all they were. A good example of this is Montague S. Giuseppi, Naturalization of Foreign Protestants in the American and West Indian Colonies..., 1921, (Baltimore: Genealogical Publishing Co., 1964 reprint). Another is William H. Egle, Names of Foreigners Who Took the Oath of Allegiance To the Province and State of Pennsylvania, 1727-1775, with the Foreign Arrivals, 1786-1880, 1892, (Baltimore: Genealogical Publishing Co., 1967 reprint).

The Fourteenth Amendment guaranteed national citizenship and extended it to all persons born or naturalized in the U.S. and subject to its jurisdiction. (This still excluded tribal Indians, natives of unincorporated territories and children of foreign ambassadors.)

There was no comprehensive regulation of naturalization until 1906 when Congress established the Bureau of Immigration and Naturalization[9] and formulated a specific procedure to be followed concurrently by this new bureau and the courts with naturalization jurisdiction. Before 1906 naturalization matters were entirely within the jurisdiction of the courts.

The process of naturalization is quite cumbersome and the records have suffered somewhat because of the overlapping jurisdictions. Some groups have been working to bring about a modernization of the system with only one agency being responsible. The present process of naturalization requires the alien first to file a petition for naturalization with the Immigration and Naturalization Service. (These records go back to the creation of the Bureau in 1906 and are confidential.) Until recently a declaration of intention, often called "first papers," has also been required. Following an

---

[9.] The name was changed in 1933 to the Immigration and Naturalization Service in the Department of Labor, and it was transferred to the Justice Department in 1940.

investigation by the Immigration and Naturalization Service (which can be waived) the applicant files a petition for naturalization with the clerk of the court where he resides. Next he is examined by someone from the office of the Immigration and Naturalization Service, following which he must appear before the judge of the court for a final hearing. At the hearing he must be recommended by an Immigration and Naturalization Service representative. An oath of allegiance is taken and a certificate of naturalization is issued.

The main difference between this procedure and the procedure followed prior to 1906 is that the court took care of the whole process in the earlier period.

Naturalization proceedings can take place in any U. S. District Court, in any court of record of the several states and (historically) in the district or supreme courts of the territories. All proceedings are required to be recorded by the clerk of the court.

Children under 16 acquire citizenship through the naturalization of their parents and, between 1855 and the Cable Act of 1922, a woman automatically became a citizen either by marrying a citizen or by the naturalization of her husband.

In instances where territories are annexed by the United States, all residents of those territories can become citizens by collective naturalization through legislative enactment (as with Hawaii, Texas, Puerto Rico) or by treaty (as with Louisiana, Florida, Alaska, the Virgin Islands).

2. Location of the records. The records of naturalizations in the U.S. District Courts are mostly still in the courts but are, in some cases, in the custody of various Federal Record Centers. The records of naturalizations in the state courts are still in the courts' custody almost without exception. [10] The records are open to public use but, because of certain restrictive legislation, they cannot be copied. (This does not prevent the abstracting of information from them.)

The Works Projects Administration (WPA) undertook a project in the 1930's to make photocopies of pre-1906 naturalization records and to index them, but the project managed to cover only the courts in four New England states—Maine, Massachusetts, New Hampshire and Rhode Island—before it was terminated. These 5" x 8" photocopies, covering the period 1787 to 1906, are in the National Archives together with a card index (Soundex system as described in Chapter Ten). The forms in these files (as the naturalization files of any court) usually contain information on...

... place and date of birth and of arrival in the United

---

[10]. About two-thirds of the naturalizations take place in 200 federal courts with the other one-third taking place in about 1,800 state courts.

States, place of residence at the time of applying for citizenship, and sometimes the name of the ship on which the immigrant arrived and his occupation. [11]

However, the restriction on making copies also applies to these records.

If your ancestor lived in New Jersey you will find naturalization records from 1749 through 1810 in the State Library, Archives and History Division, at Trenton. Also in New Jersey the WPA made a "Guide to Naturalization Records" in the courts of that state (December 1941) as part of their program to inventory vital statistics records. In Massachusetts naturalizations from 1885 to 1931 are on file in the Archives Division at the State House in Boston.

3. Special helps. In a case where the citizen who had been naturalized, or the alien who was seeking naturalization, filed a homestead claim or applied for a passport, these applications (homestead and passport) are normally in the National Archives. They give the name of the court where the naturalization took place, and they may prove to be valuable if you do not know the location of that event.

You might also receive assistance from the 1870 federal census. It indicated whether or not males over 21 were U.S. citizens. If an immigrant is reported as a citizen you know that there must be naturalization papers somewhere.

Anytime you know that your ancestor was a naturalized citizen it is worth-while to spend whatever time is necessary to locate the record of that naturalization. This record can bridge the gap to the ancestral home in the Old World. Remember, however, that persons born in the U.S. are citizens even though their immigrant parents may never have sought naturalization. If your immigrant ancestor did not seek American citizenship there will be no such record.

V. SPECIAL NOTE ON VIRGINIA

Many genealogists have difficulty in Virginia research because they fail to allow for the idiosyncrasies of her court system. They try to treat her like any other southern state, never looking for records anywhere except in the county. This may work fine most of the time, but if you will carefully note some of the lists of various courts we give in this chapter and in the chapters on wills and land records, you will see that there are

---

[11.] Meredith B. Colket, Jr., and Frank E. Bridgers, Guide to Genealogical Records in the National Archives (Washington, D.C.: The National Archives, 1964), p. 141.

some significant exceptions in Virginia, and some date back a long way. This means that some very important records are not found in the county courthouses but rather in the cities. A city in Virginia is a municipality which is independent of the county in its total operation.

Once incorporated as a city, a Virginia municipality establishes its own courts and government separate and distinct from the county in which it is geographically situated. The following table shows Virginia's independent cities, as they are called, the counties within whose boundaries they are located and the dates of their incorporation. The dates in parentheses are the dates they were incorporated as towns.

CITY	COUNTY WHERE GEOGRAPHICALLY LOCATED	INCORPORATION DATE
Alexandria	Fairfax and Arlington counties	(1779) 1852
Bristol	Washington County	(1856) 1890 (from town of Goodson)
Buena Vista	Rockbridge County	(1890) 1892
Charlottesville	Albemarle County	(1801) 1888
Chesapeake	formerly Norfolk County (extinct)	1963 (by merger of Norfolk County and City of South Norfolk)
Clifton Forge	Alleghany County	(1884) 1906
Colonial Heights	Chesterfield County	(1926) 1948
Covington	Alleghany County	(1833) 1954
Danville	Pittsylvania County	(1830) 1890 (North Danville added in 1869)
Emporia	Greenville County	1967
Fairfax	Fairfax County	(1874) 1961 (formerly called Providence)
Falls Church	Fairfax County	(1875) 1948
Franklin	Southampton County	(1876) 1961
Fredericksburg	Spotsylvania County	(1782) 1879
Galax	Carroll and Grayson counties	(1906) 1954 (formerly called Bonepart)
Hampton	formerly Elizabeth City County (extinct)	(1849) 1908 (Elizabeth City Co. and town of Phoebus added in 1952)
Harrisonburg	Rockingham County	(1849) 1916

CITY	COUNTY WHERE GEOGRAPHICALLY LOCATED	INCORPORATION DATE
Hopewell	Prince George County	1916 (City Point added in 1923)
Lexington	Rockbridge County	1966
Lynchburg	Campbell County	(1805) 1852
Martinsville	Henry County	(1873) 1928
Newport News	formerly Warwick County (extinct)	1896 (city of Warwick added in 1958)
Norfolk	formerly Norfolk County (extinct)	(1737) 1845 (Berkeley added in 1906)
Norton	Wise County	(1894) 1954 (formerly called Prince's Flat)
Petersburg	Dinwiddie and Prince George counties	(1784) 1850 (Blandford, Pocahontas and Ravensworth added in 1784)
Portsmouth (now in Chesapeake)	formerly Norfolk County (extinct)	(1836) 1858
Radford	Montgomery County	(1887) 1892 (formerly called Central City)
Richmond	Henrico and Chesterfield counties	(1782) 1842 (added Manchester—or South Richmond—in 1910 and Barton Heights, Fairmount and Highland Park in 1914)
Roanoke	Roanoke County	(1874) 1902 (formerly called Big Lick)
Salem	Roanoke County	1968
South Boston	Halifax County	(1884) 1960
South Norfolk	(see Chesapeake)	
Staunton	Augusta County	(1801) 1871
Suffolk	Nansemond County	(1808) 1910
Virginia Beach	formerly Princess Anne County (extinct)	(1906) 1952 (Princess Anne

CITY	COUNTY WHERE GEOGRAPHICALLY LOCATED	INCORPORATION DATE
		County added in 1963)
Warwick	(see Newport News)	
Waynesboro	Augusta County	(1834) 1948 (Basic City added in 1923)
Williamsburg	James City and York counties	(1722) 1884
Winchester	Frederick County	(1779) 1784 (formerly called Fredericktown)

In several of the above cities the records date back to their incorporation as cities and in many instances to their incorporation as towns. If your ancestors lived within the area of any of these cities after their incorporation that fact is probably important to your research.

Though these independent cities are legally separated from county jurisdiction we have listed the counties in which they are situated to facilitate your locating them. Many of them, in fact, are the seats of county government in those counties. They include Charlottesville (Albemarle County), Covington (Alleghany County), Emporia (Greensville County), Fairfax (Fairfax County), Martinsville (Henry County), Richmond (Henrico County), Salem (Roanoke County), Staunton (Augusta County), Suffolk (Nansemond County), Williamsburg (James City County) and Winchester (Frederick County).

As the above list attests, many of these independent cities have only recently achieved such status and, at present, have negligible genealogical significance but, in the interest of completeness, we have listed all of them. And you can be certain that the end is not yet.

Some of the old Virginia counties no longer exist because they have been absorbed by the independent cities. In such cases the records of these counties are in the custody of the city courts. These extinct counties include:

Alexandria County	Became Arlington County in 1920. Much of the area is now in the city of Alexandria.
Elizabeth City County	Now in the city of Hampshire (since 1952).
Norfolk County	Now in the city of Chesapeake (since 1963). (Chesapeake also has records of the former independent cities of Portsmouth and South Norfolk.)
Princess Anne County	Now in the city of Virginia Beach (since 1963).
Warwick County	Now in the city of Newport News (since 1958).

All court records, including land and probate records, are in the jurisdiction of the courts (mainly the Corporation Courts) of these cities and are not in the county courts. The only cities whose courts are not called Corporation Courts are:

Hampton	Court of Law and Chancery.
Norfolk	Circuit Court and Court of Law and Chancery have concurrent jurisdiction.
Portsmouth	Court of Hustings.
Richmond	Chancery Court has jurisdiction north of James River and Hustings Court has jurisdiction south of the river.
Roanoke	Law and Chancery Court and Circuit and Hustings Court have concurrent authority.

A useful book for understanding Virginia and her history is A Hornbook of Virginia History (Richmond: The Virginia State Library, 1965). We recommend it to anyone who has Virginia ancestry.

VI. CONCLUSION

In most states court records of one type or another go back to the very beginning, thus providing a quite-useful genealogical source. However, many of the most valuable court records—the older records and case files —are stored in out-of-the-way places because they are not in current use and space is scarce. Often the present records custodian is unaware of the location (and frequently the existence) of such records. In some cases the WPA inventories of the various county courthouses are useful, but often the information therein, which was current in the early 1940's, is somewhat antiquated. In searching for these records the genealogist will do well to employ diligence and imagination.

Court reports of the various courts of appeal in the states also provide a way to locate some court records. These reports are composed of the published opinions of the judges in the appellate courts to which the cases have been brought. They are accessible through the use of court digests which provide a table of cases (by both plaintiffs and defendants) as well as a subject (or point-of-law) index to the reports. The reports are no substitute for the case files of either the trial courts or the appellate courts, but they do provide a way to get at the case files. They give the docket number of each case, the name of the court reviewing it and the date of the court's decision, all of which are helpful in locating briefs and case files.

In addition to the state reports, since the 1880's the comprehensive reporters and digests of the seven regions of the National Reporter Series, the four federal court series and the supplemental reports for New York

State (and more recently California) are also important. The regional reporters include some cases from the state appellate courts which are not in the state reports, as they contain reports of cases from all courts of appellate jurisdiction. The state reports (with a few exceptions) are usually restricted to cases in the state Supreme Court.

What may be a useful tool is the table of cases in the American Digest (West Publishing Co.). Of special note are volumes 21 through 25 of the 1911 edition of this publication wherein is printed "A Complete Table of American Cases from 1658 to 1906." Subsequent editions (published every 10 years) update this table. The tables are particularly helpful if the surname you seek is uncommon.

All of the various court reports and digests can usually be found in law libraries (at the local courthouse), and occasionally in other libraries.

An aid to finding the proper digests is Appendix 3 of Frederick Charles Hicks, Materials and Methods of Legal Research, 3rd rev. ed. (Rochester, N. Y.: The Lawyers Co-operative Publishing Co., 1942). This appendix contains a list of the various volumes of court reports, arranged by state.

The records and files of some court actions are voluminous. You may find hundreds of pages of various kinds of papers in the file of just one case. In such situations it is certainly impractical for you to copy all of this material into your notes; however, you will find it worthwhile to go through the papers and abstract everything of significance. It has been our experience that the complaint of the plaintiff (the portion at the beginning of the case where the cause is explained, also sometimes called the petition, declaration or statement of claim), the plea of the defendant (or answer to the complaint) and the decree (the final judgment) are usually of the most genealogical significance. This, however, is not to discount the value of other information in the file.

Court records, with some justifiable exceptions, are completely open to the public use. If they are not on film for the locality you need (and they usually are not) you should contact the court or pay a personal visit to the courthouse. And, as you have observed from some of the examples used in earlier chapters, other records often tell of the existence of important court records.

To the informed user of court records, we wish (in fact, we almost promise) good luck. These records are loaded.

CHAPTER NINETEEN

CHURCH RECORDS

The story is told of the old cowboy who visited the Grand Canyon for the first time. He is reported tying his horse to a tree then sauntering out to the ledge to look down into the canyon. "Ah took one look," he said, "and then ah wished ah'd tied m'self to the tree and let the horse look down into the canyon."

This is about the way American church records affect many researchers. These records constitute a vast, relatively-unexplored and little-known genealogical source, and they can be awesome to the average genealogist. However, they are different from the Grand Canyon in that they are usually not as easy to locate—and that is our biggest problem.

We are not trying to say that no one has ever made good use of American church records (that would certainly be an error), but rather that these church records quite generally present some unique problems which significantly limit our use of them as a research source. In New England and the northern colonial states, however, church records present few problems and have wider use than is typical elsewhere in the country.

I. TYPES OF RECORDS

In many respects the records of most churches are not unlike vital records. They deal with the same essential identifying data—births, marriages, deaths—only in a slightly different way. Rather than the actual birth, the church ordinarily reports the baptism or christening—usually a few days later. Instead of a marriage license or bond, the church keeps a record of the actual marriage and of the banns. And instead of the death, the church is more likely to record the burial. But because of the near proximity of these dates—timewise—they serve the same purpose, and they were generally kept in a much earlier time period than were civil vital records. These three—christenings, marriages and burials—are usually the most important, and certainly the most widely used, church records in genealogical research. They are ordinarily kept in books called registers.

Another kind of church record that has special genealogical value is the record which indicates removal to or arrival from another congregation. Most churches kept records of this type so that faithful members would be welcomed into the church when they moved to a new location, but each church had a different name for them. The Society of Friends (Quakers) called them certificates of removal, the Protestant Episcopal Church (Church of England) called them letters of transfer, the Baptists called them letters of admission, the Congregationalists called them dismissions and the Latter-day Saints (Mormons) called them certificates of membership.

These records are useful because they allow a family to be traced with relative ease from one locality to another, sometimes a very difficult matter without this assistance. The problem with them is that they are usually incomplete.

Other types of church records include confirmations, lists of communicants, membership lists, excommunications—all of which are frequently recorded in the registers—plus vestry minutes and proceedings (Protestant Episcopal Church), sessions minutes (Presbyterian Church) and other minutes which include financial reports, disciplinary actions and fines toward backsliders, and (for the Friends) disownments and manumissions.

It might be well to mention it now, though we will discuss it more thoroughly later, but the nature of church records is greatly affected by the position (and by this we do not mean geographical location) of the church in the community. In places where there is a state church (one which is recognized by law as the official church and is supported by the government) the church records are usually much better and are more often complete. This emphasizes one of the chief problems of American church records as a genealogical source: The U. S. has a complete separation of church and state. Politically this is wonderful, but genealogically it has disadvantages.

During the colonial period our nation did experience the existence of state churches in some of the colonies. For example, many of the New England colonies adhered to the Congregational Church; in Virginia the English (Protestant Episcopal) Church was the official church. Other colonies —notably Georgia, Maryland and South Carolina—also held the P. E. Church as a state church at various times. In New Netherland the Dutch Reformed Church was the state church.

America was truly unique in her religious development. During settlement she combined persons from many European nations, who brought with them the religions of their homelands and tried to make those religions dominant. The English tried hard—the colonies were mostly English so there was an extra advantage. However, any advantage proved small, especially after the passing of the Toleration Act by William III in 1689. State churches did exist but they did not stand unchallenged, and the only remedy left to the framers of the Constitution, in light of the multiplicity of churches and of national origins, was to separate completely the powers of church and government. Thus there was never a national church in the United States though some state establishments persisted long after the Revolution (especially in New England).

II. THE NATURE OF THE RECORDS

Perhaps the best way to explain the true nature of church records is to show examples of them. For our examples we have drawn from the Congregational Church in New England (Maine), from the Protestant Episcopal (P.E.) Church in the South (Virginia), from the Lutheran Church in the central-Atlantic states (Pennsylvania), from the Baptist Church and from the Society of Friends. Remember that these are only examples and that church records often vary considerably even within the same denomination. There is frequently extensive variance in records of the same congregation when a new minister or a new clerk took over the record-keeping duties.

A. CONGREGATIONAL CHURCH

Let's begin with a Congregational Church—the Second Church of Kittery (Maine). This church, as most Congregational Churches, kept a record of baptisms, but note that these are not always baptisms of infants and that some important information was not included in the record:

1. Baptisms.

> 1725—Ap—David Libby Junr
> Ester his wife
> Mary Smal Jos: wife
> Eban^r Libby
> Sept^r—Joseph son of Joseph Harn^d Junr—
> Decem^r—Catharine my Daughter [the minister]
> Feb.—Saml & Hep^h child^n of Saml Hanscom in Private
> 1726—July.—Two Children of Nathan Spinney—
> Edward Chapman son Simon
> 31—Jno Libby & Ephra^m Libby, adult—
> Elisha son of John Libby
> Mary Daughter of Richd King
> 1727. May—Eleanor Daughter of Deacon Tetherly
> June 25—Nathl son of Peter Staple—
> July 3d Sab—Tho: Knight—
> Sept 3—David Libby & Son David
> Saml Son of Samuel Winget on her acc^t—

A few years later the information was a little more detailed, but not much:

1764
Aug 29 Gabriel son of William Tetherly

Eunice dau of John Spinney J[r]

Sep 24   Jotham, son of Samuel Emery

Oct 1   Nathan Bartlett, Jr, son of Nathan

1765 Apr 21 J. Gowen, wife of William Gowen

May 12   John Kennard owned the covenant & had his child bap-
         tized named John

June 9   Mary child of Mr. Tho Hammcnd & wife who renewed
         their baptismal covenant

July 14 Joshua son of Jonathan More. 3d Sabbath in Oct Joseph
         son of William Stacy

Oct 10   Joel & David sons of Ephraim Libby, Jr.

Nov 23   Samuel son of Tobias Shapleigh

2. Communicants.

The following is from an undated list (sometime between 1727 and 1746)
of "Males Belonging to the Communion." Such lists were also made of female communicants, but they did not often state the given names of married
women—only "Mrs.":

Joseph Hamond	Edward Chapman mov'd
Nic[o] Shapleigh	Christopher Sargent mov'd
Sam[l] Hill	Robert Staple
Daniel Fogg	James Staple jun[r]
John Staple	Phylip Cooms mov'd
Stephen Tobley	Josiah Paul
William Tetherly	Jeremiah Paul mov'd

3. Dismissions.

Also recorded among sundry notes which the minister kept of the
church's (and his own) activities are records of persons moving in and out.
These are called dismissions:

June 1749—Had Deacon Simon Emerys Dissmission from the
      Church of Berwick Read to the Brethren, and then voted
      for receiving him into communion with us—

July 30, 1778—Jerusha Hanscom was dismissed from this chh
      & recommended to the 2nd chh of Berwick.

July 7, 1817—Sarah Thimison was dismissed from this chh and
      recommended to the chh of X[t] in Temple.

4. Notes.

As mentioned earlier, the ministers in this particular church kept notes in journal form of some of the church's activities. There is not a lot of information in these of value to the genealogist, but they should be considered. The following notes are typical:

Novemb^r 6—1721—
The chh met at the House of Brother James Staple, in order to make choice of Two Suitable Persons for Deacons: And after Prayer to the Great Head of the chh, for Direction in this Important affair—the Members by written votes, chose William Tetherly, & James Staples for this offices.

Octob^r 6, 1727
Being ye Lords Day: After the Public Exercises were over I Stay'd ye Brethren of ye chh, & Laid before them ye Error which I apprehended those of o^r Brethren, viz. Ham^d, Tobey, Rogers, Hanscom, Tob: Leighton, in withdrawing communion from this chh & in Continuing in their Separation from it: observed to them y^t they had broken their Covenant with us which was to Submit to ye watch & Discipline of this chh, & walk orderly & in Comunion with us: and Laid before them our Duty; which was to call them to an acc^t & proceed with them in a way of admonition in the first place, Publickly before the chh to bring them to a sense of y^r disorderly doings.

In addition to these notes and to the lists of communicants given earlier, this church also kept a list of persons admitted to full communion with the church, as follows:

1746, May 18, Admitted Abigail Wittum wife of Eben^r—
1747, Augt 30. Admitted Cumbo, a Negro woman of Capt Bartletts.—
1748, Ap^l 10. Admitted Wid^o Judith Gowen—
1751, Augt 4. Jane Remick, wife of Nath Remick—
1754. July. Samuel Fernald—
1754. Decem^r 1: John Heard Bartlett: who had a Liberal Education at Harvard Colledge.—
1756 June, Joanna Preble the wife of Edward Preble.

5. Burials and marriages.

In this particular church there are no records of burials and marriages preserved, though this is not the case in all Congregational churches.

B. THE PROTESTANT EPISCOPAL CHURCH (CHURCH OF ENGLAND)

The Protestant Episcopal Church has generally kept quite good records in America, but many of them have not been preserved. For our example we have chosen two separate churches—the Augusta Parish in Augusta County, Virginia, where we will take a comprehensive look at vestry minutes [1] and the Immanuel Church in Hanover County, Virginia, where we will also peek at the vestry minutes, but shall be chiefly concerned with church registers.

1. Vestry minutes.

The P. E. Church in colonial times had a very close connection with the civil government of Virginia as we have already discussed, and many things you will find in the records of the vestry you might more typically find in civil court records if you were in some other part of the country or in a later time period. One example which we will not illustrate but will only mention is the record involved with the processioning of land. This involves the formality of determining the limits and boundaries (metes and bounds) of the several private estates within the parish. The processions tell the amount of land (number of acres) that each person owns. Another good example is the record kept of orphans and illegitimate children.

2. The poor, orphans and illegitimate children.

The church, through the vestry, was responsible for the material sustenance and physical well-being of the parish members and kept careful records of the manner in which this obligation was discharged. In addition to the widows, the physically incapable and the habitually poor, children who were incapable of providing for themselves were objects of special concern and a large portion of vestry minute space was often devoted to them. Bastardy bonds, such as the following, are quite common and can be of great genealogical value:

1748/9   KNOW all men by These Presence that we Christo-
Feby 14th pher Finney and William Armstrong are held and
           firmly bound unto James Lockhart and John Madison
           Churchwardens for the Parish of Augusta in the just
           and full sum of Fifty Pounds Curr[t] money of Virginia
           to which Payment will and truly to be made and done

---

[1] The vestry is a group of church members who oversee and manage the temporal affairs of the church.

we bind us and Each of our Heirs and Assigns firmly by these Presents as witness our Hands and Seals this 14th day of February 1748/9.

THE CONDITION of this obligation is such that whereas Sarah Simmons Single Woman hath this day before me Charged Christopher Finney Taylor for getting Her with Child which Child when Born will be a Bastard and may be Burdensome To our S^d Parish of Augusta if the said Finney shall be and appear at our next Court to be held for s^d County then & there to do what may be by the s^d Child then this obligation to be void or Else to Remain in force and Virtue in Law & c.

Taken before me ⎱ (signed) Christopher Finney
Robt Cunningham ⎰ (signed) Wm Armstrong

Also, as a means of removing the care of children from the church, it was common to find apprenticeship records wherein an orphan or an illegitimate child (the record usually indicated which) was bound as an apprentice to some responsible party. (Some illegitimate children were apprenticed to their reputed fathers.) Following is an apprenticeship document for a child who was deserted:

THIS INDENTURE Witnesseth that we James Lockhart and John Archer Churchwardens of Augusta County at the November Court In the Year of our Lord MDCCL it was agreed that the Churchwardens bind out an orphan Child belonging to Nicholas Smith named Peter Smith and as he is now Run away it appearing to the Court that all his Children is like to become Burdonsome to the Parish of Augusta there being no Persons to care of ye sd Children it is ordered y^t ye Churchwardens bind out the sd Peter Smith to Elijah McClenachan who appeared in Court & agreed to take the sd Peter Smith According to Law Pursuent To which they bind him unto ye s^d Elijah McClenachan to serve him his Heirs or assigns untill he shall be full Twenty one years of Age he being now Four years of Age during all which Term ye sd Peter Smith his sd master and mistress shall Faithfully serve their Secrets keep their Lawful commands everywhere gladly obey he shall do no Damage to his master or Mistress he shall not Waste his S^d master or mistresses Goods nor lend them unlawfully to any He shall not commit Fornication nor Contract matrimony during ye sd Term he shall not Play at Cards Dice or any unlawful Game he shall not absent himself Day nor night from his said Master or mistresses service unlawfully nor haunt

Ale Houses Taverns or Play Houses but in all things behave himself as a Faithful servant out to do & ye sd Elijah McClenachan
shall Teach or cause him to be Taught to Read write and Cast
up Acct[S] & shall Provide for & Procure to him meat Drink
Washing & apparel & all other necessaries fitting for such an
apprentice the sd Term and for the true Performance of every
the said Covenants & agreements either of the Parties bind themselves to the others firmly by these Presents In witness whereof
this XXIJ Day of November 1752 & the sd Elijah McClenachan
shall give sd Peter Smith when free such freedom dues as the
Law directs likewise to Learn him or cause him to be instructed
in the Cooper Trade or some other & c.

Signed Sealed and delivered   (signed) James Lockhart
In Presence of——   (signed) John Archer
W[m] Preston   (signed) Elijah McClenachan

3. Money.

The vestry minutes are also concerned with the incoming of money
from various sources:

1753	Dr To the Parish of Augusta	
To Cash paid... by Mr John Madison	£ 30 – 0 – 0
To Ditto by William Henderson a fine	2 – 10 – 0
To Ditto by Widow Smily a fine	2 – 10 – 0
To Ditto by James Greenlee his servants fine	2 – 10 – 0
To Ditto by Andrew Beard for swearing	0 – 10 – 0
To Ditto by Robert Gwin his Daughters fine	0 – 10 – 0
To Ditto collected by James Greenlee Constable for swearing	1 – 0 – 0
To Ditto by John Mason Constable for swearing	0 – 10 – 0
To Ditto by Henry Gay his Daughters fine	2 – 10 – 0
To Jean Campbells Fine	2 – 10 – 0
To a Deposit in his Hands the 6th Aug[t] 1750	52 – 14 – 5
To Interest on the same 2 years	5 – 4 – 0
To Viter Mauck's part of the Quitrent money	4 – 18 – 3
To Cash of John Graham for swearing	1 – 0 – 0
To Cash pd.. by David Stuart late Sheriff	1 – 12 – 3

They were also concerned with the outgoing of that same money:

2 Nov 1752

David Stuart Sheriff Produced an Acc^t against this Parish out of which he is allowed the sum of £1"15"2 and ordered that he be Paid the same.

Ordered that Margaret Frame be allowed the sum of £6"0"0 for the maintainance of one of Her Children this insuing year it appearing To this Vestry that it is an Object of Charity.

It appears to this Vestry that Hewan Mathers is an object of Charity it is therefore ordered that he be allowed £4 for this Present Year to be laid out at the Discretion of the Church-wardens for Cloaths only

Ordered that the Revd John Jones be allowed at the rate of £50 p^r annum to commince from the first Day of Sepr 1752 It appearing to this Vestry that the Glebe Buildings are not yet Finished and the said Jones having acquainted this Vestry that John Lewis Gen^t (the undertaker of the same) Agrees to allow him at the Rate of £20" p^r annum until the same be Finished, for which he declares himself Satisfied and ac-quits this Vestry and Parish of any further charge for the same.

Ordered that a Reader of this Parish be allowed the sum of £6"5 yearly and that the Revd Mr Jones have a Liberty to Choose the same to officiate at ye Court House.

Ordered that Wm Preston be allowed the Sum of £5" p^r Annum to serve as a Clerk for this Vestry and that, to Com-mence from the first Sepr 1752.

Ordered that a Register Book be Procured for the use of this Parish and Delivered to the Revd Mr Jones.

And...

		s	d
1753	To Cash pd the Revd John Jones as Hd Rect £50 "	0 "	0
	To Cash to CoLo James Patton (Asst) Rect 9 "	19 "	7
	To Hewan Mathers one of the Poor of this		
	Parish 4 "	0 "	0
	To 2 3/4 Gallons of Wine for the Sacrament 1 "	7 "	6
	To Diging a Cellar in the Glebe House 2 "	5 "	0
	To Robert McClenachan H^d order of Vestry 2 "	13 "	4
	To David Stuart & Wm Hinds for carriage		
	of the vestry books 1 "	10 "	0
	To Julian Mauck for keep a Blind Woman 1 "	4 "	3
	To Patrick Porterfield for Nursing an		
	Orphan Child 9 "	4 "	0
	To Widow Thing for Burying John Lowdon 4 "	10 "	0

To the Quitrents of the Glebe Land for the
      Years 1747: 48: 49: 50 " 51 & 52   1 " 9 " 11 1/2
To Cash to Thomas Moffit at Sundrys one
      of the Poor   4 " 13 " 4
To Peter Mauck on Account of a Blind
      Woman   9 " 6 " 9
To Lambert Booper an Object of Charity   2 " 12 " 10

4. Other matters.

Various other types of notes are also found in vestry minutes. The following is particularly reminiscent of documents arising out of the "poor laws" of England which required that the parish of origin (called "parish of settlement") be responsible for their poor regardless of where they may remove themselves:

August 6th 1750
    On the information of CoLᵒ John Buckanan that one _____
[sic] Morrice is lately come into this Parish with a numerous Family who is likely to become chargeable to this Parish Its ordered that the Churchwardens move the said Morrice to the place from whence he came——According to Law and bring in their Charge for the same at the laying of the next Parish Levy unless he give Security for indemnifying the said Parish.

Even biographical material can be found in vestry minutes upon occasion. In the minutes of the Immanuel Church, Hanover County, Virginia, on October 21, 1878, there was recorded an obituary for one of the churchwardens or vestrymen. It was copied from the Southern Churchman:

BASSETT——Departed this life on the 25th of August, 1878, at his residence, Clover Lia in the county of Hanover, George Washington Bassett, Esqr, in the seventy ninth year of his age. By the death of Mr. Bassett, a prominent and valient member of the old, fashioned Virginia gentry has been taken away from the few who still survive and the church has been deprived of a wise and devoted member.
    Mr Bassett was descended from the ancient and honorable family of the Bassetts of Eltham in the county of New Kent, which for two centuries exercised so prominent an influence in their native county and was so active in the civil and, ecclesiastical affairs of Virginia. The sister of Mrs. Washington, Miss Anna Maria Dandridge, married Mr. Bassett's grandfather and between the families of Mount Vernon and Eltham there was always

maintained the most intimate and cordial relations. Early in life
Mr. Bassett became a communicant of the Episcopal Church and
at once manifested the most active zeal for its prosperity in the
neighborhood in which he resided. He sat in many of the con-
ventions of the diocese and was always found in hearty coopera-
tion with those ------- and, devoted, men to whom so much of
the prosperity and advancement of the church in Virginia is
firstly due.

In the year of 1843, soon after his removal, to his estate in
Hanover, Mr. Bassett became much concerned at the prostrate
condition of the Church in his neighborhood, and the adjoining
counties of King William and New Kent. The parishes had died
out and been without rectors or church services for more than
half a century. With extraordinary patience and self denial Mr.
Bassett awakened the interest and aid of the few Churchmen
scattered over the large extent of the country and, the church
was reorganized and a clergyman appointed, to labor in the lower
part of Hanover County, two parishes in King William and one in
New Kent.

Mr. Bassett's money, his time and, personal influence were
issued unsparingly bestowed, and, his faithful services were
much abundantly rewarded.

He saw the Church of his fathers happily restablished and
with slight interruptions it has continued to prosper to this day.
So far as ------- judgment may venture it seems certain that
but for Mr. Bassett's exertions the Church would, have died out
utterly or remained ------- and, useless as he found it in this
part of Virginia.

Like so large and sorrowful a number of the prominent families in old, Virginia, Mr. Bassett sustained severe damage to
his temporal prosperity from the effects of the late war and,
other causes beyond his control. Estates held from a long line
of honored ancestry were almost wholly ------- but his patient
submission to his Master's dispensations and his unmurmuring
acquiescence in what had befallen him without any hope of amel-
ioration were most touching and edifying to witness.

No complaints ever fell from his lips and he seemed heart-
ily thankful for the comforts yet left to him in his declining years.

For heaven his last days were his best days, and it is a
most precious memory to his many friends, that the religion of
his early manhood was so full of steadfastness and afforded, so
many precious consolations when he was wasted and feeble and
slowly passing away to his rest in heaven.

The community of which Mr. Bassett was so conspicuous a

member for so many years will long remember his as a -------
friend, a hospitable, sympathising neighbor, and though not a
perfect, yet an humbel minded, earnest and devoted, Christian.

5. Registers of the P. E. Church.

The registers of the Immanuel Protestant Episcopal Church are quite
typical of those kept in other churches of the same denomination, though,
as we said earlier, there is no set pattern—they vary even with the minister. Let's look at some register entries:

a. Baptisms.

Name of Infant	Name of Parents	Name of Sponsors	Date and Age
William Braxton	Carter & Ellen Roy	Parents	1857 April 1 yr
Carter			1857 April 3 yr
William Roy	Thomas H. & Susan Carter	W^m H Roy & Sally V B Tabb	1857 June 5 yrs
James Bernard	Thos & Sally Q. Gardiner	E. P. Meridith	1857 July 10 2 yrs
Blanch Bell	Mrs McGehee	Mother & uncles	1857 Sep 8 yrs

Note this Baptism was at Wht Sulphur Springs. The parties of
Bolvin County, Miss. (Post Office Victoria)

Charles Pinkney	Thos & Sally Q Gardiner	E. P. Meredith	1858 May 29 3 mo
Edmon Fitzhugh	Rob^o W. & H. V. B. Tomlin	Parents	1858 July 9 yrs
Thomas Nelson Carter	Thomas H. & Susan Carter	Mrs. Ann Wickham Mrs Ann Carter	1858 Nov

These baptisms contain quite complete information, but later baptisms
are somewhat more informative:

At Hempstead July 5th 1873—
    Ellen Douglas, daughter of W. W. & Fanny Gordon
    Born Aug 11th 1873 [sic]
1874: Nov 16. At the house of James S. & Delia Kelley their
    child Mary Egbert born May 6th last
    Sponsors, Mrs B. B. Bassett & Mrs Annette L. Ingle
    Rev J. E. Ingle of the Diocese of Maryland officiating

1876: Apr 28th—At Mrs Blake's.   King William Co.
    Rush Aldridge Hunt
    Son of Jones Rush Lincoln (and Elizabeth Aldridge Blake
    his wife deceased)
    born Ap 8 1866
    Sponsors Rev E. A. Dalrymple STD, Miss Sophia L.
    Lincoln—by proxy.
Oct 14th at Hampstead, New Kent.
    Laura Robinson daughter of W. W. & Fanny Gordon
    born July 10th 1876.
1877
Oct 5th at the Rectory.
    Lydia Bock, daughter of Francis E. & Emma Keene
    Habersham
    born Sept 20th
    Sponsors: Mrs Emma Keene, Miss Ella Habersham,
    Newton Keene, by proxy.

b. Confirmations.

Confirmations tell us very little—just names and dates:

Name of Candidates	By Whom Administered	Date
Ella Moore Bassett	Rt Rev Wm Meade D.D.	1857 Nov.
Augusta Lewis	"	"
Sarah Ann Baker	"	"
Thos. H. Carter	"	1860 Nov. 4th
Mary M. L. Newton	"	" "
Henry Franklin Baker	"	" "
Mary Louisa "	"	" "
Maria Carter Wormly	"	" "
Bettie A. Polaka	Confirmed in Lexington, Ky	
May Dabney	" Charlottesville, Va	
O. T. Baker	Rt Rev J. Johns D.D.	1866 Nov.
Robt H. "	"	"
Margt E. "		"
Susan C. L. "	"	"
Anna J. "	"	"
Maria Dabney	"	
Sallie C. Darricotte	"	

c. Communicants.

1.	Geo W. Bassett sen	
2.	Betty Barnett Bassett	
3.	Geo W. Bassett Jr.	
—	Judith F. F. Bassett	Removed
4.	Carter Warner Wormley	
5.	Ellen Bankhead Wormley	
6.	Sallie Lightfoot Wormley	
—	Turner	Removed to Frederick, M^d
7.	Mary Sheet	
8.	Susan E. Carter	Withdrawn
—	Robert W. Tomlin	Died July 22^d 1862
9.	Wm A.R. Brockenborough	
—	William Sayre	Removed
—	Elizabeth Sayre	Died Dec 8th 1860
—	Mildred Ruffin	Removed to Frankfort, Ky
—	Margaret Tyler	Transferred to St Peters Parish
—	Betty Tyler	Transferred to St Peters Parish
10.	Wm A Baker	Died June 24, 1873
11.	Sarah A. Baker	
12.	Judith O. Johnson	
—	Sally A. Gardiner	Removed to Kanawha 1860
—	Virginia T. Carroway	Removed and dead
—	Ella M. Bassett	Removed to Jefferson C. Nov 1860
13.	Annette L. Bassett	
14.	Sarah A.E. Baker	Removed to California
15.	Sarah Eliza Blake	Withdrawn

d. Marriages.

Names of Parties	Where Married	Date
Wm A. Tignor & Ann E. Clifton	Immanuel Church	1857 Oct 13th
John Peris Points & Elizth Garlick Tyler	Turwood Hannvill	1858 April 18th 11: AM

Names of Parties	Where Married	Date
Henry J. C. Vass & Lavinia Via	Black Creek Church	1858 April 18th 3 PM
Wm Robt Boyd & Marg^t Farley Smith	Immanuel Church	1859 Sept 28 10: AM.
Barnett Bassett Sayre & Mildred Campbell Ruffin	Marlbourne	1859 October 4 12 AM

e. Deaths and funerals.

Wm Roy infant son of Dr Thos & Susan Carter died Sunday May
    2^d and buried at Pampatake on Monday May 3^d [1857]
James Tyler died July -- 1857 and buried by Mr Points
Mrs _____ White aged about 100 buried Oct 2/58
Mrs Bently Waker   Apr 12/59
Miss Polly White   June   "
Elisha White   69   Nov 23^d "
C. W. Robt Wate   abt 60   Aug 11 1860
Mrs Eliz. Sayre   died on 8th Decr buried Decr 10th at
    Marlbourne
This infant son of Mrs Sayre 19   "
Susan Cath^n daughter of Mrs Blake died 25th & buried 27th Aug 61

Later funeral and death records are typically better than the earlier
ones:

1876 March 25th
    Mrs Harriet Clopton, aged 78, was buried at the cemetery
    near the dwelling house of her son
March 31—In New Kent County from his residence at The White
    House. William A. Cooke—aged about 30.
April 25th—At Hampstead, New Kent, Virginia—Jane Farland
    eldest daughter of Wm W. Gordon Esq.—aged seventeen
    years. One who belonged to be with Christ!
1877—March 1st. Mrs Maria D. Woodee a recent Communicant
    of this Church, aged 27 or 28 years was buried at Shinmer
    [?] Hill this day.
1878—Feb 13: Mr James Tucker a citizen of Hanover Co., aged
    62, died, It is said of the disease of the heart suddenly
Apr. 24. Mrs. Judith Johnson—aged 71
August 27th—George W. Bassett Sr.
    Born Aug 23, 1800—Died Aug 25, 1878. A Communicant
    from early life and Warden of Immanuel Church from its
    organization. When he moved to the County, he found the

Colonial Church extinct, and by his efforts, and liberal aid, was Immanuel Church built subsequently—
He lies in its cemetery,—May his rest be peace.

Nov 7—Ramaliel Philips, son of William and Caroline Philips, died Nov 6th 1878, aged 19 years, buried in the cemetery of Immanuel

C. THE LUTHERAN CHURCH

The Lutheran Church was the dominant religion in many areas during the early history of this country, and it had a large following in other areas. Lutheran records are generally quite complete but, as with the records of other churches, much depends on the minister or clerk. Also, Lutheran Church records are not unlike the records of some other churches, notably some of the branches of the Reformed Church. For our examples we have chosen the records of the Goshenhoppen Lutheran Church, Montgomery County, Pennsylvania.

1. Register of families.

The register of families contains detailed information on all members of the congregation and their families. It is arranged by family and looks like this:

The names of the Members of the Congregation their wives and Children, began in the year 1751.

1. John Michael Reiher, age 62 years, born 1689 father John Michael Reiher, Mother Annie Catherine, from Rohrbach near Zinze in Courtebarg. Anno 1732 he came to America. He married

    (1) In the year 1708, Anna Maria, daughter of Dietrich See-land and Amelia, of Nurnberg, died 1742.

    (2) In the year 1743, Maria Catherine, Reformed, born 1713, died 1750, daughter of Henrich Schneider of Asohpissen in the Palatinate and of Catharine daughter of Abraham Schneider.

    (3) In 1751, Sept 12, Maria Christine, born 1718, Nov 18 at Borna in Electoral Saxony, daughter of George Gerlach and Susanna, who is now with her daughter. Married (1) John Christopher Hoepler, died Aug 18, 1750 at sea, where he was buried.

    The children of this marriage are as follows:
    1. John Christian, born 1739, Jan 18, bapt 29 ditto
    2. John George, born 1743, Nov 17. Bapt Nov 18
    3. John Gottleib, born 1748, Jan 23, bapt Jan 25

    4. John Henry, born 1750, Dec 11, bapt Dec 20

In the year 1750, she with her mother and parents in law came to America and married (2) Michael Reiher. Michael Reiher has the following children of the first and second marriage.

    1. Anna Maria, died
    2. John Carl, born 1711, Dec 15, bapt. Dec 17
    3. Anna Maria, born 1712, Dec 5, bapt Dec 8
    4. John Martin, born 1716, Jan 9, bapt Jan 11
    5. Anna Sarah, born 1718, March 24
    6. Anna Catharine, born 1729, Dec 6
    7. Anna Barbara, born 1745
    8. George Philip, born 1750

2. Lists of communicants.

This is a periodic list of persons who received communion, made approximately every two or three months. In this case the names were arranged more or less alphabetically:

Nov 4 1751
    1. Bausberger, Laurence
    2. Bauersax, John Nicholas
    3. Bausmann, Conrad
    4. _____ Anna Eva, his wife
    5. Berckheimer, Leonhard
    6. _____ Catharine, his wife
    7. Berckheimer, Valentine
    8. Bering, Adam
    9. Bittner, Henry
  10. _____ Christinea, his wife

    *   *   *

3. Confirmations.

The following list is dated June 24, 1752:

    1. Elias Schneider, age 18 years, son of Conrad Schneider, see p. _____
    2. John Martin Schmidt, age 17 years, son of Henry Schmidt.
    3. Peter Gabel, 14 years, son of Philip Gabel, see p. _____
    4. Christian Hoepler, 13 years, son of John Christopher Hoepler, see p. _____

5. George Philip Gabel, 12 years, son of Philip Gabel, see p. _____

6. Michael Schneider, 16 years, son of Conrad Schneider, see p. _____

7. Anna Margaret Klein, 23 years, wife of John Klein.

8. Elizabeth Schmid, 17 years, da. of Martin Schmid

9. Maria Agatha Klingele, 17 years, da. of Georg Frederick Klingel and wife Maria Agnes, of Conestoga, living at Samuel Schuler's

10. Evan Margaret, 15 years, da. of Philip Kresler; her mother Barbara is dead.

4. Marriages.

(1751)

1. John George Goerkes, single, Lutheran, admitted to the Lord's Supper with his father William Goerkes living in New York, married Anna Zipperle, single, Lutheran, da. of the late Frederick Zipperle and Catharine of Rhinesbeck, who lived at George Weigele, bro. of her mother, Banns published (1) in Old Goshenhoppen, June 30, (2) at same place July 14, (3) at Falkner Swamp July 21. Married at Old Goshenhoppen, July 23, in the church with a wedding sermon. The text was taken from Tobit 4:1-7, 13-16.

Later marriage records have much less detail:

(1780)

Jan 11.	George Schwenck	and	Susanna Weis
Febr 8.	George Lemle	and	Barbara Haas
May 11.	Henry Graf	and	Charlotte Schwarz
July 18	Jacob Gros	and	Susanna Klein

5. Baptisms.

There was not much change in the information or format in the baptism records over the years. They are all about like these:

(1751)

CHILDREN	PARENTS	SPONSORS
Elisabeth	Jacob Grotz	Henry Bittner
b. July 7, 1751	and Elizabeth	and Christina
bapt Aug 4	at Shippack	fr Shippack

CHILDREN	PARENTS	SPONSORS
Anna Margaret b. July 24, 1751 bapt Aug 4	Henry Bittner and Christine	Jacob Grotz and wf Elizabeth

*   *   *

There was also a special record kept of the baptisms of illegitimate children:

Names of the baptized children, who were born out of wedlock.
George Philip, born Febr 16, 1753, bapt Febr 25 1753 in the schoolhouse. His father is said to be Henry Lips, a servant across the river. The mother is single, named Elizabeth, living at John Fischer's, Godparents: Philip Wenzel and wife Christine, both newcomers.
Anna Elizabeth, born Dec 27, 1754, bapt. March 9, 1755. Parents: His father is said to be John Peter Kabel His Mother Anna Barbara Kircher, da of the late John George Kircher, single.
Godparents: John Frederick Kircher, single and Elizabeth Schwenck, single, da of the late Peter Schwenck.
Barbara, born July 21, 1763.
Parents: John Daub, died and Catharina
Sponsors: John Kantz and wife Barbara
Manli, born 1767, parents: Michael Gaugler and Catharine Gaugler. Sponsors: Kilian Fischer and Elizabeth Nuagesser.

6. Dead who were buried publicly.

1. Eva Margaret, born 1751, March—died Jan 31, 1752, buried Febr 2nd, in cemetery in front of the Old Goshenhoppen Church, on Sunday before the morning service. Parents: John Jacob Kayser and Anna Maria, Ref.
2. Jacob Eckmann, age 65 years, born 1687, from Switzerland, the Canton of H. Gall, born in Runnelshorse, Reformed. Father Librich Eckman, who left only one son, Jacob, and his widow Anna Maria. Anno 1752, July 3 he died and was buried in our Church yard at Old Goshenhoppen on July 4, 1752.

The same is true of the burials as was true of the marriages—the later ones have less detail:

1776
> On April 5, was buried Catharina, da of Henry Hemsinger school-
> master here, her age 2 years, 8 months.
> On May 31, was buried Catharine, da of the late Herman Waische,
> her age 5 years, 10 months.
> On June 6, was buried Catharine, da of George Boyer, her age
> 3 years less 5 weeks.

D. THE BAPTIST CHURCH

The Baptist Church records that we are going to examine with you (briefly) are those of the Woodbury Baptist Church in Cannon County, Tennessee. The records are called "minutes" and the entries are diverse. They include financial accounts, lists of converts (name only), notations of letters of admission, annual membership lists (also name only) and accounts of church business meetings. Following are the minutes of a typical business meeting:

> Saturday   Jan. 26, 1889
> Baptist Church of Christ met in Conferance at Woodbury
> Minutes of last meeting called for and Read and approved. No
> unfinished business refured to. Bro. J.R. Rushing anonce the
> minutes of last association. Are on the table, and all can get
> them that want to. Bro. D.B. Vance give notice of the death of
> Sister Juda A. Ferrell. A notice from the Clerk of North Fork,
> Missionary Baptist Church notify the church of this place that
> Bro. Wm. St. John and wife was Received into that church Oct.
> 1888 by letter granted them by this church. By motion and 2nd
> Bro. J.G. Moore, Bro. J.C. New, Bro. D.B. Vance appointed
> as a commity to examine the windows of the church, come upon
> some plan of Repairing the same. Investigate the cost of Repairs
> and Report to the church next meeting. A motion was made to
> appoint a commitee to see Sister Sue Talley about Dancing. Bro.
> Moderator appoint the Deakons of the church as the commity.
> By motion church vote to cloth the committy with the authority
> to interview all other disorderly members. Bro. J.D. New made
> a financial report to the church moved and 2nd...

E. THE SOCIETY OF FRIENDS (QUAKERS)

The last denomination from whose records we will draw specific examples is the Quakers. Regardless of where you go you will find consistency in the nature of the Friends' records. They do not vary extensively either with the passage of time or from one locality to another. The records are based on the "Meeting" system. The local congregation meets weekly and is called a Weekly Meeting. Each Weekly Meeting group has a Preparative Meeting wherein the business of the congregation belongs. A Monthly Meeting is comprised of several Weekly Meetings and is the meeting wherein most of the business of the church is transacted and recorded. There are both men's and women's Monthly Meetings. It is the Monthly Meeting records that are generally considered to be of the most genealogical value, though other records do have some value.

Several Monthly Meetings make up a Quarterly Meeting and several Quarterly Meetings come together to make up a Yearly Meeting, and some branches of the organization have Three-Year Meetings. These latter three are mainly administrative divisions and their records are not so useful to us.

Thomas W. Marshall, writing in the introduction to Hinshaw's Encyclopedia of American Quaker Genealogy (Vol. I), made the following observations about Quaker records:

> The records kept by Friends Monthly Meetings during the eighteenth and nineteenth centuries usually consisted of a record of births and deaths, a record of marriage certificates, and minutes covering all proceedings and discussions coming before the monthly sessions of the meeting. As the men and women met separately, two sets of minutes were kept. In some meetings the marriage records were kept in the same book with the birth and death records; in others they were kept in a separate book. The birth and death records are never complete. In some cases whole families are omitted; sometimes the older children of a family are recorded and the younger ones omitted. The percentage of births recorded appears to be considerably higher than that of deaths. In only a few meetings was it the practice to record the birth dates and parentage of the father and mother of a family. Place of birth was not usually recorded, for either parents or children.
>
> None of the earlier meeting records contains a list of the membership. When a monthly meeting was divided to establish a new one, all members of the old meeting who lived within the verge of the new automatically became members of the new meeting without any list of their names being entered in the records of either meeting. A person who became a member in this way, unless he took some active part in the affairs of the meeting, was married, or was complained of for some breach of discipline, might continue in membership until the end of his life without his name ever appearing in the records.
>
> The records of marriage certificates are much more com-

plete than birth and death records. In a few meetings every marriage accomplished in the meeting is fully recorded. Others
are nearly complete, —with only a few marriages missing. Since
the regular procedure in the marriage involved two appearances
of the couple before both men's and women's meetings prior to
marriage and subsequent reports of the committees appointed to
attend the marriage ceremony, there is ample record of each
marriage in the minutes even though recording of the marriage
certificate may have been overlooked. The record in the minutes, however, does not give the names of the parents of the
persons married nor the exact date of the marriage. The report
of the committee that the marriage had been accomplished was
made in the next succeeding meeting, thus fixing the date within
a month.

The minutes of sessions of the monthly meetings cover many
subjects... During the periods of migration the minutes relating
to certificates of membership received and issued are the most
numerous and have the greatest interest. Records of disciplinary action against members for violation of the rules of the Society occupy much space. Members were "dealt with" on a
great variety of complaints, including fiddling and dancing,
drinking intoxicating liquor to excess, serving in the militia or
other armed forces, using profane language, fighting, failure to
meet financial obligations, marrying contrary to the order used
by Friends, deviation from plainness in apparel or speech, joining another religious society, etc. Unless the offending member
expressed sorrow for his misconduct and brought a signed paper
condemning the same, he was usually disowned. The number so
disowned runs into thousands. Many of them, after a shorter or
longer time, produced the necessary paper of condemnation and
were reinstated in membership. A minute showing that a person
presented a satisfactory paper condemning his misconduct, implies that he was retained or reinstated in membership, as the
case might be, whether the fact is specifically stated or not.
Often, following the disownment of a member (perhaps many
years later) the minutes may record a request for membership
coming from a person of the same name, but with no reference
to previous membership or disownment. In such cases it is
usually impossible to tell whether the two minutes refer to the
same person or to two individuals with the same name. A great
many of those who were disowned never asked to be reinstated
but remained outside the Society for the rest of their lives. The
names of these persons never appear in the records again.

When individual members of families removed from one

monthly meeting to another they were furnished removal certificates setting forth the fact of their membership in good standing and recommending them to the fellowship of the monthly meeting to which they were removing. In the earlier days these certificates were usually prepared and signed in advance and carried by the members to their new place of abode. Later, it appears to have become more the custom to wait until the new home had been established and then send back a request that the certificate be forwarded. A condition to the granting of a certificate was that the member's "outward affairs" be satisfactorily settled. The certificate usually stated that this had been done. When a certificate was issued to a family the fact was generally recorded in the men's minutes so far as it applied to the husband and sons, and in the women's minutes as it applied to the mother and daughters. The names of children were frequently omitted in the minutes of the issuing meeting but were usually recorded by the receiving meeting. The fact that John Jones and family (men's minutes) and Mary Jones and daughters (women's minutes) were granted certificates to the same meeting on the same day does not guarantee that John and Mary were husband and wife. Such an assumption would be correct in the majority of cases but would sometimes be erroneous. Confirmatory evidence should always be sought.

If a man and woman contemplating marriage were members of different monthly meetings they made their declarations of intention in the meeting of which the woman was a member. The man was required to bring a certificate from his meeting stating that he was a member in good standing and free from marriage engagements with others. This certificate did not transfer his membership to the woman's meeting, but only made it possible for him to marry there. After marriage, the wife usually obtained a certificate, issued in her married name, transferring her membership to her husband's meeting.

Marriage contrary to the Friends' order, variously referred to in the minutes as "marriage by a priest," "outgoing in marriage," "marriage contrary to good order," "marriage out of unity," "marriage contrary to discipline," etc., and spoken of in every day speech as "marriage out of the meeting," was the cause of more complaints and disownments than any other single offense... Unfortunately the minutes rarely give the name of the person to whom the offending member was married. The record relating to a woman usually refers to her as Mary Jones, formerly Brown, thus giving a clue which is not available in the case of a man. In a large percentage of cases of marriage con-